lonely planet

St Petersburg

"All you've got to do is decide to go
and the hardest part is over.

So go!"

TONY WHEELER, COFOUNDER – LONELY PLANET

THIS EDITION WRITTEN AND RESEARCHED BY

Tom Masters, Simon Richmond

Contents

Plan Your Trip 1

Explore St Petersburg 38

Understand St Petersburg 169

Survival Guide 215

St Petersburg Maps 252

LOOK DIE BILDAGENTUR DER FOTOGRAFEN GMBH / ALAMY ©

Left: Water Avenue, Grand Palace (p141)

Above: Winter Palace, the Hermitage (p44)

Right: Church on the Spilled Blood (p64)

IZZET KERIBAR / LONELY PLANET IMAGES ©

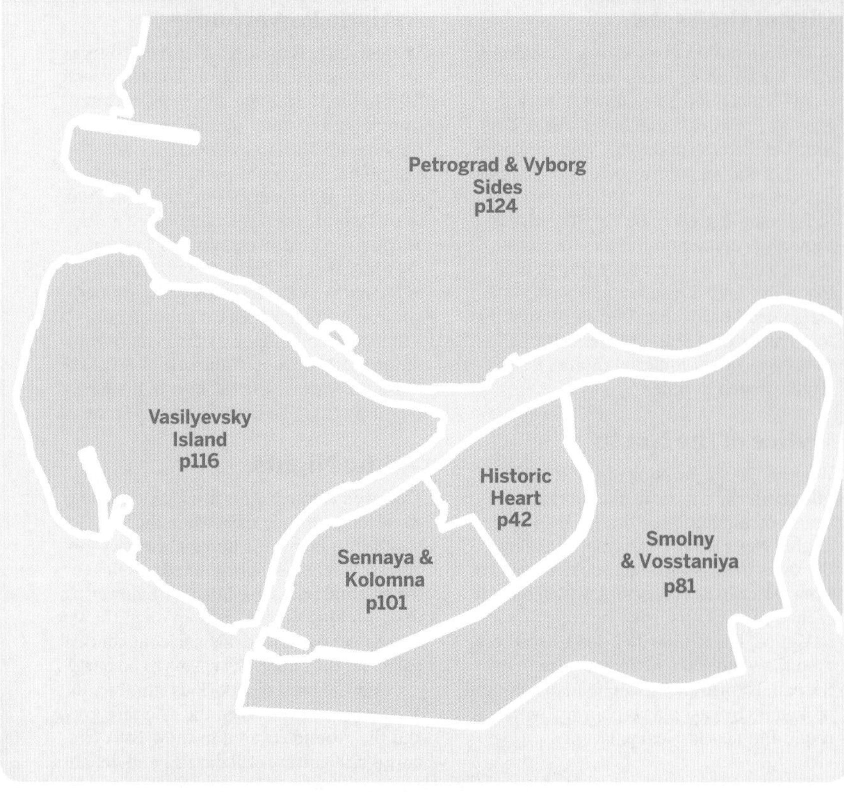

Welcome to St Petersburg

Built on a swamp, the imperial capital is today a dazzling metropolis whose sheer grandeur never fails to amaze.

City of the Tsars

Built from nothing by westward-looking Peter the Great, St Petersburg was to be from its inception a display of imperial Russia's growing status in the world. Fine-tuned by Peter's successors, who employed a host of Italian architects to add fabulous palaces and cathedrals to the city's layout, St Petersburg grew to be the Romanovs' showcase capital and Russia's first great, modern city. You can walk through the incredible gilded results today, just as the tsars would have done. Despite all that history has thrown at it, St Petersburg still feels every bit an imperial capital, a city largely frozen in time.

Venice of the North

Whether you're crossing one of the 342 bridges in the city, cruising the elegant canals or watching the bridges over the mighty Neva River rise at night to allow the ships to pass through, you're never far from water in St Petersburg, which has earned the city unsurprising comparisons to Venice. The similarities don't stop there, though: wander the historic centre to see the canals lined by Italianate mansions and broken up by vast plazas adorned with baroque and neoclassical palaces.

Artistic Powerhouse

St Petersburg is an almost unrivalled treasure trove of art and culture. You can spend days in the Hermitage, seeing everything from Egyptian mummies to Picassos, while the Russian Museum, spread over four sumptuous palaces, is perhaps the best collection of Russian art in the world. Add to this world-class ballet and opera at the Mariinsky Theatre, classical concerts at the Shostakovich Philharmonia and a slew of big-name music festivals over summer, and you won't be stuck for cultural nourishment. If contemporary art is more your thing, there's also the fantastic new Erarta Museum, showcasing the best in modern Russian art, and a buzzing gallery scene.

White Nights

The city's White Nights are legendary: those long summer days when the sun barely dips below the horizon. Revelry begins in May, when spring finally comes to the city and parks are filled with flowering trees, and peaks in mid-June, when the sky doesn't get dark, festivals pack out concert halls and the entire city seems to be partying over the brief but glorious summer. But don't worry – even when the skies are grey and the ground covered in snow, St Petersburg's rich culture still dazzles and delights.

Why I Love St Petersburg

By Tom Masters, Author

There is something about St Petersburg that gets under your skin. Despite preferring Moscow when I first came to Russia 15 years ago, St Petersburg lingered; its colours and incredible light stayed with me; its history haunted me. When I came to live in Russia in 2000, I didn't hesitate for a moment to choose St Petersburg as the city to settle in. Today what excites me about the city is the growing underground art and music scene, the hedonistic atmosphere and the sense that great things are once again happening here. The city is emerging from Moscow's shadow and there's never been such a good time to visit.

For more about our authors, see p272.

Above: Catherine Palace (p145)

St Petersburg's Top 10

CATRIONA BASS RUSSIAN IMAGES / ALAMY ©

White Nights (p21)

1 The ultimate St Petersburg experience is during mid-June when the sun slumps lazily towards the horizon, but never fully sets, meaning that the magical nights are a wonderful whitish-grey. At this time Petersburgers indulge themselves in plenty of all-night revelry, several festivals take place and the entire city enjoys an uncharacteristically relaxed atmosphere. Though it's the busiest time to visit the city, and most hotels are booked up weeks in advance, there's nothing quite like it, so don't miss out – even if you come in May or July you'll be impressed by how late the sun stays out!

Month by Month

The Hermitage (p44)

2 Perhaps the world's greatest museum, this iconic establishment's vast collection is quite simply mind-boggling, with Egyptian mummies, more Rembrandts than the Louvre, and a collection of early-20th-century art that is unrivalled by almost any other in the world. As if this wasn't enough, your entry ticket allows you to walk around the fascinating apartments and dazzling staterooms of the Romanovs. And there are still the other museum sites: the Winter Palace of Peter I, General Staff Building, Menshikov Palace, Imperial Porcelain factory and the excellent Hermitage Storage Facility.

Historic Heart

ROBERTO GEROMETTA / LONELY PLANET IMAGES ©

RICHARD I'ANSON / LONELY PLANET IMAGES ©

IZET KERIBAR / LONELY PLANET IMAGES ©

St Isaac's View *(p103)*

3 No other viewpoint of the historic centre beats the one from the stunning gold dome of St Isaac's Cathedral, which rises majestically over the uniformly sized Italianate palaces and mansions around the Admiralty. Well worth the climb up the 262 steps, a panorama of the city opens up to you – with fantastic views over the river, the Winter Palace and the *Bronze Horseman*. The cathedral's interior is also well worth seeing, with a wonderfully over-the-top iconostasis framed by columns of marble, malachite and lazurite.

Sennaya & Kolomna

Russian Museum *(p57)*

4 Even though the Hermitage is unrivalled as St Petersburg's most impressive museum, that shouldn't stop you from visiting this lesser-known treasure trove of Russian art, spread out over four stunning palaces in the centre of the city. The main building, Mikhailovsky Palace, presents a fascinating collection of Russian art from medieval icons to 20th-century avant-garde masterpieces, while the Marble Palace houses a wing of the Ludwig Museum, and the Stroganov Palace has some of the most spectacular interiors in the city.

Historic Heart

Church on the Spilled Blood *(p64)*

5 The spellbinding Church on the Spilled Blood never fails to impress visitors. The church was built to commemorate the death of Tsar Alexander II, who, in an event that gave the church its unusual name, was attacked here by a terrorist group and later died of his injuries in 1881. Despite its grizzly heritage, the glittering, multicoloured onion domes and intricate interior mosaics are quite simply stunning, and have to be seen to be believed.

Historic Heart

Tsarskoe Selo *(p145)*

6 Arguably the most beautiful of the tsarist palace areas that surround St Petersburg, Tsarskoe Selo (the Tsar's Village) is an idyllic place for a day trip. Arrive in good time to see the lavish interiors of the Catherine Palace including the famous Amber Room, enjoy the gorgeous formal gardens and have a picnic lunch in the landscaped park where Catherine the Great so loved to walk. Nearby is the scenic estate and palace of Pavlovsk, also well worth a visit and a beautiful place to escape the crowds.

Day Trips

Mariinsky Ballet *(p113)*

7 What could be more Russian than seeing a ballet at the city's famous Mariinsky Theatre? Formerly known as the Kirov, where Soviet stars such as Nureyev and Baryshnikov danced, today the Mariinsky is one of the premier ballet troupes in the world. Tickets to see shows here are always sought-after, so book online before you travel to ensure you don't miss out during your stay. Even if ballet isn't your thing, the historic building is a sight in its own right, as is the next-door New Mariinsky Theatre, Russia's first new ballet house since the revolution.

Sennaya & Kolomna

6

SERGEY KULIKOV / AFP / GETTY IMAGES ©

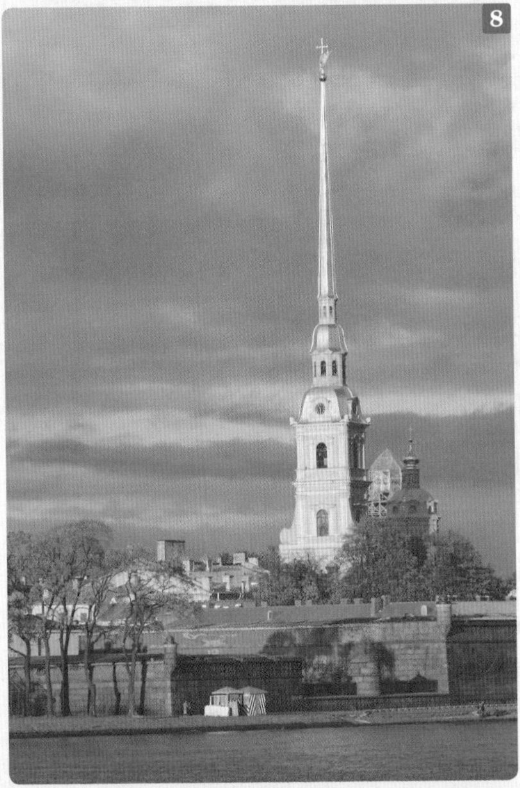

WIN INITIATIVE / GETTY IMAGES ©

Peter & Paul Fortress *(p126)*

8 The city's first major building is on little Zayachy Island, where Peter the Great first broke ground for St Petersburg. It's immediately recognisable from its extraordinary golden spire, visible all over the city centre at an incredible (for the 18th century) 122m high. A visit to this large complex is a must for history buffs: you'll see the tombs of the Romanovs, visit an excellent history museum and even be able to relax on a surprisingly decent beach with stellar Hermitage views!

Petrograd & Vyborg Sides

Cruise the Canals *(p65)*

9 St Petersburg is, quite simply, a city that is best appreciated from the water. Despite Peter's efforts to make the population use boats as the main means of transport, boat transport never quite caught on in the 'Venice of the North'. Even so, it's well worth paying for a canal or river trip, offered all over the city day and night, so that you can drift down the charming canals, see some offbeat architectural gems and ride on the mighty Neva.

Historic Heart

ANDREY KEKYALYAYNEN / ALAMY ©

ITAR-TASS / ALAMY ©

Taking a Banya *(p32)*

10 For real cultural immersion, head to one of St Petersburg's *bani* (steam baths) and get the detox of a lifetime. In between basking in the infernal wet heat of the *banya*, having your toxins removed through a sound birch-twig whipping and then plunging into ice cold water, this is a great place to relax and chat with locals for whom the weekly *banya* is a semisacred rite.

☆ ***Entertainment***

What's New

Erarta Museum of Contemporary Art

Out in the wastelands of Vasilyevsky Island is this fantastic new museum of contemporary Russian art, the very first of its kind in St Petersburg. (p118)

Loft Project ETAGI

The converted Smolinsky Bread Factory is now an innovative arts space, cultural centre, hotel and restaurant with lots of exciting events and a fantastic summer drinking terrace. (p87)

House of Music

The former palace of Grand Duke Alexey Alexandrovich has been beautifully restored and now houses the House of Music (Dom Muzyki), which can be visited on a popular guided tour or for one of the regular concerts held here. (p110)

W Hotel

One of the world's coolest hotel brands opened in St Petersburg in summer 2011, and its property in the historic heart is a stunner, complete with an Alain Ducasse restaurant, rooftop cocktail lounge and superb spa. (p159)

Dom Beat

Whether you seek cocktails, coffee, delicious food or just a cool vibe, head to Dom Beat – it's the place that the city's movers and shakers are all talking about. (p91)

Metro Line 5

St Petersburg's limited metro system has grand plans to expand, and now the city's fifth line is open, providing a useful new stop in the centre of town just a stone's throw from the Hermitage!

Ligovsky Prospekt

In the past few years this rather shabby and run-down central St Petersburg street has become the centre of the city's artistic and cultural underbelly and is full of bars, clubs and galleries.

Trinity Cathedral

Fully restored after a terrible fire destroyed its huge main dome, this historic cathedral now looks better than ever with its blue cupola covered with yellow stars. (p105)

Cosmonaut

Housed in a converted Soviet cinema, this excellent new music venue has hosted some interesting live shows and arts festivals and is setting a new standard for local concert halls. (p97)

Galeria & Nevsky Centre

Not to be eclipsed by consumerist Moscow, two enormous shopping centres have recently opened either side of Pl Vosstaniya. Galeria (p99) has a huge number of stores, while the smaller Nevksy Centre (p99) has the best supermarket in the city.

For more recommendations and reviews, see **lonelyplanet.com/stpetersburg**

Need to Know

Currency
Ruble (r) R40 = €1, R28 = US$1

Language
Russian

Visas
Nearly all visitors need a visa, which will require an invitation. Tourist visas are generally single entry and valid for 30 days.

Money
ATMs are widespread, and credit cards accepted in most good restaurants and shops.

Mobile Phones
Local SIM cards can be bought for very little and used in GSM-compatible phones. Nearly all phones will be able to roam in Russia.

Time
St Petersburg uses Moscow time, which is GMT+3 in winter and GMT+4 in summer.

Tourist Information
St Petersburg Tourist Information Centre (14 ul Sadovaya; 9am-7pm; M Nevsky Prospekt) Maps, tours, information and advice for travellers. English spoken.

Your Daily Budget
The following are average costs per day.

Budget under €60
- Dorm bed €15
- Supermarket and business lunches for food
- Cheap theatre ticket €15

Midrange €60–€200
- Double room €60
- Two-course dinner with wine €40
- Theatre ticket €30

Top end over €200
- Four-star hotel double room €150
- Three-course dinner with wine €100
- Best seats at the Mariinsky €100

Advance Planning
Three months Get working on your visa – this can be done last minute, but it's far cheaper if you do it in good time. Book hotel rooms for the White Nights.

One month Book hotel rooms during the rest of the year, Mariinsky tickets during the summer months.

One week Buy your Hermitage ticket online and print it out. Train tickets to Moscow are worth buying before you arrive for ease and choice.

A few days Dinner reservations at popular restaurants.

Useful Websites
- **St Petersburg Tourist Information** (http://eng.ispb.info)
- **The St Petersburg Times** (www.sptimes.ru)
- **In Your Pocket St Petersburg** (www.inyourpocket.com/russia/st-petersburg)
- **Way to Russia** (www.waytorussia.net)

WHEN TO GO

May to September is best, with White Nights the peak. Winter is cold and dark, but beautiful. Go in early May and September to avoid the crowds.

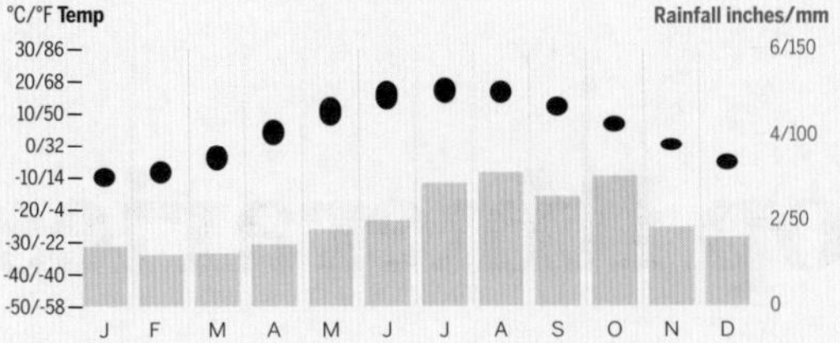

Arriving in St Petersburg

Pulkovo Airport Taxi R700, bus to the metro R21, metro R25

Moscow Station Easy connection to the nearby Pl Vosstaniya (Line 1) and Mayakovskaya (Line 3) metro stations

Finland Station Direct connection to the Pl Lenina (Line 1) metro station

By Boat Taxis are easily caught at all cruise terminals in St Petersburg. Expect to pay around R200–300 for a trip into the city centre.

For much more on **arrival**, see p216.

Getting Around

➡ **Metro** The quickest way to get around the city. All signs are in Roman as well as Cyrillic letters. Runs from 5am until 12.30am.

➡ **Bus & marshrutka** Despite no signs written in Latin letters, there are lots of useful bus routes where the metro doesn't run. You can always buy tickets on board.

➡ **Taxi** Taxis can be ordered easily by your hotel front desk or you flag down a car and negotiate a price – just hold out your hand (palm down) and a car will stop. Reckon on R200 to R300 per trip in the centre of the city.

For much more on **getting around**, see p219.

Sleeping

St Petersburg has seen an explosion of hotels in recent years and now everything from great hostels to international luxury hotel brands can be found easily. However, if you are travelling in summer (particularly during the White Nights) you'll need to book several months in advance to get the best possible deal.

Hostels are now very plentiful in the city, although standards can vary hugely between them. Even though most have rules about noise, they can still be loud, communal experiences.

Mini-hotels are a local speciality – usually housed in old apartments with fewer than six rooms – and can be charming and great value.

Hotels in St Petersburg come in all stripes, but tend to be relatively expensive (moving to eye-wateringly so in four- and five-star categories). The best deals are often available on hotel websites.

For much more on **sleeping**, see p156.

RUSSIAN VISAS

Nearly everyone needs a visa to go to Russia, and while it's not the major headache it's often portrayed to be, it's still a pain to organise and the main disincentive for travelling to Russia that there is. You'll need to get your hotel or hostel to send you an invite, send or take it (along with an application form and passport photo) to the Russian embassy in your home country and leave your passport there for several days. Annoying and fiddly, but worth it! For more information, see p227.

Top Itineraries

Day One

Historic Heart (p42)

Begin your first day in St Petersburg by taking a stroll down Nevsky pr, the city's vast central avenue that connects the Hermitage to the Alexander Nevsky Lavra at the far end. From the Nevsky Prospekt metro station, drop into the Church on the Spilled Blood, the Kazan Cathedral and end up at the dazzling ensemble of Palace Square, the Winter Palace and the General Staff Building.

Lunch Where better to eat than on the eponymous terrace of Terrassa (p73).

Sennaya & Kolomna (p101)

Wander down the Moyka to **St Isaac's Cathedral**, visit the astonishingly elaborate interiors and then climb to the top of the dome for superb views of the city. Continue down the Moyka to **Yusupov Palace** and the **Mariinsky Theatre**, ending up at the beautiful sky-blue **Nikolsky Cathedral**. Drop into **Entrée** for coffee and cake.

Dinner Book ahead for gorgeous Teplo (p111).

Historic Heart (p42)

If it's a weekend, head down to **Dumskaya ul** for a raucous time with locals who like to congregate here for drinking, dancing and general debauchery. For something a little more elegant, have a cocktail at the **Grand Hotel Europe**.

Day Two

Historic Heart (p42)

After a hearty breakfast, head to the **Hermitage** with a packed lunch in hand, and get ready for a day of artistic exhilaration. Choose the parts of the collection you want to see, though leave some room for on-the-spot decision making – the exhibition is so enormous that you'll inevitably discover new painters and eras you weren't planning on seeing. As well as the art, don't miss the staterooms, and allow yourself plenty of rest stops to avoid exhaustion.

Lunch Bring your own sandwich or face the expensive Hermitage cafe.

Historic Heart (p42)

You may still want to spend a few hours in the museum and make the most of your day ticket. After lunch, wander to the **Mars Field** or through the **Mikhailovsky Gardens** before picking up a **sightseeing cruise** around the canals – the best way to sightsee without having to do any more walking!

Dinner Enjoy Italian at Park Giuseppe (p73).

Sennaya & Kolomna (p101)

If you've booked ahead, dress up to spend the evening watching a ballet from the classical repertoire of the **Mariinsky Theatre**. Even if you haven't booked, it's usually quite possible to do so last minute in one of the other theatres in town. For a post-Mariinsky drink, head to **Hundertwasser Bar**.

Day Three

Petrograd & Vyborg Sides (p124)

Begin day three with a trip to the beautiful Petrograd Side. Start with a visit to the **Peter and Paul Fortress** to see where the city began, wander past the **mosque** and perhaps drop in to see either **Peter's Cabin** or the very interesting **Museum of Political History**. Wander down **Kamennoostrovsky pr** to take in the Style Moderne architecture.

Lunch Enjoy a relaxed and stylish lunch at Mesto (p135).

Vasilyevsky Island (p116)

After lunch, walk across to Vasilyevsky Island, and wander the historic ensemble around the **Strelka**. Visit the fascinating **Kunstkamera**, Peter the Great's personal cabinet of curiosities, and drop in to the very interesting **Menshikov Palace** to see the oldest standing palace in the city. If you enjoy contemporary art, continue on to the excellent **Erarta Museum of Contemporary Art**, which is definitely worth the hassle of a *marshrutka* ride to get to.

Dinner Dine in understated Russian elegance at Restoran (p122).

Smolny & Vosstaniya (p81)

Head south to happening Vosstaniya to gallery-, bar- and gig-hop around **Ligovsky pr**. See some new artwork at **Loft Project ETAGI**, enjoy a drink in the sand and some table football at **Dyuni** or see some live music at underground club **Zoccolo**.

Day Four

Day Trips from St Petersburg (p140)

Head out of the city early to spend the day in tsarist opulence. Go first to **Tsarskoe Selo** in order to visit the **Catherine Palace** during its opening hours for individuals (as opposed to groups) and have a walk in the gardens. If you're still wanting more, **Pavlovsk** is a quick bus ride away and the park is even wilder and more beautiful.

Lunch Back in town, head to Garçon (p72) on Kanal Griboyedov.

Historic Heart (p42)

After lunch, head for the **Russian Museum**, the perfect complement to the Hermitage. This spectacular (and far more manageable) museum showcases seven centuries of Russian art from church icons to the avant-garde. Buy the full ticket and add on the **Stroganov Palace**, **Marble Palace** and **Mikhailovsky Castle** for some fabulous interiors too.

Dinner Dine with the cool kids at fabulous Dom Beat (p91).

Smolny & Vosstaniya (p81)

Enjoy the bars around ul Rubinshteyna – have a drink at **Terminal Bar**, then perhaps see some live bands at **Manhattan**. For more music, have a Soviet-era dance at **Petrovich**, or head to alternative favourite **Griboyedov** for some electronic music or **Kitaysky Lyotchik Dzhao Da** for some guitar-based sounds.

If You Like...

Art

Hermitage There's nowhere else quite like the Hermitage, perhaps the world's greatest art collection. (p44)

Russian Museum This fantastic survey of all Russian art is also essential, even if you know nothing about it before going. (p57)

Erarta Museum of Contemporary Art Stunning new museum of modern Russian art on Vasilyevsky Island. (p118)

Loft Project ETAGI One of the city's coolest galleries is housed in an old bread factory on Ligovsky pr. (p87)

Rizzordi Art Foundation Fantastic new temporary art space in the middle of nowhere. (p88)

Pushkinskaya 10 The one-time centre of the city's alternative scene has aged a little, but it's still a must for art lovers. (p88)

Hermitage Storage Facility In case you came out of the Hermitage wanting more, this state-of-the-art space will definitely sate you. (p132)

Architecture

Winter Palace It's hard to beat this spectacular piece of baroque excess. (p67)

Church on the Spilled Blood See the multicoloured onion domes that have come to represent the city. (p64)

Peterhof The spectacular fountains and views of the palace from Water Ave are breathtaking. (p141)

Water Avenue, Grand Palace (p141)

Smolny Cathedral This soaring sky-blue Rastrelli masterpiece never fails to awe. (p84)

Singer Building Style Moderne at the heart of neoclassical Nevsky pr. (p68)

Chesme Church This unique, striated red and white church is well worth the trek out of the city centre! (p90)

House of Soviets An unbeatable example of Soviet architectural taste in southern St Petersburg. (p90)

Russian Literature

Site of Pushkin's Duel A sight of great tragedy for anyone who knows the work of Russia's national poet. (p135)

Dostoevsky Museum A wander around Dostoevsky's apartment is a fascinating insight into the writer. (p87)

Raskolnikov House See *Crime and Punishment* come to life in the seedy streets of Sennaya. (p104)

Nabokov Museum See the house immortalised by the *Lolita* author in his autobiography *Speak, Memory*. (p108)

Anna Akhmatova Museum This museum honours the most quintessential Leningrad poet and survivor of the great terror. (p84)

Bronze Horseman Brought to life in Pushkin's eponymous epic poem, the sculpture that inspired him is a must-see. (p106)

Alexandrinsky Theatre See the theatre where Chekhov's *Seagull* was first performed to terrible reviews. (p77)

Icons & Incense

Kazan Cathedral See the dramatic interior of this Orthodox stunner. (p65)

Sampsonievsky Cathedral One of the most impressive iconostases in the city. (p134)

Nikolsky Cathedral Perhaps the prettiest church in the city, this place is stunning both outside and in. (p107)

Church on the Spilled Blood Dazzling domes, incredible mosaics. (p64)

Alexander Nevsky Monastery One of Russia's most important religious centres. (p83)

Buddhist Temple Incense also burns at the world's most northerly *datsan*. (p134)

Soviet History

Finland Station Where Lenin famously arrived to lead the October coup. (p134)

Cruiser Aurora The ship that fired a blank round to signal the start of the October Revolution. (p131)

Winter Palace Where the provisional government was arrested. (p67)

Smolny Institute The home of Soviet power, and still the seat of the city's governor today. (p86)

Kirov Museum Home of Sergei Kirov, Stalin's ill-fated man in Leningrad. (p130)

Monument to the Heroic Defenders of Leningrad The moving memorial to the 900-day Nazi blockade. (p90)

For more top St Petersburg spots, see

- Eating (p25)
- Drinking & Nightlife (p28)
- Entertainment (p31)
- Shopping (p35)

Parks & Gardens

Kirovsky Islands Three beautiful islands almost totally given over to wild parkland. (p131)

Pavlovsk The best tsarist palace to wander around. (p147)

Gatchina Wild and extremely beautiful, this is also a wonderful place for a ramble. (p148)

Mikhailovsky Gardens The most beautiful park in the centre of St Petersburg. (p57)

Botanical Gardens A fascinating botanical garden that's a real pleasure to walk around. (p130)

Russian Culture

Mariinsky Theatre There's nowhere like the Mariinsky for great ballet and opera. (p107)

Feel Yourself Russian A surprisingly excellent Russian folk music and dance show. (p114)

Molokhovets' Dream Look no further if you want to experience the very best of Russian cuisine. (p89)

Russian Museum A one-stop shop for Russian art and culture. (p57)

Banya The ultimate Russian experience – naked and sweaty in a steam bath with locals! (p32)

Russian Vodka Museum An excellent look at the 'little water' that is important to Russians. (p107)

Month by Month

TOP EVENTS

Mariinsky Ballet Festival April

City Day May

Victory Day May

White Nights June

Arts Square Winter Festival December

January

Deep in the Russian winter, the days may be short and dark but the city often looks magical as snow continues to fall regularly.

Orthodox Christmas

Russia celebrates Orthodox Christmas (Rozhdestvo) on 6 January. Exclusively a religious holiday, it is not widely celebrated, although services are held at churches and cathedrals around the city.

February

Intensely cold, with snow and ice still everywhere, February is a great time to see Petersburg in full winter garb, as long as you don't mind the short days!

Maslenitsa

Akin to Mardi Gras, this celebration kicks off Orthodox Lent and involves eating lots of bliny. Exact dates depend on the dates of Orthodox Easter, but it is usually in February or early March.

March

You can still expect snow on the ground, though in warmer years March can also see the beginning of the thaw.

International Women's Day

Russia's favourite holiday – 8 March – was founded to honour the women's movement. These days, men buy champagne, flowers and chocolates for their better halves – and for all the women in their lives.

April

Finally the thaw comes, but you might prefer snow to the grey slush that can engulf the city in April! Orthodox Easter and the Mariinsky Ballet Festival brighten the scene, however.

Easter

Easter Sunday kicks off with celebratory midnight services in which churches are jam-packed. Afterwards, people eat special dome-shaped cakes known as *kulichy* and exchange beautifully painted wooden Easter eggs.

Mariinsky Ballet Festival

The city's principal dance theatre hosts a week-long international festival, where the cream of Russian ballet dancers showcase their talents.

May

Spring is finally here, and with it a slew of holidays in the first two weeks of the month. Late May is a great time to come to St Petersburg before the summer crowds arrive.

Victory Day

Celebrating the end of WWII, 9 May is a day of huge local importance, when residents remember the 900-day Nazi blockade. Crowds assemble at Piskaryovskoe Cemetery (p134) to commemorate the victims, and a parade along

Nevsky pr culminates in fireworks over the Neva in the evening.

City Day

Mass celebrations are held throughout the city centre on 27 May, the city's official birthday, known as *den goroda* (city day). Brass bands, folk-dancing and mass drunkenness are the salient features of this perennial favourite, which marks Peter the Great's founding of the city in 1703.

June

This is St Petersburg's high season, and there's certainly no shortage of things to do, as the nights are white, spirits are high and the city has an almost surreal atmosphere.

Festival of Festivals

St Petersburg's annual international film festival is held during the White Nights in late June. Co-sponsored by Lenfilm and hosted at cinemas around the city, the festival is a noncompetitive showcase of the best Russian and world cinema.

Stars of White Nights Festival

From late May until mid-July, this annual festival showcases world premieres of opera and ballet. Performances are held around the city, especially at the Mariinsky Theatre. The festival culminates in a fabulous ball at Tsarskoe Selo, which draws the event to a close.

July & August

High summer is hot and bright – a great time to see the city in all its vividly painted, Italianate glory. There are few festivals in July and August, but with weather like this, who needs them?

Navy Day

On 25 July St Petersburg celebrates its thousands of naval officers and rich maritime history with a flotilla of boats on the Neva outside the Admiralty and a general party along the banks of the river – great if you like a man in uniform.

September & October

Two great months to visit – September is still usually warm and tourist numbers are dropping off, while October is cool, if not yet cold, with even fewer visitors.

Early Music Festival

This musical festival aims to revive forgotten masterpieces from the Middle Ages, the Renaissance and the baroque era. The festival features a baroque opera, as well as performances by the Catherine the Great Orchestra. Musicians perform at various venues from mid-September until early October.

November

Winter is already here in November and you can expect to see the first snow on the ground, which gives the city a magical look.

Day of Reconciliation & Accord

The former October Revolution day – 7 November – is still an official holiday, although it is hardly acknowledged. It still is, however, a big day for flag-waving and protesting by old-school Communist Party members, especially in front of Gostiny Dvor (p70).

December

Christmas isn't such a big deal in Russia (and it's in January anyway), but New Year's Eve is huge. St Petersburg is freezing, snowy and magical.

Arts Square Winter Festival

Maestro Yury Temirknaov presides over this musical highlight, which takes place every year at the Shostakovich Philharmonia. For 10 days in late December and early January, artists stage both classical and contemporary works, including symphonic music and opera.

New Year

Petersburgers see in the New Year (Novy God) by trading gifts, drinking champagne and listening to the Kremlin chimes on the radio or TV. A great time to see Russians at their merry best!

With Kids

With its focus on art, history and architecture, St Petersburg may not be an obvious place to bring children, but there are actually plenty of activities that children will love, especially during the summer months when the whole city is something of an outdoor playground.

Accessible Sights

Top museums for children include the Museum of Zoology (p120), with thousands of stuffed animals (including several mammoths) on display; the Museum of Railway Technology (p105), where you can go aboard old steam trains; the ghoulish Kunstkamera (p118), which is not suitable for smaller kids; and the Artillery Museum (p130), which is great for any children who love tanks. Two fascinating old Soviet naval craft on Vasilyevsky Island can be great fun to explore: take a tour of the *Krasin* (p120), an Arctic icebreaker, or the *People's Will* (p121), a Soviet D-2 submarine now open to the public. Suitable for all ages is the terrific St Petersburg State Circus (p78) on the Fontanka, for which you can buy tickets at short notice.

The Great Outdoors

The Kirovsky Islands (p131), on the Petrograd Side, are an excellent place to get away with the kids. Amusement parks, boats and bikes for hire, and lots of open space make this a great option just a short journey from the centre of the city. Kids will love the fountains at Peterhof (p141), as well as the hydrofoil ride to get out there. Alexandrovsky Park (p130), on the Petrograd Side, is a great place for youngsters too – with the zoo, planetarium and plenty of other diversions among the trees. Another fun outdoor activity is taking a boat trip on the beautiful canals of the historic heart.

Child-friendly Eating

Restaurants have changed enormously in the past couple of decades, and now there are a host of family-friendly eateries with playrooms, children's menus and high chairs for babies. Some of our favourites include Teplo (p111), Botanika (p89), Sadko (p111), Stroganoff Steak House (p112) and Makarov (p90). For child-friendly snacks on the hoof, try ubiquitous bliny stands Teremok (p26), found all over the city, for cheap and delicious sweet or savoury pancakes.

Puppet Shows

Russia has a proud tradition of puppetry and St Petersburg boasts two renowned theatres, both with large repertoires that will appeal to adults and children, and to non-Russian speakers and Russian speakers alike. The excellent Bolshoy Puppet Theatre (p97) has been producing wonderfully innovative shows since its inception in the dark days of Stalinism, becoming a much-loved local institution. It currently boasts 22 shows for children – including an excellent version of *The Little Prince*. The Demmeni Marionette Theatre (p78) is also an excellent venue, with a large range of shows, including *Gulliver's Travels* and *Puppets and Clowns* (a lively hour-long circus-style show performed by puppets). Do check with the theatre which shows are suitable for children – both do literary and arty performances aimed solely at adults as well.

Like a Local

Foreigners are still conspicuous in St Petersburg. Until you've learned to push your way through the crowds on Nevsky pr and bark at waiters you'll remain clearly marked out. Here are some tips to enjoy the city as a local nevertheless.

Metro Etiquette

When on the escalators going down to the platforms, be aware that you stand on the right, while you run on the left – walkers will be unceremoniously bundled past! While getting on and off the trains is done in the rudest possible way (leave the carriage fast before the crowds waiting to board charge in), once inside a metro carriage it's all positively chivalrous: most young men won't even sit down when there are empty seats. But should you be seated and any female over the age of 40 boards the train, then leap up immediately to offer your seat and don't expect to be thanked...

Russian Prices

It's a familiar scenario to anyone who's been in Russia for some time: you line up and pay to get into a museum only to realise you're paying twice (or even three or four times) the price locals are charged. The excuses you'll hear are all based on the supposed limitless wealth of foreigners and the endemic poverty of Russians, something that just doesn't ring true these days. Your best response is to try for the Russian price – just say 'adEEn' (one) gruffly and hand over the money and you might get lucky. Don't even bother at the Hermitage, however, where you'll need a Russian passport to get the local rate (25% of the foreigner price!).

Eating & Drinking Like a Local

Locals still disappear to their local *stolovaya* (canteen) at lunchtime for a supremely cheap (and usually very unexciting) meal. These places, a hangover from the Soviet times, are usually not signposted and tend to be located in basements and courtyards, but if you stumble across one you'll usually be very welcome to partake. Experiences don't come much more local than this one. Likewise, the local equivalent to a pub is the *ryumochnaya*, where traditionally an all-male clientele knocks back glasses of vodka and nibbles on dried fish. While generally dark and uninviting places, there's nothing to stop you visiting one, and recently there has been a spate of fashionable conversions of old Soviet-era *ryumochnaya* into modern, inviting and cool places to come and enjoy a drink or two, where women will feel comfortable, and which even serve drinks beyond vodka.

See How Locals Really Live

If you really want to get out and see how the majority of locals live, then hop on the metro and head to any of the end stations on almost any line – you'll find yourself emerge into Soviet neighbourhoods that look quite different to anything you'll see in the centre. While not beautiful, they can be interesting to walk around to get a sense of daily life for millions. Try getting out at Ozerki, Kupchino, Avtovo or Leninsky Prospekt.

For Free

There's no getting around it: St Petersburg is no longer a cheap destination. Sadly, hotels and dining are expensive, as are admission prices to many essential sights, where you'll often be charged at least twice as much as locals. Here are our tips for how to save when you can.

Discounts

If you're a student, get an ISIC card before you travel, as most places won't accept any other form of student card as evidence of your status. If you want to see a lot of the Hermitage, it's well worth booking the two-day ticket online, which is great value and allows you to visit the museum's other, lesser-known buildings at no extra charge. Senior citizens and children also sometimes get free entry, but will need to bring some proof of age with them, such as a passport.

Free Entry

You can visit the Hermitage (p44) for free on the first Thursday of each month. Yelagin Island (p132) is free on weekdays, while the Nabokov Museum (p108), the Geological Museum (p121), Pushkinskaya 10 (p88), Cruiser Aurora (p131), Kazan Cathedral (p65), Sampsonievsky Cathedral (p134), Nikolsky Cathedral (p107), Sigmund Freud Museum of Dreams (p131), Alexander Nevsky Monastery (p83), Grand Choral Synagogue (p108), Piskaryovskoe Cemetery (p134) and Monument to the Heroic Defenders of Leningrad (p90) are always free.

As well as these excellent museums and sights, there's a wealth of gorgeous parks that make great picnic spots. In central St Petersburg try the charming Mikhailovsky Gardens (p57), the wide open spaces of the Mars Field (p69), the overgrown beauty of the gardens at the Alexander Nevsky Monastery (p83) and the spacious and pleasant Tauride Gardens (p84) in Smolny – all free and perfect on a sunny day.

Money Saving

Try to get the Russian price wherever possible – if you have a local friend, go along with them and keep quiet at the ticket office. If you'll use the metro a lot, buy a magnetic card (R30) and buy trips in bulk to save money. Eat business lunches *(biznes lanch)* in restaurants, which are great value and very filling. Book in good time for the ballet to get the best choice of seats and not to be limited to the most expensive.

Cheap Frills

Even though there's relatively little for free in St Petersburg, there are plenty of sights that are very reasonably priced. Try the Hermitage's other branches, each of which can be visited for a reasonable R60, or the Mendeleev Museum (p120; R30), Stieglitz Museum (p85; R60) and Kirov Museum (p130; R90), all excellent value for money.

Eating

There has never been a better time to eat out in St Petersburg as the range and quality of ingredients increases each year and old stereotypes about Soviet food now seem like bizarre anachronisms. Petersburgers have well and truly caught the foodie bug, and while little of good quality is cheap in this town, the choice is now bigger than ever.

Getting Serious About Food

It may have taken two decades since the end of communism, but finally St Petersburg has become a place where good food is prized and defined not by its high price tag but rather by the talents of the chef. Fresh ingredients, inventive combinations, the use of herbs and spices (other than the ubiquitous dill) and a wider range of flavours have finally come to the city's dining tables, and while there's still plenty of mediocre food out there, visitors today are spoiled for choice. We've never had an easier time recommending restaurants. However, good places are rarely the most obvious, and you may have to reserve for the very best.

Modern Russian

Russian food, it's fair to say, has an image problem – and if you're not careful you can easily end up with dill-smothered soups, under-seasoned and over-cooked meats, and salads that are more mayonnaise than vegetable. But fret not: there is great Russian cooking to be had in St Petersburg now – both traditional and modern, and increasingly a combination of the two. Russian chefs have been rediscovering their own culinary history, and have been slowly moving away from the dozen or so standard offerings that are ubiquitous on the country's menus. They're preparing rarer or even forgotten dishes such as venison and duck cooked in subtle and interesting ways and combined with herbs and fresh vegetables.

International Cuisine

There was a time when international cuisine in St Petersburg was limited to the odd Georgian or Italian (read: bad pizza) place. Next came sushi in the late 1990s, which is still universally adored by locals and can be found on every corner (and even on the menu of many non-Japanese places!). These days the choice is far greater, with plenty of excellent French, German, Italian and pan-Asian places. More common, however, is the international menu, where Russian dishes, pizza, sushi and noodles all compete for your attention. In many cases this means that all four are pretty average, but increasingly there are places that know what they're doing with multiple cuisines.

Vegetarian Options

There is also a surprisingly good variety on offer for vegetarians, both at mainstream restaurants and at an increasing number of meat-free places. Fish is plentiful and fresh in St Petersburg, so it offers an excellent alternative for pescetarians. Most importantly, there is no shortage of starch in Russia. Bread, bliny and potatoes are always on the menu, and they are filling. During the 40 days before Orthodox Easter (*veliky post* in Russian), many restaurants offer a menu that is happily animal-free. St Petersburg also boasts Troitsky Most, an excellent chain of vegetarian cafes that are all over the city. Moreover, one of the city's most pleasant and friendly restaurants is the charming Botanika.

NEED TO KNOW

Price Ranges

In our listings we've used the following price codes to represent the cost of a main course:

€	less than R500
€€	R500–1000
€€€	more than R1000

Opening Hours

Nearly all restaurants are open seven days a week, generally from around 11am or noon until at least 11pm. Many restaurants open 'until the last customer' – a fairly nonspecific term that means as long as someone is still ordering, they'll stay open.

Reservations

The vast majority of restaurants don't require reservations, though they can be handy on Friday or Saturday evening or for weekend breakfasts in popular places. We note in individual reviews when it's a good idea to reserve a table.

Service

Service tends to be well-intentioned but rarely very good outside fancy places where it can often be over-attentive. The main problem you'll have is that most waiting staff's English is limited, so a few words of Russian will always help.

Tipping

In little cafes and cheap eats, tipping is not expected, though you can easily round up the amount you pay if you're happy with the service. Anywhere more upmarket will usually expect a 10% tip.

English Menus

These are a lifeline for non-Russian speakers and are available in nearly all smarter restaurants, though they're often not available in cheaper cafes (and when they are, they are very badly translated). Bring along a sense of humour and adventure!

Supermarket Sweep

Along with a real upswing in restaurant food quality has come a noticeable improvement in what's on offer in the shops. No longer does your shopping experience consist largely of queuing and asking a ferocious sales assistant to show you the *'produkty'*. These days there are excellent supermarkets stocking everything from organic hummus to freshly baked baguettes, and while you'll pay for the pleasure, food shopping in St Petersburg is a breeze.

Fast Food: Russian-Style

There is no shortage of American fast-food chains around St Petersburg, but there are also a few uniquely Russian chains that are every bit as popular as their Western counterparts. Perfect for travellers who are short on time and/or cash, these options offer a somewhat authentic Russian experience at a low price. Outlets are located around the city:

Chaynaya Lozhka (Чайная ложка; www.teaspoon.ru; mains R30-100; ⌚9am-9pm) An excellent bliny, soup and salad joint. Among the 20 outlets in St Petersburg are those in Smolny (Map p258; pr Chernyshevskogo 9; Ⓜ Chernyshevskaya), Vasilyevsky Island (Map p266; Sredny pr 44; Ⓜ Vasileostrovskaya) and Petrograd Side (Map p268; Kamennoostrovsky pr 40; Ⓜ Petrogradskaya).

Teremok (Теремок; www.teremok.ru; bliny R40-100; ⌚10am-10pm) Sprinkled all over the city, these kiosks and sit-down restaurants are superb value. A couple to look out for in the centre are on Nevsky pr (Map p254; Nevsky pr 60; Ⓜ Gostiny Dvor) and ul Bolshaya Morskaya (Map p254; ul Bolshaya Morskaya 11; Ⓜ Admiralteyskaya).

U Tyoshi na Blinakh (У тёщи на блинах; bliny R50-150; ⌚24hr) There are numerous outlets in this cafeteria-style chain, including Sennaya & Kolomna (Map p264; ul Sadovaya 33; Ⓜ Sennaya Pl), Vosstaniya (Map p260; Zagorodny pr 18; Ⓜ Vladimirskaya) and Petrograd Side (Map p268; Sytninskaya ul 16; Ⓜ Gorkovskaya).

Eating by Neighbourhood

- **Historic Heart** Hidden gems among many mediocre places.
- **Smolny & Vosstaniya** Cool and innovative dining options abound.
- **Sennaya & Kolomna** Has some of the city's best restaurants.
- **Vasilyevsky Island** Great Russian and international dining.
- **Petrograd & Vyborg Sides** Great choices on the Petrograd side.

Lonely Planet's Top Choices

Teplo (p111) Charming, welcoming and eccentric, this great spot is a perennial favourite.

Dom Beat (p91) Retro-funky and eclectic, Dom Beat exudes cool and has a delicious menu.

Sadko (p111) Pre- or post-theatre dinner institution with singing waiters.

Botanika (p89) Vegetarian spot with a wonderful atmosphere and gorgeous, inventive food.

Istoriya (p89) Passionately run Russian restaurant with excellent fresh seafood.

Molokhovets' Dream (p89) Traditional Russian cooking with a gourmet edge.

Best by Budget

€

Soup Vino (p72)

Sumeta (p110)

Stolle (p72)

Garçon (p72)

€€

Makarov (p90)

Les Amis de Jean-Jacques Rousseau (p91)

Entrecôte (p73)

Terrassa (p73)

€€€

MiX in St Petersburg (p72)

Noble Nest (p112)

Il Grappolo (p90)

Matrosskaya Tishina (p92)

Best by Cuisine

Russian Chekhov (p135)

Georgian Tbiliso (p136)

Italian Il Grappolo (p90)

French Entrecôte (p73)

International Mansard (p111)

Best for Breakfast

Kompot Café (p89)

Stolle (p72)

Makarov (p90)

The Idiot (p111)

Garçon (p72)

Coolest Tables

Mesto (p135)

Fartuk (p92)

Restoran (p122)

Chekhov (p135)

Best Coffee & Cake

Entrée (p111)

Schümli (p112)

Black & White (p123)

Café Singer (p76)

Stolle (p72)

Best Budget Eats

Troitsky Most (p73)

Pelmeny Bar (p74)

Pirogovoy Dvorik (p74)

Yolki Palki (p75)

Best Bites Near the Sights

The Hermitage NEP (p74)

Church on the Spilled Blood Stolle (p72)

St Isaac's Cathedral The Idiot (p111)

Peter and Paul Fortress Mesto (p135)

Best for Romance

Fiolet (p72)

Mansard (p111)

Noble Nest (p112)

Entrée (p111)

Backstage (p112)

Best for Atmosphere

Sadko (p111)

Fartuk (p92)

Schastye (p92)

Les Amis de Jean-Jacques Rousseau (p136)

Zoom Café (p73)

Drinking & Nightlife

'Drinking is the joy of the Rus. We cannot live without it.' With these words Vladimir of Kiev, father of the Russian state, is said to have rejected abstinent Islam on his people's behalf in the 10th century. And the grateful Russian people have confirmed old Vlad's assessment, as drinking remains an integral part of Russian culture and society.

Little Water

The word 'vodka' is the diminutive of *voda,* the Russian word for water, so it means something like 'a wee drop'. Russians sometimes drink vodka in moderation, but more often it's tipped down in swift shots, often followed by a pickle (snacking apparently stops you from getting drunk). Russky Standard and Stolichnaya are two good brands of vodka that are commonly available. It's very rare to get bad vodka in a restaurant, so do not fear if you don't recognise the brand name (there are many). However, if the vodka isn't served cold, send it back immediately.

Many visitors to St Petersburg are surprised to learn that *pivo* (beer) is actually Russia's most popular alcoholic drink. The market leader is Baltika, a Scandinavian joint-venture with Russian management, based in St Petersburg. Another very popular local brand is Vasileostrovskaya, named after Vasilyevsky Island, where it is brewed.

Where to Drink

Back in the day, the equivalent of the local pub was a *ryumochnaya,* which comes from the word *ryumka* (shot). These were pretty grim places, serving up *sto gramm* (100 grams), but not much else. Most people preferred to drink at home, surrounded by friends and family.

In recent years, St Petersburg's drinking possibilities have expanded exponentially. Now, drinkers can take their pick from wine bars, cocktail bars, pubs, sports bars, microbreweries and more. In summer months, there is an additional assortment of *letny sady* (summer gardens) scattered around town. It's also perfectly acceptable to go into almost any restaurant and just order drinks.

Nightlife in St Petersburg

Like so many aspects of city life, nightlife in St Petersburg has changed beyond recognition in the past decade. Gone are most of the elitist, flashy and downright tacky nightclubs that came to be the norm during the late 1990s, and in their place is now a sophisticated array of live music joints, jazz venues, dance clubs, stylish bars and busy gay hotspots, all looking very European in comparison to their gaudy forebears.

Undoubtedly the centre of the city's party culture is ul Dumskaya, a side street off Nevsky pr that has transformed into St Petersburg's unofficial drinking street. Indeed, after midnight at the weekends, it's a sight to see. The bars on this street and in the immediate area are the busiest and best known in the city. For more bohemian venues, head south to Vosstaniya, where you'll find lots of hipsterish bars and clubs in and around Ligovsky pr.

Finding Out Where to Go

Other than the recommendations in this book, it's well worth checking the latest reviews in the **St Petersburg Times** (www.sptimes.ru) and **In Your Pocket** (www.inyourpocket.com/russia/st-petersburg). If you speak Russian, then both **Time Out St Petersburg** (www.timeout.ru) and **Afisha** (www.afisha.ru/spb) have full club listings as well as bar reviews.

Face Control

This wonderful piece of Russ-glish came about during the 1990s, when Russia's new rich started to party and wanted to do so in great exclusivity, thus creating an entire social class of intimidating doormen whose job was to ensure you were well dressed enough to enter a venue. It's quite rare these days (though security is nearly always present), but if you're turned away from a venue, it means your face (and probably the rest of you) has been controlled and found wanting.

Cafes

A few Russian coffeeshop chains have followed their Western counterparts and opened up outlets on every corner. Rest assured, you will never be far from a Coffee House (Кофе Хауз), Ideal Cup (Идеальная Чашка) or Shokoladnitsa (Шокаладница). But the independent cafes listed in this guide earn higher marks for atmosphere and artistry.

Drinking & Nightlife by Neighbourhood

➡ **Historic Heart** An endless choice of smart cafes, cool bars and busy clubs centred on Dumskaya ul.

➡ **Smolny & Vosstaniya** The city's coolest district is the preferred haunt of hipsters, serious musicians and clubbers.

➡ **Sennaya & Kolomna** Despite being decidedly quiet for the most part, there are a few excellent bars here.

➡ **Vasilyevsky Island** This residential area isn't noted for nightlife, but its big student population means it's never sleepy.

➡ **Petrograd & Vyborg Sides** It's rather quiet after dark north of the Neva, but Petrograd is home to the excellent Tunnel Club.

NEED TO KNOW

Opening Hours

Most pubs and bars are open very late indeed – typically from 6pm until 6am, although many use the cunningly unclear phrase 'until the last customer' (ie as long as you're still buying the drinks, the staff will be there to serve them to you). Cafes are usually open from early in the morning until the late evening – typically from 8am to 10pm. Clubs open around 11pm and close around 7am.

Service & Tipping

In most cafes and bars you'll be waited upon. Only in rougher, more crowded places will you usually have to go to the bar yourself. You'll rarely be expected to tip, unless you're in a very high-end place.

Legality

It's perfectly acceptable to drink in public in Russia, even on the way to work. Alcohol is legal on the street, but it's banned in the metro. The legal drinking age is 18 in Russia, though it's rarely enforced. Note that it is illegal for shops to sell alcohol between 11pm and 7am – so buy drinks in advance or you'll have to drink in a bar or restaurant between these times.

Smoking

There are also virtually no smoking restrictions in clubs, bars or cafes here and the majority of people light up on a night out, as you'll notice very quickly if you're not a fan of smoking.

Lonely Planet's Top Choices

Kitaysky Lyotchik (p95) One of the best live music venues in town and a great bar to boot.

Dom Beat (p94) Retro-funky and eclectic, this is where to kick back with a cocktail in style.

Dyuni (p94) Come and join the fun in this hipster sandpit.

Golubaya Ustritsa (p75) St Petersburg's coolest gay bar has them hanging from the rafters (literally).

Petrovich (p96) Relive the Soviet era through old pop songs and dancing.

Griboyedov (p94) Still St Petersburg's coolest electronic music club.

Best Cocktail Bars

MiXup Bar (p75)

Lobby Bar, Grand Hotel Europe (p76)

Barakobamabar (p75)

Radiobaby (p75)

Best Bars By Neighbourhood

Datscha (Historic Heart; p77)

Dyuni (Smolny & Vosstaniya; p94)

Hundertwasser Bar (Sennaya & Kolomna; p113)

Helsinki Bar (Vasilyevsky Island; p123)

Torn Off Balls (Petrograd & Vyborg Sides; p137)

Best St Petersburg Clubs

Tunnel Club (p137)

Mod Club (p75)

The Club (p95)

Radiobaby (p75)

Best for Beer

Grad Petrov (p122)

Hundertwasser Bar (p113)

Shamrock (p113)

Tinkoff (p76)

Terminal Bar (p94)

Best Bohemian Hangouts

Zhopa (p93)

Datscha (p77)

Dusche (p96)

Stirka (p112)

Belgrad (p77)

Best Drinks with a View

Terrassa (p73)

Café Singer (p76)

MiXup Bar (p75)

Igrateka (p94)

Best Gay Venues

Golubaya Ustritsa (Blue Oyster; p75)

Central Station (p76)

The Club (p95)

Malevich (p114)

Entertainment

The classical performing arts are one of the biggest draws to St Petersburg. Highly acclaimed professional artists stage productions in elegant theatres around the city, many of which have been recently revamped and look marvellous. Seeing a Russian opera, ballet or classical music performance in a magnificent baroque theatre is a highlight of any trip.

The Glorious Mariinsky

The Mariinsky Theatre (often still known outside Russia by its prerevolutionary name, the Kirov) gave the world Nijinsky, Nureyev and Baryshnikov among many, many others, and is understandably every visitor's first choice for entertainment in St Petersburg. Under the artistic direction of Valery Gergiev, the theatre has gone from strength to strength, and the 2012 opening of the vast New Mariinsky Theatre (next door to the 1860 Mariinsky Theatre) will certainly put the institution back on the world map of great ballet and opera houses.

Ballet & Opera

Beyond the Mariinsky, there's no shortage of ballet and opera in St Petersburg. The key is to check which troupes are performing or to look for specific directors, as it's not hard to find a turkey of a production, even of the Russian classics. Critics complain that the Russian renditions of well-known Western works often seem naive and over-stylised, so steer clear of Mozart. If you tire of Russian classics, keep your eye out for more modern productions and premieres, which are also staged at the Alexandrinsky and Mikhailovsky Theatres.

Far more likely to be good are productions of Tchaikovsky, Prokofiev, Rimsky-Korsakov or Shostakovich, all regulars on the playbills at most theatres. Choreography and staging of classics is usually traditional (some might even say uninventive), but that's why they're classics. Check *St Petersburg Times* reviews and listings for what's on during your visit.

Tickets

While ballet and opera productions remain an incredible bargain in other parts of the country, performing arts in St Petersburg don't come cheap. The Mariinsky, the Hermitage Theatre and the Yusupov Palace Theatre continue to charge foreigners big mark-ups on the Russian price (though, for the sake of legality, officially it's Russians who get the huge discount on the foreigner price). Generally speaking, even the foreigners' prices are still less than you would normally pay in Western Europe for a similar performance, and rest assured that the cheapest tickets in the 'nosebleed' section are dirt cheap, no matter what your passport says.

The standard way to buy tickets is from a theatre kiosk (театральная касса); these kiosks can be found scattered all over the city, or you can buy from the individual theatre box offices. You can also buy tickets online through many of the theatre's own websites, which is a good way to ensure you have seats for shows you want to see when you're in St Petersburg. Last-minute tickets are generally easy to find, with the exception of the Mariinsky and anywhere during the White Nights: book well in advance in both cases.

Classical Music

It's not unusual to see highly talented musicians working the crowds inside the metro stations, violinists single-handedly performing Vivaldi's *Four Seasons* and flautists whistling away at Mozart or Bach. That such talented musicians are busking in the streets (or under the streets, as the case may

NEED TO KNOW

Prices

Expect to pay a minimum of R500 for ballet and opera tickets – these will usually be for a seat with a restricted view in 'the gods' (the upper balconies), and the price will rise by R250 to R500 with each floor lower you go. The very best seats in the house at the Mariinsky will go for up to R3000, while an average seat will go for R1800. Classical concerts will generally be cheaper than ballet and opera, but will remain pricey if they're held in prestigious venues such as the Shostakovich Philharmonia or the Mariinsky Concert Hall: reckon on paying around R500 to R1000. Theatre tickets are far less expensive, starting from around R150 to R800.

Performance Times

Most ballet, opera and theatre performances begin at 7pm or 7.30pm. Come in good time to absorb the atmosphere (woe betide you if you're late – you'll have to face the wrath of the fearsome babushkas who ensure order in the theatre). During the White Nights, many theatres have two evening performances to meet the enormous demand for tickets, so you may find you can get tickets for a second show at 9pm.

Etiquette

Definitely dress up for the ballet, opera or theatre: Russians are dolled up to the nines on these occasions, and you'll stick out like a sore thumb if you aren't.

be) is testament to the incredible talent and training of Russian music students – and to the lack of resources of their cultural institutions. While it's possible to hear a good show in the metro station, a visit to one of the local orchestra halls is highly recommended. Besides the more famous musical venues, small-scale concerts are often hosted at the Maltiyskaya Capella within the Vorontsov Palace (p70), the Hermitage Theatre (p77) and the Glinka Capella (p77).

Theatre

Due to the language barrier, drama and comedy are less alluring prospects than music and dance. Nonetheless, St Petersburg has a long tradition in theatre, which remains vibrant today. Dozens of venues host local, national and international acting troupes. Performances are almost exclusively in Russian, but the repertoire is vast, from William Shakespeare to Anton Chekhov and everything in between.

While nearly all the drama is in Russian, there are occasional festivals in foreign languages and some Russian productions with subtitles. However, even if you go and see a play in Russian, the incredible 19th-century interiors and the sense of occasion surrounding the performances make for an interesting night out, even if you only stay for the first half (tickets are generally cheap enough to make this perfectly feasible).

To entertain your kids the good old-fashioned Russian way, take them to the circus or to one of the many impressive puppet theatres in town.

Banya

If you're looking for a completely different and uniquely Russian experience, then head to your nearest *banya* (steam bath). Enter the *parilka* (steam room) stark naked and sit back and watch the mercury rise (yes, the *banya* is normally segregated by gender, unless you book a private one with friends). To eliminate toxins and improve circulation, bathers beat each other with a bundle of birch branches, known as *veniki*. When you can't take the heat, retreat. A public *banya* allows access to a plunge pool, usually filled with ice-cold water. The contrast in temperature is invigorating, energising and purifying.

The *banya* has always been essential for surviving the coldest Russian months. Apparently, in the early days, Peter the Great was often sighted running naked from the bathhouse to jump in the Neva. A *banya* is not complete without a table spread with snacks, or at least a thermos of tea. And just when you think you have recovered, it's time to repeat the process. As they say in Russia, *S lyogkim parom* – easy steaming!

Cinema

For a city with such an illustrious cinematic history, St Petersburg has relatively few cinemas, and sadly nearly all foreign films are dubbed into Russian (and often poorly at that). Yet subtitled films are occasion-

Entertainment by Neighbourhood

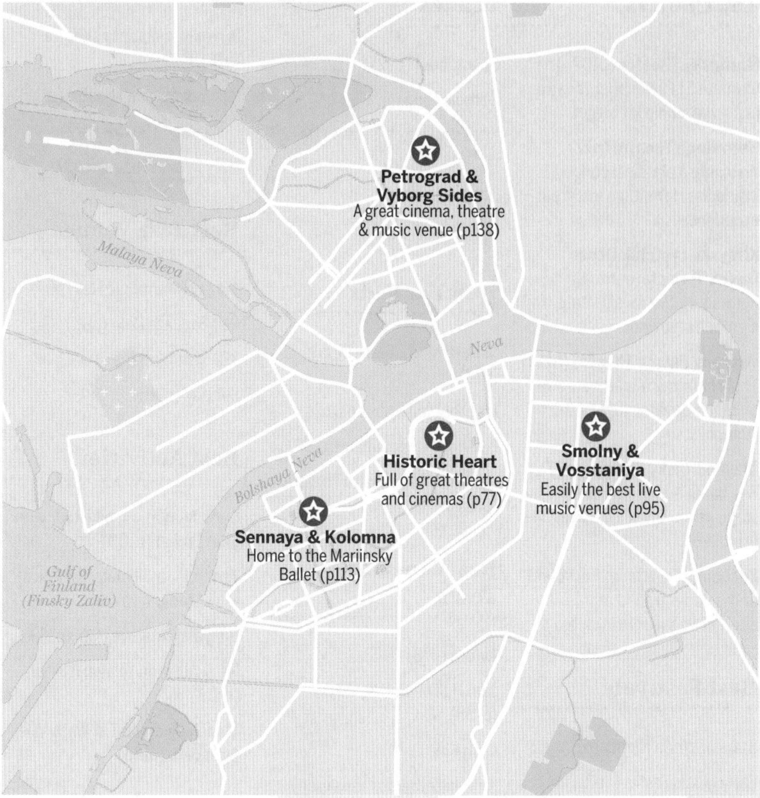

ally shown; check the *St Petersburg Times* for current listings. Also, there are several foreign film festivals run by cultural centres such as the Alliance Française, Goethe Institute and British Council, with films often shown in the original language.

Sports

St Petersburg's two twin sporting loves are football and ice hockey, and you can get tickets to see one or the other almost year round. The city's beloved football team, **Zenit** (www.fc-zenit.ru) plays regularly at its Petrovsky Stadium (p139) home, while the city's ice hockey team is **SKA** (Army Sports Club; www.ska.spb.ru), whose home ground is the Ice Palace (p100). Both teams attract an almost scary amount of loyalty in locals, as you'll see if you're near either of the grounds after an important match.

Lonely Planet's Top Choices

Mariinsky Theatre (p107) The ultimate St Petersburg theatre just got a whole lot bigger.

Hermitage Theatre (p77) Watching a classical concert inside the Hermitage is a great experience.

Kitaysky Lyotchik Dzhao Da (p95) Our favourite St Petersburg live music venue and a great bar to boot.

Yusupov Palace Theatre (p113) This charming mini theatre was once the private stage of the Yusupovs.

Alexandrinsky Theatre (p77) See ballet and drama on the stage where Chekhov's Seagull premiered.

Zoccolo (p96) Catch the sound of the underground at this alternative live music club.

Best Festivals

Stars of White Nights (p21)

Early Music Festival (p21)

Mariinsky Ballet Festival (p20)

Arts Square Winter Festival (p21)

Best Banyas

Degtyarniye Bani (p100)

Krugliye Bani (p139)

Kazachiye Bani (p115)

Mytninskiye Bani (p100)

Best Live Music Venues

Cosmonaut (p97)

Zoccolo (p96)

Kitaysky Lyotchik Dzhao Da (p95)

Dusche (p96)

Fish Fabrique (p97)

Best For Kids

St Petersburg State Circus (p78)

Feel Yourself Russian (p114)

Bolshoy Puppet Theatre (p97)

Demmeni Marionette Theatre (p78)

Best Cinemas in Town

Avrora (p78)

Jam Hall on Petrogradsky (p138)

Dom Kino (p78)

Kinoteatr Khudozhestvernny (p98)

Best for Classical Music

Glinka Capella House (p77)

Rimsky-Korsakov Conservatory (p114)

Mariinsky Concert Hall (p113)

Shostakovich Philharmonia (p77)

Best Small Theatres

Priyut Komedianta Theatre (p78)

Yusupov Palace Theatre (p113)

Hermitage Theatre (p77)

Maly Drama Theatre (p97)

Best Jazz Venues

Jazz Philharmonic Hall (p97)

Red Fox Jazz Café (p96)

JFC Jazz Club (p96)

Sunduk (p96)

Best Activities

Sunday-morning bike tour with Skat Prokat (p100)

Zenith football match at Petrovsky Stadium (p139)

Banya at Krugliye Bani (p139)

Ice skating on Yelagin Island (p139)

Splashing around at Waterville Aquapark (p123)

Shopping

St Petersburg's shopping scene today still lags way behind Moscow's glitzy capitalist paradise, but it's a massive improvement on the past with something for everyone hidden in an ever-increasing array of new shops. Recent trends have included Soviet chic and retro fashions, a glut of high-class new shopping centres and smart department stores as well as the perennials of Russian culture: plenty for curio hunters of all stripes.

Souvenirs

The city heaves with shops selling that most archetypal souvenir of Russia, the *matryoshka* (nesting doll). Most of these are overpriced and mass-produced: you have to really know what you're doing to find a unique one. One obvious place to shop is at the large Souvenir Market (p80) next to the Church on the Spilled Blood. It's certainly touristy, but the sheer number of sellers here means you can haggle and prices remain competitive. Other good places for souvenirs include Staraya Kniga (p79) for books, maps and postcards, Imperial Porcelain (p99) for Russia's famous tea sets, Yakhont (p79) for Fabergé-style jewellery and the Mariinsky Art Shop (p114) for a large selection of ballet- and opera-related gifts.

Shopping Centres

Shopping centres, for so long considered something rather Muscovite and tacky in St Petersburg, have finally become big business in the northern capital. First came somewhat central Sennaya (p115) and then the somewhat grand Vladimirsky Passage (p99), but very recently two massive palaces to consumerism have opened up on either side of Pl Vosstaniya, right in the heart of the city. The sheer size of Galeria (p99) is something to behold, and with its international designer names as well as local brands it's definitely the easiest one-stop shop for shopping in St Petersburg today. Nearby Nevsky Centre (p99) is smaller, but equally impressive, housing the first true department store in the city, Stockmann, and the best supermarket in the city in its basement.

Local Fashion

There's a small but enterprising fashion industry in St Petersburg with a few local designers blazing the trail and selling classy and creative clothing designs. While it has taken a long time for them to get any real recognition in a market obsessed with European labels, in the past few years it has become very fashionable to buy Russian fashion in Russia. Local fashion week, called 'Defile on the Neva', features local designers including Lilya Kissilenko, Natalya Soldatova and Tatyana Sulimina, all of whom have boutiques in the city. For international fashion labels, look no further than the Hermitage end of Nevsky pr and the super glamorous Bolshaya Konyushennaya ul, where you'll see many world-famous brands have set up shop.

Secondhand & Vintage

Sekond-khand (Секонд-ханд) is all the rage in St Petersburg, with fabrics and designs from the Soviet era now being very fashionable among people born after the fall of the Berlin Wall. In fact, many of the stores import secondhand clothing from Europe, such is the demand, and you'll see signs (in Russian) all over the city, telling you where to find the latest arrivals.

Soviet chic is so in that it goes way beyond clothing – accessories, music, art and (let's face it) a lot of plain junk is on sale all over the city, simply because it's from that era. If you're into Soviet bric-a-brac, then simply head to Udelnaya Fair (p138) on a Sunday for a truly mind-blowing array of Soviet junk and the odd real treasure.

NEED TO KNOW

Opening Hours

Most shops are open seven days a week, typically from 10am to 6pm Monday to Friday, and from 10am to 7pm at the weekends. These times vary of course, with many places opening earlier and closing later. In this guide we note the opening hours of shops only when they vary from these standard times.

Credit Cards

You can usually guess which shops take plastic and which don't, though it's always worth asking. In general, smarter, larger shops will nearly always take major credit cards, though an increasing number of smaller places and supermarkets now do too. If you plan to use your credit card, bring a passport or driving licence; otherwise many stores won't allow you to use it.

Caviar

It might be the glamorous face of Russian shopping, but the environmentally conscious will stay well clear of black caviar, which is widely available in food shops across the city. Sturgeon overfishing in the Caspian Sea has reached crisis levels and the international trade of caviar from wild sturgeon has been banned since 2006. That said, plenty of wild sturgeon roe ends up in shops in Russia, so think twice before buying it to bring home as a souvenir.

Markets & Supermarkets

Markets in St Petersburg are by far the best places to find high-quality, fresh fruit and vegetables, though they aren't always particularly well located. Try Sennoy Market (p115), Sytny Market (p138), Kuznechny Market (p99) and Maltsevsky Market (p100), where there's always a great selection – though be sure to haggle.

Most people these days shop in large, Western-style supermarkets. Unfortunately, it really pays to shop in one of the big ones in St Petersburg, as small and even medium-sized supermarkets are frustratingly understocked and lack the most basic of fresh products. The very best supermarkets in the city are expensive but worth the extra effort and expense – there's sumptuous Stockmann (p99), elite favourite Lend (p99), Galeria's enormous Okey (p99) and the rather out-of-the-way, but fantastically stocked French hypermarket Auchan (p100). Passable local supermarket chains you'll find all over the city include Lenta (Лента), Dixy (Дикси) and Nakhodka (Находка).

Shopping by Neighbourhood

➡ **Historic Heart** The city's commercial heart positively throbs with shopping possibilities, from thrift store to department store.

➡ **Smolny & Vosstaniya** Dominated by two enormous shopping centres, there's nevertheless plenty of unique shopping here too.

➡ **Sennaya & Kolomna** This quiet neighbourhood offers some truly offbeat, quirky and arty shopping experiences.

➡ **Vasilyevsky Island** Despite being very residential, Vasilyevsky Island is not known for shopping and has nothing to offer travellers.

➡ **Petrograd & Vyborg Sides** You have to look for it, but you'll find some great fashion and souvenir shopping here.

Lonely Planet's Top Choices

Gostiny Dvor (p70) Discover one of the world's oldest shopping malls.

Dom Knigi (p79) This beautiful building is one of Nevsky's most impressive.

Mariinsky Art Shop (p114) Bring a piece of the ballet home with you after the performance.

Staraya Kniga (p79) Antiquarian fun at this bookshop that also sells old maps and postcards.

Udelnaya Fair (p138) Find the gems among the junk at this amazing, sprawling place.

Best Souvenirs

Matryoshka (nesting doll) from Souvenir Market (p80)

Samovar from Tula Samovars (p100)

Fabergé style jewellery from Yakhont (p79)

Russian army uniform from Military Shop (p79)

Soviet kitsch from Udelnaya Fair (p138)

Best Shopping Streets

Nevsky pr (Historic Heart)

Bankovsky per (Historic Heart)

Zagarodny pr (Smolny & Vosstaniya)

Kanal Griboyedova (Historic Heart)

Pushkinskaya ul (Smolny & Vosstaniya)

Bolshoy pr (Petrograd Side)

Best Fashion Shops

Day & Night (p138)

Grand Palace (p142)

Kisselenko Fashion Salon (p98)

Prostranstvo Kultury (p80)

The People Showroom (p80)

Best Bookshops

Dom Knigi (p79)

Staraya Kniga (p79)

Writers' Bookshop (p79)

Anglia Books (p98)

Bukvoed (p79)

Best Art Shopping

Dom Knigi (p79)

Hermitage Shop (p42)

Pushkinskaya 10 (p88)

Borey Art Centre (p98)

Best Farmers Markets

Kuznechny Market (p99)

Sennoy Market (p115)

Sytny Market (p138)

Maltsevsky Market (p100)

Best Quirky Shopping

OFF (p98)

Tula Samovars (p100)

Military Shop (p79)

Staraya Kniga (p79)

Explore St Petersburg

ST PETERSBURG TOP SIGHTS

St Isaac's Cathedral (p103)

Neighbourhoods at a Glance

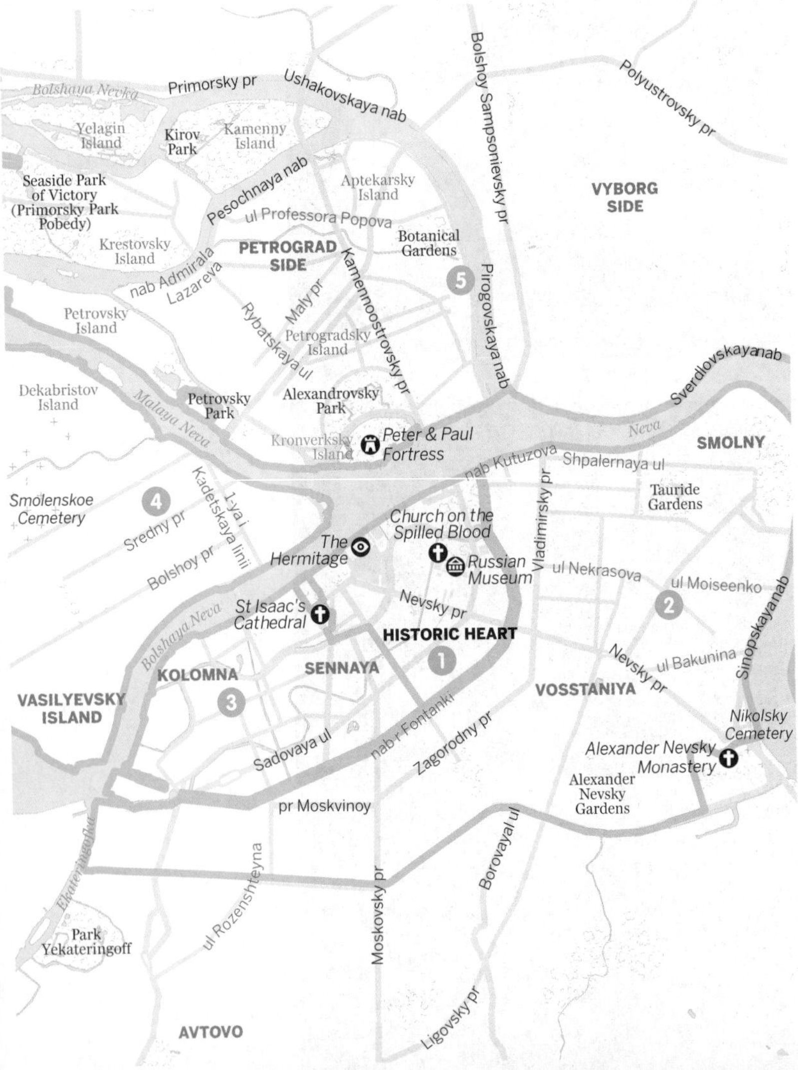

1 Historic Heart (p42)

The heart of the city is the area between the Neva River and the Fontanka River. It is cut in two by Nevsky pr, the city's vast main avenue, and separated from Sennaya and Kolomna by Gorokhovaya ul. The most famous sights are packed together extraordinarily tightly here, including the Hermitage, Kazan Cathedral and the Church on the Spilled Blood. It's a fast-paced, crowded part of the city and is its commercial as well as its tourist heart. A majority of the city's best hotels and good restaurants can be found here, and whether you stay here or not, it's where you'll inevitably spend much of your time in St Petersburg.

2 Smolny & Vosstaniya (p81)

This agglomeration of four districts (Smolny, Liteyny, Vosstaniya and Vladimirskaya) is also part of the city centre. The Smolny peninsula is a well-heeled residential district dominated by the Smolny Cathedral, while next-door Liteyny is centred on Liteyny pr, a commercial street between the Smolny and the Fontanka River. South of Nevsky pr are Vosstaniya and Vladimirskaya. Vosstaniya is the focus of St Petersburg's nascent underground scene, while Vladimirskaya, named after the stunning Vladimirsky Cathedral, is a mercantile district full of shopping, markets and a clutch of quirky museums.

3 Sennaya & Kolomna (p101)

These two areas adjoin the Historic Heart and are almost as historic themselves, even though they're quite different from one another. Sennaya is centred on Sennaya Pl (the Haymarket), a traditionally poor area immortalised in Dostoevsky's *Crime and Punishment* and one that has somehow retained its seedy and down-at-heel air despite a big attempt to redevelop it. Kolomna is the largest of seven islands and a quiet, rather out-of-the-way place, although one steeped in history and great beauty. It contains the world-famous Mariinsky Theatre and more canals and rivers than any other part of the city.

4 Vasilyevsky Island (p116)

The concentration of historical sights at Vasilyevsky Island's eastern edge was originally set to be the administrative heart of the city under Peter the Great, but the plan was never carried out and today the island is largely residential, with a uniform grid system and several busy shopping streets. The western edge of the island is more empty and industrial, but houses the fantastic new Erarta Museum of Contemporary Art, the main reason to come out here.

5 Petrograd & Vyborg Sides (p124)

The Petrograd Side is a fascinating place that includes everything from the Peter and Paul Fortress to an impressive clutch of Style Moderne buildings lining its main drag. The Petrograd Side also hosts St Petersburg's beautiful mosque, many interesting museums and huge swathes of parkland on the Kirov Islands, the city's largest green lung. The Vyborg Side, home to the Finland Station, is famous for its role in Soviet history and can be a little bleak. That said, a walk around the ugly but fascinating postindustrial landscape here will appeal to anyone with palace fatigue, and a few interesting sights make coming out here worthwhile.

Historic Heart

Neighbourhood Top Five

❶ Spend an entire day in the **Hermitage** (p44), taking a tour through millennia of art and culture from around the world, get lost in the apartments of the Romanovs, see the latest temporary exhibits in the Great Hall and take a tour of the dazzling Golden Rooms.

❷ Gawp at the view of the **Church on the Spilled Blood** (p64) from Kanal Griboyedov, and then be awestruck by the mosaics inside.

❸ See perhaps the world's best collection of Russian art at the fantastic **Russian Museum** (p57).

❹ Take a **cruise** (p65) on the rivers and canals of the Historic Heart, the best way to see this watery city!

❺ Enter the embrace of the architectural mishmash that is the **Kazan Cathedral** (p65) and see atmospheric Orthodox ritual in full swing inside.

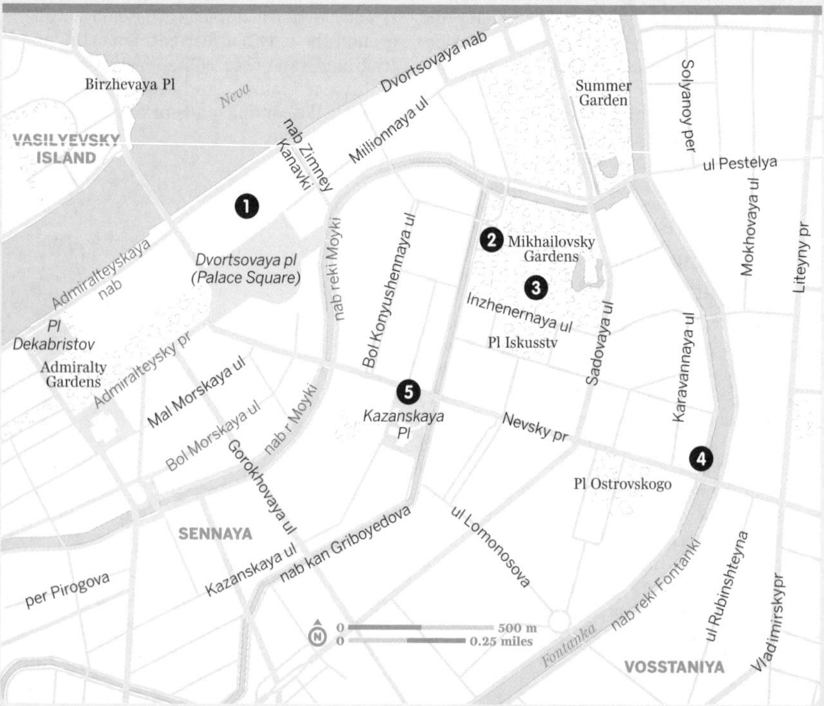

For more detail of this area, see Map p254

Explore: Historic Heart

Home to most of St Petersburg's top sights, the Historic Heart is where most people will spend most of their time in the city. The area is packed full of palaces, churches, museums, canals and parks, and there's almost no limit to the amount of things to see and do here.

A good place to start is impressive Palace Sq, where you'll see the Hermitage in all its glory along with the amazing panorama of the General Staff Building and the great Neva River: an unforgettable St Petersburg first impression. From there, cherry-pick your way through the rest of the neighbourhood over a couple of days or so.

Nevsky pr, the city's main avenue, dominates every itinerary of course, and you'll find yourself back on its crowded pavements throughout your visit, whether you like it or not. Do try to spend some time off the main drag though, as this fascinating district deserves to be fully explored.

Local Life

- **Parks** On a sunny day the vast Mars Field (p69) is a great place for a picnic and some sunbathing, especially while the ever-popular nearby Summer Garden remains under restoration. Another alternative is the lovely Mikhailovsky Gardens (p57), behind the Russian Museum.
- **Free Art** Locals flock to the Hermitage (p44) on the first Thursday of each month when entrance is free, although the crowds can be huge!
- **Hangouts** At the weekend the bars on ul Dumskaya (p77) are party central for St Petersburg's cool kids and a local experience not to be missed. The even more 'in the know' crowd hangs out in the bars around nearby Bankovsky per.

Getting There & Away

- **Metro** This neighbourhood is served by three metro stations: the interconnecting Nevsky Prospekt (Line 2) and Gostiny Dvor (Line 3) and the brand-new Admiralteyskaya (Line 5), right around the corner from the Hermitage.
- **Trolleybus** The number 7 bus, which runs the length of Nevsky pr, goes past Palace Sq and then crosses Dvortsovy most to Vasilyevsky Island.
- **Marshrutka** Very useful for getting up or down Nevsky pr in a matter of minutes, hundreds of minibuses run this route – but to check they don't turn off halfway, ask the driver if they go down 'vyess Nyevsky' (all of Nevsky pr).

Lonely Planet's Top Tip

Due to a long-standing problem with empty tables at lunchtime, even pretty upmarket restaurants in the historic heart offer excellent-value *biznes lanch* (business lunch), a set meal (often with elements of choice) that can be enjoyed between noon and 4pm. Even when lunch deals aren't offered, many places offer reductions of up to 20% on meal prices if you eat before the evening, making this a great time to eat out for those on a tight budget.

Best Places to Eat

- MiX in St Petersburg (p72)
- Terrassa (p73)
- Soup Vino (p72)
- Baku (p73)

For reviews, see p72

Best Places to Drink

- Radiobaby (p75)
- Datscha (p77)
- MiXup Bar (p75)
- Bar Without a Name (p75)

For reviews, see p75

Best Parks

- Summer Garden (p69)
- Mars Field (p69)
- Mikhailovsky Gardens (p57)
- Ploshchad Ostrovskogo (p70)

For reviews, see p65

IVANOV_ARK / DREAMSTIME ©

TOP SIGHTS
THE HERMITAGE

The State Hermitage Museum, the geographic and tourism centrepiece of St Petersburg, is one of the world's greatest art collections and usually most visitors' first stop in the city, even if it is simply to admire the baroque Winter Palace and the extraordinary ensemble of buildings that surround it. No other institution so embodies the opulence and extravagance of the Romanovs, and yet today, for the price of admission, anybody can parade down the grand staircases and across parquet floors, gawking at crystal chandeliers, gilded furniture and an art collection that cannot fail to amaze.

DON'T MISS...

- da Vinci (Room 214)
- Rembrandt (Room 254)
- Monet (Room 319)
- Matisse (Rooms 343–45)
- Picasso (Rooms 348–49)

PRACTICALITIES

- Map p254
- ☎710 9079
- www.hermitagemuseum.org
- Dvortsovaya pl 2
- adult/student R400/free
- ⏲10.30am-6pm Tue-Sat, until 5pm Sun
- Ⓜ Admiralteyskaya

The Western European Collection

Each year, millions of art lovers flock to the Hermitage to feast their eyes on the Western European collection. Occupying more than 120 rooms, the collection does not miss much: Spanish, Flemish, Dutch, French, English and German art are all covered from the 15th to the 18th centuries, while the Italian collection goes back all the way to the 13th century, including the Florentine and Venetian Renaissance, with priceless works by Leonardo da Vinci, Raphael, Michelangelo and Titian. A real highlight is the enormous collection of Dutch and Flemish painting, in particular the spectacular assortment of Rembrandt, most notably his masterpiece *Return of the Prodigal Son.*

Impressionism & Post-Impressionism

Another undeniable highlight of the Hermitage is the collection of French and German paintings from the 19th and 20th centuries. This collection of impressionist and post-impressionist paintings is arguably the best in the world, especially considering recent additions: much of this artwork was displayed for the first time in the 1990s, when the museum revealed some fabulous art hoards kept secret since seizure by the Red Army from Germany at the end of WWII. It is now displayed under the title 'Hidden Treasures Revealed' and can be found on the 2nd floor of the Winter Palace. The rooms on the 3rd floor, devoted to Monet, Cézanne, Renoir, Van Gogh and Gaugin, are some of the museum's most impressive.

Modern European Painting

The 3rd floor of the Winter Palace is hallowed ground for anyone passionate about early-20th-century art. Huge caches of Matisse and Picasso masterpieces, including several paintings from Picasso's blue period, crown the collection's modern end, alongside works by Kandinsky, Malevich, Léger and many other important names from the era. Matisse's huge primitivist canvases *Music* and *The Dance* are other important highlights, along with his famous *Portrait of the Artist's Wife*. If the wealth of the collection itself seems limitless, imagine that there's about 20 times more still in its vaults.

VISITING THE HERMITAGE

The Hermitage is a dynamic institution. Displays change, renovations continue, specific pieces go on tour, and temporary exhibitions occupy particular rooms, displacing whatever normally resides there, so be prepared for slight changes to the following.

First Floor Exhibits

To get here you'll need to go up to the 2nd floor and then down via the stairs between Rooms 153 and 156 or between Rooms 289 and 288.

Rooms 1–26: Prehistoric Artefacts

The prehistoric collection at the Hermitage contains thousands of artefacts dating from as far back as the Palaeolithic era (500,000 to 12,000 BC). Most of the items were excavated from different regions of the USSR during the Soviet era. The following are the highlights:

Room 12 Carved petroglyphs (dating to 2000 BC) were taken from the northeastern shores of Lake Onega after archaeological expeditions in 1935.

Rooms 13–14 Excavations of a burial mound in the northern Caucasus include the corpse of a nomadic chief, lavishly dressed and covered in jewels.

HERMITAGE TIPS

Reserve tickets online (www.hermitagemuseum.org) and print out the receipt before you travel to St Petersburg. Your voucher is not tied to any date, so you can go anytime during your trip. Walk straight into the Hermitage and collect your ticket without waiting in line – magic. Choose what you take inside the museum carefully – leave jackets and bags in the cloakroom, though be aware that you can't go back for anything without leaving the museum. Handbags and plastic bags are allowed in the Hermitage, but backpacks aren't.

Bring a sandwich or some snacks and a bottle of water with you: you can't leave the museum for lunch without buying a second ticket to go back in, and both the eating options in the Hermitage are rather pitiful and overpriced.

A HALF-DAY TOUR

Successfully visiting the State Hermitage Museum, with its four vast interconnecting palaces, and some 365 rooms of displays, is an art form in itself. Our half-day tour of the highlights can be easily done in four hours, or can also be extended to a full day.

Once past ticket control, take a right at the end of the Rastrelli Gallery to see Room 101, the fantastic Egyptian collection. Return the way you came and then head up the incredibly grand **Jordan Staircase** 1 to the Neva Enfilade and the Great Enfilade for the impressive staterooms, the Romanov's private apartments and the **Palace Church** 2 . Head back towards the Jordan Staircase via Rooms 153 and 151 for a full survey of the Romanovs in portrait form. Next visit Hidden Treasures Revealed, a superb survey of late-19th and early-20th-century French art, before proceeding to the Pavilion Hall to see the amazing Peacock Clock. Take in the Renaissance in the Italian rooms, where you shouldn't miss masterpieces by **Da Vinci** 3 and **Caravaggio** 4 , and should see both the absorbing Spanish and Dutch art collections, the latter culminating in the **Rembrandt** 5 orgy of Room 254. Finally, walk through the Great Enfilade, take the staircase to the 3rd floor and end your tour with the modern collection from the impressionists, including a superb room of **Monet** 6 and two show-stopping rooms of **Picasso** 7.

TOP TIPS

➡ **Queues** Reserve tickets online to skip the long lines.

➡ **Dining** Bring a sandwich and a bottle of water with you: the cafe is dire.

➡ **Footwear** Wear comfortable shoes.

➡ **Cloakroom** Bear in mind the only one is before ticket control, so you can't go back and pick up a sweater.

Picasso
The Absinthe Drinker, Room 348
Picasso's blue period is represented in the Hermitage by four paintings, of which this is arguably the most significant. Painted when Picasso was just 22 years old, it is a stunning portrayal of human loneliness.

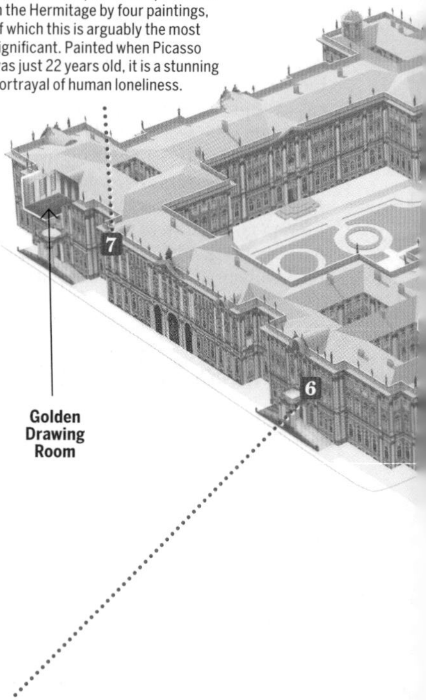

Monet
Waterloo Bridge, Effect of Mist, Room 319
The Monets in Room 319 make up a sublime ensemble, but no painting is more subtle and delicate than this one, painted from the artist's suite at the Savoy Hotel and depicting the extraordinary light during a foggy morning in London.

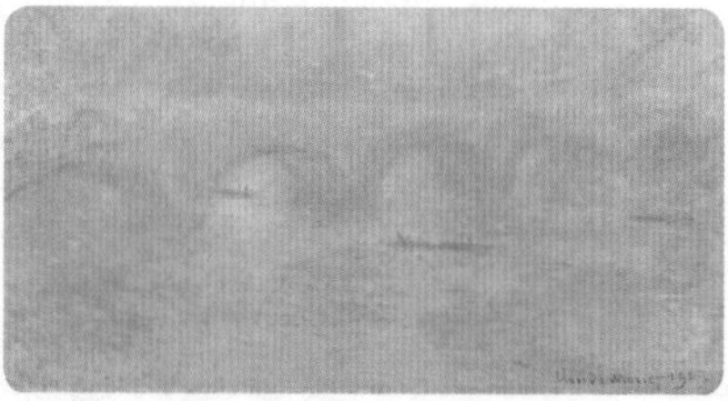

LEE FOSTER / LONELY PLANET IMAGES ©

Jordan Staircase

Originally designed by Rastrelli, this incredibly lavish staircase is named for the celebration of Christ's baptism in the River Jordan, for which the imperial family would descend the stairs annually to the Neva River.

Rembrandt

Return of the Prodigal Son, Room 254
Perhaps the most famous painting in the Hermitage is this colossal psychological masterpiece. Inspired by the Bible story, the scene of a wayward son returning to his father is a moving portrait of contrition and forgiveness.

DANITA DELIMONT / ALAMY ©

Da Vinci

Madonna and Child (Madonna Litta), Room 214
One of just a handful of paintings known to be the work of Leonardo da Vinci, the *Madonna Litta* makes an interesting counterpart to the Hermitage's other Da Vinci painting, the *Benois Madonna*.

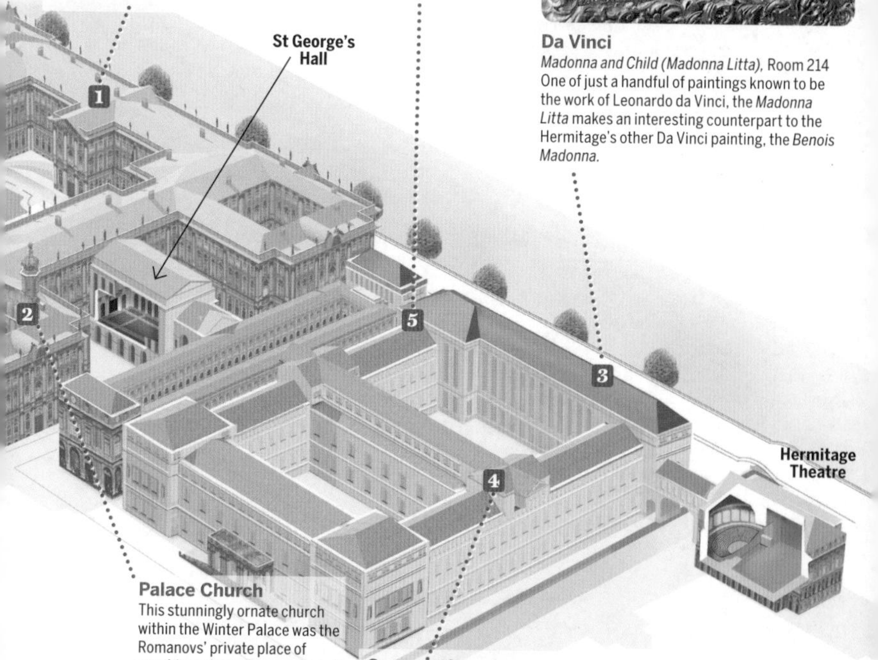

Palace Church

This stunningly ornate church within the Winter Palace was the Romanovs' private place of worship and saw the marriage of the last tsar, Nicholas II, to Alexandra Fyodorovna in 1895.

Caravaggio

Lute-Player, Room 237
The Hermitage's only Caravaggio is one of three versions of this painting in existence (the other two are in private collections). Caravaggio apparently described the work as the best piece he'd ever painted.

DAVID PARKER / ALAMY ©

IGOR GOLOVNOV / ALAMY ©

THE HERMITAGE — 1ST FLOOR

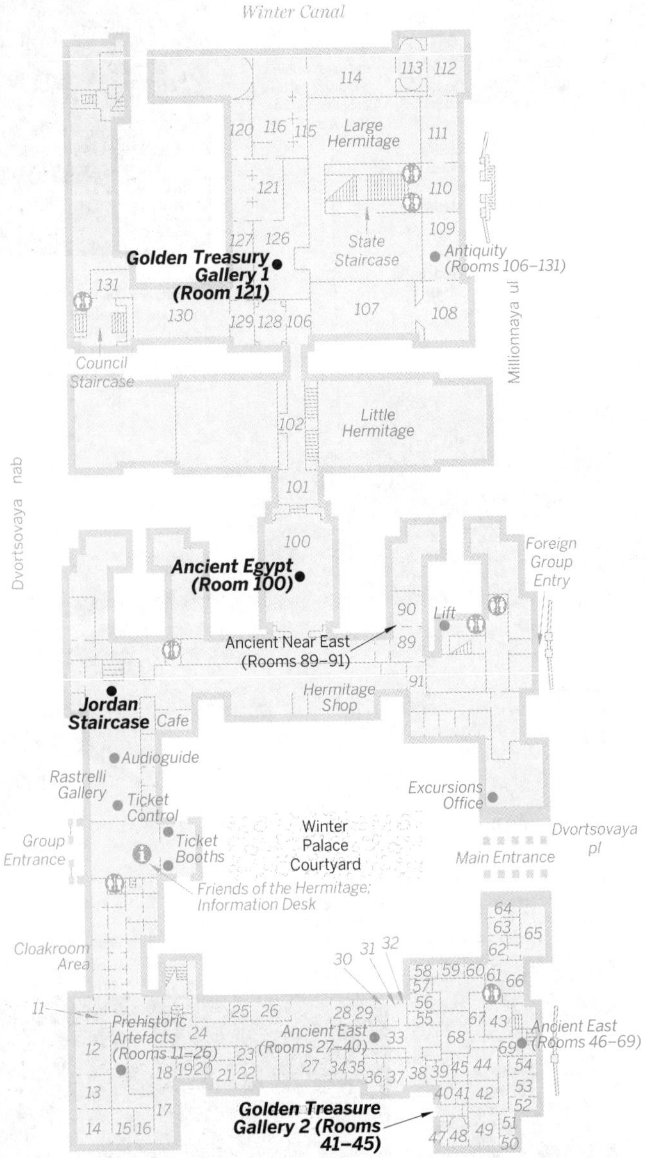

Golden Drawing Room (p53), Winter Palace

Room 26 This room contains human corpses that are more than 2000 years old, as well as a fantastically reconstructed wooden cart.

Rooms 27–40 & 46–69: Ancient East

Recently redesigned, these excellent galleries present exhibits from Central Asia, Siberia and the Caucasus, dating as far back as the 10th century BC. Rooms 47 to 51 feature impressive 7th- and 8th-century relics from Panjakent in present-day Tajikistan, while Rooms 67 to 69 feature art and artefacts of the Golden Horde, which swept through Russia in the 13th and 14th centuries.

Rooms 89–91: Ancient Near East

These rooms house a very impressive collection of cuneiform texts from Babylon and Assyrian limestone reliefs.

Room 100: Ancient Egypt

This large hall houses an incredible collection of ancient Egyptian artefacts uncovered by Russian archaeologists. The display spans the Egyptian era from the Old Kingdom (3000–2400 BC) to the New Empire (1580–1050 BC). The amazing ancient papyrus texts include *The Shipwrecked Sailor,* a secular text that dates to 1900 BC. There are many painted sarcophagi and tombstones carved with hieroglyphics, as well as a fascinating mummy from the 10th century BC.

THE HERMITAGE GOLD ROOMS

Known as the **Golden Rooms** (☎571 3420; admission R350; ⏰11am-4pm Tue-Sat, until 3pm Sun), these additional two special collections within the Hermitage are open only by guided tour, for which you should either call ahead to reserve a place, or buy a ticket at the entrance. The focus is a hoard of fabulous Scythian and Greek gold and silver from the Caucasus, Crimea and Ukraine, dating from the 7th to 2nd centuries BC, but you'll also see fabulous jewellery from Western Europe, and pieces from as far apart as China, India and Iran.

If you want to escape the crowds, check out Rooms 1 to 65 on the 1st floor of the Hermitage, which contain prehistoric relics as well as treasures from Siberia, Central Asia and the Caucasus. Due to the layout of the museum, you have to go up to the 2nd floor and then back down the stairs on the other side of the main entrance to get here. Because of this, you'll find you have many of the galleries down here almost entirely to yourself.

THE HERMITAGE — 2ND FLOOR

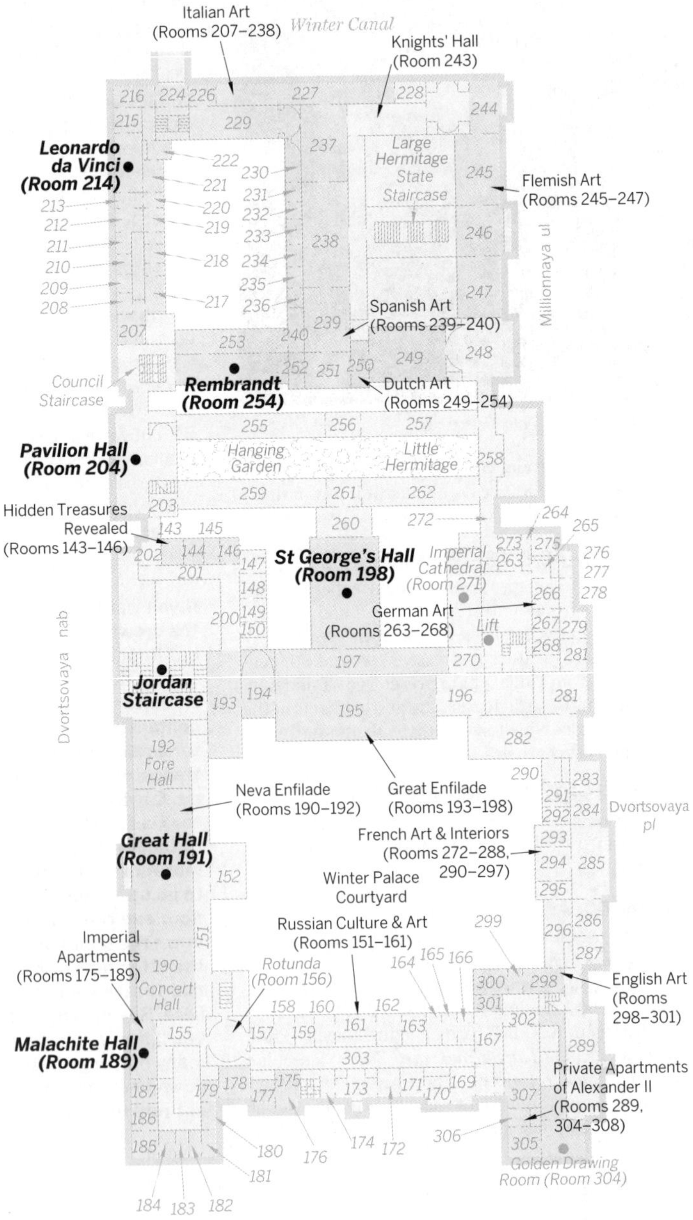
Italian Art (Rooms 207–238)
Winter Canal
Knights' Hall (Room 243)
Leonardo da Vinci (Room 214)
Large Hermitage State Staircase
Flemish Art (Rooms 245–247)
Millionnaya ul
Spanish Art (Rooms 239–240)
Council Staircase
Rembrandt (Room 254)
Dutch Art (Rooms 249–254)
Pavilion Hall (Room 204)
Hanging Garden
Little Hermitage
Hidden Treasures Revealed (Rooms 143–146)
St George's Hall (Room 198)
Imperial Cathedral (Room 271)
German Art (Rooms 263–268)
Lift
Dvortsovaya nab
Jordan Staircase
Fore Hall
Neva Enfilade (Rooms 190–192)
Great Enfilade (Rooms 193–198)
Dvortsovaya pl
French Art & Interiors (Rooms 272–288, 290–297)
Great Hall (Room 191)
Winter Palace Courtyard
Russian Culture & Art (Rooms 151–161)
Imperial Apartments (Rooms 175–189)
Concert Hall
Rotunda (Room 156)
English Art (Rooms 298–301)
Malachite Hall (Room 189)
Private Apartments of Alexander II (Rooms 289, 304–308)
Golden Drawing Room (Room 304)

Rooms 106–131: Antiquity

The Hermitage has more than 100,000 items from Ancient Greece and Rome, including thousands of painted vases, antique gemstones, Roman sculpture and Greek gold.

Room 107 The Jupiter Hall is a sumptuous space with portraits of sculptors on the ceiling.

Room 108 Designed by German neoclassicist architect von Klenze to imitate a Roman courtyard.

Room 109 Peter I acquired the sculpture *Tauride Venus* from Pope Clement XI. This piece – a Roman copy of a Greek original – was the first antique sculpture ever brought to Russia.

Room 111 Another impressive design by von Klenze, this one was intended to be a library (which explains the philosophers' profiles).

Room 130 Hall of Twenty Columns, containing a fabulous collection of Greco-Roman clay urns.

Second Floor Highlights

The 2nd floor houses many of the Hermitage's highlights, including its unbeatable Western European collection and its grandest state rooms.

Rooms 143–146: Hidden Treasures Revealed

These 19th- and 20th-century French oil paintings were confiscated by the Red Army from private collections in Germany. The collection, including works by Monet, Manet, Degas, Renoir, Pissaro, Cézanne, Seurat, Gaugin and Van Gogh, is stunning. If you like this, there is more on the 3rd floor.

Rooms 151–161: Russian Culture & Art

Most of the western wing of the Winter Palace contains the huge collection from ancient Rus (10th to 15th centuries) up through to the 18th century, including artefacts, icons, portraits and furniture.

Rooms 151 & 153 This long corridor, broken up by a vast clock, contains portraits of all the Russian tsars from Peter the Great to Nicholas II.

Rooms 155–156 Moorish Dining Room and Rotunda.

Rooms 157–162 The Petrovsky Gallery displays personal effects and equipment used by Peter the Great, as well as some beautiful early-18th-century furniture. Look for the ivory chandelier that was partly built by Peter himself.

Room 161 In 1880 there was an attempt on the life of Alexander II in this room. A young revolutionary, Khalturin, planted a bomb in the room below. It killed 11 soldiers when it went off, although the tsar had wandered into another room at the time.

PAVILION HALL

A highlight of the Hermitage is the ceremonial Pavilion Hall (Room 204), an airy white-and-gold room sparkling with 28 chandeliers. The south windows look on to Catherine the Great's hanging garden, while the north overlooks the Neva. The amazing floor mosaic in front of the windows is copied from a Roman bath. The centrepiece, though, is the incredible Peacock Clock, created by James Fox in 1772. A revolving dial in one of the toadstools tells the time, and on the hour (when it's working) the peacock spreads its wings and the toadstools, owl and cock come to life. The Peacock Clock is exercised on a monthly basis, but otherwise it's retired.

There is good provision of toilets throughout the Hermitage – don't make the rookie mistake of thinking that those at the foot of the Jordan Staircase as you enter are the only ones available, as the lines (especially for women) can be very long indeed.

Rooms 175–189: Imperial Apartments

This series of rooms represents the private apartments of the last tsar, Nicholas II and the imperial family. Many of these rooms were completed in 1894, and they now show off elaborate 19th-century interiors.

Room 178 Nicholas II spent much of his time in this wonderful Gothic library, topped with a sublime walnut ceiling.

Room 181 The relatively small and intimate Pompeii dining room.

Room 187 The griffin-motif furniture in this palace drawing room dates from 1805.

Room 188 This small dining room is where the Provisional Government was arrested by the Bolsheviks in 1917.

Room 189 Two tonnes of gorgeous green columns, boxes, bowls and urns have earned this room the name 'Malachite Hall', and it is one of the most striking rooms in the entire palace. The handiwork of architect Alexander Bryullov, it was completed in 1839. Three figurines on the wall represent Day, Night and Poetry. This was where the last meeting of the 1917 Provisional Government occurred, on the fateful nights of 25 and 26 October 1917; they were arrested soon after, in the Small Dining Room next door.

Rooms 190–192: Neva Enfilade

These grand ceremonial halls are used for temporary exhibitions.

Room 190 This Concert Hall was used for small soirees. The enormous ornate silver tomb was commissioned by Empress Elizabeth for the remains of Alexander Nevsky.

Room 191 As many as 5000 guests could be entertained in the Great Hall (also called Nicholas Hall). The palace's largest room was the scene of imperial winter balls.

Room 192 This anteroom was used for pre-ball champagne buffets.

Rooms 193–198: Great Enfilade

You'll find more staterooms here.

Room 193 Field Marshals' Hall is known for its military-themed chandelier and its portraits of six of Russia's great military leaders. This is where the disastrous fire of 1837 broke out.

Room 194 The Hall of Peter the Great contains his none-too-comfy throne.

Room 195 This gilt Armorial Hall contains chandeliers engraved with the coat-of-arms of all the Russian provinces.

Room 197 The 1812 War Gallery is hung with 332 portraits of Russian and allied Napoleonic war leaders.

Room 198 St George's Hall was the staterooms where the imperial throne used to sit. With white Carrara marble imported from Italy and floors crafted from the wood of 16 different tree species, it is a splendid affair.

Rooms 207–238: Italian Art

Covering 30-plus rooms, the Hermitage's collection of Italian art traverses the 13th to the 18th centuries. The highlights are certainly the works by the Renaissance artists: Leonardo da Vinci, Raphael, Giorgione and Titian. Look also for Botticelli, Caravaggio and Tiepolo.

Room 207 The earliest example in this collection is *The Crucifixion,* painted by Ugolino Di Tedice in the second half of the 13th century.

Jordan Staircase, Winter Palace

Room 214 Of a dozen or so original paintings by da Vinci that exist in the world, two are here. The very different *Benois Madonna* (1478) and *Madonna Litta* (1490) are named after their last owners. For years, the latter was considered lost. However, in 1909, the Russian architect Leon Benois surprised the art world when he revealed that it was part of his father-in-law's collection.

Room 217 Giorgione is one of the most mysterious painters of the Renaissance, as only a few paintings exist that are known for certain to be his work. A portrait of idealised beauty, *Judith* is said to represent the inseparability of life and death.

Room 221 The work of Titian, the best representative of the Venetian school during the 16th century, is featured here: *Dana* and *St Sebastian* are widely accepted as two of his masterpieces.

Rooms 226–227: Loggia of Raphael When Catherine the Great visited the Vatican she was so impressed that she commissioned Quarenghi to create this copy of a Vatican gallery; a team of Raphael's students recreated the master's murals on canvas. Note the occasional Russification on these versions: the two-headed eagle of the Romanov dynasty replaces the papal coat-of-arms.

Room 229 Here you'll enjoy two pieces by Raphael, *The Holy Family* and *Madonna and Child,* as well as many pieces by his disciples. This room usually contains the Hermitage's only piece by Michelangelo, a marble statue of a crouching boy.

JORDAN STAIRCASE

The main staircase of the Winter Palace – a magnificent creation of Bartolomeo Rastrelli – is a great introduction to the opulence of the tsars and was originally known as the Ambassadorial Staircase. However, in the 19th century it became known as the Jordan Staircase as every year on 6 January the imperial family would descend these stairs to the Neva River for the celebration of Christ's baptism in the River Jordan. The tradition was to cut a hole in the ice and ladle out a cup of water, which was then blessed by the Metropolitan of St Petersburg and ceremoniously drunk by the emperor.

Rooms 289 and 304–308 comprise the private apartments of Tsar Alexander II. His wife Maria Alexandrovna had most of them redesigned to her liking when she moved here in the 1840s. Most spectacular is Room 304, the Golden Drawing Room, which features a fabulous gilt ceiling and a marble fireplace with an intricate mosaic over the mantle.

THE HERMITAGE — 3RD FLOOR

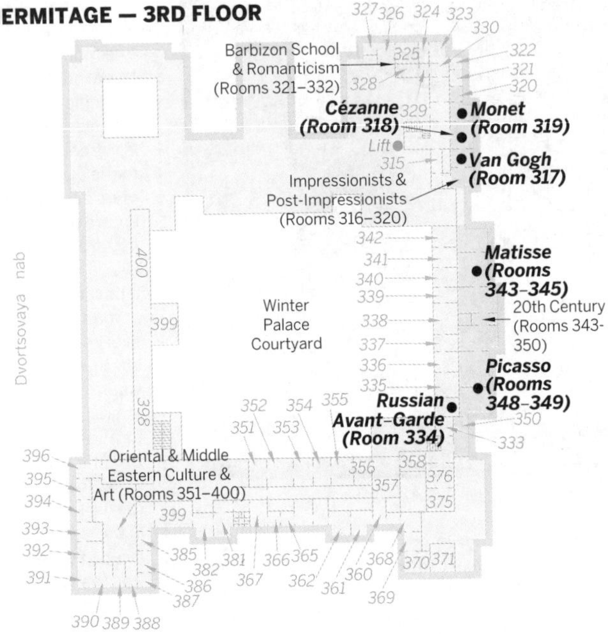

Rooms 237–238 These Italian Skylight Halls are bathed in natural light, which highlights the ornately moulded ceilings.

Rooms 239–240: Spanish Art

Ranging from the 16th to the 18th centuries, this collection includes the most noteworthy artists of this 'Golden Age' of Spanish painting: Murillo, Ribera and, of course, Velázquez. The collection also includes two remarkable paintings from the 16th century: the marvellous *St Peter and St Paul,* by El Greco; and *St Sebastian Cured by St Irene,* by Ribera.

Room 243: Knights' Hall

Nicholas I started collecting artistic weapons and armaments from around the world. Here is the Western European collection, featuring four impressive 16th-century German knights sitting atop their armoured horses.

Rooms 245–247: Flemish Art

These three rooms dedicated to 17th-century Flanders are almost entirely consumed by three artists: Peter Paul Rubens, Anthony Van Dyck and Frans Snyders.

Rooms 249–254: Dutch Art

Dating from the 17th and 18th centuries, the Dutch collection contains more than 1000 pieces. The 26 paintings by Rembrandt in Room 254 nearly outshine anything else in these rooms. The collection traces his career, starting with *Flora* and *The Descent from the Cross,* which are noticeably lighter but more detailed. His later work tends to be darker and more penetrating, such as the celebrated *The Return of the Prodigal Son.* Painted in 1669, it arguably represents the height of Rembrandt's mastery of psychology in his paintings. The solemn baroque masterpiece is a moving portrait of unquestioning parental love and mercy.

Rooms 263–268: German Art

This small collection of German art ranges from the 15th to the 18th centuries. Among the earliest works there are five paintings by Lucas Cranach the Elder.

Room 271: Imperial Cathedral

The private imperial cathedral (closed at the time of writing for renovation) was the site of many royal weddings, funerals and other ceremonies, including the wedding of Nicholas II to Alexandra in 1894.

Rooms 272–288 & 290–297: French Art & Interiors

These rooms trace the development of French art from the 15th to the 18th centuries, including tapestries, ceramics, metalwork and paintings. Look for rooms devoted to Nicholas Poussin, founder of French Classicism, and Claude Lorrain, master of the Classical landscape. Room 282, Alexander Hall, is another testament to the victory over Napoleon in 1812.

Rooms 298–301: English Art

These rooms showcase 15th- to 18th-century English art. Highlights include *The Infant Hercules Strangling the Serpents,* by Sir Joshua Reynolds, which was commissioned by Catherine the Great to symbolise the growing strength of Russia. *Portrait of a Lady in Blue,* by Thomas Gainsborough, is perhaps the most famous piece in the collection.

Third Floor Highlights

The 3rd floor will amaze anyone with an interest in 20th-century art. Featuring everything from Impressionism to cubism, these galleries are many people's favourite.

Rooms 316–320: Impressionists & Post-Impressionists

Inspired by Romanticism, a group of painters in the 1860s began experimenting with painting modern life and landscapes, endeavouring to capture the overall effect of a scene instead of being overly concerned with details. The new trend – radical in its time – was known as Impressionism. After Impressionism, artists continued to use thick brush strokes, vivid colours and real-life subject matter, but they were more likely to use sharp lines and distorted shapes.

Room 316 Gaugin is famed for the primitive paintings that he created in Tahiti.

RUSSIAN ARK

Russian film director Alexander Sokurov celebrated the Hermitage's history in his highly lauded film *Russian Ark* (2002). The viewer sees through the eyes of an unnamed narrator, a ghost who resides in the Winter Palace. The other character is a 19th-century visitor, the Marquis de Custine, who wrote extensively about his travels to Russia. In one unedited sweep (the film was the first-ever feature length production to be shot in one continuous take), the narrator guides the 'European' through 33 rooms of the Winter Palace and 300 years of Russian history.

Kazimir Malevich's *Black Square* (Room 334) is the most striking painting of the Petrograd avant-garde. Malevich created several variants of the simple black square against a white background throughout his career, of which this is the fourth and last. It was taken by many as a nihilistic declaration of the 'end of painting', causing both awe and outrage.

Room 317 Spectacular Van Goghs including *Thatched Cottages* (1890) and the dreamy *Memory of the Garden at Etten* (1888) are on display here.

Room 318 This remarkable room has some of Cézanne's most famous pictures, including *Mont Sainte-Victoire, Lady in Blue* and *The Smoker*. Pissarro's *Blvd Montmartre, Sunny Afternoon* (1897) is also here.

Room 319 Feast your eyes on the paintings by Claude Monet, including his early work *Lady in a Garden*. One of the most extraordinary paintings in the entire Hermitage collection is his later work, *Waterloo Bridge, Effect of Mist* (1903). The room also has three sculptures by Rodin.

Room 320 Five Renoir paintings are here, including the celebrated *Portrait of the Actress Jeanne Samary* (1878) and the iconic *Child With a Whip* (1885).

Rooms 321–331: Barbizon School & Romanticism

Romanticism was the prevailing school of art in the 19th century and Delacroix is the most celebrated French Romantic painter. Prime examples of his style can be seen in *Moroccan Saddling a Horse* and *Lion Hunt in Morocco* (Room 321).

The Barbizon School, named for the village where this group of artists settled, reacted against this romanticism, making a move towards realism. Gustav Courbet, Jean-Baptiste Camille Corot, Théôdore Rousseau and Jean-François Millet are all represented (Rooms 321 to 322).

Room 334: Russian Avant-Garde

This is the only room in the entire Hermitage to feature 20th-century Russian art (most is housed in the Russian Museum). Look for some examples of Kandinsky's early work, as well as paintings by Kazimir Malevich. This is the permanent home of the *Black Square* (1915), which went missing during the Soviet period, mysteriously reappearing in southern Russia in 1993. Oligarch Vladimir Potanin bought the painting for $US1 million and donated it to the Hermitage in 2002.

Rooms 343–350: 20th Century

Arguably, the collection culminates in these rooms, where you can see as many as 37 paintings by Matisse and almost as many by Picasso. Henri Matisse was initially classified as a Fauvist: indeed you can see work by his contemporaries in Room 350. But he continued to paint in his own particular style, even as Fauvism declined in the early 20th century. Around this time, Matisse met Pablo Picasso and the two became lifelong friends. Picasso is best known as the founder and master of cubism; but again, his work spanned many styles.

Rooms 343–345 A turning point for Matisse – and perhaps his most famous work – is *The Dance* (1910). The intense colours and the dancing nudes convey intense feelings of freedom. This panel – along with the accompanying *The Music* – was painted specifically for Russian businessman Sergei Shchukin. While these panels are certainly commanding, don't miss *The Red Room* and *Portrait of the Artist's Wife*.

Rooms 348–349 Picasso's blue period is characterised by sombre paintings in shades of blue. When he was only 22, he painted *The Absinthe Drinker*, a haunting portrait of loneliness and isolation. The sensuous *Dance with Veils* (1907) and *Woman with a Fan* (1908) are excellent representations of his cubist work, as are the ceramics on display here.

Rooms 351–400: Oriental & Middle Eastern Culture & Art

These 50 rooms display ancient art from the Far East, including China and Tibet, Indonesia, Mongolia and India. Also on display are art and artefacts from Syria, Iran, Iraq, Egypt and Turkey.

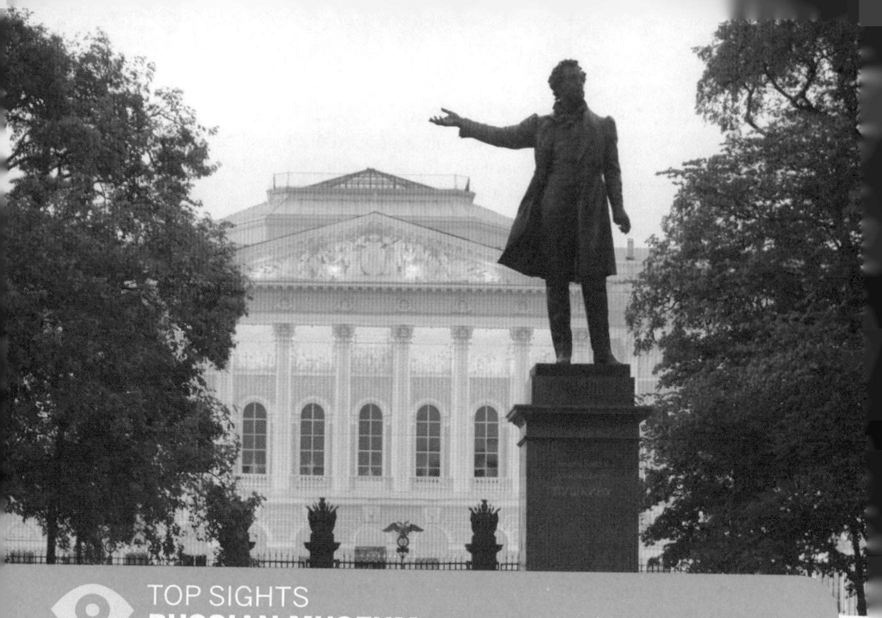

LOU JONES / LONELY PLANET IMAGES ©

TOP SIGHTS
RUSSIAN MUSEUM

Even if your time in St Petersburg is limited, don't miss this world-class museum's overview of eight centuries of Russian art. It's easily done in a half-day visit, unlike the vast and sometimes overwhelming Hermitage. While the Hermitage spreads its net across the cultures of the world, the Russian Museum – as its name suggests – focuses solely on Russian art, from ancient church icons to modern painting. The collection is magnificent and although it lacks some of the better-known paintings that can be found in Moscow's Tretyakov State Gallery, the Russian Museum's range is arguably more balanced.

The Museum's Locations

Mikhailovsky Palace was designed by Carlo Rossi and built between 1819 and 1825. It was a gift for Grand Duke Mikhail (brother of Tsars Alexander I and Nicholas I) as compensation for missing out on the throne. Nicholas II opened it as a public gallery on 7 March 1898. The museum originated from the collection begun by Tsar Alexander III, whose bust greets you on the magnificent main staircase.

The museum's Benois Wing houses the modern collection and was constructed between 1914 and 1919. It is now connected to the original palace and is accessible through an entrance on nab kanala Griboyedova. In 2002 all 8.7 hectares of the **Mikhailovsky Gardens** (⏲10am-10pm May-Sep, 10am-8pm Oct-Mar, closed Apr) were redesigned according to the original 19th-century plans. The gardens are absolutely lovely and offer the most impressive perspective of Mikhailovsky Palace.

DON'T MISS...

- *Peter I Interrogating Tsarevich Alexey in Peterhof* – Nicholas Ghe
- *Barge Haulers on the Volga* – Ilya Repin
- *The Last Day of Pompeii* – Karl Bryullov
- *Portrait of the Poetess Anna Akhmatova* – Nathan Altman

PRACTICALITIES

- Map p254
- www.rusmuseum.ru
- Inzhenernaya ul 4
- adult/student R300/150, combined 24hr ticket for all four palaces of the Russian Museum adult/student R600/300
- ⏲10am-6pm Wed-Sun, 10am-5pm Mon
- Ⓜ Nevsky Prospekt

THE PALACES OF THE RUSSIAN MUSEUM

As well as the magnificent Mikhailovsky Palace, the Russian Museum's main building, the museum also owns three other impressive palaces in the city centre, boasting temporary exhibits, permanent collections and grand staterooms. These are the Marble Palace (p66), the Stroganov Palace (p65) and Mikhailovsky Castle (p66). A good-value joint ticket for all four venues is valid for 24 hours. Of the palaces, the Marble Palace has the best art collection, while the Stroganov Palace has the best interiors.

Enter the museum via the ground floor entrance to the right of the main facade. Pick up a museum map before ascending the magnificent main staircase to the 1st floor, as this is where the chronological ordering of the exhibits begins.

The Museum's Collection

The collection is ordered chronologically from medieval icons to the present day. It starts on the 2nd floor and finishes on the 1st floor.

Rooms 1–4: Religious Icons

The first four rooms of the museum encapsulate a succinct but brilliant history of Russian icon painting, including work from the three major schools of Russian icon painting: Novgorod, and Pskov. Room 2 has *St Nicholas and Scenes of His Life*, while Room 3 features Russian master Andrei Rublev's massive *Peter and Paul* as well as his *Presentation of Christ in the Temple*. Room 4 is notable in its departure from earlier styles. Compare *Old Testament Trinity with Scenes from Genesis* with the completely atypical *Our Father* (1669).

Rooms 5–7: Petrine & Post-Petrine Art

Peter was a great patron of the arts and almost single-handedly brought the Western eye to Russian painting, as witnessed by the massive jump in style from ecclesiastical to secular subjects between Rooms 4 and 5. The room includes three busts of Peter and two portraits.

Room 6 includes some charmingly odd canvases in very strange shapes as well as mosaic portraits of both Peter and Catherine the Great, as well as of Elizabeth I, Peter's daughter. The centre of the room is taken up by a huge portrait of the ill-fated Peter III, although look out for the impressive bust of Prince Menshikov. Room 7 has an amazingly ornate ceiling. The room houses a sculpture of *Empress Anna with an Arab Boy* and a few impressive tapestries, including one that depicts Peter the Great at the Battle of Poltava, his greatest military victory.

Rooms 8–11: The Rise of the Academy

These rooms display the early works of the St Petersburg Academy of Arts. These artists borrowed the European classical aesthetic for their work. Look for portraits in Rooms 8 and 10 (including two portraits and a full-sized sculpture of Catherine the Great) and biblical themes in Room 9.

Room 11 is the Rossi-designed White Hall, which was Grand Duke Mikhail's drawing room. Here, the interior is the art – in this case representing the Empire epoch. It's wonderfully ornate and shiny – a perfect place to host musical greats like Strauss and Berlioz, who performed here.

Rooms 12–17: Dominance of the Academy

By the early 19th century the Academy of Arts was more and more influenced by Italian themes, given the unfashionability of France. In Room 12 look for

RUSSIAN MUSEUM — 1ST FLOOR

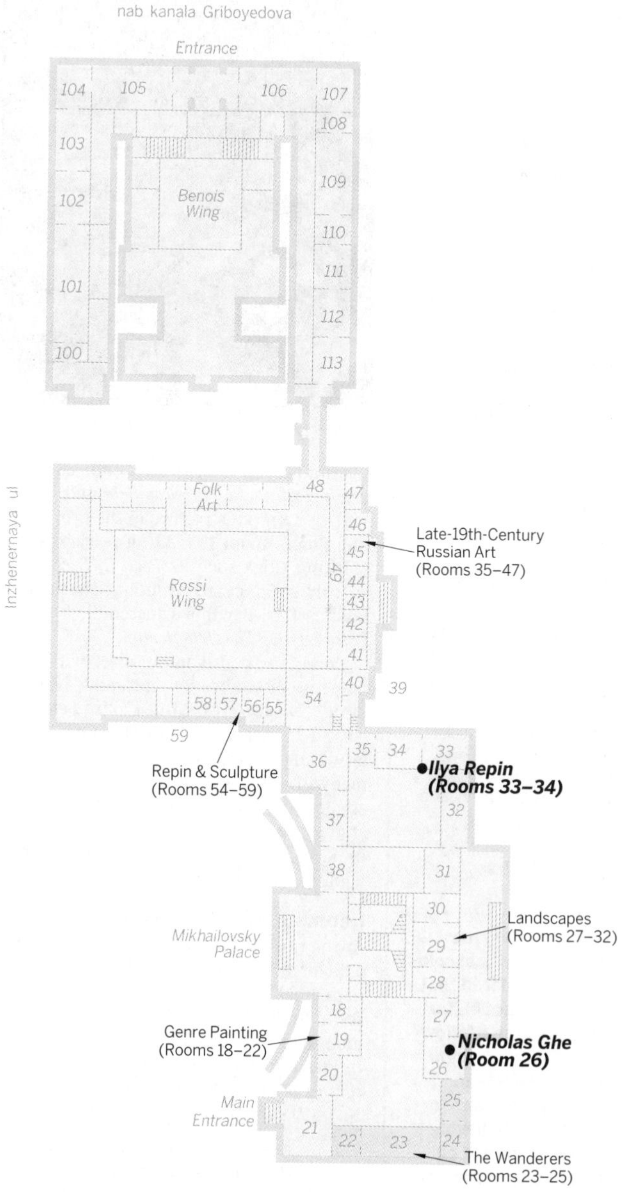
nab kanala Griboyedova
Entrance
104
105
106
107
108
103
109
102
Benois Wing
110
111
101
112
100
113
Inzhenernaya ul
Folk Art
48
47
46
45
Late-19th-Century Russian Art (Rooms 35–47)
Rossi Wing
49
44
43
42
41
40
39
58
57
56
55
54
59
Repin & Sculpture (Rooms 54–59)
36
35
34
33
Ilya Repin (Rooms 33–34)
37
32
38
31
30
Mikhailovsky Palace
29
Landscapes (Rooms 27–32)
28
18
27
Genre Painting (Rooms 18–22)
19
Nicholas Ghe (Room 26)
26
20
25
Main Entrance
21
22
23
24
The Wanderers (Rooms 23–25)

PETER I INTERROGATING TSAREVICH ALEXEY IN PETERHOF

One of Russian art's most famous historical paintings, Nicholas Ghe's masterpiece relates to the tumultuous relationship between Peter the Great and his son. Peter could not understand Alexey's character, so different from his own, and Alexey grew to hate his father's overbearing ways. Alexey foolishly went abroad and sought support from foreign leaders to place him on the Russian throne. Peter, paranoid by his later years, managed to convince Alexey to return home unpunished if he renounced his right to the succession. While Alexey kept his side of the bargain, Peter had his own son tortured to death as he tried to extract information about 'plotters' against him. This picture expertly captures the gulf between the two men, and foreshadows Alexey's brutal end in the Peter and Paul Fortress.

Ghe's painting met with such critical coldness he declared that art should not be for sale, became a follower of Tolstoy, bought a farm and began painting portraits for a pittance, believing everyone should be able to pay to preserve their image.

Original study for the Bronze Horseman (p106), *Etienne Falconet*

Vladimir Borovikovsky's magnificent *Catherine II Promenading in Tsarskoe Selo* and his *Portrait of Murtaza Kuli,* his picture of the brother of the Persian Shah. Room 13 is fill of peasant subjects with uplifting titles such as *Peeling Beetroot.* Room 14 is truly spectacular, including enormous canvases such as Karl Bryullov's incredible *The Last Day of Pompeii* and *The Crucifixion.*

Room 15 is also impressive, with the far wall made up of studies for Alexander Ivanov's masterpiece *The Appearance of Christ Before the People* (1837–57), which hangs in Moscow's Tretyakov Gallery. Ivanov spent 20 years on this work, but it was met with a negative critical reception. However, later generations appreciated the work, and even these studies, many of which mark a notable departure in terms of detail and representation. Room 17 pays tribute to the Academy Council.

Rooms 18–22: Genre Painting

At the turn of the 19th century, it became fashionable for 'genre painting' to look to themes from (an incredibly idealised) rural Russia, which you can see in Rooms 18 to 20. Room 21 contains some enormous canvases: *Phrina at the Poseidon Celebration in Elesium* by Genrikh Semiradsky, *Christian Martyrs at the Colosseum* by Konstantin Flavitsky and *Nero's Death* by Vasily Smirnov.

Rooms 23–25: The Wanderers

The Wanderers (Peredvizhniki) were a group of academy artists who saw their future outside the strict confines of that institution. They wandered among the people, painting scenes of realism that had never been seen before in Russian art. Look for brilliant works by Perov, including *Hunters at Rest* and the scathing *Monastery Refectory* (both works are often on loan, however).

Room 26: Nicholas Ghe

Ghe's masterpiece, *Peter I Interrogating Tsarevich Alexey in Peterhof,* is here. Ghe's other work, such as *Christ and his Disciples Come into the Garden of Gethsemane* and *The Last Supper,* are equally dark.

Rooms 27–32: Landscapes

Contemporaries of the Wanderers, landscape artists such as Ivan Shishkin (Room 27) were still popular. These rooms also document the rise of populist art, which had a strong social conscience and sought to educate the public. The best examples of this are Vladimir Makovsky's *The Condemned* and Konstantin Savitsky's *To War* (Room 31).

Rooms 33–34: Ilya Repin

This room contains several masterpieces by Ilya Repin (1844–1930), one of Russia's most famous painters. The iconic *Barge Haulers on the Volga* is sadly often on loan abroad, but even if this incredible picture isn't here, look for *Cossacks Writing a Letter to the Turkish Sultan* and his marvellous portrait of a barefoot Leo Tolstoy.

Rooms 35–47: Late-19th-Century Russian Art

These rooms display the large number of contradictory styles that were fashionable in St Petersburg before the explosion of the avant-garde. These include Vasily Surikov, a master of the historical painting that was in vogue in the late 19th century. His portrayals of *Yermak's Conquest of Siberia* and *Suvorov Crossing the Alps* (Room 36) are particularly romantic, but the lifelike rendition of Cossack rebel *Stepan Razin* (Room 37) is undoubtedly his most evocative.

Rooms 48–49: Antokolsky's Historical Paintings

Mark Antokolsky's *Ivan the Terrible* and *Death of Socrates* are on display either side of a souvenir stand. From here you enter the Benois Wing to your right or continue straight ahead for the comprehensive account of Russian folk art, featuring everything from kitchen equipment to window frames. The long corridor in Room 49 showcases posters from past exhibits at the Russian Museum.

Rooms 54–59: Repin & Sculpture

Room 54 features Repin's enormous rendition of the *Ceremonial Sitting of the State Council on 7 May 1901, Marking the Centenary of Its Foundation.* Around the walls are individual portraits of its members. Rooms 55 to 59 contain sculptures in storage, but behind glass walls, so still visible. Most interesting here is Etienne Falconet's model for his *Bronze Horseman.*

Rooms 66–71: Early-20th-Century Art

Room 66 is the home of the father of modern Russian art, Mikhail Vrubel (1856–1910). Some of his ground-breaking works include *Lady in Lilac, Epic Hero (Bogatyr)* and *Demon in Flight.* Rooms 67 to 71 include works by an array of important early-20th-century painters including Kuzma Petrov-Vodkin, Nikolai Sapunin, Mikhail Nesterov and Boris Kustodiev, whose *Merchant's Wife at Tea* is perhaps the most well-known picture here.

ILYA REPIN

Considered by most Russians to be the greatest artist the nation has ever produced, Ilya Repin (1844–1930) was originally a member of the Wanderers, but he outgrew the movement. He went on to produce key works of Russian realist and populist art. His masterpiece is *Barge Haulers on the Volga,* an unrivalled portrait of human misery and enslavement in rural Russia.

Repin spent the last years of his life at his idiosyncratic dacha Penates in a Gulf of Finland town now named Repino in his honour. Today it's a museum and possible to visit by taking the bus from outside the Ploshchad Lenina metro station.

Rooms 72–78: Russian Avant-Garde Painting

Between 1905 and 1917, the Russian art world experienced an explosion of creative inspiration that defied the stylistic categorisation that had existed before. Room 72 is home to Nathan Altman's gorgeous, semi-cubist *Portrait of the Poetess Anna Akhmatova* (Room 72), painted in 1914, and it remains one of his most famous works even though Akhmatova apparently didn't care for it herself. In the same room is Altman's striking *Self Portrait* (1911). Room 74 contains primitivist paintings by artist couple Natalya Goncharova and Mikhail Larionov.

Futurism and suprematism, including Malevich's *Red Square, Head of a Peasant* and *Black Square,* can be found in Rooms 75 to 76, while Room 77 is devoted to constructivism and features works by Rodchenko and Vladimir Lebedev. Room 78 displays the bright, ethereal work of Pavel Filonov.

Room 79: Kuzma Petrov-Vodkin

Spanning two centuries and surviving the Russian Revolution, Kuzma Petrov-Vodkin (1878–1939) was a unique painter. His work conveys a dreamlike atmosphere, much of it with homoerotic overtones. See *Mother of God* (1914–15) and another *Portrait of Anna Akhmatova* (1922).

Rooms 80–81: Early Soviet Art

Most paintings from the Stalin era may have been censored beyond meaning, but there are some interesting portraits of daily life here, such as Alexander Samokhvalov's *Militarised Komsomol* (1932–33) and various pictures from WWII showing heroic resistance and national unity. Room 81 ends with Vyacheslav Pakulin's beautiful *Nevsky on 9th July 1945,* depicting troops returning from the war.

Rooms 82–109: Late Soviet Art & Temporary Exhibits

With Stalin gone and the 'thaw' under way in the 1950s, Soviet art recovered somewhat from the severity of socialist realism. Idealised images of rural life and peasants still feature very strongly, however. These rooms are often used for special exhibitions, while Rooms 87 to 94 were being refurbished at the time of writing.

Rooms 23–25: The Wanderers

The Wanderers (Peredvizhniki) were a group of academy artists who saw their future outside the strict confines of that institution. They wandered among the people, painting scenes of realism that had never been seen before in Russian art. Look for brilliant works by Perov, including *Hunters at Rest* and the scathing *Monastery Refectory* (both works are often on loan, however).

Room 26: Nicholas Ghe

Ghe's masterpiece, *Peter I Interrogating Tsarevich Alexey in Peterhof,* is here. Ghe's other work, such as *Christ and his Disciples Come into the Garden of Gethsemane* and *The Last Supper,* are equally dark.

Rooms 27–32: Landscapes

Contemporaries of the Wanderers, landscape artists such as Ivan Shishkin (Room 27) were still popular. These rooms also document the rise of populist art, which had a strong social conscience and sought to educate the public. The best examples of this are Vladimir Makovsky's *The Condemned* and Konstantin Savitsky's *To War* (Room 31).

Rooms 33–34: Ilya Repin

This room contains several masterpieces by Ilya Repin (1844–1930), one of Russia's most famous painters. The iconic *Barge Haulers on the Volga* is sadly often on loan abroad, but even if this incredible picture isn't here, look for *Cossacks Writing a Letter to the Turkish Sultan* and his marvellous portrait of a barefoot Leo Tolstoy.

Rooms 35–47: Late-19th-Century Russian Art

These rooms display the large number of contradictory styles that were fashionable in St Petersburg before the explosion of the avant-garde. These include Vasily Surikov, a master of the historical painting that was in vogue in the late 19th century. His portrayals of *Yermak's Conquest of Siberia* and *Suvorov Crossing the Alps* (Room 36) are particularly romantic, but the lifelike rendition of Cossack rebel *Stepan Razin* (Room 37) is undoubtedly his most evocative.

Rooms 48–49: Antokolsky's Historical Paintings

Mark Antokolsky's *Ivan the Terrible* and *Death of Socrates* are on display either side of a souvenir stand. From here you enter the Benois Wing to your right or continue straight ahead for the comprehensive account of Russian folk art, featuring everything from kitchen equipment to window frames. The long corridor in Room 49 showcases posters from past exhibits at the Russian Museum.

Rooms 54–59: Repin & Sculpture

Room 54 features Repin's enormous rendition of the *Ceremonial Sitting of the State Council on 7 May 1901, Marking the Centenary of Its Foundation.* Around the walls are individual portraits of its members. Rooms 55 to 59 contain sculptures in storage, but behind glass walls, so still visible. Most interesting here is Etienne Falconet's model for his *Bronze Horseman.*

Rooms 66–71: Early-20th-Century Art

Room 66 is the home of the father of modern Russian art, Mikhail Vrubel (1856–1910). Some of his ground-breaking works include *Lady in Lilac, Epic Hero (Bogatyr)* and *Demon in Flight.* Rooms 67 to 71 include works by an array of important early-20th-century painters including Kuzma Petrov-Vodkin, Nikolai Sapunin, Mikhail Nesterov and Boris Kustodiev, whose *Merchant's Wife at Tea* is perhaps the most well-known picture here.

ILYA REPIN

Considered by most Russians to be the greatest artist the nation has ever produced, Ilya Repin (1844–1930) was originally a member of the Wanderers, but he outgrew the movement. He went on to produce key works of Russian realist and populist art. His masterpiece is *Barge Haulers on the Volga*, an unrivalled portrait of human misery and enslavement in rural Russia.

Repin spent the last years of his life at his idiosyncratic dacha Penates in a Gulf of Finland town now named Repino in his honour. Today it's a museum and possible to visit by taking the bus from outside the Ploshchad Lenina metro station.

Rooms 72–78: Russian Avant-Garde Painting

Between 1905 and 1917, the Russian art world experienced an explosion of creative inspiration that defied the stylistic categorisation that had existed before. Room 72 is home to Nathan Altman's gorgeous, semi-cubist *Portrait of the Poetess Anna Akhmatova* (Room 72), painted in 1914, and it remains one of his most famous works even though Akhmatova apparently didn't care for it herself. In the same room is Altman's striking *Self Portrait* (1911). Room 74 contains primitivist paintings by artist couple Natalya Goncharova and Mikhail Larionov.

Futurism and suprematism, including Malevich's *Red Square, Head of a Peasant* and *Black Square,* can be found in Rooms 75 to 76, while Room 77 is devoted to constructivism and features works by Rodchenko and Vladimir Lebedev. Room 78 displays the bright, ethereal work of Pavel Filonov.

Room 79: Kuzma Petrov-Vodkin

Spanning two centuries and surviving the Russian Revolution, Kuzma Petrov-Vodkin (1878–1939) was a unique painter. His work conveys a dreamlike atmosphere, much of it with homoerotic overtones. See *Mother of God* (1914–15) and another *Portrait of Anna Akhmatova* (1922).

Rooms 80–81: Early Soviet Art

Most paintings from the Stalin era may have been censored beyond meaning, but there are some interesting portraits of daily life here, such as Alexander Samokhvalov's *Militarised Komsomol* (1932–33) and various pictures from WWII showing heroic resistance and national unity. Room 81 ends with Vyacheslav Pakulin's beautiful *Nevsky on 9th July 1945,* depicting troops returning from the war.

Rooms 82–109: Late Soviet Art & Temporary Exhibits

With Stalin gone and the 'thaw' under way in the 1950s, Soviet art recovered somewhat from the severity of socialist realism. Idealised images of rural life and peasants still feature very strongly, however. These rooms are often used for special exhibitions, while Rooms 87 to 94 were being refurbished at the time of writing.

RUSSIAN MUSEUM — 2ND FLOOR

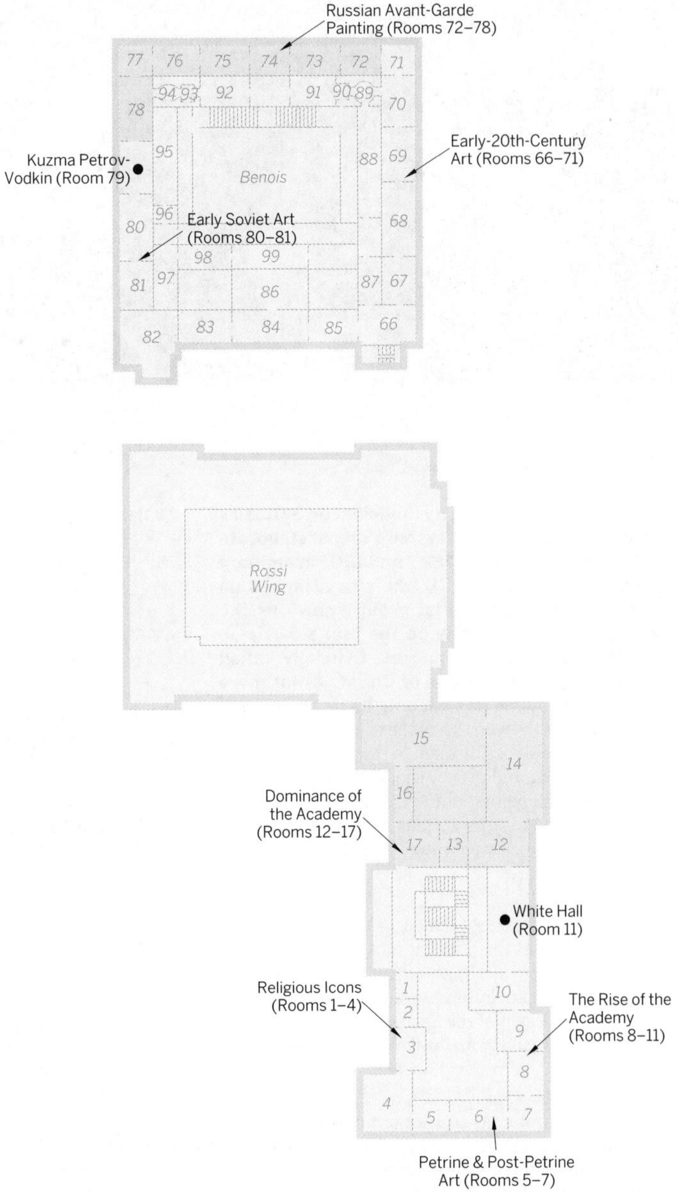
Russian Avant-Garde Painting (Rooms 72–78)
77
76
75
74
73
72
71
94
93
92
91
90
89
70
78
Kuzma Petrov-Vodkin (Room 79)
95
Benois
88
69
Early-20th-Century Art (Rooms 66–71)
96
Early Soviet Art (Rooms 80–81)
80
68
98
99
81
97
86
87
67
82
83
84
85
66
Rossi Wing
15
14
16
Dominance of the Academy (Rooms 12–17)
17
13
12
White Hall (Room 11)
Religious Icons (Rooms 1–4)
1
2
3
10
9
The Rise of the Academy (Rooms 8–11)
8
4
5
6
7
Petrine & Post-Petrine Art (Rooms 5–7)

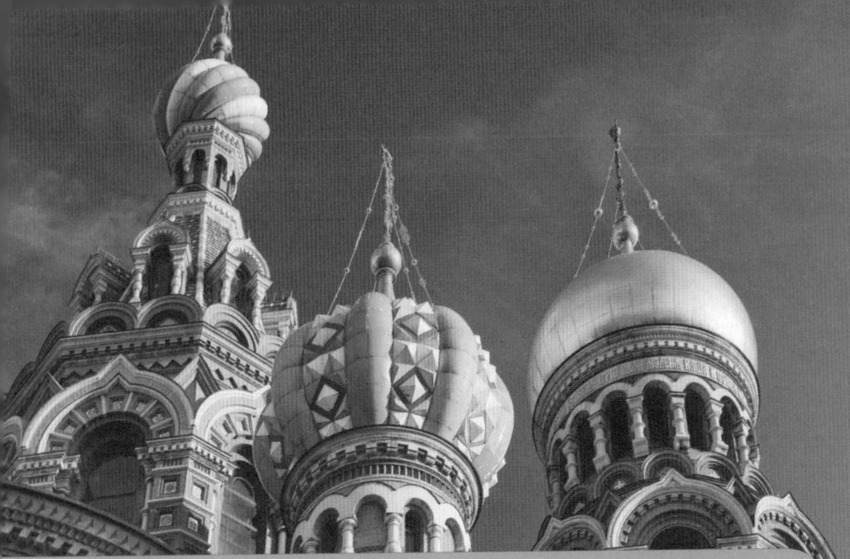

IZZET KERIBAR / LONELY PLANET IMAGES ©

TOP SIGHTS
CHURCH ON THE SPILLED BLOOD

This multidomed dazzler, partly modelled on St Basil's Cathedral in Moscow, is St Petersburg's most elaborate church. It was built between 1883 and 1907 in memory of reformist Tsar Alexander II, who was attacked on this spot in 1881 by a terrorist group known as the People's Will. The bomb blew up the tsar's carriage, and he later died from his injuries. Officially called the Church of the Resurrection of Christ, its far more striking colloquial name has become its de facto one.

It was the Bolsheviks who threw the ornate doors of this amazing candy-cake structure open to the people. Not built to withstand the wear and tear by thousands of visitors, its interior suffered. Following Stalin's closure of churches in the 1930s, it was used to store various items, from potatoes to theatre sets, and quickly fell into disrepair.

Restored Beauty

Decades of abuse and neglect ended in the 1970s and the church is now famed as the one that took 24 years to build and 27 to restore. It reopened in 1997 to much fanfare and the 7000 sq metres of mosaics lining its walls are spectacular. In the western apse, the spot of the assassination is marked by a small but beautiful canopy made of rhodonite and jasper.

DON'T MISS...

- The steeple
- Canopy marking the spot of the assassination
- The mosaic murals
- The 20 granite plaques on the outside
- Taking a photo from the footbridge

PRACTICALITIES

- Map p254
- www.cathedral.ru
- adult/student R250/150
- 10am-6pm Thu-Tue
- M Nevsky Prospekt

The Exterior

The superbly polychromatic exterior of this Russian Revival marvel is unique in the city. The 20 granite plaques on the facade record, in gold letters, the main events of Alexander's reign. The mosaic panels about halfway up detail scenes from the New Testament, and the 144 mosaic coats of arms each represent the provinces, regions and towns of the Russian Empire of Alexander's time.

SIGHTS

HERMITAGE MUSEUM

See p44.

RUSSIAN MUSEUM MUSEUM

See p57.

CHURCH ON THE SPILLED BLOOD CHURCH

See p64.

ANGLO TOURISMO BOAT TOURS

(☎325 9906; www.anglotourismo.com) You can find boat tours on every canal and river in St Petersburg, and there's a huge number of companies offering cruises all over the historic heart on the Moyka and Kanal Griboyedova – all with similar prices and itineraries. However, Anglo Tourismo is the only operator to run all their tours in English, and you'll pay the same rate (R500) per tour as you would for a Russian-language one, so it's well worth heading down to the embarkation point at nab reki Fontanki 27 (just off Nevsky pr) to take the one-hour boat tours that leave every two hours on the hour from 11am until 7pm. Night boat tours (R700) are also available.

PALACE SQUARE SQUARE

Map p254 (Дворцовая пл; Ⓜ Admiralteyskaya) It is no secret where St Petersburg's heart lies. Although it's no longer the hub of the city, there can be little doubt that the vast expanse where Nevsky pr meets the Neva River and Dvortsovaya nab is simply one of the most striking squares in the world, still redolent of imperial grandeur almost a century after the end of the Romanov dynasty. For the most amazing first impression, walk from Nevsky pr, up Bolshaya Morskaya ul and under the triumphal arch.

The square's most impressive building is the incredible green, white and gold **Winter Palace** (Zimny Dvorets), a rococo profusion of columns, windows and recesses, topped by rows of larger-than-life statues. A residence of tsars from 1762 to 1917, it's now the largest part of the Hermitage (p44).

In the centre of the square, the 47.5m **Alexander Column** was designed in 1834 by Montferrand. Named after Alexander I, it commemorates the 1812 victory over Napoleon. On windy days, contemplate that the pillar is held on its pedestal by gravity alone!

Curving an incredible 580m around the south side of the square is the Carlo Rossi–designed General Staff Building (p66) of the Russian Army (1819–29). The two great blocks are joined by a **triumphal arch** over Bolshaya Morskaya ul. The arch is topped by the Chariot of Glory, another monument to the Napoleonic Wars.

On Bloody Sunday (9 January 1905), tsarist troops fired on workers who were peaceably gathered in the square, sparking the 1905 revolution. And it was across Dvortsovaya pl that the much-exaggerated storming of the Winter Palace took place during the 1917 October Revolution.

KAZAN CATHEDRAL CATHEDRAL

Map p254 (Казанский собор; www.kazansky-spb.ru, in Russian; Kazanskaya pl; admission free; ⏰11am-7pm; Ⓜ Nevsky Prospekt) Atypical of St Petersburg churches, the neoclassical Kazan Cathedral was commissioned by Tsar Paul shortly before he was murdered in a coup. It reflects his eccentric desire to unite Catholicism and Orthodoxy in a kind of 'super-Christianity' as well as his fascination with the Knights of Malta, of which he was a member. The cathedral's great, 111m-long colonnaded arms reach out towards Nevsky pr, encircling a pleasant garden that is studded with statues. Andrei Voronikhin, a former serf, built the cathedral between 1801 and 1811 and his design was influenced by St Peter's in Rome. His original plan was to build a second, mirror version of the cathedral opposite it on the other side of Nevsky pr, but this never materialised.

Look for the victorious Napoleonic War field marshal Mikhail Kutuzov (whose remains are buried inside the cathedral) and his friend and aide Mikhail Barclay de Tolly.

Inside, the cathedral is dark and traditionally orthodox, with a daunting 80m-high dome. There is usually a long queue of believers waiting to kiss the icon of Our Lady of Kazan, a copy of one of Russia's most important icons.

STROGANOV PALACE PALACE

Map p254 (Строгановский дворец; www.rusmuseum.ru; Nevsky pr 17; adult/student R300/150, combined 24hr ticket for all four palaces of the Russian Museum adult/student R600/300; ⏰10am-5pm Wed-Mon; Ⓜ Nevsky Prospekt) One of the city's loveliest baroque exteriors, the salmon-pink Stroganov Palace was designed by court favourite Bartolomeo Rastrelli in 1753 for one of the city's leading aristocratic families. Most famously, the Stroganov's chef created a beef dish served in a sour cream and mushroom sauce that became known to the world as 'beef stroganoff'. The building has been superbly restored by the Russian Museum, and you can visit the impressive state rooms upstairs, where the Arabesque Dining Room, the Mineralogical Study and the Rastrelli Hall, with its vast frieze ceiling, are the obvious highlights. Downstairs there are temporary exhibits and an internet cafe.

MARBLE PALACE — PALACE

Map p254 (Мраморный дворец; www.rusmuseum.ru; Millionnaya ul 5/1; adult/student R300/150, combined 24hr ticket for all four palaces of the Russian Museum adult/student R600/300; 10am-5pm Wed-Mon; M Nevsky Prospekt) Between Mars Field and the Neva, this palace is an architectural gem by Antonio Rinaldi, who used 36 kinds of marble, and took pains to bleed them seamlessly into one another. Built between 1768 and 1785, it was a gift from Catherine the Great to Grigory Orlov for suppressing a Moscow rebellion. Formerly the Lenin Museum under the Soviets, it is now a branch of the Russian Museum featuring rotating exhibitions of contemporary art and a permanent display of paintings from the Ludwig Museum in Cologne that includes works by Picasso, Warhol, Basquiat and Liechtenstein. The interiors aren't quite as lavish as elsewhere in the Russian Museum, but there are still highlights: the Gala Staircase, made of subtly changing grey Urals marble; and the impressive Marble Hall, whose walls are made up of lapis-lazuli and marble in a range of colours from yellow to pink.

An amusing equestrian statue of Alexander III stands plumply in the courtyard outside the main entrance; it became the butt of many jokes after it was erected in 1909 (originally outside Moscow Station). Even his son Nicholas II thought of shipping it off to Irkutsk, but when rumours started that he wanted to send his dad into Siberian exile, he changed his mind. Sculptor Paolo Trubetskoy said of his work, 'I don't care about politics. I simply depicted one animal on another.'

MIKHAILOVSKY CASTLE — CASTLE

Map p254 (Михайловский замок; www.rusmuseum.ru; Sadovaya ul 2; adult/student R300/150, combined 24hr ticket for all four palaces of the Russian Museum adult/student R600/300; 10am-5pm Wed-Mon; M Gostiny Dvor) A much greater Summer Palace used to stand at the southern end of the Summer Garden. But Rastrelli's fairy-tale wooden creation for Empress Elizabeth was knocked down in the 1790s to make way for the bulky Mikhailovsky Castle (Engineer's Castle). The son of Catherine the Great, Tsar Paul I, was born in the wooden palace and he wanted his own residence on the same spot. He had the current edifice built complete with defensive moat as he (quite rightly) feared assassination. But this erratic, cruel tsar only got 40 days in his new abode before he was suffocated in his bedroom in 1801.

The style is a bizarre take on a medieval castle, quite unlike any other building in the city. In 1823 it became a military engineering school (hence its Soviet-era name, Engineer's Castle, or Inzhenerny Zamok), whose most famous pupil was Fyodor Dostoevsky. Nowadays the original name, Mikhailovsky Castle, is generally used, though don't confuse it with the nearby Mikhailovsky Palace, the Russian Museum's main building.

Now a wing of the Russian Museum, the castle's ground floor is used for temporary exhibits, while upstairs there's a permanent display of work by foreign artists working in Russia in the 18th and early 19th centuries as well as a few finely restored state rooms, including the lavish burgundy throne room of Tsar Paul I's wife Maria Fyodorovna.

PUSHKIN FLAT-MUSEUM — MUSEUM

Map p254 (Музей-квартира А.С. Пушкина; www.museumpushkin.ru; nab reki Moyki 12; adult/student R200/80; 10.30am-5.30pm Wed-Sun; M Admiralteyskaya) Alexander Pushkin, Russia's national poet, had his last home here on one of the prettiest curves of the Moyka River. He only lived here four months, but this is where the poet died after his duel in 1837 (see the boxed text, p67). The little house is now the Pushkin Flat-Museum, which has been reconstructed to look exactly as it did in the poet's last days. On display are his death mask, a lock of his hair and the waistcoat he wore when he died. You can only visit on a tour (run hourly on the hour), and these are given in Russian only.

GENERAL STAFF BUILDING — MUSEUM

Map p254 (Генеральный штаб; www.hermitagemuseum.org; Dvortsovaya pl 6-8; adult/student R60/free; 10.30am-6pm Tue-Sun; M Admiralteyskaya) The western wing of this magnificent building on Dvortsovaya pl was formerly used by the Ministry of Foreign

LIFE IMITATING ART

Russian literature is filled with jaded heroes, stubborn heroines, unrequited loves and tragic deaths. None inspires more abhorrence and empathy than Yevgeny Onegin, the title character in Alexander Pushkin's epic poem.

Yevgeny Onegin is a world-weary St Petersburg socialite who rejects the love of devoted Tatiana but seduces her sister Olga. Unfortunately, Olga is betrothed to his best friend, Lensky, who challenges our antihero to a duel. Both rivals have misgivings, but pride forces the pair to fight, and Lensky is slain.

Is it a coincidence that Pushkin – the national bard and pride of St Petersburg – was himself slain in a duel? His killer was a French nobleman, Baron Georges d'Anthès, who had publicly courted Pushkin's beautiful wife, Natalya Goncharova.

Oddly enough, d'Anthès married Natalya's sister, Ekaterina – perhaps as a ruse. But Pushkin was not persuaded. After an anonymous letter was circulated, nominating the poet as the 'Grand Master of the Order of Cuckolds', the only honourable response was a fight to the death.

History has not clarified this nasty affair: some still speculate that d'Anthès acted under the influence of Tsar Nicholas I, who found the famed poet's radical politics inconvenient; others imply that the tsar himself may have had a thing for Natalya, a notorious flirt. One thing's for sure: it ended badly for Pushkin.

On a cold night in February 1837, having eaten his final meal at the Literatornoye Kafe on Nevsky pr, Pushkin set off by sled to a remote woodland to meet his adversary (see p135). He was shot and died two days later at his home on the Moyka River (see p66).

Unlike the remorseful Yevgeny Onegin, who recognises his foolishness in rejecting Tatiana and must live with his love unrequited and his soul sorrowful, things did not go so badly for d'Anthès. By way of punishment, he was stripped of his rank and forced to leave Russia. He returned to France with his wife (who supposedly never doubted his loyalty), and the two lived out their days in apparent wedded bliss.

This ironic ending does not go over well with Russian romantics. Needless to say, d'Anthès is a much-maligned character in Russian history, sometimes dismissed as a tsarist stooge, a hidden homosexual or a French spy (and perhaps all three).

Affairs, including private apartments for the minister himself. The fabulous Carlo Rossi-designed interiors have been meticulously maintained, and today house exhibition halls displaying items from the Hermitage collection. Here, the art of 20th-century French painters Pierre Bonnard and Maurice Denis is on permanent display. Monarchists will appreciate the 'heraldic eagle', also featured in 600-plus examples of graphics, paintings and applied arts from Russia and Western Europe.

WINTER PALACE OF PETER I — MUSEUM

Map p254 (Зимний дворец Пётра Первого; www.hermitagemuseum.org; Dvortsovaya nab 32; adult/student R60/free; ⌚10.30am-5pm Tue-Sun; Ⓜ Admiralteyskaya) Opened as a part of the Hermitage in 1992, this palace on the Neva was the principal residence of Peter the Great, and he died here in 1725. When Giacomo Quarenghi built the Hermitage Theatre on this site between 1783 and 1789, he preserved parts of the palace and grounds. Between 1976 and 1986, excavations beneath the theatre stage uncovered a large fragment of the former state courtyard, as well as several suites of palace apartments. Today, the courtyard is used to display Peter's official carriage and sledge. Some of the chamber rooms have been restored to their appearance during Peter's era, complete with Dutch tiles and parquet floors, and are used to exhibit some of Peter's personal items from the Hermitage collection. The admission price includes a useful audio-guide in the language of your choice.

ADMIRALTY — HISTORICAL BUILDING

Map p254 (Адмиралтейство; Admiralteysky proezd 1; ⌚closed to the public; Ⓜ Admiralteyskaya) Across the road from Dvortsovaya pl, the gilded spire of the old Admiralty is a prime St Petersburg landmark. It is visible from Gorokhovaya ul, Voznesensky pr and

Nevsky pr, as all of these roads radiate outwards from this central point. Despite the spire's solid gold appearance, it's actually made from wood and was almost rotted through before restoration efforts began in 1996. From 1711 to 1917, this spot was the headquarters of the Russian navy; now it houses the country's largest military naval college and is currently undergoing much-needed exterior restoration.

The Admiralty was reconstructed between 1806 and 1823 to the designs of Andreyan Zakharov. With its rows of white columns and its plentiful reliefs and statuary, it is a foremost example of the Russian Empire style. Get a close look at the globe-toting nymphs flanking the main gate. The green gardens, laid out from 1872 to 1874, are dotted with statues of Glinka, Lermontov, Gogol and other cultural figures, as well as a refreshing fountain that dates to 1877.

It's a lovely place to sit and stroll, but the building itself is closed to visitors.

SINGER BUILDING HISTORICAL BUILDING

Map p254 (Nevsky pr 28; Ⓜ Nevsky Prospekt) Opposite the Kazan Cathedral stands one of St Petersburg's most marvellous buildings, the headquarters of the Singer sewing machine company, which opened a factory in the Russian capital in 1904. The building also housed the American consulate for a few years prior to WWI. These days, the Singer Building provides a home to St Petersburg's premier bookstore, Dom Knigi (p79), and the attractive Café Singer (p76) with superb views of the Kazan Cathedral.

BRIDGES IN THE BURG

The never-ending network of canals and waterways in St Petersburg has resulted in some innovatively designed bridges over the years. With the exception of the new Big Obukhovsky, all of the *mosty* (bridges) across the Neva are drawbridges. They are raised every evening at designated times to let the ships pass, a spectacle that draws starry-eyed lovers and stranded night birds (see p221 for the schedule). But some of the most charming bridges are the smaller structures that span the canals around the city. Of St Petersburg's hundreds of bridges, here are a few of our favourites:

Anichkov most (Аничков мост; Map p254) St Petersburg's most striking bridge features rearing horses at all four corners, symbolising man's struggle with and taming of nature.

Bankovsky most (Банковский мост; Map p254) This beauty is suspended by cables emerging from the mouths of golden-winged griffins. The name – meaning Bank Bridge, something that does not quite fit this whimsical creation – comes from the Assignment Bank (now a further-education institute), which stands on one side of the bridge.

Most Lomonosova (Мост Ломоносова; Map p254) Four Doric towers contain the mechanism that pulls up the moveable central section, allowing boat traffic to pass along the Fontanka underneath.

Lviny most (Львиный мост; Map p264) Another suspension bridge, this one is supported by two pairs of regal lions, which give the bridge its name.

Panteleymonovsky most (Пантелеймоновский мост; Map p254) At the confluence of the Moyka and the Fontanka, this beauty features lamp posts bedecked with the double-headed eagle and railings adorned with the coat of arms.

1-y Inzhenerny most (Первый Инженерный мост; Map p254) While there is no shortage of adornment on the cast-iron bridge leading to Mikhailovsky Castle (p66), the highlight is the Chizhik-Pyzhik, the statue of the little bird that hovers over the Moyka.

Siniy most (Синий мост; Blue Bridge; Map p254), **Krasny most** (Красный мост; Red Bridge; Map p254), **Zelyony most** (Зелёный мост; Green Bridge; Map p254) **&** **Pevchesky most** (Певческий мост; formerly known as Yellow Bridge; Map p254) These colour-coded bridges cross the Moyka at intervals between Isaakievskaya pl and Dvortsovaya pl.

PLOSHCHAD ISKUSSTV SQUARE

Map p254 (Площадь Искусств; Ⓜ Nevsky Prospekt) Just a block east of the Kanal Griboyedov is the quiet pl Iskusstv (Arts Sq), named after the cluster of museums and concert halls that surrounds it. In the 1820s and 1830s, Carlo Rossi designed this square and the lovely Mikhailovskaya ul, which joins it to Nevsky pr. A **statue of Pushkin**, erected in 1957, stands in the middle of the tree-lined square, which is surrounded by the Shostakovich Philharmonia (p77), Mikhailovsky Theatre (p77), Russian Museum (p57) and Museum of Ethnography (p70).

MUSEUM OF THE HISTORY OF POLITICAL POLICE MUSEUM

Map p254 (Музей политической полиции; www.polithistory.ru; Gorokhovaya ul 2; adult/student R150/60; ⏲10am-6pm Mon-Fri; Ⓜ Admiralteyskaya) In the very same building that housed the tsarist and the Bolshevik secret police offices, this small museum recounts the history of this controversial institution. An annexe of the Museum of Political History (p129), it includes one room that recreates the office of Felix Dzerzhinsky, founder of the Cheka (Bolshevik secret police). Each of the remaining three rooms is devoted to the secret police during a different period of history: the tsarist police, the Cheka and the KGB. Exhibitions are heavy on photographs and documents, but some of them are fascinating. Some explanatory materials are available in English.

ROSPHOTO STATE PHOTOGRAPHY CENTRE GALLERY

Map p254 (РОСФОТО; www.rosphoto.org; Bolshaya Morskaya ul 35; admission R100; ⏲11am-7pm; Ⓜ Admiralteyskaya) This exhibition hall showcases rotating exhibitions of photography, videography and other mixed media drawn from all over Russia and around the world. It's definitely one of the best spaces for seeing contemporary photographic work in St Petersburg. Recent shows have included photos of life in Moscow from the second half of the 20th century and a fascinating comparison of photographs from the Russian and Mexican revolutions.

SUMMER GARDEN PARK

Map p254 (Летний сад; Ⓜ Gostiny Dvor) Central St Petersburg's loveliest and oldest park, the Summer Garden is on its own island between Mars Field and the Fontanka River (you can normally enter at the northern or southern end). At the time of writing the garden was shut for a total renovation and is due to reopen in 2012. Early-18th-century architects designed the garden in a Dutch baroque style, following a geometric plan, with fountains, pavilions and sculptures studding the grounds. The ornate cast-iron fence with the granite posts was a later addition, built between 1771 and 1784. The gardens functioned as a private retreat for Peter the Great before becoming a strolling place for St Petersburg's 19th-century leisured classes. Only in the 20th century were commoners admitted.

SUMMER PALACE OF PETER I PALACE

Map p254 (Летний дворец Пётра Первого; Ⓜ Gostiny Dvor) The modest, two-storey Summer Palace, in the northeastern corner of the Summer Garden, was St Petersburg's first 'palace', which may seem like a slight misnomer for a remarkably small building. The 14-room baroque palace was built for Peter between 1704 and 1714 by Domenico Trezzini and includes bas-reliefs of Russian naval victories on the walls. It was closed for refurbishment at the time of writing, and should reopen in 2012.

MARS FIELD PARK

Map p254 (Марсово поле; nab Lebyazhey kanavki; Ⓜ Gostiny Dvor) Once the scene of 19th-century military parades, the grassy Mars Field lies immediately west of the Summer Garden (south of Troitsky most). Formerly known as the Tsarina's Meadow (Tsaritsyn lug), it's a popular spot for strollers. At its centre, an **eternal flame** burns for the victims of the 1917 revolution and the ensuing civil war. Don't take a short cut across the grass – you may be walking on the graves of the victims or of later communist luminaries also buried here.

LUTHERAN CHURCH CHURCH

Map p254 (Nevsky pr 22; ⏲9am-7pm; Ⓜ Nevsky Prospekt) Tucked in a recess between Bolshaya and Malaya Konyushennaya uls is the lovely Lutheran Church that was built for St Petersburg's thriving German community in the 1830s. Distinguished by a four-column portico and topped with a discreet cupola, it was turned into a swimming pool in the 1950s (the high diving board was placed in the apse) – but is that worse than using it to store vegetables, as it had been since the 1930s? The church is open to visitors, having since been restored beautifully.

GOSTINY DVOR — HISTORICAL BUILDING

Map p254 (Гостиный двор; www.gostinydvor.ru, in Russian; Nevsky pr 35; ⏲10am-10pm; Ⓜ Gostiny Dvor) The arcades of Gostiny Dvor department store stand facing the clock tower of the **former Town Duma** (Town Parliament) on Dumskaya ul, which was the seat of the prerevolutionary city government. One of the world's first indoor shopping malls, the 'Merchant Yard' dates from between 1757 and 1785 and stretches 230m along Nevsky pr (its perimeter is more than 1km long). This Rastrelli creation is not as elaborate as some of his other work, finished as it was by Vallin de la Mothe in a more sober neoclassical style.

These days, Gostiny Dvor is a rather unfashionable shopping spot (see p79), which has never really recaptured the pre-eminence it enjoyed in Soviet times. Opposite Gostiny Dvor across Sadovaya ul is the **Vorontsov Palace** (1749–57), another noble town house by Rastrelli. From 1810 it was the most elite military school in the empire and it's still used as a military school for young cadets. The palace is occasionally opened for concerts and such, details of which are posted out the front.

BRODSKY HOUSE-MUSEUM — MUSEUM

Map p254 (Музей-квартира И.И. Бродского; www.nimrah.ru/musbrod, in Russian; pl Iskusstv 3; adult/student R200/100; ⏲11am-6pm Wed-Sun; Ⓜ Nevsky Prospekt) This is the former home of Isaak Brodsky, Repin's favourite student and one of the favoured artists of the revolution (not to be confused with Joseph Brodsky, one of the least favourite poets of the same regime). Besides being a painter himself, Brodsky was also an avid collector, and his house-museum contains his collection of thousands of works, including lesser-known paintings by top 19th-century artists such as Repin, Levitan and Kramskoy.

MUSEUM OF ETHNOGRAPHY — MUSEUM

Map p254 (Музей этнографии; www.ethnomuseum.ru; Inzhenernaya ul 4/1; adult/student R300/150, English group tour R1500; ⏲10.30am-6pm Tue-Sun; Ⓜ Gostiny Dvor) In an impressive classical building on pl Iskusstv, this excellent museum displays the traditional crafts, customs and beliefs of more than 150 cultures that make up Russia's fragile ethnic mosaic. There's a bit of leftover Soviet propaganda going on here, but it's a marvellous collection: the sections on Transcaucasia and Central Asia are fascinating, with rugs and two full-size yurts (nomads' portable tent-houses). The Special Storeroom has some great weapons and rare devotional objects. The museum's centrepiece is the magnificent Marble Hall, a 1000-sq-metre gallery surrounded by pink Karelian-marble columns.

ARMENIAN CHURCH OF ST CATHERINE — CHURCH

Map p254 (Церковь св. Екатерины; Nevsky pr 42; ⏲8am-6.30pm Mon-Fri, 9.30am-1.30pm Sat; Ⓜ Nevsky Prospekt) Continuing with a tradition of non-Orthodox churches being built on Nevsky pr, the Armenian merchant Ovanes Lazarian paid for the city's first Armenian church to be erected here in 1771. It was designed and built by German architect Georg Veldten and completed in 1780. The Soviet regime deemed it reasonable to bash the place to bits and install a 2nd floor, which blocked the view of the cupola. Since then the church has been fully restored, and it's open to visitors.

PLOSHCHAD OSTROVSKOGO — SQUARE

Map p254 (Площадь Островского; Ⓜ Gostiny Dvor) Ringed with important cultural institutions, pl Ostrovskogo (Ostrovsky Sq) is named for Alexander Ostrovsky (1823–86), a celebrated 19th-century playwright. An enormous **statue of Catherine the Great** (1873) stands amid the chess, backgammon and mah-jong players who crowd the benches here. At the Empress' heels are renowned statesmen of the 19th century, including her lovers Orlov, Potemkin and Suvorov. This airy square, commonly referred to as Cathy's Garden (Katkin Sad), was created by Carlo Rossi in the 1820s and 1830s.

The most prominent building on the square is Rossi's neoclassical Alexandrinsky Theatre (p77). In 1896, at the opening night of Anton Chekhov's *The Seagull*, the play was so badly received here that the playwright fled to wander anonymously among the crowds on Nevsky pr.

The square's west side is taken up by the lavish **National Library of Russia**, St Petersburg's biggest with some 31 million items, nearly a sixth of which are in foreign languages.

Rossi's ensemble continues behind the theatre on ul Zodchego Rossi. It is proportion deified: the buildings are 22m wide, 22m apart and 220m long. The **Vaganova School of Choreography** at No 2 is the Kirov Ballet's training school, where Pavlova, Nijinsky, Nureyev and others learned their art.

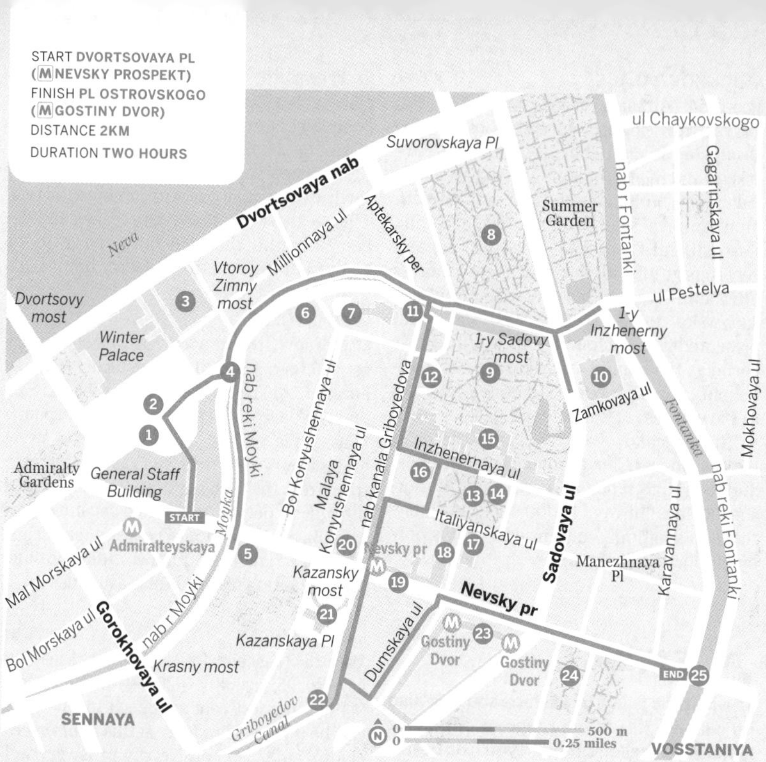

Neighbourhood Walk

Historic Heart

Approach magnificent 1 **Dvortsovaya pl** (Palace Sq) from Bolshaya Morskaya ul. Turning the corner from Nevsky pr, behold the 2 **Alexander Column**, perfectly framed under the triumphal arch. The surrounding buildings are part of the 3 **Hermitage**.

At the 4 **Moyka River** look northwest for a wonderful view of the Neva; to the south is Bartolomeo Rastrelli's lavish 5 **Stroganov Palace**. Head north along nab reki Moyki to No 12, the final residence of Russia's most celebrated poet and now the 6 **Pushkin Flat-Museum**.

7 **Konyushennaya pl** is dominated by crumbling 18th-century court stables. Formerly the imperial guard parade grounds 8 **Mars Field** became a burial ground for revolution and civil war victims. South is the shady canal-side 9 **Mikhailovsky Gardens** and southeast the unusual 10 **Mikhailovsky Castle**, part of the Russian Museum.

Near the intersection of the Moyka and Kanal Griboyedova, 11 **Teatralny most** gives a spectacular perspective on the 12 **Church on the Spilled Blood**.

Centred on a stoic 13 **statue of Pushkin**, pretty 14 **pl Iskusstv** (Arts Sq) is ringed by celebrated cultural institutions, including the 15 **Russian Museum** (p57), 16 **Mikhailovsky Theatre** and 17 **Shostakovich Philharmonia**, as well as the historic 18 **Grand Hotel Europe**.

The corner of 19 **Nevsky pr** and this canal is a landmark. The old 20 **Singer Building** provides a whimsical contrast to the formidable 21 **Kazan Cathedral** opposite. Behind it, 22 **Bankovsky most** is the city's most picturesque and photographed bridge.

Crowds pour out of the metro station at 23 **Gostiny Dvor**, the 18th-century trading arcade still serving shoppers. The National Library of Russia, Alexandrinsky Theatre and Anichkov Palace surround 24 **pl Ostrovskogo** (Ostrovsky Sq), named for the playwright. Beyond the square on Nevsky pr the elaborate 25 **Anichkov most**, flanked by rearing horses, crosses the Fontanka.

ANICHKOV PALACE PALACE

Map p254 (Аничков дворец; ☎310 4395; nab reki Fontanki; ⏲by appointment; Ⓜ Gostiny Dvor) Occupying an entire block between pl Ostrovskogo and the Fontanka River, the Anichkov Palace was built between 1741 and 1750, with input from a slew of architects, including Rastrelli and Rossi. The palace was twice a generous gift for services rendered: Empress Elizabeth gave it to her favourite Count Razumovsky and later Catherine the Great presented it to Potemkin. This was also Tsar Nicholas II's favourite place to stay in St Petersburg – he far preferred the cosy interiors to the vastness of the Winter Palace.

The Anichkov Palace became the city's largest Pioneer Club headquarters after 1936 and to this day it houses more than 100 after-school clubs for over 10,000 children. Today there's a small museum inside, but it is only open sporadically for tours.

EATING

The historic heart of St Petersburg is also its culinary heart: the range of options is generally excellent, though you'll do better to get off Nevsky pr itself, which tends to be pricey and of average quality (with a few notable exceptions).

TOP CHOICE MIX IN ST PETERSBURG INTERNATIONAL €€€

Map p254 (☎610 6166; www.wstpetersburg.com; Voznesensky pr 6; mains R1000-1500; ⏲noon-3pm & 7pm-midnight; Ⓜ Admiralteyskaya; 📶📋) A sign of the changing times, MiX is St Petersburg's first celebrity chef restaurant, and the first Russian venture of French cookery star Alain Ducasse. Though it's inside the new W Hotel, to one side of St Isaac's Cathedral, it feels nothing like a hotel restaurant. It has its own entrance from the street, several glamorous rooms surrounding an open kitchen and a huge wine cellar. Sublime yet simple dishes tend to be French in essence with an international or Russian edge. Service and atmosphere are both top-notch, making this one of St Petersburg's hottest tables of the moment.

TOP CHOICE SOUP VINO ITALIAN €

Map p254 (Суп вино; www.supvino.ru; Kazanskaya ul 24; mains R200-500; Ⓜ Nevsky Prospekt; 📋✍) This tiny place is a foodie dream by St Petersburg standards. Fresh daily specials such as artichoke salad and gazpacho complement a large range of both soup and wine – a strange combination, maybe, but the owners explain that they don't necessarily expect customers to combine the two. There's also a range of pasta dishes and delicious panini that can be taken away or enjoyed in the cute, wood-heavy premises.

TOP CHOICE STOLLE BAKERY €

Map p254 (Столле; www.stolle.ru; Konyushenny per 1/6; pies R50-200; ⏲8am-10pm; Ⓜ Nevsky Prospekt; ✍) The delicious, freshly baked Saxon-style pies *(stolle)* at this cool, atmospheric place are legendary, and a selection of sweet and savoury offerings sits on the counter, fresh from the oven anytime of day. It may be difficult to decide (rabbit and mushroom or salmon; apricot or apple?) but you really can't go wrong. There are further outlets around the city, and takeaway is also available.

TOP CHOICE GARÇON FRENCH €

Map p254 (Гарсон; www.garcon.ru; nab kanala Griboyedova 25; sandwiches R200; Ⓜ Nevsky Prospekt; 📋) Finding a decent sandwich in this town can be a Herculean feat, so this *boulangerie* chain's outlet just off Nevsky pr is very welcome indeed. Freshly made sandwiches in freshly baked baguettes, not to mention a great range of cakes and other treats, are all available to have here or take away.

CAFÉ KING PONG ASIAN €€

Map p254 (www.kingpong.ru; Bolshaya Morskaya ul 16; mains R300-600; Ⓜ Admiralteyskaya; 📶📋✍) From the team that brings you the excellent Soup Vino and Testo comes this innovative and fun pan-Asian diner, occupying sleek and luminous premises with a retro-glamorous feel just off Nevsky. The large menu is of very good quality and takes in dim sum, noodles, soups and rice dishes.

FIOLET INTERNATIONAL €€€

Map p254 (nab reki Fontanki 55; mains R500-1000; Ⓜ Gostiny Dvor; 📶📋✍) The restaurant of the excellent Rossi Hotel is a destination in its own right, a beautiful contemporary space with plush leather sofas, wooden floorboards and a popular summer terrace overlooking the Fontanka. The Asian-European menu includes such delights as fresh oysters and miso-marinated beef with Tobiko caviar rolls. Service can be sniffy, but otherwise this place is a winner.

SHARLOT CAFÉ INTERNATIONAL €€

Map p254 (Шарлоткафе; www.sharlotcafe.ru; ul Kazanskaya 2; mains R350-700; Nevsky Prospekt;) This stylish, bright and spacious cafe has wooden floors, deeply distressed walls and understated old-world furnishings. Its mouth-watering pictorial menu has lots of salads, antipasti, sandwiches, pasta, seafood, grilled fish and meats. It's also a great place for breakfast, served until 4pm each day.

TERRASSA EUROPEAN €€

Map p254 (937 6837; www.terrassa.ru; Kazanskaya ul 3a; mains R450-1000; 11am-1am, from noon Sat & Sun; Nevsky Prospekt;) On the top floor of a modern shopping centre, this sleek and buzzing place is centred on its namesake terrace, a wide porch boasting unbelievable views of the Kazan Cathedral, Nevsky pr and the Church on the Spilled Blood. It is a spectacular setting and you'll usually need reservations to sit on the terrace, but you can just drop by and hope to get lucky. Inside, the atmosphere is Old World but understated. The focus is clearly on the food; if you have any doubt, take a peek inside the open kitchen, where chefs are busy preparing fresh fusion cuisine, exhibiting influences from Italy, Asia and beyond. There's a good breakfast menu available from 11am to 1pm Monday to Friday.

ZOOM CAFÉ EUROPEAN €€

Map p254 (www.cafezoom.ru; Gorokhovaya ul 22; meals R100-400; 9am-midnight Mon-Sat, 1pm-midnight Sun; Sennaya Pl;) A perennially popular cafe with a funky feel and an interesting menu, Zoom does everything from Japanese-style chicken in teriyaki sauce to potato pancakes with salmon and cream cheese. Light pink walls are adorned with B&W photos, while well-stocked bookshelves and a range of board games encourage lingering. A great lunch spot.

BAKU AZERI €€€

Map p254 (www.baku-spb.ru; Sadovaya ul 12/23; mains R300-1600; Gostiny Dvor;) No expense has been spared on the decor here: tiled walls, arched doorways and throw pillows whisk you to Azerbaijan – exactly what's intended. Try famous Azeri shashlyk (kebabs), traditional *plov* (rice and lamb spiced with cumin and raisins), as well as delicious *kutab* (thin pancakes stuffed with different fillings). Service is deferential, and there's an upstairs room if you don't fancy the nightly live music downstairs.

PARK GIUSEPPE ITALIAN €€€

Map p254 (Парк Джузеппе; www.park-restaurant.ru; nab kanala Griboyedova 2B; mains R450-1000; Nevsky Prospekt;) Enjoying a fantastic location wedged between the Mikhailovsky Gardens and the Church on the Spilled Blood, this smart Italian restaurant is great for a sumptuous meal after a hard day's sightseeing. Spread over two spacious and bright rooms, it serves up inventive dishes such as black cod fillet with courgette (zucchini) and dried tomato crostini and rabbit in mushroom sauce with tagliatelle.

ENTRECÔTE FRENCH €€

Map p254 (www.probka.org; Bolshaya Morskaya ul 25; mains R400-700; 9am-midnight; Admiralteyskaya;) The very stylish design of this French steakhouse draws you in, with traditional white linen tablecloths under an exposed brick interior with sleek minimalist touches. Ribeye steaks, including Wagyu, are the speciality here, though there's a full menu of modern French cooking and decent breakfasts too.

TANDOORI NIGHTS INDIAN €€

Map p254 (Voznesensky pr 4; meals R350-850; Admiralteyskaya;) The city's most stylish Indian restaurant is also among its most authentic, offering a mix of traditional and modern recipes road-tested by a top London Indian chef before he opened this restaurant in Russia. It's a great choice for vegetarians.

THE OTHER SIDE INTERNATIONAL €€

Map p254 (www.theotherside.ru; Bolshaya Konyushennaya ul 1; mains R200-400, snacks R100-200; Nevsky Prospekt;) Calling itself a 'gastro bar and refuge', this popular expat hangout has a friendly atmosphere and an interesting bar menu as well as regular live music and even pub quizzes. While used by many as a bar, it's well worth trying the food here, which ranges from chilli con carne to Indian spiced chicken in mint sauce. There's also a selection of sandwiches and wraps that are very good value.

TROITSKY MOST VEGETARIAN €

Map p254 (nab reki Moyki 30; mains R50-100; 10am-10pm; Nevsky Prospekt) This is the most central branch of the excellent veggie-cafe chain, and a true lifeline for non-meat eaters. Overlooking the Moyka, just moments from Nevsky, it serves up the same excellent fare, including great vegetarian lasagne.

NE GORUY GEORGIAN €€

Map p254 (Не горюй; www.negoruy.ru; Kirpichny per 3; mains R200-500; Admiralteyskaya;) The strangely named 'Don't Grieve' is actually a great little Georgian spot in the heart of the city centre where you can fill up on *khachapuri* (Georgian cheese bread) and lots of other spicy and delicious dishes from the Caucasus.

NEP RUSSIAN €€

Map p254 (571 7591; www.neprestoran.ru; nab reki Moyki 37; mains R250-500; Admiralteyskaya;) NEP celebrates the early 1920s, a period of entrepreneurial activity and relative liberalism under Lenin's 'New Economic Policy'. The restaurant's hip, jazz-age style evokes a kind of vaudevillian luxury, as does the tasty Russian and Thai menu. There's live music and cabaret plays from 8.30pm Wednesday to Sunday, for which reservations are a good idea.

KILIKIA ARMENIAN €€

Map p254 (www.kilikia.restoran.ru; Gorokhovaya ul 26/40; mains R200-600; 10.30am-6am; Sennaya Pl;) An excellent option for the late-night munchies, Kilikia is famous for its shashlyk, which, despite its wildly inauthentic pictorial menu, is the real thing – deliciously seasoned, fresh meat served with a range of traditional Armenian dishes. There's live music between 8pm and 11pm each night.

KOROVABAR STEAKHOUSE €€

Map p254 (Karavannaya ul 8; mains R500-800; noon-1am Sun-Thu, 1pm-3am Fri & Sat; Gostiny Dvor) Named after the bar in *A Clockwork Orange*, this place boasts an excellent selection of steaks (cooked as you prefer, though they are resolutely anti-well done), as well as a number of other dishes (vegetarians will be fine here) and an excellent wine list.

KAVKAZ BAR CAUCASIAN €€

Map p254 (www.kavkazbar.ru; Karavannaya ul 18; mains R350-700; 11am-1am; Gostiny Dvor;) This survivor is one of St Petersburg's most established restaurants, and though it does still serve up very good food, it has barely changed in the past decade. The portions are generous though and the food – served on large wooden platters – is consistently delectable. The bar menu is far cheaper and better value for a quick lunch than the menu in the main restaurant itself.

YAKATORIYA JAPANESE €€

Map p254 (www.yakitoriya.spb.ru; pl Ostrovskogo 5/7; mains R200-400; 8am-midnight Sun-Thu, until 6am Fri & Sat; Gostiny Dvor;) With its efficient service and excellent fresh fish, this popular chain's Nevsky pr location is its most central and it features an actual sushi bar, which is ideal for solo diners. The woody interior is slick and modern, with a slightly upmarket atmosphere.

PELMENY BAR RUSSIAN €

Map p254 (Пельмени Бар; Gorokhovaya ul 3; mains R200-300; 11am-11pm; Admiralteyskaya) Specialising in the old Siberian standard *pelmeni* (dumplings), this kitschy cafe with unsmiling staff serves them up with beef, pork, salmon or mushrooms. Choose a soup or a salad as a starter, and you've got a filling and good-value Russian meal.

FAT FRIAR RUSSIAN €€

Map p254 (Толстый Фраер; www.tolstiy-fraer.ru; Dumskaya ul 2; mains R150-350; 10am-1am, until 3am Fri & Sat; Nevsky Prospekt) Now with branches around the city, this beer hall's handiest venue is on the city's most famous party street and provides a fun hideaway for some comfort food and a Baltika beer. The food is nothing special here, but it's tasty and filling and a real Russian experience.

BUSHE BAKERY €

Map p254 (Буше; Malaya Morskaya ul 7; cakes R50-150; 9am-9pm; Admiralteyskaya) This handy Austrian chain of bakeries is a great spot for a cheap, delicious breakfast or for a coffee-and-cake stop between museums. Lines can be long, but the goods are deservedly popular.

KALINKA MALINKA RUSSIAN €€€

Map p254 (Калинка малинка; Italiyanskaya ul 5; mains R500-900; Nevsky Prospekt;) Rather pricey but charming in a kitschy sort of way, this long-standing traditional restaurant is in a basement on pl Iskusstv (Arts Sq). It specialises in country cooking and the interior resembles a cosy country house. Try homemade *solyanka* (pickled vegetable and potato soup) or rabbit à la Russe for a great introduction to traditional cuisine. Live folk music will accompany your evening meal.

PIROGOVOY DVORIK BAKERY €

Map p254 (Пироговой дворик; www.pirogov-dvorik.ru; nab kanala Griboyedova 22; pies R20-50; 10am-11pm; Nevsky Prospekt;) For those on a serious budget, this bargain-basement version of Stolle (p72) is a great place for a seriously cheap lunch. Even the pie fillings are almost identical to Stolle's, but for a fraction of the price (and charm!).

MAMA ROMA ITALIAN €€

Map p254 (www.mamaroma.ru; Karavannaya ul 3/35; mains R200-300; ⌚8am-1am; MGostiny Dvor;) Mama's menu is almost too long, as it's hard to choose between the grilled meats and fish, the hardy home-made pastas and the crispy thin pizzas topped with your favourite meats and cheeses. This is a chain with multiple outlets across the city.

YOLKI PALKI RUSSIAN €

Map p254 (Ёлки-Палки; www.elki-palki.ru, in Russian; Malaya Konyushennaya ul 9; meals R200-400; ⌚24hr; MNevsky Prospekt;) Decorated with stuffed animals and fake trees, this place's wooden interior is supposedly reminiscent of the Russian countryside, and its menu specialises in reliable, affordable Russian classics. The salad bar is the main drawcard – a huge selection for a fixed price, with no waiting and no deciphering Russian menus. It's an excellent option for vegetarians.

DRINKING & NIGHTLIFE

RADIOBABY BAR

Map p254 (www.radiobaby.com; Kazanskaya ul 7; ⌚6pm-6am; MNevsky Prospekt) This super-sleek new addition to the city nightlife is tricky to find – go through the arch at Kazanskaya 5 (not 7 – that's just the street address), then turn left through a second arch, and you'll find the bar on your right. It's well worth the effort though. A large barnlike bar is divided into several different rooms, each with distinct atmospheres. There's cool lighting throughout, a 'no techno, no house' music policy, table football, a cool crowd and an atmosphere of eternal hedonism. There are DJs from 10pm each night, after which the place becomes more a club than a bar (and there's a cover to match).

TOP CHOICE **BAR WITHOUT A NAME** BAR

Map p254 (Bankovsky per 3; ⌚6pm-6am; MSennaya Pl) This local favourite is just tricky enough to find to ensure that it stays cool. Walk past Friends Hostel into the courtyard behind it, take the first right and follow your ears: music will be coming from one of the basements – this is the bar with no name. Downstairs there are two low-slung rooms, one with a bar, busy dance floor and DJ, the second with the ubiquitous table football and plenty of comfy sofas to lounge about on. It's a cool, friendly and relaxed place where people come to drink and dance.

TOP CHOICE **MIXUP BAR** BAR

Map p254 (www.wstpetersburg.com; Voznesensky pr 6; ⌚1pm-midnight Sun-Thu, until 2am Fri & Sat; MAdmiralteyskaya) This superb new cocktail bar tops off St Petersburg's most fashionable hotel and offers fantastic city views from its Antonio Citterio–designed lounge area to be enjoyed over top-notch cocktails. One floor up is the MiXup Terrace, an even cooler outdoor space with seating in cosy cabanas and views straight onto St Isaac's Cathedral. Definitely the classiest place in town for cocktail hour.

BARAKOBAMABAR BAR

Map p254 (www.barakobamabar.ru; Konyushennaya pl 2; ⌚6pm-6am; MNevsky Prospekt) It can be more a case of 'no you can't' than 'yes we can' at this smart place (with the unfortunately mispelled presidential name), where face control can be pretty selective, so dress stylishly if you want to party here. In the summer months there's a great outdoor bar and dance floor, while inside there are a couple of cosy bars and a hookah lounge spread over two floors, both always full of beautiful young things. It's right at the back through the complex at Konyushennaya pl 2 – walk through the courtyard and continue to veer right.

MOD CLUB NIGHTCLUB

Map p254 (www.modclub.info; nab kanala Griboyedova 7; cover Fri & Sat R100-300; ⌚6pm-6am; MNevsky Prospekt) A popular spot for students and other indie types who appreciate the fun and friendly atmosphere, the groovy mix of music (live and spun) and added entertainment such as novus tables (a billiards-type game that is increasingly popular in Russia). Laid-back and great fun, this is a solid choice for a night out.

GOLUBAYA USTRITSA GAY BAR

Map p254 (www.boyster.ru, in Russian; ul Lomonosova 1; ⌚6pm-6am; MNevsky Prospekt) A self-styled 'trash bar', the Blue Oyster is named after the leather bar that so prominently featured in the 1980s *Police Academy* movies. But instead of daddies slow dancing you'll find a young and totally uninhibited crowd knocking back the vodka and (quite literally) hanging from the rafters. Loud, lewd and lots of fun, this is by far the coolest gay place in town.

BERMUDY BAR DISCO BAR

Map p254 (Bankovsky per 6; 6pm-6am; Sennaya Pl) Resurrecting the time-honoured St Petersburg practice of dancing on the tables, this friendly bar does indeed become more of a disco than a bar after midnight. With low prices, good cocktails, table football and a trashy, fun atmosphere, Bermudy is an anything-goes destination if you want a late night.

CENTRAL STATION GAY CLUB

Map p254 (www.centralstation.ru; ul Lomonosova 1/28; admission before midnight free, after midnight R100-1000; noon-6am; Gostiny Dvor) This flashy gay club is huge, with several bars and dance floors, as well as a men-only dark room. It's the absolute centre of the St Petersburg gay scene, so there are busy events on throughout the week, including Female Station (a lesbian night) on Wednesday. During the day, it's open as a restaurant and lounge.

FOLKS BAR

Map p254 (www.folksbar.ru; ul Lomonosova 2; 7pm-6am; Nevsky Prospekt) This new addition to the now notorious stretch of bars around Dumskaya ul is a firm favourite with students, who pack this place out in the evenings. Spread over three floors, you'll usually be able to find a vibe and music genre for you. Late at night, face control can be tough.

TINKOFF BREWERY

Map p254 (www.tinkof.ru; Kazanskaya ul 7; noon-2am; Nevsky Prospekt) Set inside a microbrewery that also does a good line in German food, Tinkoff is a great place to sample one of eight beers brewed on-site and enjoy the live music in this unusual industrial space. Service can be hit and miss, but both the food and beer are excellent.

TRIBUNAL BAR BAR

Map p254 (www.tribunal.ru; Karavannaya ul 26; 9pm-6am; Gostiny Dvor) This is something of a St Petersburg institution, famous for the debauchery and decadence that sets in as soon as the crowd has had enough to drink. Scantily clad women dancing on the bar are practically guaranteed, making this a popular stop for lone male visitors.

LOBBY BAR BAR

Map p254 (www.grandhoteleurope.com; Mikhailovskaya ul 1/7; 9am-1am; Nevsky Prospekt) If classical elegance, a buzzing atmosphere and a pianist tinkling the ivories on a grand piano is more your scene, then head for the fabulous lobby bar of the Grand Hotel Europe for a perfectly made cocktail. Prices are steep, but what else would you expect from St Petersburg's most famous hotel?

STRAY DOG CAFÉ CAFE

Map p254 (Кафе Бродячая собака; pl Iskusstv 5; 11.30am-midnight; Nevsky Prospekt) Back in the days of the St Petersburg avant-garde, this atmospheric, underground cafe was the gathering place for poets and playwrights such as Anna Akhmatova and Vladimir Mayakovsky. These days, the crowd isn't so bohemian, but the cafe still hosts occasional poetry readings and acoustic music performances and has a lovely ambience.

CAFÉ SINGER CAFE

Map p254 (Кафе Зингер; Nevsky pr 28; 9am-11pm; Nevsky Prospekt) On the 2nd floor of the iconic Singer Building is this great cafe, with fantastic views of the Kazan Cathedral and the bustle of Nevsky pr through its huge windows. As well as a sumptuous cake counter there's actually a more formal dining area around the corner, where you can order from a largely Russian menu.

LOMONOSOV BAR

Map p254 (ul Lomonosova 1; 6pm-6am; Nevsky Prospekt) Branding itself 'St Petersburg's most alcoholic and democratic bar', this raucous joint is actually rather smarter than its even more raucous neighbours on Dumskaya ul. With free karaoke and even (perhaps rather ambitiously?) some poles for dancing above the bar, this place goes all night.

ENTERTAINMENT

SHOSTAKOVICH PHILHARMONIA — CLASSICAL MUSIC

Map p254 (www.philharmonia.spb.ru; Ⓜ Nevsky Prospekt) Under the artistic direction of world-famous conductor Yury Temirkanov, the St Petersburg Philharmonic Orchestra represents the finest in orchestral music. The **Bolshoy Zal** (Grand Hall; Mikhailovskaya ul 2) on pl Iskusstv is the venue for a full program of symphonic performances, while the nearby **Maly Zal** (Small Hall; Nevsky pr 30) hosts smaller ensembles. Both venues are used for numerous music festivals, including the superb Early Music Festival (p21).

HERMITAGE THEATRE — BALLET & OPERA

Map p254 (www.hermitageballet.com; Dvortsovaya nab 34; Ⓜ Admiralteyskaya) This austere neoclassical theatre – once the private theatre of the imperial family – stands on the site of the original Winter Palace of Peter I. At the behest of Catherine the Great, Giacomo Quarenghi designed the theatre to resemble an amphitheatre, with statues of Apollo and the Muses occupying the niches. During the Soviet period, this hall was used more often for lectures and such, but it reopened as a theatre in the 1980s. The venue is small, and tickets are often sold out, so book early if you'd like to see a ballet or opera in this intimate space.

MIKHAILOVSKY THEATRE — BALLET & OPERA

Map p254 (www.mikhailovsky.ru; pl Iskusstv 1; Ⓜ Nevsky Prospekt) While not quite as grand as the Mariinsky, this stage still delivers the Russian ballet or operatic experience, complete with multitiered theatre, frescoed ceiling and elaborate concerts. The inspiring pl Iskusstv (Arts Sq; p69) is a lovely setting for this respected venue, which is home to the State Academic Opera & Ballet Company. It's generally easier and cheaper to get tickets to the performances staged here than those at the Mariinsky.

GLINKA CAPELLA HOUSE — CLASSICAL MUSIC

Map p254 (www.glinka-capella.ru, in Russian; nab reki Moyki 20; Ⓜ Admiralteyskaya) This historic hall is beautifully located on the Moyka and was constructed for Russia's oldest professional choir, the Emperor Court Choir Capella, founded in 1473. Originally based in Moscow, it was transferred to St Petersburg upon the order of Peter the Great in 1703. These days, performances focus on choral and organ music.

ALEXANDRINSKY THEATRE — THEATRE

Map p254 (www.alexandrinsky.ru; pl Ostrovskogo 2; Ⓜ Gostiny Dvor) Formerly the Pushkin State Drama Theatre, this magnificent venue is just one part of an immaculate architectural ensemble designed by Carlo Rossi (see pl Ostrovskogo, p70). The theatre's interior

ST PETERSBURG'S DRINKING STREET – A QUICK GUIDE

If you are up for a night of bar-hopping, you can't do better than **Dumskaya ulitsa** (Map p254; Dumskaya ul 9; ⌚noon-6am; Ⓜ Gostiny Dvor), around which dozens of St Petersburg's hottest spots for drinking and dancing are crammed into a crumbling, classical facade. A couple of these places are (or were) owned by Anton Belyankin and Andrei Gradovich – two members of the local ska band Dva Samolyota – which pretty much guarantees great music and a cool vibe.

While rumours continue that Dumskaya ul is slated as the city's next big renovation project, at the moment it's all still here, so come at weekends to party with a young, alternative and very up-for-it crowd. One tip: arrive early (before 11pm) to get a stamp from the bars, as they tend to fill up later and you may have trouble getting in. Directly facing these bars in the shopping centre in the middle of the street are three clubs, Ludovic, Shine and Punch – where all the loud music is coming from. These are the favoured hangouts of a young teen crowd who come to listen to brain-meltingly loud Russian pop.

If you prefer a different vibe, try one of these:

Datscha Shabby chic decor, cheap drinks and a strict 'no house or techno' policy.

Fidel This funky place is a sort of musical and alcoholic tribute to the ruler who 'outlived six presidents of America and six leaders of the Soviet Union and Russia'.

Belgrad *Bel*-yankin and *Grad*-ovich. Get it? This is your best bet for live music. DJs start playing at 10pm while bands start at midnight.

oozes 19th-century elegance and style, and it's worth taking a peek even if you don't see a production here. This is where Anton Chekhov premiered *The Seagull,* which was pretty much universally hated by the public and critics alike. These days, the company has a huge repertoire, ranging from Russian folktales to Shakespearean tragedies.

THE OTHER SIDE LIVE MUSIC

Map p254 (www.theotherside.ru; Bolshaya Konyushennaya ul 1; ⌚noon-last customer; Ⓜ Nevsky Prospekt) This expat mainstay is a solid option for drinks with a fun crowd and features live musical entertainment most nights of the week: count on everything from jazz to blues and funk. Concerts start at 8pm during the week, or 10pm at the weekend.

BOLSHOY DRAMA THEATRE THEATRE

Map p254 (BDT; www.bdt.spb.ru, in Russian; nab reki Fontanki 65; Ⓜ Sennaya Ploshchad) The BDT became the city's most innovative and exciting theatre under the direction of Georgi Tovstonogov between the 1960s and the 1980s. His 1957 staging of Fyodor Dostoevsky's *The Idiot* is still remembered as one of the peaks of Soviet theatre. Today the theatre has a reputable repertoire and is a good place to see Russian drama. It's one of the city's grandest theatres, and its location on the Fontanka River is delightful.

KOMISSARZHEVSKAYA THEATRE THEATRE

Map p254 (www.teatrvfk.ru, in Russian; Italiyanskaya ul 19; Ⓜ Gostiny Dvor) This theatre is named after Vera Komissarzhevskaya, a great St Petersburg actress who gained her reputation as leading lady in Vsevolod Meyerhold performances during the late 19th century. In the early years of the 20th century, Komissarzhevskaya founded an acting troupe that performed in the Passage concert hall, staging plays by all of the famous playwrights of the day, including Maxim Gorky and Anton Chekhov. Revived in the midst of the Siege, the theatre was renamed in honour of the great actress. These days, headed by artistic director Viktor Novikov, it is known for its modern treatment of classic plays.

PRIYUT KOMEDIANTA THEATRE THEATRE

Map p254 (www.pkteatr.ru, in Russian; Sadovaya ul 27/9; Ⓜ Sennaya Ploshchad) This delightful theatre's name means 'the actor's shelter' and it does a pretty good job of fulfilling its role, providing refuge for some of the city's best up-and-coming directors and producers. It was founded by actor Yury Tomashevsky in the late 1980s, when the city turned over a defunct cinema that the group still uses.

AVRORA CINEMA

Map p254 (www.avrora.spb.ru; Nevsky pr 60; Ⓜ Gostiny Dvor) Opening in 1913 as the Piccadilly Picture House, this was the city's most fashionable cinema in the early years of Russian film, and it has retained its position pretty consistently ever since. Renamed the more Soviet-sounding Avrora in 1932, it was here that a young Dmitry Shostakovich played piano accompaniment to silent movies. Today it's one of the best cinemas in town, and most premieres (to which you can nearly always buy tickets) take place here. Most foreign films are dubbed into Russian, though sometimes you'll find the odd subtitled one.

DOM KINO CINEMA

Map p254 (www.domkino.spb.ru; Karavannaya ul 12; Ⓜ Gostiny Dvor) This cinema shows arty Russian and foreign films, plus some higher-brow Hollywood productions. It is also where the British Council holds its British Film Festival. Despite a refit, the whole place remains remarkably Soviet in a charming way.

DEMMENI MARIONETTE THEATRE PUPPET THEATRE

Map p254 (www.demmeni.ru, in Russian; Nevsky pr 52; Ⓜ Gostiny Dvor) Since 1917, this venue under the arches on central Nevsky is the city's oldest professional puppet theatre. Mainly for children, the shows are well produced and professionally performed.

ST PETERSBURG STATE CIRCUS CIRCUS

Map p254 (www.circus.spb.ru; nab reki Fontanki 3; Ⓜ Gostiny Dvor) The oldest and best-established circus in the city, dating to 1827, occupies an ornate building on the Fontanka River. The performances, running about 2½ hours, usually tell a story based on a fairy tale or folklore. This venue also hosts circus troupes from other cities and countries.

SHOPPING

Not only the historic heart, but also the commercial heart, this district is bursting with credit-maxing designer digs, eye-catching boutiques, filled-

to-the-brim bookstores and run-of-the-mill souvenir shops. Nevsky pr is, of course, the city's main shopping street, although the real gems and best bargains are hidden away in the smaller surrounding streets.

BUKVOED — BOOKS

Map p254 (Буквоед; www.bookvoed.ru, in Russian; Nevsky pr 13; 9am-11pm; Admiralteyskaya) St Petersburg's premier bookshop chain has branches around the city. This is one of the smaller outlets, but it is centrally located and it carries a good selection of maps, art books, posters, calendars and postcards, as well as a smaller selection of English-language literature.

DOM KNIGI — BOOKS

Map p254 (Дом книги; www.spbdk.ru; Nevsky pr 28; 9am-midnight; Nevsky Prospekt) The stalwart of the city's bookshops is Dom Knigi, housed in the wonderful, whimsical Singer Building (p68). For years, this was the only place in the city that carried a decent selection of literature, and it is still an inviting place to browse. On the 1st floor, you'll find lots of English-language coffee-table books that make good souvenirs. The 2nd floor houses a great cafe with superb views onto Nevsky pr and the Kazan Cathedral.

WRITERS' BOOKSHOP — BOOKS

Map p254 (Книжная лавка писателей; Nevsky pr 66; Gostiny Dvor) Specialising in foreign literature, this place is one of the few that carries Lonely Planet guides. You'll also find an excellent selection of English-language literature, including English translations of Russian classics and contemporary bestsellers.

WILD ORCHID — CLOTHING, ACCESSORIES

Map p254 (Дикая Орхидея; www.wildorchid.ru; Nevsky pr 44; 10am-10pm; Nevsky Prospekt) Underwear is yet another measure of Russia's amazing transition to capitalism. Gone are the days of one-size-fits-all, baggy cotton briefs; sensational, sexy lingerie is on sale all over St Petersburg. This top-of-the-line store carries devastatingly sensual and expensive lingerie by European designers.

VINISSIMO — FOOD & DRINK

Map p254 (571 3405; www.bonvin.ru, in Russian; nab kanala Griboyedova 29; noon-9pm Mon-Sat; Nevsky Prospekt) With low ceilings and exposed brickwork, this little wine cellar is an atmospheric place to pick out a *bon vin*. There is no shortage of *grands crus* and pricey reserves if you are shopping for a special occasion, but head to the sale rack in the centre of the store for excellent French, Spanish and Italian wines that you can afford to drink every day.

STARAYA KNIGA — BOOKS

Map p254 (Старая книга; Nevsky pr 3; 10am-7pm; Admiralteyskaya) This long-established antique bookseller is a fascinating place to rummage around. The stock ranges from fancy, mint-edition books to secondhand, well-worn Soviet editions, maps and art, and is a great place to look for an unusual, unique souvenir.

YAKHONT — JEWELLERY

Map p254 (Яхонт; Bolshaya Morskaya ul 24; 10am-8pm; Nevsky Prospekt) From this building, Carl Fabergé dazzled the imperial family and the rest of the world with his extraordinary bespoke designs. Yakhont has no link to the Fabergé family, but it is carrying on the tradition anyway. This long, dark salon provides an impressive showcase of their work.

MILITARY SHOP — MILITARY

Map p254 (Товар для военных; www.voentorg spb.ru; Sadovaya ul 26; 10am-7pm; Gostiny Dvor) In a city with men in uniform on every street corner, this is where you can get yours (the uniform that is!). Buy stripy sailor tops, embroidered badges, big boots, camouflage jackets and snappy caps at decent prices. Look for the circular green and gold sign with 'Military Shop' written in English; the entrance is in the courtyard.

GOSTINY DVOR — SHOPPING CENTRE

Map p254 (Гостиный двор; www.bgd.ru, in Russian; Nevsky pr 35; 10am-10pm; Gostiny Dvor) One of the oldest shopping arcades in the world, Gostiny Dvor (Merchant Yard) was built in the mid-18th century. After a decade-long renovation, the exterior is already looking like it needs a serious repaint, while the interior retains a largely Soviet feel. On the ground floor, endless corridors of counters showcase everything from stereos to souvenirs. Upstairs you will find some fancier fashion outlets, and the most likely places you'll want to shop.

GRAND PALACE — SHOPPING CENTRE

Map p254 (Гранд Палас; www.grand-palace.ru, in Russian; Nevsky pr 44; 11am-9pm; Gostiny

Dvor) This palatial shopping centre was created for the New Russian shopping classes, who expect nothing less than grand and glittering. The biggest names in fashion may have moved on to Bolshaya Konyushennaya ul, but the Grand Palace remains home to Sonia Rykiel, Swarowski, Nina Ricci and local brand Wild Orchid, not to mention the fanciest free toilets in the city.

PASSAGE SHOPPING CENTRE

Map p254 (Пассаж; www.passage.spb.ru; Nevsky pr 48; 10am-9pm; M Gostiny Dvor) This old-fashioned arcade, lined with boutiques and souvenir shops, runs between Nevsky pr and Italiyanskaya ul. The shopping here is not particularly unique, but it is a pleasant, atmospheric place to stroll, similar to Moscow's world-famous GUM.

PROSTRANSTVO KULTURY FASHION

Map p254 (Пространство культуры; 3rd fl, Nevsky pr 48; 10am-9pm; M Gostiny Dvor) This shop, inside the Passage shopping centre, is well worth noting separately, as it contains several small independent boutiques producing local accessories including bags, jewellery, watches and cool clothing ranging from secondhand to hand-printed t-shirts. Enter Passage through the door on the right, near the entrance to the underpass and then go to the top floor of the building.

THE PEOPLE SHOWROOM FASHION

Map p254 (Bankovsky per 3/4; M Sennaya Pl) You'll have to ring the bell to gain admittance to this oh-so-stylish boutique, but once you're in, it's inviting and friendly and the staff go to great lengths to get you what you want. The showroom stocks Russian and international designer gear at surprisingly reasonable prices.

RETRO SHOP SECONDHAND

Map p254 (Karavannaya ul 22; M Gostiny Dvor) Tucked away in the side of an arch just moments from Nevsky is this little shop, which has lots of quirky old things for sale, from near-antique Soviet records to charming bric-a-brac and ephemera from days gone by.

SOUVENIR MARKET SOUVENIRS

Map p254 (nab kanala Griboyedova 1; sunrise-sunset; M Nevsky Prospekt) You're unlikely to find any incredible bargains at the sanitised market behind the Church on the Spilled Blood, but you will find a great selection of handicrafts, Soviet paraphernalia and other souvenirs. You are encouraged to haggle with the vendors, some of whom are also the artists, and don't worry – the vendors speak enough English to barter back.

Smolny & Vosstaniya

SMOLNY | LITEYNY | VOSSTANIYA | VLADIMIRSKAYA

Neighbourhood Top Five

❶ Explore the beating heart of Orthodox St Petersburg in the complex of churches at the **Alexander Nevsky Monastery** (p83) and see the last resting place of many of Russia's greatest artists in the atmospheric cemeteries.

❷ Climb the extraordinary baroque spires of the **Smolny Cathedral** (p84) for great views of the city.

❸ Savour the superb collection of gorgeous objects at the **Museum of Decorative & Applied Arts** (p85).

❹ Visit **Cathedral of the Transfiguration Of Our Saviour** (p84) and **Vladimirsky Cathedral** (p87), the least known but most beautiful churches.

❺ See the room where Fyodor Dostoevsky wrote *The Brothers Karamazov* at the fascinating **Dostoevsky Museum** (p87).

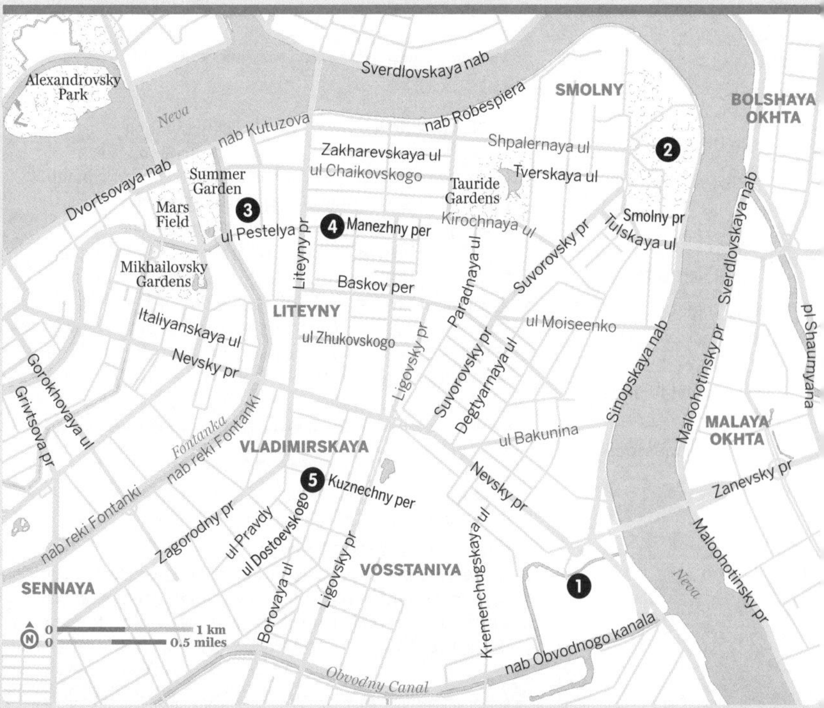

For more detail of this area, see Map p258 and p260

Lonely Planet's Top Tip

Avoid hanging around the entrance to the Moscow Station on pl Vosstaniya. It's a favoured police hangout for document checks and, in some cases, shakedowns. You're unlikely to have problems (if you have your passport with you), but it's just a pain and best avoided.

Best Places to Eat

- Istoriya (p89)
- Bistro Garçon (p92)
- Kompot Café (p89)
- Botanika (p89)
- Dom Beat (p91)

For reviews, see p89

Best Places to Drink

- Dyuni (p94)
- XXXX (p94)
- Griboyedov (p94)
- Terminal Bar (p94)
- Dom Beat (p91)

For reviews, see p93

Best Galleries

- Loft Project ETAGI (p87)
- Pushkinskaya 10 (p88)
- Art re.flex (p99)
- Rizzordi Art Foundation (p88)

For reviews, see p84

Explore: Smolny & Vosstaniya

This area, bisected by the second half of Nevsky pr, breaks down into four districts: Smolny, Liteyny, Vosstaniya and Vladimirskaya. An extremely varied place, it contains the closest thing St Petersburg has to a creative hub, as well as its political and diplomatic heart.

The Liteyny and Smolny districts sit side-by-side east of the Historic Heart, tucked inside a swooping curve of the Neva River on its left bank. These neighbourhoods take their names from the industries that once dominated this area: *liteyny* means 'foundry' and *smol* means 'tar', although these evocative names hardly capture the atmosphere of these quaint but quiet neighbourhoods today.

On the south side of Nevsky the historic neighbourhood of Vladimirskaya is dominated by the grand, gold-domed cathedral of the same name. This is a busy, commercial area full of shops and several quirky museums.

Nevsky pr continues east to pl Vosstaniya (Uprising Sq), so called because the February Revolution began here in 1917. Although it is a geographically large area, it contains swathes of industrial wasteland, as well as St Petersburg's busiest railway station, Moscow Station (Moskovsky Vokzal). Nevsky pr ends at pl Alexandra Nevskogo, named after the city's patron saint, who defeated the Swedes in the area during the 12th century. On this square stands the ancient and revered Alexander Nevsky Monastery, the oldest monastery in the city.

Local Life

- **Creative Kicks** Make the most of being in St Petersburg's most creative area: enjoy an exhibition at Loft Project ETAGI (p87), see a band at Kitaysky Lyotchik Dzhao Da (p95) and buy art at Borey Art Centre (p98).
- **Shop Till You Drop** Smolny and Vosstaniya boast two of the city's biggest shopping centres – vast Galeria (p99) and smaller, but equally flashy Nevsky Centre (p99).
- **Musical Thrills** See local rock bands perform at Zoccolo (p96), Fish Fabrique (p97) and Dusche (p96), and chill at St Petersburg's two best jazz clubs: JFC (p96) and Red Fox Jazz Café (p96).

Getting There & Away

- **Metro** Accessed by Pl Vosstaniya/Mayakovskaya, Vladimirskaya/Dostoevskaya, Pl Alexandra Nevskogo, Chernyshevskaya and Ligovsky Prospekt.
- **Marshrutka** Handy for getting up or down Nevsky pr in minutes, hundreds of minibuses run this route – check they don't turn off halfway by asking the driver if they go down 'vyes Nyevsky' (all of Nevsky pr).

TOP SIGHTS
ALEXANDER NEVSKY MONASTERY

Named after the patron saint of St Petersburg who led the Russian victory over the Swedes in 1240, the Alexander Nevsky Monastery is the city's oldest and most eminent religious institution. Today it is a working monastery that attracts scores of devout believers, as well as being the burial place of some of Russia's most famous artistic figures.

Founding the monastery in 1710, Peter the Great sought to link St Petersburg to the historic battle against the Swedes, and thus to underscore Russia's long history with the newly captured region. Even though the site of Nevsky's victory was further upstream by the mouth of the Izhora River, the monastery became the centre of the Nevsky cult and his remains were transferred here from Vladimir in 1724. In 1797 the monastery became a *lavra,* the most senior grade of Russian Orthodox monasteries.

You can wander freely around most of the grounds and churches, but you must buy tickets to enter the two most famous cemeteries.

DON'T MISS...

- Seeing the greats in the Tikhvin Cemetery
- The iconostasis in the Trinity Cathedral
- Alexander Nevsky Gardens
- The Nikolsky Cemetery

PRACTICALITIES

- Map p260
- www.lavra.spb.ru
- Pl Alexandra Nevskogo
- Cemeteries R200, State Museum of Urban Sculpture R100
- ⌚Artists' Necropolis 9.30am-9pm, 18th Century Necropolis 9.30am-6pm
- ⓂPloshchad Alexandra Nevskogo

Cemeteries

Coming into the monastery complex, you'll first arrive at the Tikhvin and Lazarus Cemeteries, burial place to some of Russia's most famous names. You'll find Dostoevsky, Tchaikovsky, Rimsky-Korsakov, Borodin and Mussorgsky within the walls of the **Tikhvin Cemetery** (also called the Artists' Necropolis), which is on your right after you enter the monastery's main gate. Across the way in the **Lazarus Cemetery** (or 18th Century Cemetery), you'll find even more atmospheric graves, though fewer famous names – look out for polymath Mikhail Lomonosov, as well as the graves of the St Petersburg architects Quarenghi, Stasov and Rossi.

The cemeteries are now part of the rather misleadingly named State Museum of Urban Sculpture, which also has an exhibit inside the **Annunciation Church** (admission R100), where you'll find the tombs of many minor royals and tsarist generals.

Monastery Complex

The monastery itself is within a further wall beyond the cemeteries. The centrepiece is the classical **Trinity Cathedral**, which was built between 1776 and 1790. Hundreds crowd in here on 12 September to celebrate the feast of St Alexander Nevsky, whose remains are in the silver reliquary by the elaborate main iconostasis. Behind the cathedral is the **Nikolsky Cemetery**, a beautiful spot with a little stream running through it, where more recently deceased Petersburgers can be found, including former mayor Anatoly Sobchak and murdered Duma deputy Galina Starovoytova.

Opposite the cathedral is the **Metropolitan's House** (built 1775–78), the official residence of the spiritual leader of St Petersburg's Russian Orthodox community. In the surrounding grounds is a smaller cemetery where leading Communist (ie atheist) Party officials and luminaries are buried. On the far right of the grounds facing the canal is St Petersburg's **Orthodox Academy**, one of only a handful in Russia (the main one is at Sergiev Posad, near Moscow).

SIGHTS

Smolny & Liteyny

SMOLNY CATHEDRAL CATHEDRAL

Map p258 (Смольный собор; pl Rastrelli 3/1; adult/student R150/90, bell tower R100; ⏲10am-7pm Thu-Tue; Ⓜ Chernyshevskaya) If baroque is your thing, then look no further than the sky-blue Smolny Cathedral, an unrivalled masterpiece of the genre that ranks among Bartolomeo Rastrelli's most amazing creations. The cathedral is the centrepiece of a convent mostly built to Rastrelli's designs between 1748 and 1757. His inspiration was to combine baroque details with the forest of towers and onion domes typical of an old Russian monastery. There's special genius in the proportions of the cathedral (it gives the impression of soaring upwards), to which the convent buildings are a perfect foil.

In stark contrast, the interior is a disappointingly austere plain white as it is no longer a working church, but serves instead as a concert hall and exhibition space. If you're lucky there may well be rehearsals for concerts going on while you visit, to which you're welcome to listen, otherwise it's not really worth paying to enter the cathedral itself.

By contrast, however, it's definitely worth paying to climb the 277 steps to one (or both) of the two 63m-high bell towers for stupendous views over the city.

TAURIDE PALACE & GARDENS PARK

Map p258 (Таврический сад; Ⓜ Chernyshevskaya) Catherine the Great had this fabulous baroque palace built in 1783 for Grigory Potemkin, a famed general and one of her lovers. The palace takes its name from the Ukrainian region of Crimea (once called Tavria), which Potemkin conquered. The palace was a thank you for that acquisition, among other things. Catherine's bitter son, Paul I, turned the palace into a barracks after his ascension to the throne in 1796, which ruined most of the lavish interiors. Between 1906 and 1917 the State Duma, the Provisional Government and the Petrograd Soviet all met here; in the 1930s it housed the All-Union Agricultural Communist University, a fate that would have no doubt horrified Catherine the Great. Today it is home to the Parliamentary Assembly of the Member States of the CIS (Commonwealth of Independent States). It is not open to the public.

The gardens, on the other hand, are open to all. Once the romping grounds of the tsarina, the palace gardens have since become – in true Soviet style – a park for the people (also called **City Children's Park**). The tree-lined dirt paths and picturesque pond make for a pleasant place to stroll, while children can enjoy climbing on the playground equipment or take their chances on some rusty rides.

Just east of the gardens, on Shpalernaya ul, is one of the last remaining **statues of Felix Dzerzhinsky**, founder of the infamous Cheka (Bolshevik secret police), KGB predecessor.

ANNA AKHMATOVA MUSEUM IN THE FOUNTAIN HOUSE MUSEUM

Map p258 (Музей Анны Ахматовой в Фонтанном Доме; www.akhmatova.spb.ru; Liteyny pr 53; admission R100, audio tour R100; ⏲10.30am-6.30pm Tue-Sun, 1-9pm Wed; Ⓜ Gostiny Dvor) Housed in the south wing of the Sheremetyev Palace (built 1750–55), this touching and fascinating literary museum celebrates the life and work of Anna Akhmatova, St Petersburg's most famous 20th-century poet. Akhmatova lived here from 1924 until 1952, as this was the apartment of her common-law husband Nikolai Punin. The apartment is on the 2nd floor and is filled with mementos of the poet and correspondence with other writers. The atmosphere is peaceful and contemplative. It's also an interesting chance to see the interior of an (albeit atypical) apartment from the early to mid-20th century.

Admission also includes the **Josef Brodsky American Study**. Brodsky did not live here, but his connection with Akhmatova was strong. For lack of a better location, his office has been recreated here, complete with furniture and other 'artefacts' from his adopted home in Massachusetts.

Downstairs is a bookshop and video room where you can watch documentaries on the lives of Akhmatova and her contemporaries over a coffee.

CATHEDRAL OF THE TRANSFIGURATION OF OUR SAVIOUR CATHEDRAL

Map p258 (Спасо-Преображенский собор; Preobrazhenskaya pl; Ⓜ Chernyshevskaya) The interior of this marvellous 1743 cathedral, which has been beautifully restored and repainted both outside and in, is one of the most gilded in the city. The grand gates bear the imperial double-headed eagle in vast golden busts, reflecting the fact that the cathedral was built on the site where the Preobrazhensky Guards (the monarch's personal protection unit) had their headquarters. Architect Vasily Stasov rebuilt the cathedral from 1827 to 1829 in the neoclassical style. It is dedicated to the victory over the Turks in 1828–29; note the captured Turkish guns in the gate surrounding the cathedral.

MUSEUM OF DECORATIVE & APPLIED ARTS — MUSEUM

Map p258 (Музей прикладного искусства; www.spbghpa.ru; Solyanoy per 15; adult/student R60/30; ⏲11am-4.30pm Tue-Sat; Ⓜ Chernyshevskaya) Also known as the **Stieglitz Museum**, this fascinating establishment is as beautiful as you would expect a decorative arts museum to be. A vast array of gorgeous objects is on display, from medieval handcrafted furniture to 18th-century Russian tiled stoves and contemporary works by the students of the Applied Arts School next door. Their surroundings merely match their magnificence. This museum is less visited than some of its counterparts in the city, but the quiet, off-the-beaten-track atmosphere only adds to its appeal.

In 1878 the millionaire Baron Stieglitz founded the School of Technical Design and wanted to surround his students with world-class art to inspire them. He began a collection that was continued by his son and was to include a unique array of European and Oriental glassware, porcelains, tapestries, furniture and paintings. It eventually grew into one of Europe's richest private collections. Between 1885 and 1895, a building designed by architect Maximilian Messmacher was built to house the collection and this building also became a masterpiece. Each hall is decorated in its own unique style, including Italian, Renaissance, Flemish and baroque. The **Terem Room**, in the style of the medieval Terem Palace of Moscow's Kremlin, is an opulent knockout.

After the revolution the school was closed, the museum's collection redistributed to the Hermitage and the Russian Museum, and most of the lavish interiors brutally painted or plastered over, even destroyed (one room was used as a sports hall). The painstaking renovation continues to this day, despite receiving no state funding.

Just finding the museum can be tricky; enter through the academy building (the second entrance as you walk up Solyanoy per from ul Pestelya). Tell the guard that you want to go to the museum *(v moozáy)*, then go up the main staircase, turn right at the top, walk through two halls and then go down the staircase to your left. All signs are in Russian only.

MUSEUM OF THE DEFENCE & BLOCKADE OF LENINGRAD — MUSEUM

Map p258 (Государственный мемориальный музей обороны и блокады Ленинграда; Solyanoy per 9; admission R200; ⏲10am-5pm Thu-Tue, closed last Thu of month; Ⓜ Chernyshevskaya) This museum opened just three months after the blockade was lifted in January 1944 and boasted 37,000 exhibits, including real tanks and aeroplanes. But three years later, during Stalin's repression of the city, the museum was shut, its director shot, and most of the exhibits destroyed or redistributed. Not until 1985's glasnost was an attempt made once again to gather documents to reopen the museum; this happened in 1989. The grim but engrossing displays contain donations from survivors, propaganda posters from the time and many photos depicting life and death during the blockade.

SHEREMETYEV PALACE — MUSEUM

Map p258 (Шереметьевский дворец; www.theatremuseum.ru; nab reki Fontanki 34; admission R250; ⏲noon-7pm Wed-Sun; Ⓜ Gostiny Dvor) Splendid wrought-iron gates facing the Fontanka River guard the entrance to the Sheremetyev Palace (built 1750–55), now a branch of the **State Museum of Theatre & Music**, which has a collection of musical instruments from the 19th and 20th centuries. The Sheremetyev family was famous for the concerts and theatre performances they hosted at their palace, which was a centre of musical life in the capital in the 18th century. Upstairs, the rooms have been wonderfully restored, which gives an impression of the cultural life of the time. Occasional concerts are still held here.

ANNA AKHMATOVA MONUMENT — MONUMENT

Map p258 (Памятник Анне Ахматовой; nab Robespierre; Ⓜ Chernyshevskaya) This moving statue of St Petersburg's most famous 20th-century poet was unveiled in 2006, across the river from the notorious Kresty holding prison, to mark the 40th anniversary of Akhmatova's death. The location is no coincidence – Kresty Prison was where

Akhmatova herself queued for days in the snow for news of her son after his multiple arrests during Stalin's terror. The inscription on the monument comes from her epic poem 'Requiem' (1935–40), in which she describes life during the purges. It reads: 'That's why I pray not for myself/But for all of you who stood there with me/Through fiercest cold and scorching July heat/Under a towering, completely blind red wall.'

SMOLNY INSTITUTE — HISTORIC BUILDING

Map p258 (Смольный институт; pl Proletarskoy Diktatury 3; by appointment only 10am-6pm Mon-Fri; Chernyshevskaya) Built by Giacomo Quarenghi between 1806 and 1808 as a school for aristocratic girls, the Smolny Institute was thrust into the limelight in 1917 when it became the headquarters for the Bolshevik Central Committee and the Petrograd Soviet. From here, Trotsky and Lenin directed the October Revolution, and in the **Hall of Acts** (Aktovy zal) on 25 October, the All-Russian Congress of Soviets conferred power on a Bolshevik government led by Lenin. The Smolny Institute served as the seat of power until March 1918. In 1934, the powerful Leningrad Party chief Sergei Kirov was assassinated in its corridors, on orders from Stalin, sparking the notorious Leningrad purges (see p189). Today St Petersburg's governor runs the city from here.

FLORAL EXHIBITION HALL — PARKS & GARDENS

Map p258 (Выставочный зал цветы; Potyomkinskaya ul 2; adult/student R30/20; 11am-8pm Tue-Sun, 2-8pm Mon; Chernyshevskaya) One of the finest ways to momentarily escape from a St Petersburg winter is to head for the Floral Exhibition Hall, an indoor tropical paradise just northwest of the Tauride Gardens. There's also an impressive **Butterfly House** (adult/student R180/120) on the premises.

CHURCH OF ST JOHN THE BAPTIST — MUSEUM

Map p258 (Храм Иоанна Богослова; ul Nekrasova 31; 9am-6pm; Mayakovskaya) This extraordinary building has one of the most striking exteriors in the city – its Byzantine facade is totally incongruous with the rest of the street, although few people seem to notice it, hemmed in on both sides by other terraced buildings on ul Nekrasova. The church was used until recently as a hospital. Take the stairs to the 2nd floor where you can see the small church and chat with the charming nuns who look after it.

MUSEUM OF EROTICA — MUSEUM

Map p258 (Музей Эротики; ul Furshtatskaya 47; admission R100; 8am-9pm Mon-Fri, 9am-6pm Sat & Sun; Chernyshevskaya) It is odd enough that a museum should be housed in a venereal disease clinic, but even more surprising is that the chief attraction is a 30cm-long grey, embalmed penis that allegedly belonged to Rasputin. The chief of the prostate research centre of the Russian Academy of Natural Sciences, Igor Knyazkin, assembled this collection of sexually themed trinkets his patients had given him over the years. At the very least, it gives patients something to do in the waiting room. Other exhibits include the bone of a sea lion's penis and various statuettes of people and animals in a variety of sexual positions.

WORLD OF WATER MUSEUM — MUSEUM

Map p258 (Мир воды; Shpalernaya ul 56; adult/student R250/100; 10am-6pm Wed-Sun; Chernyshevskaya) The handsomely restored complex of 19th-century brick buildings between Tauride Gardens and the Neva River houses St Petersburg's water treatment company Vodokanal and its museum. The 1st floor has an interesting multimedia exhibition about what goes on underneath St Petersburg. The upper floors of the water tower contain historical exhibitions, including the construction of waterways in the city and the water system during the blockade. Displays are slick and informative, though only in Russian.

BOLSHOY DOM — HISTORICAL BUILDING

Map p258 (Большой дом; Liteyny pr 4; closed to the public; Chernyshevskaya) Noi Trotsky's monolithic design for the local KGB headquarters (and current Interior Ministry headquarters) is referred to by everyone as the 'Bolshoy Dom' or 'Big House'. It's a fierce-looking block of granite built in 1932 in the late-constructivist style and was once a byword for fear among the people of the city: most people who were taken here during the purges were never heard of again. Employees who have worked here include Vladimir Putin during his days as a KGB man. The Bolshoy Dom made the news in 2010, when the political art collective Voina (War) drew a 65m-long penis on the nearby Liteyny Bridge, which, when the bridge was raised, made a very clear statement towards the FSB.

Vladimirskaya & Vosstaniya

ALEXANDER NEVSKY MONASTERY MONASTERY

See p83.

VLADIMIRSKY CATHEDRAL CATHEDRAL

Map p260 (Владимирский собор; Vladimirsky pr 20; admission free; ⌚8am-6pm, services 6pm daily; Ⓜ Vladimirskaya) This fantastic, five-domed cathedral, ascribed to Domenico Trezzini, is the namesake of this neighbourhood. Incorporating both baroque and neoclassical elements, the cathedral was built in the 1760s, with Giacomo Quarenghi's neoclassical bell tower added later in the century. Apparently Fyodor Dostoevsky was a parishioner here (convenient, as he lived around the corner). The cathedral was closed in 1932 and the Soviets turned it into an underwear factory; but in 1990 it was reconsecrated and reconstructed, and it has resumed its originally intended function. These days it is one of the busiest cathedrals in town, as evidenced by the hordes of babushkas and beggars outside. Nonetheless, it's worth weaving your way through the outstretched hands to admire the cathedral's interiors (upstairs). The baroque iconostasis was originally installed in the private chapel of the Anichkov Palace (p72), but was transferred here in 1808. For an impressive perspective on the onion domes, have a drink in the 7th-floor Raskolnikov bar of the Hotel Dostoevsky across the road.

DOSTOEVSKY MUSEUM MUSEUM

Map p260 (Литературномемориальный музей Ф.М. Достоевского; www.md.spb.ru; Kuznechny per 5/2; adult/student R160/80, audio tour R170; ⌚11am-6pm Tue-Sun; Ⓜ Vladimirskaya) Fyodor Dostoevsky lived in flats all over the city, mostly in Sennaya, but his final residence is this 'memorial flat' where he lived from 1878 until he died in 1881. The apartment remains as it was when the Dostoevsky family lived here, including the study where he wrote *The Brothers Karamazov,* and the office of Anna Grigorievna, his wife, who recopied, edited and sold all of his books. Two rooms of the museum are devoted to his novels; literature fans will want to pay close attention to the map of Dostoevsky's Petersburg, which details the locations of characters and events in his various works. A rather gloomy sculpted likeness of the man himself (as if there's any other kind) is just outside the nearby Vladimirskaya metro station.

LOFT PROJECT ETAGI GALLERY COMPLEX

Map p260 (Лофт проект ЭТАЖИ; www.loftprojectetagi.ru; Ligovsky pr 74; ⌚noon-10pm; Ⓜ Ligovsky Prospekt) Perhaps St Petersburg's most interesting and exciting artistic space, this fantastic conversion

CASUALTIES OF WAR

Art collective Voina ('War') have long enjoyed something of a cult following in Russia for pulling a series of stunts with subversive messages and – very unusually for modern Russia – a strong political edge. Previously in Moscow their members threw homeless cats over the counter of McDonald's 'to help snap the workers out of the dull routine of menial labour', and in St Petersburg their members had overturned police cars as a protest against ingrained corruption.

But on the night of 14 June 2010, the group took on the ultimate force in modern Russia, the Federal Security Bureau (FSB, the post-Soviet name for the KGB) to wonderful, comic effect. Members painted a 63m-long penis on the surface of the Liteyny Bridge, which then rose that evening, erecting the phallus right in front of the Bolshoy Dom (see p86) – the ultimate message of defiance to an organisation that still exercises enormous power in Russia. Voina quickly became global art stars, a status confirmed by British street artist Banksy pledging money to bail out members of the group subsequently arrested in November 2010.

The absurdity doesn't end there. Despite their obvious anti-establishment message, Voina received the Russian government's own Innovation 2011 award at the same time that several of its members were being tried for disorder offences. The group are largely in hiding from the authorities today, but remain active. You can track their progress at en.free-voina.org of the former Smolninsky Bread Factory has plenty to keep you interested, including many of the original factory fittings seamlessly merged with the thoroughly contemporary design. There are three galleries here, two exhibition spaces, a couple of shops, a hostel and a cafe-bar, **Café Green Room** (p92), with a great summer terrace. Come by to check out what's going on in St Petersburg's contemporary art scene – go through the little entrance with the turnstile and ETAGI is in the courtyard.

PUSHKINSKAYA 10 — GALLERY

Map p260 (Пушкинская 10; en.p-10.ru; Ligovsky pr 53; admission free; 3-7pm Wed-Sun; Ploshchad Vosstaniya) This legendary locale is a required stop for anyone who is interested in the contemporary art and music scene in St Petersburg. The former apartment block – affectionately called by its street address despite the fact that the public entrance is actually on Ligovsky pr – contains studio and gallery space, as well as the cool music clubs **Fish Fabrique** (p97) and **Fabrique Nouvelle** and the **Experimental Sound Gallery (GEZ-21)** (p97), plus an assortment of other shops and galleries. It offers a unique opportunity to hang out with local musicians and artists, who are always eager to talk about their work.

The story of Pushkinskaya 10 goes back to 1988, when a group of artists/squatters took over the condemned apartment block. The decrepit building became 'underground central', as artists and musicians moved in to set up studios, others stopped by to hang out with them, and outsiders became curious about the creative activity going on inside.

The main galleries, the **Museum of Non-Conformist Art** and the **New Academy of Fine Arts Museum**, are on the 4th floor. Smaller galleries are scattered throughout the building, and the artists often open their studios to visitors, especially on Saturday afternoons. A highlight is the **Temple of Love, Peace & Music** (ground fl; 6-8pm Fri). Collector Kolya Vasin (Russia's most famous Beatles fan) has an amazing array of John Lennon paraphernalia, which he shares with other fans on designated days.

It's possible to arrange a free tour of the building in English. Call Anastasia on 911 977 3850 to book a time.

WORTH A DETOUR

RIZZORDI ART FOUNDATION

If you've visited the galleries of Ligovsky pr and Vosstaniya and you're still looking for some more contemporary art, head out to the **Rizzordi Art Foundation** (www.rizzordi.org; Kurlyandskaya ul 49; admission free; 2-8pm Tue-Sun; Baltiiskaya), the most exciting contemporary art venue in the city to date. Opening in summer 2011, this impressive factory conversion is worth seeing in itself; it's a huge space taking up the top two floors of a disused 19th-century brewery. Very interesting temporary exhibits from local up-and-coming artists are showcased here. Half the adventure is just getting to the site (not to mention the incredible post-industrial wasteland you have to travel through). It's a 30-minute walk from Baltiiskaya metro, or you can take bus 49 from Sennaya pl towards Dvinskaya ul and get off at Kurlyandskaya ul, the second stop after you cross the Fontanka River.

RIMSKY-KORSAKOV FLAT-MUSEUM — MUSEUM

Map p260 (Мемориальный музей-квартира Римского-Корсакова; www.theatremuseum.ru; Zagorodny pr 28; admission R100, audio-guide R100; 11am-6pm Wed-Sun; Vladimirskaya) Home of Nikolai Rimsky-Korsakov for the last 15 years of his life (1893–1908), this is where he composed 11 of his 15 operas, including the *Fairy Tale of the Tsar Sultan* and the *Golden Rooster*. The memorial flat (a branch of the State Museum of Theatre & Music) includes four rooms that have been lovingly restored to their original appearance, including the composer's study. A Becker grand piano graces the living room, played over the years by Rachmaninov, Glazunov, Scriabin, Stravinsky – and of course Rimsky-Korsakov himself.

The composer maintained a tradition of hosting musical soirees at his home; this tradition continues today, with concerts on Thursday afternoons at 4pm (although you are unlikely to see Chaliapin perform here today). Enter from the courtyard.

MUSEUM OF THE ARCTIC & ANTARCTIC MUSEUM

Map p260 (Музей Арктики и Антарктики; www.polarmuseum.sp.ru, in Russian; ul Marata 24A; adult/student R150/50; 10am-6pm Wed-Sun; Vladimirskaya) Inside the former Old Believers' Church of St Nicholas, this little museum is devoted to Soviet polar explorations. The self-proclaimed highlight of the museum is the 'polar philatelic collection' – a huge selection of postcards sent by various expeditions and stamps with polar themes. Apart from stuffed polar bears, the most impressive exhibit is a wooden boatplane hanging from the ceiling.

POLICE HISTORY MUSEUM MUSEUM

Map p260 (Музей истории милиции; 717 9536; Poltavskaya ul 12; by appointment only; Ploshchad Vosstaniya) The interesting but little-known Police History Museum chronicles the history of criminality and law enforcement by the Ministry of Internal Affairs in Leningrad/St Petersburg. This balanced, fascinating exhibition, featuring photos, costumes and weapons in several large halls, will acquaint you with interesting titbits about gang bosses and the Mafia's reign of terror in the 1920s, through to the fight to control illegal abortions and alcohol production. You can only visit on a Russian-language guided tour, and foreign individuals will usually be allowed to join groups for free if you call ahead and are flexible about when you come.

BREAD MUSEUM MUSEUM

Map p260 (Музей хлеба; www.colobki.ru, in Russian; Ligovsky pr 73; adult/student R70/35; 10am-5pm Tue-Sat; Ploshchad Vosstaniya) This funky little museum pays tribute to 'our daily bread' and the role it has played in history (of the city and of the world). A model bakery exhibits the equipment that was used to make bread for the city's poorest classes in the 19th century. A special exhibition on the Siege of Leningrad offers an example of a daily ration of bread during WWII.

NEW EXHIBITION HALL EXHIBITION HALL

Map p260 (Новый выставочный зал; Nevsky pr 179/2; admission R100; noon-6pm Sat-Wed; Ploshchad Alexandra Nevskogo) This small, two-storey exhibition space is used as a venue for temporary contemporary art exhibits. Exhibitions change monthly, usually showcasing Russian artists, as well as some works by influential 20th-century artists.

EATING

Liteyny & Smolny

TOP CHOICE BOTANIKA VEGETARIAN €€

Map p258 (Ботаника; www.cafebotanika.ru; ul Pestelya 7; mains R200-450; Gostiny Dvor;) Enjoying perhaps the friendliest and most laid-back atmosphere of any restaurant in St Petersburg, this vegetarian charmer wins on all counts. The menu takes in Russian, Indian, Italian and Japanese dishes, all of which are very well realised, service is friendly, English is spoken and there's even a playroom and dedicated menu for the kids. Highly recommended.

TOP CHOICE MOLOKHOVETS' DREAM RUSSIAN €€€

Map p258 (Мечта Молоховец; 929 2247; www.molokhovets.ru; ul Radishcheva 10; mains R1200-1600; Ploshchad Vosstaniya;) Inspired by the cookbook of Elena Molokhovets (see p93), the Russian Mrs Beeton, the menu here covers all the classics from borsch to beef stroganoff, as well as less frequently seen dishes such as goose breast in forest berry sauce and veal cutlets in mushroom ragu. Start with berry kissel, a delicious sweet soup of brambles and wine, and don't bypass the speciality, *koulibiaca*, a golden pastry pie of fish or rabbit. Whatever you have here, you can be sure it's the definitive version – this place is something of an institution locally and takes its food very seriously. Book ahead for dinner.

TOP CHOICE KOMPOT CAFÉ INTERNATIONAL €€

Map p258 (Первое, второе и компот; www.kompotcafe.ru; ul Zhukovskogo 10; mains R200-600; Ploshchad Vosstaniya;) This stylish new restaurant has three different rooms decked out in thoroughly different stylish decors (though it remains unmistakably Russian, as evidenced by the giant TV in the main room). There's a great menu, which stretches from breakfasts served all day long to soups, sandwiches, pies and a range of international mains running from chilli con carne to 'funky tomato bouillabaisse'.

ISTORIYA SEAFOOD €€€

Map p258 (История; ul Belinskogo 8; mains R600-800; Gostiny Dvor;) Istoriya represents a very welcome new approach to food in St Petersburg. The friendly chef and

WORTH A DETOUR

THE SOVIET SOUTH

Sprawling southern St Petersburg was once planned to be the centre of Stalin's new Leningrad, and anyone interested in Stalinist architecture should make the easy trip down here to Moskovskaya metro station for a wander around and to see a clutch of sights all within easy walking distance.

Right outside the metro station you'll see the **House of Soviets** (Дом Советов; Moskovsky pr 212; closed to the public), a staggeringly bombastic Stalinist beauty. Planned to be the central administrative building of Stalin's Leningrad, it was built with the leader's neoclassical tastes in mind. Begun by Noi Trotsky in 1936, it was not finished until after the war, by which time Trotsky had been purged. Nonetheless, this magnificently sinister building is a great example of Stalinist design, with its columns and bas-reliefs and an enormous frieze running across the top. Today it houses the Moskovsky Region's local administration.

Due south from here down Moskovsky pr is the striking **Monument to the Heroic Defenders of Leningrad** (Памятник героическим защитникам Ленинграда; pl Pobedy; admission free; 10am-5pm Thu-Tue; M Moskovskaya). Centred around a 48m-high obelisk, the monument, unveiled in 1975, is a sculptural ensemble of bronze statues symbolising the city's encirclement and eventual victory in WWII. On a lower level, a bronze ring 40m in diameter symbolises the city's encirclement; a very moving sculpture stands in the centre. Haunting symphonic music creates a sombre atmosphere to guide you downstairs to the underground exhibition in a huge, mausoleum-like interior. Here, the glow of 900 bronze lamps creates an eeriness matched by the sound of a metronome (the only sound heard by Leningraders on their radios throughout the war save for emergency announcements), showing that the city's heart was still beating. Twelve thematically assembled showcases feature items from the war and siege. An electrified relief map in the centre of the room shows the shifting front lines of the war.

Finally, if all this Soviet architecture makes you yearn for something a little more traditional, then wander back north past the House of Soviets to the beautiful **Chesme Church** (Чесменская церковь; ul Lensoveta 12; admission free; 10am-7pm; M Moskovskaya), one of the city's most wonderful buildings. This red-and-white Gothic beauty looks not unlike a candy cane, with long, vertical white stripes giving the impression that it's rising straight up from the earth like a mirage and shooting upwards. Designed by Yury Felten, it was built between 1777 and 1780 in honour of the Battle of Chesme (1770). The church's remote location is due to the fact that Catherine was on this spot when news arrived of her great victory over the Turks. Ever capricious, Catherine ordered that a shrine be built on the spot to preserve this great moment in Russian history. It now seems particularly incongruous with its surroundings, as Stalin's ill-fated city centre has since grown up around it.

owner will talk you through the fish and seafood-dominated menu and tell you what's best each day. With fresh oysters and lobster coming in twice a week, this upmarket yet somewhat kitschy restaurant is definitely the best in town for seafood lovers, although there is plenty of meat on the menu too.

MAKAROV — RUSSIAN €€

Map p258 (Макаров; 327 0053; Manezhny per 2; mains R500-800; 9am-11pm Tue-Fri, 11am-11pm Sat-Mon; M Chernyshevskaya;) A very welcome addition to the dearth of good restaurants in this part of town is this charming place, which has an interesting menu of Russian food with a modern slant. Unfortunately there are no English menus and even those in Russian are hard to read as they're handwritten, so ordering can be tricky. That said, it's well worth the effort – on a sunny day, the seats outside on the terrace are hot property. Good breakfasts are served daily until noon, and until 2pm on weekends (reservations are essential). There's also a child's playroom.

IL GRAPPOLO — ITALIAN €€€

Map p258 (www.probka.org; ul Belinskogo 5; mains R450-1500; 1pm-1am; M Gostiny Dvor;) This very upmarket Italian restaurant sits above Probka wine bar (p94), and is a real treat, featuring traditional home-cooking with a gourmet slant (pizza with black truffles, and cream of asparagus and prawn soup, for example) and a fantastic accompanying wine list. The 2nd-floor dining room is bathed in natural light and is one of the chicest venues in St Petersburg, with crisp linen tablecloths and views onto the church across the street.

VOX ITALIAN €€€

Map p258 (www.voxresto.ru; ul Pestelya 4; mains R400-1000; MChernyshevskaya) On a quaint corner of the pedestrian-friendly Stolyarny per and ul Pestelya, Vox has a great terrace which makes a perfect spot for lunch or dinner during the summer months. The upscale interior, with white linens and stripped-down decor, provides a suitably sexy environment for sublime antipasti, pastas, meats and seafood. Service is very professional and food is top-notch.

JAKOV CAKES €

Map p258 (ul Chernyshevskog 3; cakes from R150; 9am-8pm; MChernyshevskaya) This fantastic cake shop is a real treat for the well-heeled residents of the Smolny. Beautifully presented pastries, tarts, macaroons and handmade chocolates await, and while most people take them away, you can eat in and enjoy a coffee here too.

GIN NO TAKI JAPANESE €€

Map p258 (www.ginnotaki.ru; pr Chernyshevskogo 17; mains R200-500; 11am-midnight; MChernyshevskaya) In a city awash with wannabe Japanese restaurants, this large and lively operation is one of the most authentic, with a wide range of sushi, sashimi, kebabs, tempura and bento box lunches. A photo menu makes ordering no hassle at all, and their homemade Japanese beer is an excellent accompaniment to any meal.

SUNDUK INTERNATIONAL €€

Map p258 (www.cafesunduk.ru; Furshtatskaya ul 42; mains R170-750; MChernyshevskaya) This 'art cafe' is tucked into a tiny basement, its two rooms crowded with mismatched furniture, musical instruments, carefully posed mannequins and lots of other junk (or 'art'), creating a bohemian atmosphere. The European menu has a good selection of meat and fish, with plenty of Russian classics, plus the odd Asian dish to spice things up. There is live music nightly – see p96.

FAT FRIAR RUSSIAN €

Map p258 (Толстый Фраер; www.tolstiy-fraer.ru; ul Belinskogo 13; mains R150-350; 10am-1am Sun-Thu, until 3am Fri & Sat; MMayakovskaya) The original branch of this citywide chain is a great place for late-night dining. There's another branch (p74) in the historic heart.

BALTIC BREAD BAKERY €

Map p258 (Балтийский хлеб; www.baltic-bread.ru; Grechesky pr 25; breakfast R200; 10am-9pm; MPloshchad Vosstaniya) This outstanding bakery-cafe is an excellent place to stop for breakfast, lunch or a late-afternoon coffee break. Seating is limited, so take your order *soboy* ('to go') and head to Tauride Gardens. There is another outlet in Vladimirsky Passage (p93) and one on the Petrograd Side (p137).

Vladimirskaya & Vosstaniya

TOP CHOICE **DOM BEAT** INTERNATIONAL €€

Map p260 (Дом Быта; www.dombeat.ru; ul Razyezzhaya 12; mains R300-500; MLigovsky Prospekt) As if naming St Petersburg's coolest bar, lounge and restaurant after a Soviet all-purpose store and then dressing the model-gorgeous staff in tailored pastiches of factory uniforms wasn't a solid enough start, the sleek, retro-humorous interior, sumptuous menu and great atmosphere add up to make this one of the best eating choices in town. As well as great breakfasts (served until 7pm!), there's a wide choice of dishes ranging from top-notch Asian cuisine to modern takes on Russian meals and international bar food.

LES AMIS DE JEAN-JACQUES ROUSSEAU FRENCH €€

Map p260 (Жан-Жак Руссо; www.jan-jak.com; ul Marata 10; mains R300-600; MMayakovskaya) This is the most conveniently located of the two St Petersburg branches of this smart French bistro. With a pleasant terrace outside and a burgundy and hunter green interior that could be that of your favourite Parisian cafe, this restaurant has an authentic and delicious menu taking in all the classic brasserie dishes, from *magret de canard* to boeuf Bourguignon. There's also lots of affordable wine available by the glass.

FARTUK INTERNATIONAL €€

Map p260 (Фартук; ul Rubinshteyna 15/17; mains R200-300; Ⓜ Mayakovskaya;) Despite its unfortunate name, Fartuk is a beautifully designed place with tiled floors and old-world-meets-industrial fittings. The crowd here is cool and the menu is interesting: wok-cooked chicken with ginger and coriander sits next to freshly made bruschetta, soups and steaks.

CAFÉ GREEN ROOM INTERNATIONAL €

Map p260 (www.loftprojectetagi.ru; Ligovsky pr 74; mains R100-200; 9am-11pm Sun-Thu, until 6am Fri & Sat; Ⓜ Ligovsky Prospekt;) The in-house cafe of the super cool Loft Project ETAGI, you'll find this place on the 3rd floor (from the street go through turnstile checkpoint and through the courtyard). The centrepiece here is a fantastic summer terrace, even though there are ridiculously few chairs and tables outside for some reason. Inside it's an airy, cool cafe space with a menu that's simple, tasty and excellent value, including filling breakfasts, sandwiches and traditional Russian dishes such as borsch and *manty* (giant ravioli).

SCHASTYE ITALIAN €€

Map p260 (Счастье; www.schaste-est.com; ul Rubinshteyna 15/17; mains R200-700; 8am-midnight, until 6am Fri & Sat; Ⓜ Mayakovskaya;) 'Happiness' comes in several forms here: a multiroomed venue full of cosy nooks and crannies to huddle up in, an expansive and interesting Italian menu, delicious pastries and sweets piled up on plates around the place, and lavish and thoroughly warm (if somewhat random) decor.

MOPS THAI €€

Map p260 (www.mopscafe.ru; ul Rubinshteyna 12; mains R300-700; 1pm-midnight Tue-Sun; Ⓜ Mayakovskaya;) The first and only dedicated Thai restaurant in the city is a visual treat: the elegant dining room is all white painted floorboards and linen tablecloths embellished with gorgeous Thai furniture. Quality was good when we ate here, though dishes tend to be on the small side. The same restaurant also houses a luxurious Thai spa (see p100).

MATROSSKAYA TISHINA SEAFOOD €€€

Map p260 (Матросская Тишина; 764 4413; ul Marata 54; meals R500-1000; Ⓜ Ligovsky Prospekt;) This long-standing, high-quality seafood restaurant is one of the city's very best, even though it doesn't look like much from the street. There's a large gourmet menu including a sumptuous *Table Russe* (R4850 for two people) as well as a far more wallet-friendly à la carte menu (try the sole *meunière* with almonds and lemon or the giant prawns flambéed in Talisker), and a great wine list. Reservations are a good idea.

BISTRO GARÇON FRENCH €€

Map p260 (www.garcon.ru; Nevsky pr 95; mains R250-500; 10am-midnight; Ⓜ Ploshchad Vosstaniya;) This gorgeous little bistro is smart and unpretentious, with low lighting, upscale but still charming decor, and professional staff. Prices are reasonable given the excellent standard of the cooking (and Parisian chef). While this is the main restaurant of the group in town, you can find its bakeries, which serve up excellent sandwiches, all over St Petersburg.

CAT CAFÉ GEORGIAN €€

Map p260 (Кафе Кэт; Stremyannaya ul 22/3; mains R300-700; Ⓜ Mayakovskaya;) With vines hanging from the ceiling to evoke the Caucasian countryside, this popular and reliable restaurant dishes up Georgian favourites such as hearty *khinkali* (meat dumplings), decadent *khachapuri* (cheese bread) and delectable rolled aubergine with walnuts. Sadly, it's not cheap (Georgian products are hard to come by due to a Russian trade embargo since the 2008 war), but few people leave unimpressed.

IMBIR RUSSIAN €€

Map p260 (Имбирь; Zagorodny pr 15; mains R400-600; Ⓜ Dostoevskaya;) Effortlessly cool, Imbir combines ornate imperial elements with contemporary design to brilliant effect. With a great atmosphere, it's always full. The hip local crowd come here for dark coffee and creative cooking, all of which is reasonably priced. There's a full bar too, and the place usually stays open until the small hours at the weekends.

SHINOK UKRAINIAN €€

Map p260 (Шинок; www.spshinok.ru; Zagorodny pr 13; mains R300-600; 11am-5am; Ⓜ Dostoevskaya) Tucked into a folksy interior filled with embroidered linens and painted wooden handicrafts, Shinok is a fun, friendly and kitsch place to sample Ukrainian fare. The waiters may look like Ukrainian peasants, but they speak English and are eager to please. Country cooking such as hearty soups and meat-filled *vareniki* (dumplings) will sate your appetite, and there is live folk music nightly at 8.30pm.

IL PATIO ITALIAN €€

Map p260 (www.ilpatio.ru; Nevsky pr 182; pizza R200-400; MPloshchad Alexandra Nevskogo;) There are not too many places to eat at the far end of Nevsky pr. Fortunately, Russia's favourite pizza chain comes through for hungry travellers who want to grab lunch after visiting the monastery.

TROITSKY MOST VEGETARIAN €

Map p260 (Zagorodny pr 38; mains R100-250; MPushkinskaya;) The Zagorodny pr branch is one of the nicest of this chain of vegetarian cafes and it overlooks a small park. A huge selection of soups and salads, excellent pasta (including unbeatable lasagne) and other meat-free treats round out the daily-changing menu.

BALTIC BREAD BAKERY €

Map p260 (Балтийский хлеб; Vladimirsky pr 19; snacks R100-200; MDostoevskaya) This British-run bakery in the Vladimirsky Passage shopping centre is a great spot for picking up fresh bread, cakes and ready-made sandwiches on the run. You can take away or eat in the small cafe area provided.

BUSHE BAKERY €

Map p260 (Буше; ul Razyezzhaya 13; breakfast or snacks R50-150; MVladimirskaya) This Austrian bakery has developed a huge number of local devotees, thanks to its fresh-baked pastries and delicious coffee. It's a great breakfast spot if you're in the neighbourhood.

DRINKING & NIGHTLIFE

Liteyny & Smolny

TOP CHOICE **ZHOPA** BAR

Map p258 (Жопа; Pr Bakunina 6; 8pm-1am Sun-Thu, until 8am Fri & Sat; MPloshchad Vosstaniya) This funky, hip and largely unknown place is a hideaway for the cool kids. Its name means 'arse' in Russian and is fairly rude, so don't ask old ladies for directions to get here – the sign on the front door is just the

A GIFT TO YOUNG HOUSEWIVES

The most popular cookbook in 19th-century Russia was called *A Gift to Young Housewives*, a collection of favourite recipes and household management tips that turned into a bestseller. The author, Elena Molokhovets, a housewife herself, was dedicated to her 10 children, to the Orthodox Church, and to her inexperienced 'female compatriots' who might need assistance keeping their homes running smoothly.

This book was reprinted 28 times between 1861 and 1914, and Molokhovets added new recipes and helpful hints to each new edition. The last edition included literally thousands of recipes, as well as pointers on how to organise an efficient kitchen, how to set a proper table and how to clean a cast-iron pot.

Molokhovets received an enormously positive response from readers who credited her with no less than preserving their family life. The popular perception of the time was that a wife's primary responsibility was to keep her family together, and keeping her husband well fed seemed to be the key. As one reader wrote, 'a good kitchen is...not an object of luxury. It is a token of the health and well-being of the family, upon which all the remaining conditions of life depend'. Molokhovets included some of these letters in later editions as testimony to her work.

The classic cookbook was never reprinted during the Soviet period. The details of sumptuous dishes and fine table settings – let alone questions of etiquette and style – would certainly have been considered bourgeois by the Soviet regime. Yet still, copies of this ancient tome survived, passed down from mother to daughter like a family heirloom. Today, the book reads not only as a cookbook, but also as a lesson in history and sociology.

first letter: Ж. Inside it's a treasure trove of fairy lights, umbrellas hanging from the ceiling, tapestries on the walls and kitschy chandeliers. Add in great music, table football and stiff drinks and you've got one of Petersburg's coolest bars.

TOP CHOICE **PROBKA** WINE BAR

Map p258 (www.probka.org; ul Belinskogo 5; 1pm-1am; Gostiny Dvor) You'll feel you could almost be in Rome when you enter this charming wine bar just off Liteyny pr. Tile floors and terracotta walls recall an Italian *enoteca,* with its shelves stocked with wine bottles and liqueurs. Several wines are available by the glass or half-bottle, and there is a menu of light snacks, salads and pastas.

P.I.E.R.O.G.I. BAR

Map p258 (nab reki Fontanki 40; 24hr; Gostiny Dvor) This long-established Moscow chain of boho bookshop-cum-bars has now established itself in the northern capital just moments from Nevsky. It's divided into smoking and nonsmoking rooms, enjoys a very casual feel and is favoured by a young crowd. There's a full menu of international dishes (R180 to R300) and regular live music.

IGRATEKA BAR

Map p258 (Игратека; Tavrichesky Sad; 11am-11pm Sun-Thu, until 6am Fri & Sat; Chernyshevskaya) Right in the middle of the Tauride Garden, this tree house–style hideaway is definitely one of the stranger places for a cold drink. Lounge on the terrace overlooking the park, enjoy the full menu and live music in the evenings and perhaps try to get into the totally unnecessary 'VIP' section. A well-kept secret among Petersburgers in the know.

XXXX BAR

Map p258 (http://xxxxbar.ru; ul 3-ya Sovetskaya 34; noon-3am Mon-Thu, until 5am Fri-Sun; Ploshchad Vosstaniya) Now in multiple locations around the city, this is the most central of the XXXX chain of bars and you needn't look any further for a night of bawdy revelry. The low-lit saloon-style lounge is covered in photographs, flags and beer adverts, and functions as a relaxed pub with a full menu of bar food during the day. Come the evening however, it's always packed out with a young and up-for-it crowd partying until dawn, so get here in good time to ensure entry.

Vladimirskaya & Vosstaniya

TOP CHOICE **DYUNI** BAR

Map p260 (Дюны; Ligovsky pr 50; 24hr; Ploshchad Vosstaniya) St Petersburg's hippest bar in the summer of 2011 (don't worry, there will be another one along shortly), is this hipster sandpit at the back of the large warehouse complex in the courtyard of Ligovsky 50. What looks like a small suburban house sits rather incongruously here, just back from the Moscow Station train tracks. There's a cosy indoor bar and a sprawling sand-covered outside area with table football and ping pong, which keeps the cool kids happy all night in the summer months. To find it, simply continue in a straight line from the entrance to the courtyard.

TOP CHOICE **TERMINAL BAR** BAR

Map p260 (Терминал; ul Rubinshteyna 13A; 4pm-6am; Dostoevskaya) A slice of New York bohemia on one of the city's most happening streets, Terminal is great for a relaxed drink with friends, who can spread out along the length of the enormous bar, while great music (and live piano from anyone who can play) fills the long, arched room under the grey vaulted ceilings. One of our favourites.

TOP CHOICE **DOM BEAT** COCKTAIL BAR

Map p260 (Дом Быта; www.dombeat.ru; ul Razyezzhaya 12; noon-6am; Ligovsky Prospekt) The big draws at this place are the superb cocktails and wide drinks menu. Funky '70s interior, a cool crowd and tables cleared for dancing later in the evening make it a great spot. See p91 for a full review.

GRIBOYEDOV CLUB

Map p260 (www.griboedovclub.ru; Voronezhskaya ul 2a; cover R200-400; noon-6am, concerts 10pm; Ligovsky Prospekt) Griboyedov is hands-down the longest-standing and most respected music club in the city. Another club in a bomb shelter, this one was founded by local ska collective Dva Samolyota. It's a low-key bar in the early evening, gradually morphing into a dance club later in the night. Excellent music acts and international DJs play electronic, rock and dubstep. Upstairs, the plush Griboedov Hill restaurant and chill-out lounge also has occasional concerts by night and is a great place to relax.

NA ZDOROVYE!

'To your health!' is what Russians say when they throw back a shot of vodka. But this pronouncement hardly suffices as a proper toast in a public forum or an intimate drinking session among friends. A proper toast requires thoughtfulness and sincerity.

A few themes prevail. The first toast of the night often acknowledges the generosity of the host, while the second usually recognises the beauty of the ladies present. In mixed company, you can't go wrong raising your glass to international friendship *(za mezhdunarodnuyu druzhbu)* or world peace *(za miravoy mir)*. But in all cases, the toast requires a personal anecdote or a profound insight, as well as a bit of rambling preamble to make it meaningful.

In Russia, drinking vodka is a celebration of life in all its complexity – the triumph, the tragedy and the triviality. A toast is a vocalisation of that celebration, so say it like you mean it. And drink it in the same way – *zalpom* – bottoms up!

JESUS CLUB — CLUB

Map p260 (www.cometojes.us, in Russian; Ligovsky pr 50; cover free-R200; ⏲8pm-6am Fri & Sat; Ⓜ Ploshchad Vosstaniya) Another weekend destination in the Ligovsky pr 50 warehouse complex is this cool place, popular with younger clubbers and packing in the crowds at weekends to dance to techno, dubstep and other electronic styles. Most acts are local, but they occasionally get international DJs here. Walk straight down from the arch, and then turn right when you get to the open area.

THE CLUB — CLUB

Map p260 (www.the-club.fm; Scherbakov per 17; admission R300-500; ⏲11pm-6am Wed, Fri & Sat; Ⓜ Dostoevskaya) In the courtyard of the building, this chic gay-mixed club is in the basement and features a large dance floor, several bars, lots of loungelike seating and a stage where drag acts and local groups perform. In summer there's a great outdoor bar in the courtyard too. It's aimed at a wealthier, fashion-conscious crowd and is definitely at the more sophisticated end of gay clubbing.

RYUMOCHNAYA NO 1 — BAR

Map p260 (Рюмочная No 1; Pushkinskaya ul 1; ⏲11am-11pm; Ⓜ Pl Vosstaniya) The *ryumochnaya* was the generic place where comrades in the Soviet days stopped on their way to or from work to toss back a shot or two before continuing on their way. This particular one is, in keeping with current trends, a nostalgic reappropriation favoured by bohemian types who prop up the bar, perhaps ironically. It's dark, moody and studiedly Soviet – come on in and order your own *sto gram* (100 grams) – they will know what you are talking about.

PIVNAYA 0.5 — PUB

Map p260 (Пивная 0.5; www.piv05.ru; Zagorodny pr 44/2; ⏲11am-2am; Ⓜ Vladimirskaya) With classic Soviet films playing every Sunday on the big screen, this place recalls the days when the local *pivnaya* (pub) was the only choice for a brew. This particular one has gone upscale, however, with plush leather chairs and a stylish retro feel we're pretty sure was lacking 30 years ago.

ZERNO ISTINY — CAFE

Map p260 (Зерно истины; www.zerno-istiny.ru; Zagorodny pr 20; ⏲24hr; Ⓜ Vladimirskaya; 📶) This cosy coffee shop ('the grain of truth') is very passionate about the wide selection of beans and roasts they serve up. There's friendly service, a huge choice of brews and plenty of cakes to accompany your choice. Bring your own computer or borrow one from the bar to use the free wireless.

☆ ENTERTAINMENT

TOP CHOICE KITAYSKY LYOTCHIK DZHAO DA — LIVE MUSIC

Map p258 (Китайский лётчик Джао Да; www.spb.jao-da.com; ul Pestelya 7; cover R100-200 for concerts; ⏲noon-midnight; Ⓜ Gostiny Dvor) This is the St Petersburg incarnation of the well-established Moscow venue of the same name, and it's one of the very best places to see live music in the city. The premises are charming – the main bar area is bathed in light with plenty of seating and a genial buzz all day, overlooked by a replica plane swooping over the bar (the name means Chinese Pilot Dzhao Da). In the back room, there's a stage and more seating for gigs, usually with several quality indie or rock acts on each evening.

ZOCCOLO LIVE MUSIC

Map p258 (Цоколь; www.zoccolo.ru, in Russian; 3-ya Sovetskaya ul 2/3; cover R100; ⌚noon-midnight Sun-Thu, noon-6am Fri & Sat, concerts 8pm; Ⓜ Pl Vosstaniya) Zoccolo, in its urgently orange and green underground space near pl Vosstaniya, has slowly become another institution of St Petersburg's music scene. With a great atmosphere and an interesting line-up of music (indie rock, 'progressive grunge', klezmer, 'ethno-electronica' and numerous other styles you may or may not have heard of), it's easy to see why. Entry is free before 5pm, when the venue functions as an arty cafe.

DUSCHE LIVE MUSIC

Map p260 (Душе; www.dusche.ru; Ligovsky pr 50; cover free-R500; ⌚8pm-2am Sun-Thu, until 6am Fri & Sat; Ⓜ Pl Vosstaniya) Another popular and cool bar, live music venue and club in the enormous courtyard of Ligovsky 50, Dusche is owned by members of two locally famous groups, Leningrad and Spitfire. Here you'll find nightly DJs, live music as well as a laid-back party atmosphere and the occasional art show or drama performance. To find it, go through the arch into the courtyard, take the first left, then turn right, and Dusche is on your left.

PETROVICH LIVE MUSIC

Map p260 (Петрович; www.petrovich-piter.ru; ul Marata 56-58; Ⓜ Ligovsky Pr) Styling itself a club-restaurant, Petrovich, a long-running Moscow institution that has finally found its way to St Petersburg, is actually more of a music and dancing venue. The extraordinary place is crammed with Soviet paraphernalia and while it's a fun and quirky place to come for a meal (mains R350 to R850), the best reason to come is to hear the nightly live music (usually Soviet songs) and join in the fun. Saturdays is a Soviet dance night with obligatory participation – you have been warned!

JFC JAZZ CLUB JAZZ CLUB

Map p258 (☎272 9850; www.jfc-club.spb.ru, in Russian; Shpalernaya ul 33; cover R100-500; ⌚7-11pm; Ⓜ Chernyshevskaya) Very small and very New York, this cool club is the best place in the city to hear modern, innovative jazz music, as well as blues, bluegrass and various other styles (see the website for a list of what's on). The space is tiny, so book a table if you want to sit down. Otherwise, you can always stand at the bar (which is less expensive). The menu is limited to drinks and snacks.

CABARET GAY CLUB

(www.cabarespb.ru; Razyezzhaya ul 43; cover R200-500; ⌚11pm-6am Thu-Sat) This latest incarnation of a gay club that has been going in various forms for over a decade is a great place for a campy, old-school experience, complete with a very popular drag show featuring lip-synching trannies who come on stage at 2.30am each club night. Lots of silly fun, but massively popular.

NIKAKIKH ORKHIDEY LIVE MUSIC

Map p260 (Никаких Орхидей; ul Kolomenskaya 9; ⌚3pm-midnight; Ⓜ Ploshchad Vosstaniya) This charmingly off-beat piano bar in a cellar on a quiet residential street just off Nevsky is a great place to come for drinks, a full Russian menu and nightly concerts. The owner, Boris Bardash, is a well-known musician with local band Ole Lukkoye and will often take to the stage himself when local singer-songwriters aren't dropping in to do intimate sets. The mosaic portrayals of various left-wing dictators appear not to be ironic.

RED FOX JAZZ CAFÉ JAZZ CLUB

Map p258 (Красный лис; ☎275 4214; www.rfjc.ru; ul Mayakovskogo 50; cover R100-200; ⌚10am-2am Sun-Thu, until 5am Fri & Sat; Ⓜ Chernyshevskaya) The fun and friendly Red Fox Jazz Cafe is a subterranean space that showcases jazz in the old-fashioned 1920s to '50s sense: big band, bebop, ragtime and swing. Sunday changes it up with a jam session, featuring anybody who wants to participate. The menu is extensive and affordable and you can reserve a table for free.

SUNDUK LIVE MUSIC

Map p258 (Сундук; wwww.cafesunduk.ru; Furshtatskaya 42; cover for concerts R100-200; ⌚10am-last customer; Ⓜ Chernyshevskaya) This cafe promises 'art' and it delivers: live music fills up this tiny space every night from 8.30pm to 11pm. It's mostly blues and jazz, with the occasional chanteuse singing more poppy tunes. If this is not arty enough for you, check out the bathrooms. See p91 for a full restaurant review.

EXPERIMENTAL SOUND GALLERY (GEZ-21)
LIVE MUSIC

Map p260 (Галерия экспериментальной альтернативы; www.tac.spb.ru; Ligovsky pr 53, 3rd fl; cover R100-250; ⏲5-11.30pm, concerts from 9pm; Ⓜ Ploshchad Vosstaniya) You know that a place called 'experimental' is going to be out there, especially as it is part of the alternative art complex at Pushkinskaya 10 (p88). Music ranges from rock to electronic to undefinable, and there are also film screenings, readings and other expressions of creativity. The toilet contains quite an interesting gallery (of sorts).

FISH FABRIQUE
LIVE MUSIC

Map p260 (www.fishfabrique.spb.ru; Ligovsky pr 53, ground fl; ⏲3pm-6am, concerts from 8pm Thu-Sun; Ⓜ Ploshchad Vosstaniya) There are St Petersburg institutions and then there's Fish Fabrique, the museum of local boho life that has been going for two decades. Here, in the dark underbelly of Pushkinskaya 10 (p88), artists, musicians and wannabes of all ages meet to drink beer and listen to music. Nowadays, the newer Fabrique Nouvelle in the same courtyard hosts concerts nightly, while the old Fish Fabrique has them just at weekends, but whichever one you're in, you're sure to rub shoulders with an interesting crowd.

MANHATTAN
LIVE MUSIC

Map p260 (www.manhattanclub.ru; nab reki Fontanki 90; cover R200 for concerts; ⏲2pm-5am daily, concerts 8pm Wed-Sun; Ⓜ Vladimirskaya; @) This 'art-club' features live music and artistic expositions, all in a spacious renovated basement on the Fontanka River. The atmosphere is laid-back and bohemian though the party can really get going here later on. There are often a couple of bands doing sets each evening.

COSMONAUT
LIVE MUSIC

(Космонавт; www.kosmonavt.su; ul Bronnit-skaya 24; Ⓜ Tekhnologichesky Institut; ❄ 📶) This fantastic new conversion of a Soviet-era cinema in a rather nondescript part of town is the best new live music venue in St Petersburg, hosting medium-sized concerts and a current favourite with touring international bands. There's air-conditioning throughout, which is a godsend in summer, and a very comfortable VIP lounge upstairs, with seating throughout.

JAZZ PHILHARMONIC HALL
JAZZ CLUB

Map p260 (☎764 8565; www.jazz-hall.spb.ru; Zagorodny pr 27; cover R100-200; ⏲concerts 7pm Wed-Sun, Ellington Hall concerts 8pm Tue, Fri & Sat; Ⓜ Vladimirskaya) Founded by legendary jazz violinist and composer David Goloshchokin, this venue represents the more traditional side of jazz. Two resident bands perform straight jazz and Dixieland in the big hall, which seats up to 200 people. The smaller Ellington Hall is used for occasional acoustic performances. Foreign guests also appear doing mainstream and modern jazz. Drinks and light snacks available.

GRAND CONCERT HALL
CLASSICAL MUSIC

Map p258 (Большой концертный зал (БКЗ); www.bkz.ru, in Russian; Ligovsky pr 6; Ⓜ Ploshchad Vosstaniya) This massive complex near pl Vosstaniya still often goes by its former name, Oktyabrsky. Seating almost 4000 people, this is the venue for Russian stars with a national following, whether they are pop singers or ballet dancers.

SMOLNY CATHEDRAL
CLASSICAL MUSIC

Map p258 (www.cathedral.ru; pl Rastrelli 3/1; Ⓜ Chernyshevskaya) The beautiful Smolny Cathedral (p84) makes a great venue for classical concerts. While not as attractive as some of the other concert halls in the city (and certainly not as ornate as its gorgeous exterior), it is still an atmospheric place to watch a performance.

BOLSHOY PUPPET THEATRE
PUPPET SHOWS

Map p258 (Большой театр кукол; www.puppets.ru; ul Nekrasova 10; tickets R100-250; Ⓜ Chernyshevskaya) This 'big' puppet theatre is indeed the biggest in the city, and has been active since 1931. The repertoire includes a wide range of shows for children and adults.

LENSOVET THEATRE
THEATRE

Map p260 (Театр Ленсовета; www.lensov-theatre.spb.ru; Vladimirsky pr 12; Ⓜ Mayakovskaya) The Lensovet is among the more versatile theatre companies in town, staging performances of classical favourites (such as Gogol's *Government Inspector*) as well as bold new experiments (Serbian writer Biljana Srbljanović's 9/11 drama *America, Part Two*).

MALY DRAMA THEATRE
THEATRE

Map p260 (Малый драматический театр; www.mdt-dodin.ru; ul Rubinshteyna 18; Ⓜ Vladimirskaya) Also called the Theatre of Europe, the Maly is St Petersburg's most internationally celebrated theatre. Its director Lev Dodin is famed for his long version of Fyodor Dostoevsky's *The Devils,* as well as Anton Chekhov's *Play Without a Name,* which both toured the world to great acclaim.

KINOTEATR KHUDOZHESTVENNY CINEMA

Map p258 (Кинотеатр Художественный; www.poravkino.ru; Nevsky pr 67; MGostiny Dvor) This multiplex on Nevsky pr has seven screens and shows commercial blockbusters dubbed into Russian as well as mainstream Russian movies. Expect popcorn, giant sodas and the usual trapping of the multiplex experience.

SHOPPING

Smolny and Liteyny, mostly residential neighbourhoods, do not offer too much in the way of shopping, but both are arty, intellectual places, as evidenced by the proliferation of galleries and bookstores. As Nevsky pr continues east past the Fontanka River towards pl Vosstaniya, it continues to be lined with boutiques and culminates with two enormous shopping centres.

TOP CHOICE OFF SECONDHAND

Map p260 (www.offoffoff.ru, in Russian; ul Pechatnika Grigoryeva 8; noon-8pm; MLigovsky Prospekt) This bunker of fashions gone by is a paradise for anyone after some Soviet accessories, vintage jackets and secondhand clothes of varying styles. The friendly owner may take it upon herself to find just the right outfit for you – and she clearly knows what she's doing judging by her own unique appearance. There's a smaller outlet in the historic heart as part of the **Prostranstvo Kultury** (p80) boutique.

KOMMISSIONNY MAGAZIN ANTIQUES

Map p258 (Комиссионный магазин; ul Mayakovskogo 17; 10am-7pm; MMayakovskaya) It's rather generous to call this basement gem an antiques shop – much of the stock is more garage-sale worthy, but there are still some very cool bits and pieces. Everything from Soviet kitchen items to old books and antique lamps can be found here if you look hard enough.

BOREY ART CENTRE ART

Map p258 (Борей Артцентр; www.borey.ru; Liteyny pr 58; noon-8pm Tue-Sat; MMayakovskaya) There is never a dull moment at this underground (in both senses of the word) art gallery. In the front room, you'll see some fairly mainstream stuff for sale, but the back rooms always house creative contemporary exhibitions by local artists. The bookshop is one of the best in town for books on art and architecture.

PHONOTEKA MUSIC

Map p260 (Фонотека; www.phonoteka.ru, in Russian; ul Marata 28; 10am-10pm; MMayakovskaya) This cool store will thrill anyone interested in music and cinema, as it sells a very cool range of vinyls from all eras (it's particularly strong on rare Soviet discs), a great selection of CDs from around the world and a smart and discerning choice of film and documentary on DVD.

ANGLIA BOOKS BOOKS

Map p258 (nab reki Fontanki 38; MGostiny Dvor) The city's only dedicated English-language bookshop has a large selection of contemporary literature, history and travel writing. It also hosts small art and photography displays, organises book readings and generally is a cornerstone of expat life in St Petersburg.

LIBERTY ART GALLERY ART

Map p258 (www.sovietart.ru; ul Pestelya 17/25; 11am-8pm Tue-Sun; MChernyshevskaya) 'Liberty' may be an odd name for a gallery that specialises in Soviet art, but this excellent place sells paintings internationally, particularly art from the 1930s to the 1980s.

SOL-ART ART

Map p258 (www.solartgallery.com; Solyanoy per 15; 10am-6pm; MChernyshevskaya) In the sumptuous surroundings of the Museum of Decorative & Applied Arts (p85), this is a great place to buy contemporary local art.

KISSELENKO FASHION SALON CLOTHING & ACCESSORIES

Map p258 (www.kisselenko.ru; Kirochnaya ul 47; MChernyshevskaya) Designer Lilia Kisselenko uses sublimely simple fabrics to create women's clothing that is at once linear and flatteringly feminine. This is a name to watch out for; Kisselenko has established herself as St Petersburg's most eminent fashion designer through her discerning eye and highly refined fashion sensibility.

SOLDIER OF FORTUNE
MILITARY

Map p258 (Солдат Удачи; ul Nekrasova 37; ⌚11am-9pm; Ⓜ Ploshchad Vosstaniya) The extensive selection of guns and knives at this little shop is impressive, if a little frightening. Check out the knives with intricately carved handles, penknives straight out of James Bond, and machetes with names such as 'Predator Axe'. The place also carries more mundane equipment like binoculars and water bottles, as well as all manner of camouflage clothing and military souvenirs.

LA RUSSE
ANTIQUES

Map p260 (www.larusse.ru; Stremyannaya ul 3; ⌚11am-8pm; Ⓜ Mayakovskaya) This specialist in 18th- to 20th-century antiques is a real charmer, piled high with rustic old whatnots as well as more genuine antiques. You might unearth anything from a battered old samovar to an intricately painted sleigh. International shipping is no problem.

ART RE.FLEX
ART

Map p260 (www.artreflex.ru; pr Bakunina 5; ⌚noon-7pm Tue-Sat; Ⓜ Ploshchad Vosstaniya) This contemporary gallery is unique, showcasing artists of all ages, genres and experience levels. So its exhibitions mix the work of up-and-coming artists with more established names. It displays painting, graphics and sculpture, in an attempt to highlight the most interesting trends in contemporary art.

PARFIONOVA
CLOTHING & ACCESSORIES

Map p260 (www.parfionova.ru; Nevsky pr 51; ⌚noon-8pm; Ⓜ Mayakovskaya) Tatyana Parfionova was the first St Petersburg couturier to have her own fashion house back in the 1990s, when the New Russians turned up their noses at anything that was not straight from Paris or Milan. Now this local celebrity showcases her stuff at her Nevsky pr boutique, where you'll find her striking monochromatic *prêt-à-porter* designs as well as her famous crimson scarves.

IMPERIAL PORCELAIN
HOMEWARES

Map p260 (www.ipm.ru; Vladimirsky pr 7; ⌚10am-8pm; Ⓜ Vladimirskaya) This is the more convenient location of the famous porcelain factory. There is another **IPM shop** (Map p260; Nevsky pr 160; ⌚10am-8pm; Ⓜ Ploshchad Vosstaniya) midway between pl Vosstaniya and pl Alexandra Nevskogo. Prices here are higher than in the factory outlet (p138).

KUZNECHNY MARKET
MARKET

Map p260 (Кузнечный рынок; Kuznechny per 3; ⌚8am-8pm; Ⓜ Vladimirskaya) The colours and atmosphere of the city's largest fruit and vegetable market are quite the sensory experience. And the vendors – mostly from the Caucasus and Central Asia – will ply you with free samples of fresh fruits, homemade *smetana* (sour cream) and sweet honey. However, bargain hard – prices can start off very high, especially when it's clear you're not Russian.

GALERIA
SHOPPING CENTRE

Map p260 (Галерия; www.galeria.spb.ru; Ligovsky pr 30A; ⌚10am-11pm; Ⓜ Ploshchad Vosstaniya) This extraordinary place has rather changed everything for shopping in St Petersburg – there are probably more shops inside than there are elsewhere in the entire city centre. Spread over five floors, with around 300 shops (including H&M, Gap, Marks & Spencer and Zara), a multiscreen cinema, bowling alley, food hall and an enormous and excellently stocked supermarket, Okey, this really is a one-stop shop for pretty much all your shopping needs.

NEVSKY CENTRE
SHOPPING CENTRE

Map p258 (Невский Центр; www.nevskycentre.ru, in Russian; Nevsky pr 112; ⌚10am-11pm; Ⓜ Ploshchad Vosstaniya) Not nearly as big as Galeria on the other side of Pl Vosstaniya, Nevsky Centre is perhaps slightly more glamorous and upmarket. It houses some 70 shops over seven floors, including the city's largest department store, Stockmann, which includes the fabulous basement Stockmann supermarket, by far the best-stocked in the entire city. Elsewhere there's a food court and lots of independent fashion and furnishing stores.

VLADIMIRSKY PASSAGE
SHOPPING CENTRE

Map p260 (Владимирский пассаж; www.vpassage.ru, in Russian; Vladimirsky pr 19; ⌚11am-10pm; Ⓜ Vladimirskaya) Walking into this centre from the chaotic street outside you'll be forgiven for thinking you've passed through a portal to another world. Over 100 stores sell designer clothing, imported food products and other fancy stuff. Shoppers linger at sushi bars and coffee shops, though many come here for the basement supermarket, **Lend** (⌚24hr), which has everything from fresh pasta and Italian pesto to a reasonably priced bottle of Sancerre.

AUCHAN HYPERMARKET

Map p260 (Ашан; www.auchan.ru, in Russian; ul Borovaya 47; ⏲8.30am-11pm; ⓂObvodny Kanal) If you can't find something anywhere else in the city, then head for this conveniently located hypermarket, just a short walk from Obvodny Kanal metro. You'll find a huge range of food, clothing, household products and far, far more.

TULA SAMOVARS SAMOVARS

Map p260 (Тульские самовары; www.samovary.ru, in Russian; per Dzhambula 11; ⓂZvenigorodskaya) Nearly all samovars (metal containers holding boiling water) in Russia are made in the town of Tula, south of Moscow, but this beautiful showroom is the place in St Petersburg to buy a truly unique souvenir of your visit. The samovars range from small, simple designs to enormous and elaborate ones with precious stones and other embellishments.

MALTSEVSKY MARKET MARKET

Map p258 (Мальцевский рынок; ul Nekrasova 52; ⏲8am-8pm; ⓂPloshchad Vosstaniya) Bargaining is encouraged at this bright spacious market, packed with vendors selling exotic fruits and vegetables, mounds of multicoloured spices, and fresh meats, fish and fowl. In some cases, the meat is so fresh it is still being hacked off its carcass. Don't miss free samples of honey straight from the hive.

SPORTS & ACTIVITIES

PLANET FITNESS – SMOLNY GYM

Map p258 (www.fitness.ru; nab Robespiera 12; ⏲7am-11pm Mon-Fri, 9am-9pm Sat & Sun; ⓂChernyshevskaya) St Petersburg's largest chain of fitness centres now has 11 locations around the city, but the first was in Smolny. Classes include aerobics and yoga, while weights machines and cardio equipment are also available. The cardio room overlooks the Neva River, offering a lovely view as you cycle or run. Afterwards, enjoy the sauna and hot tub, or a fresh fruit drink from the juice bar.

MYTNINSKIYE BANI BANYA

Map p258 (Мытнинские бани; www.mybanya.spb.ru; Mytninskaya ul 17-19; per hr R200-800; ⏲24hr by reservation; ⓂPloshchad Vosstaniya) Unique in the city, Mytninskiye Bani is heated by a wood furnace, just like the log-cabin bathhouses that are still found in the Russian countryside. In addition to a *parilka* and plunge pool, the private 'lux' *banya* includes a swanky lounge area with leather furniture and a pool table.

DEGTYARNIYE BANI BANYA

Map p258 (Дегтярные бани; www.d1a.ru; ul Degtyarnaya 1A; per hr R300-1000; ⏲9am-midnight; ⓂPloshchad Vosstaniya) These modern baths are divided up into mixed, men's and women's sections, or you can book private *banyas* of varying degrees of luxury. Book ahead, though, as they are often full. English is spoken and the website has a helpful English-language guide to how to take a *banya* for novices.

MOPS SPA SPA

Map p258 (www.mopsspa.ru; ul Rubinshteyna 12; ⏲11am-11pm; ⓂDostoevskaya) Run by the same Thai management as the restaurant with the same name, this wonderful retreat from the roar of traffic on nearby Nevsky is a very welcome one. Choose from traditional Thai massage, facials, hair treatments, aromatherapy and stone therapy just for starters.

SKAT PROKAT CYCLING

Map p260 (☎717 6838; www.skatprokat.ru; Goncharnaya ul 7; per hr/day R150/500; ⏲1-8pm; ⓂPloshchad Vosstaniya) This tight-run outfit offers excellent Saturday- and Sunday-morning bike tours of the city (see p221). Rental bicycles are brand-new mountain bikes by the Russian company Stark, and you'll need to leave either R2000 and your passport, or R7000 as a deposit. Weekend or weekly rates are also available. Or, if you are in town for a while, this place also sells secondhand bikes.

ICE PALACE SPECTATOR SPORTS

(Ледовый дворец; www.newarena.spb.ru; pr Pyatiletok 1; ⓂProspekt Bolshevikov) The St Petersburg ice hockey team SKA play in this new stadium from September to June. Built for the World Ice Hockey Championships in 2000, this 12,000-seat stadium is a swanky state-of-the-art facility compared to other sports arenas in town and it's also a big concert venue, playing host to many international acts when they're in St Petersburg.

Sennaya & Kolomna

Neighbourhood Top Five

❶ Climb the 262 steps to the golden dome of marvellous **St Isaac's Cathedral** (p103) for breathtaking views over the Historic Heart and the Neva River. Inside, the cathedral boasts impressive baroque interiors of malachite and marble.

❷ Take in the symbol of St Petersburg among the newlyweds at the statue of the **Bronze Horseman** (p106), Catherine the Great's homage to Peter the Great.

❸ See a dazzling Russian ballet or opera classic at the iconic **Mariinsky Theatre** (p107).

❹ Marvel at the interiors and hear tales of Rasputin's grizzly end at the impressive **Yusupov Palace** (p105).

❺ Visit perhaps St Petersburg's single prettiest church, the sky-blue and gold **Nikolsky Cathedral** (p107), surrounded by canals and charming gardens.

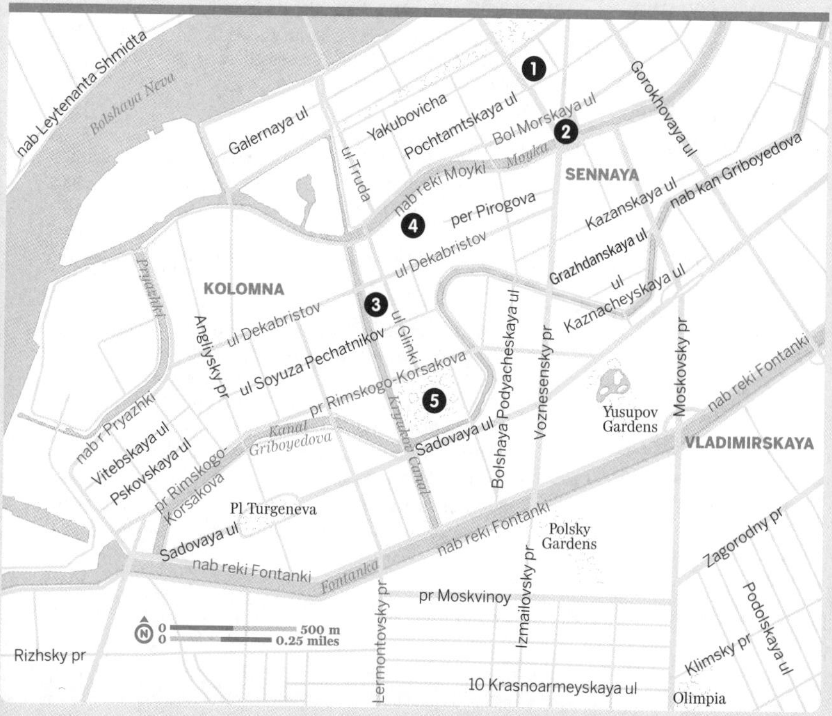

For more detail of this area, see Map p264 ➡

Lonely Planet's Top Tip

Book ahead of time to see the ballet or opera performance you're interested in at the Mariinsky Theatre (www.mariinsky.ru), especially during the White Nights, when performances of popular productions sell out months in advance. You can book and pay for tickets on the website, and then collect them at the box office before the performance, which is much better than trying to find what's available once you're in town.

Best Places to Eat

- Sadko (p111)
- Teplo (p111)
- Russian Vodka Room No 1 (p111)
- Backstage (p112)

For reviews, see p110

Best Places to Drink

- Stirka (p112)
- Hundertwasser Bar (p113)
- Bardak (p112)
- Shamrock (p113)

For reviews, see p112

Best Palaces

- Yusupov Palace (p105)
- House of Music (p110)
- Old Yusupov Palace (p104)
- Rumyantsev Mansion (p109)

For reviews, see p104

Explore: Sennaya & Kolomna

Sennaya and Kolomna are two very different areas directly to the west of Nevsky pr, both wedged between the Fontanka and Neva Rivers. Sennaya, focused on the eponymous Sennaya pl (Haymarket), is one of the city's busiest commercial neighbourhoods and is also rather rundown. The poverty so vividly brought to life in Dostoevsky's *Crime and Punishment,* may no longer be evident here any more, but you'll immediately notice that this is a poorer, scruffier part of town than the Historic Heart, with few of the embellishments.

Kolomna, named after the largest of the seven islands that make up the neighbourhood, is by contrast something of a sleepy village in the heart of the city. With no metro station and surrounded on three sides by water, it's a beautiful and relaxed backwater that also includes the world-famous Mariinsky Theatre and the soon-to-be-famous new cultural development at New Holland.

Local Life

- **Canal Life** Sennaya and Kolomna are home to some of the prettiest stretches of canal in the city, well away from the crowds. Check out the gorgeous Kryukov Canal, the far end of Kanal Griboyedov and the almost totally unknown Pryazhka River.
- **Free Concerts** Check out the Maly Zal (small hall) at the Rimsky-Korsakov Conservatory (p114), where you'll often see fantastic-quality free concerts from students and alumni.
- **Transport Issues** Get to know the bus and *marshrutka* routes if you're going to be spending any time in Kolomna, where there's no metro and distances between sights on foot can be very long.

Getting There & Away

- **Metro** Sennaya is served by the interconnecting Sennaya pl (Line 2 and 5) and Spasskaya (Line 4), the city's biggest interchange station. Kolomna is not served by the metro, so you'll need to walk from Sennaya pl or Admiralteyskaya.
- **Bus** Bus 3 connects the Mariinsky with Nevsky pr via Bolshaya Morskaya ul.
- **Marshrutka** *Marshrutka* 7 runs from Sennaya pl all the way to the far end of Sadovaya ul in Kolomna.

TOP SIGHTS
ST ISAAC'S CATHEDRAL

The golden dome of St Isaac's Cathedral dominates the St Petersburg skyline. Named after St Isaac of Dalmatia, on whose feast day Peter the Great was born, it is one of the largest domed buildings in the world. Everything about this place is enormous and designed to awe: more than 100kg of gold leaf was used to cover the 21.8m-high dome alone, while the huge granite pillars on the building's facade each weigh over 120 tonnes.

Most people bypass the museum and simply climb the 262 steps to the *kolonnada* (colonnade) around the drum of the dome. The outlook to the four corners of the city is superb, with great views over the river, the Winter Palace, pl Dekabristov and the *Bronze Horseman*. Tickets are sold separately at the kiosk on the northeast side of the cathedral.

Controversial Design

French designer Auguste Montferrand began designing the cathedral in 1818, despite the fact that he was no architect. Indeed, it was Montferrand's contacts at court that ensured the design was approved by the tsar. Local architects were outraged at the foreign upstart's commission and were quick to point out (correctly) a number of technical flaws in the plan.

The cathedral took so long to build (until 1858) that Nicholas I was able to insist on an even more grandiose structure than Montferrand had originally planned. The long construction period gave rise to a rumour among locals that the Romanov dynasty would fall were the cathedral ever completed – something that in the event happened some 60 years later. Special ships and a railway had to be built to carry the granite from Finland for the huge pillars. There's a statue of Montferrand holding a model of the cathedral on the west facade, although Nicholas I denied the architect his dying wish, to be buried here, considering it too high an honour for a mere artisan.

Lavish Interiors

The cathedral's interior is obscenely lavish. Across 4000 sq metres there are 600 sq metres of mosaics, 16,000kg of malachite, 14 types of marble and an 816-sq-metre ceiling painting by Karl Bryullov. Among the many displays inside there are some interesting photographs of the cathedral throughout its history, including one of the park outside being used to grow cabbages during the Nazi blockade.

Since 1990, after a 62-year gap, services have been held here on major religious holidays and St Isaac's may eventually return to full Church control before long. Like the Church on the Spilled Blood, St Isaac's is officially classed as a museum and as such lacks almost any religious atmosphere.

DON'T MISS...

- Climb to the dome for amazing views
- Enjoy the lavish interiors
- See the display of historic photos
- See the statue of Montferrand

PRACTICALITIES

- Map p264
- ww.cathedral.ru
- Isaakievskaya pl
- adult/student R250/150, colonnade R150
- 10am-6pm Thu-Tue
- M Admiralteyskaya

SIGHTS

Sennaya

More infamous than famous, this neighbourhood is named for the once derelict Haymarket (Sennaya pl), which was the centre of Dostoevskian St Petersburg. Sennaya was home to the poor workers and peasants who were new arrivals in the city, living in rat-infested basements and sleeping 10-to-a-room in shifts.

In honour of the city's tercentennial celebrations in 2003, the Sennaya pl received a massive overhaul, being modernised and sanitised almost beyond recognition. But the chaos around the square has not subsided, and the alleyways and waterways to the north still evoke the moodiness that Fyodor Dostoevsky portrayed so vividly.

SENNAYA PLOSHCHAD — SQUARE

Map p264 (Сенная пл; Ⓜ Sennaya Ploshchad) St Petersburg's Haymarket was once the city's filthy underbelly, immortalised by Dostoevsky, who lived all over the neighbourhood and set *Crime and Punishment* here. Until a recent face-lift, the square was overloaded with makeshift kiosks and market stalls, which made it a magnet for the homeless, beggars, pickpockets and drunks. Despite a big clean-up effort by city authorities in 2003, Sennaya pl retains a fundamental insalubriousness. Be on your guard walking around here at night.

The peripatetic Dostoevsky, who occupied around 20 residences in his 28-year stay in the city, once spent a couple of days in debtors' prison in what is now called the Senior Officers' Barracks, just across the square from the Sennaya pl metro station.

Alyona Ivanovna, the elderly moneylender murdered in *Crime and Punishment*, lived a few blocks west of here, at nab kanala Griboyedova 104. Her flat would have been no 74, on the 3rd floor.

DOSTOEVSKY HOUSES — HISTORIC BUILDINGS

Map p264 (Kaznacheyskaya ul 7; ⏲ closed to the public; Ⓜ Sennaya Ploshchad) Dostoevsky lived in three flats on this tiny street alone. From 1861 to 1863, he lived at No 1. In 1864, he spent one month living in the faded red building at No 9, before moving to No 7. Here, he lived from 1864 to 1867 and wrote *Crime and Punishment;* indeed, the route taken by the novel's antihero Raskolnikov to murder the old moneylender passed directly under his window. While this area has changed enormously, it's still possible to catch glimpses of the grim reality of slum life that pervaded this place in the mid-19th century.

RASKOLNIKOV HOUSE — HISTORIC BUILDING

Map p264 (Дом Раскольникова; Stolyarny per 5; ⏲ closed to the public; Ⓜ Sennaya Ploshchad) This innocuous house on the corner of Stolyarny per (called 'S... lane' in the book) is one of two possible locations of the attic apartment of Rodion Raskolnikov, protagonist of Dostoevsky's *Crime and Punishment.* Those who claim this is the place go further, saying that Rodion retrieved the murder weapon from a street-sweeper's storage bin inside the tunnel leading to the courtyard.

The house is marked by a sculpture of Dostoevsky. The inscription says something to the effect of 'The tragic fate of the people of this area of St Petersburg formed the foundation of Dostoevsky's passionate sermon of goodness for all mankind'.

Other Dostoevsky connoisseurs argue that it woud be more appropriate if Raskolnikov's attic apartment was located further down the street at No 9, which is otherwise unmarked.

RAILWAY MUSEUM — MUSEUM

Map p264 (Музей железнодорожного транспорта; www.railroad.ru/cmrt, in Russian; Sadovaya ul 50; adult/student/child R100/50/30; ⏲ 11am-5.30pm Sun-Thu; Ⓜ Sadovaya) This quirky museum near Sennaya pl houses a collection of scale locomotives and model railway bridges, often made by the same engineers that built the real ones. The oldest such collection in the world, the museum dates to 1809, 28 years before Russia had its first working train! It includes models of the *Yenisey Bridge,* the ship that once carried passengers and trains across Lake Baikal. No matter how many overnight trains you have ridden, you are unlikely to recognise the sumptuous 1903 Trans-Siberian wagon, complete with piano salon and bathtub.

YUSUPOV GARDENS — PARK

Map p264 (Юсуповский сад; Sadovaya ul; ⏲ sunrise-sunset; Ⓜ Sadovaya) Due west of Sennaya pl along Sadovaya ul you'll find the charming Yusupov Gardens, a pleasant park with a big lake in the middle. The flower-filled grounds are a popular place

WORTH A DETOUR

MUSEUM OF RAILWAY TECHNOLOGY

Trainspotters should hasten to view the impressive collection of decommissioned locomotives at the **Museum of Railway Technology** (nab kanala Obvodnogo 118; adult/child R200/1000; ⌚11am-5.30pm Tue-Sun; MBaltiyskaya; 🚸), behind the old Warsaw Station. Some 75 nicely painted and buffed engines and carriages dating back to the late 19th century are on display, as well as a mobile intercontinental nuclear missile launcher. This is a fantastic option for kids. To get here from the metro, turn right onto the canal and walk down to Warsaw Station. Turn right after you pass the station to find the museum.

to stroll, sit and sunbathe. The building set back behind the gardens is the **Old Yusupov Palace** (not to be confused with the Yusupov Palace on the Moyka River, where the Yusupov family moved in the 18th century). The Old Yusupov Palace is closed to the public and is used mainly for official receptions.

TRINITY CATHEDRAL CATHEDRAL

Map p264 (Троицкий собор; Izmailovsky pr 7A; ⌚9am-7pm Mon-Sat, 8am-8pm Sun, services 10am daily & 5pm Fri-Sun; MTekhnologichesky Institut) The Trinity Cathedral boasts stunning blue cupolas emblazoned with golden stars. A devastating fire in 2006 caused the central 83m-high central cupola to collapse, but it has been fully restored and now looks even better than it did before. Construction of the vast cathedral began in 1828, according to a design by Vasily Stasov. The cathedral was consecrated in 1835 and functioned as the chapel for the Izmailovsky Guards, who were garrisoned next door. In honour of the Russian victory in the Russo-Turkish War in 1878, the memorial Column of Glory was constructed out of 128 Turkish cannons. (The present monument was erected on the north side of the cathedral in 2003: it is an exact replica of the original, which was destroyed by Stalin.)

The cathedral was famed for its immense collection of icons, as well as several silver crosses dating from the 18th and 19th centuries. After the revolution, most of these treasures were looted, the ornate interiors were destroyed and the cathedral was finally closed in 1938.

Trinity Cathedral was returned to the Orthodox Church in 1990, but the interior is decidedly bare, especially compared with its previous appearance. Literature buffs will be interested to know that this is the church where Fyodor Dostoevsky married his second wife, Anna Snitkina, in 1867.

Kolomna

ST ISAAC'S CATHEDRAL CATHEDRAL

See p103.

YUSUPOV PALACE PALACE

Map p264 (Юсуповский дворец; www.yusupov-palace.ru; nab reki Moyki 94; adult/student/child R500/380/280; ⌚11am-5pm; MSpasskaya) This spectacular palace on the Moyka River has some of the most perfectly preserved 19th-century interiors in the city, in addition to a fascinating history. The palace was built by Vallin de la Mothe in the 1760s, but the current interiors date from a century later. It became the residence of the illustrious Yusupov family after they moved from another fine house on Sadovaya ul (which, confusingly, is also sometimes called the Yusupov Palace; see p104). The palace's last Yusupov owner was the eccentric Prince Felix, a high-society darling, enamoured of cross-dressing, who often attended the Mariinsky and society balls as a woman and was at one time the richest man in Russia. Most notoriously, the palace is the place where Grigory Rasputin met his gruesome end in 1916.

The palace interior is sumptuous and rich, with many halls painted in different styles and decked out with gilded chandeliers, silks, frescoes, tapestries and some fantastic furniture. The tour begins on the 2nd floor, which features an amazing ballroom and banquet hall, where musicians perform short concerts throughout the day. The highlight is the ornate rococo private theatre, which apparently has hosted artists as famed as Fyodor Chaliapin, Mikhail Glinka and Anna Pavlova. The tour continues on the ground floor, where you can't miss the fabulous Turkish Study and Moorish Drawing Room. Of the latter, Felix Yusupov wrote: 'I loved the tender Oriental luxury of this room. I used to dream here… I sat on the sofa with my mother's jewels on me and imagined myself as an Oriental satrap, surrounded by slaves.'

In 1916 Rasputin was murdered here in the grizzliest possible way by Felix Yusupov and some fellow plotters, who considered the 'mad monk' to have become too powerful (see p184).

The palace is certainly one of St Petersburg's finest, but it's very overpriced for foreigners (Russians get a far better deal) and if you want to see the room where Rasputin's murder began, you have to pay for an extra tour (adult/student R300/180), which takes place at 1.45pm daily except Sunday. There are only 20 tickets available each day, so come in good time to secure a place. The tour is in Russian only, so it's hard not to feel you're getting a bum deal, as Russians themselves pay far less. The admission price to the palace includes an audio tour in English and a number of other languages, but you'll need to leave a R1000 deposit per audioguide.

BRONZE HORSEMAN STATUE

Map p264 (Медный всадник; pl Dekabristov; Ⓜ Admiralteyskaya) The most famous statue of Peter the Great was immortalised as the Bronze Horseman in the epic poem by Alexander Pushkin. With his horse (representing Russia) rearing above the snake of treason, Peter's enormous statue stands at the river end of pl Dekabristov. The statue was sculpted over 12 years for Catherine the Great by Frenchman Etienne Falconet. Its inscription reads 'To Peter I from Catherine II – 1782'. Many have read significance into Catherine's linking of her own name with that of the city's founder: she had no legitimate claim to the throne and this statue is sometimes seen as her attempt to formalise the link (philosophical, if not hereditary) between the two monarchs. The significance of the inscription in both Latin and Cyrillic alphabets would not have been lost on the city's population, which was still in the process of Westernisation during Catherine's reign.

Falconet's original study for the magnificent sculpture can be seen in the Russian Museum (p57). Despite completing his lifework here, Falconet departed Russia a bitter, angry man. Years of arguing with the head of the Academy of Fine Arts over the finer details of the sculpture had taken its toll, and he didn't even bother staying for the unveiling.

The statue has become a much-debated philosophical symbol of the city and the main trademark of the new spirit of St Petersburg. Moreover, it's de rigueur for local newlyweds to be photographed here after their weddings, so expect to see plenty of blushing brides (see p107).

PLOSHCHAD DEKABRISTOV SQUARE

Map p264 (Пл декабристов; Ⓜ Admiralteyskaya) Centred on the famed statue of the Bronze Horseman, pl Dekabristov (Decembrists' Sq) is named after the first attempt

STREET NAMES, SIGNS & FUN WITH CYRILLIC

We use the transliteration of Russian names of streets and squares in this book to help you when deciphering Cyrillic signs and asking locals the way. To save space the following abbreviations are used:

- al – alleya (аллея; alley)
- bul – bulvar (бульвар; boulevard)
- nab – naberezhnaya (набережная; embankment)
- per – pereulok (переулок; lane or side street)
- pl – ploshchad (площадь; square)
- pr – prospekt (проспект; avenue)
- sh – shosse (шоссе; highway)
- ul – ulitsa (улица; street)

Cyrillic script is provided for all points of interest (sights, activities, restaurants, clubs, hotels etc) where there's no clear sign in English. So if you can't get a local to understand your Russian pronunciation, just point to the Cyrillic name and let them read it.

TO HAVE AND TO HOLD

No event gives more cause for celebration in Russia than a wedding. Festivities commence when the groom arrives to claim his bride. He is forced to pass a series of tests – physical feats and brain-teasers – before he can see his beloved. Once he proves his devotion, the happy couple proceeds to the department of registry for a simple ceremony, usually attended only by immediate family and close friends. Then the wedding party takes a tour of the city, laying flowers at war memorials to remember the dead, and drinking champagne at other landmarks to celebrate the living.

Newlyweds' most beloved site in St Petersburg is pl Dekabristov, where Peter the Great sits astride his horse. Here, brides and grooms, friends and family come to memorialise their wedding day in photographs. More often than not, an amateur band is on hand, playing requests from the wedding parties to earn a few roubles. Everyone is invited to partake of the bubbly, to toast the glad day and the couple's joyful future together.

at a Russian revolution: the Decembrists' Uprising of 14 December 1825. The Decembrists were young officers who were inspired by radical ideas from France during the Napoleonic campaigns and wanted to introduce constitutional monarchy. Ineptly, they set up their protest on the same day as the swearing-in ceremony of the new tsar, Nicholas I. After repeated attempts by Nicholas' ministers to reason with the rebels, they were fired upon. Many officers and bystanders died as a result. Most of the leaders later ended up on the gallows or in Siberia.

The dominant feature of pl Dekabristov is the immense facade of St Isaac's Cathedral (p103). Most of the west side of the square is occupied by the Central State Historical Archives and the new Yeltsin Presidential Library, both of which are housed in the former Senate and Synod buildings, built by Carlo Rossi between 1829 and 1834.

NIKOLSKY CATHEDRAL CATHEDRAL

Map p264 (Никольский собор; Nikolskaya pl 1/3; admission free; ⏲9am-7pm; Ⓜ Sadovaya) Just south of the Mariinsky Theatre, surrounded on two sides by canals, this ice-blue cathedral is one of the most picture-perfect in the city, beloved by locals for its baroque spires and golden domes. It was one of the few churches that continued to work during the Soviet era, when organised religion was effectively banned.

Nicknamed the Sailor's Church (Nicholas is the patron saint of sailors), it contains many 18th-century icons and a fine carved wooden iconostasis, though visitors are limited to only a small area of the church's interior. A graceful bell tower overlooks Kanal Griboyedova, which is crossed by **Staro-Nikolsky most**. From this bridge, you can see at least seven bridges, more than from any other spot in the city.

MARIINSKY THEATRE THEATRE

Map p264 (Мариинский театр; ☎326 4141; www.mariinsky.ru; Teatralnaya pl; ⏲box office 11am-7pm, tours by arrangement; Ⓜ Sadovaya) The pretty green-and-white Mariinsky Theatre has played a pivotal role in Russian ballet ever since it was built in 1859. Outside performance times you can wander into the theatre's foyer and maybe peep into its lovely auditorium. To experience the theatre as its designers intended, your best method is to buy a ticket for a performance (see p113), though private tours are sometimes available – ask at the main ticket office if these are running during your visit.

Construction of the New Mariinsky Theatre is under way directly west of the original building on the other side of the Kryukov Canal. Due to open by 2012, the theatre will seat some 2000 people and contain six stages, marking the Mariinsky's arrival in the 21st century. See p108.

Elsewhere around Teatralnaya pl you will find the illustrious music school, Rimsky-Korsakov Conservatory (p114), which faces the Mariinsky.

RUSSIAN VODKA MUSEUM MUSEUM

Map p264 (Музей русской водки; www.vodkamuseum.su; Konngvardeysky bul 4; admission with/without tour R300/150; ⏲noon-10pm; Ⓜ Admiralteyskaya) This excellent private museum tells the story of Russia's national tipple in an interesting and fun way, from the first production of 'bread wine' to the

DRAMA BACKSTAGE: THE NEW MARIINSKY THEATRE

When the Mariinsky Theatre's artistic director, Valery Gergiev, announced in 2003 that the first opera house to be built in Russia since the 1917 revolution would be constructed next door to one of Russia's most august cultural institutions, his reception in ultra-conservative St Petersburg was unsurprisingly cool.

Little did anyone know, the project would end up taking almost a decade to be realised. The extremely bold initial design by French architect Dominique Perrault was eventually abandoned (despite construction having started) due to spiralling costs and building code compliance problems. After a new competition in 2009, Canadian architects Diamond & Schmitt won the €295-million tender to build a very different structure, now due to open in 2012.

The New Mariinsky Theatre (or *Mariinka Dva* as it's known locally) is less of an architectural statement than the Perrault design (it's unlikely that it will become an icon of the city in the way that Perrault's golden cubist dome might have done), but it will be less incongruous with the surrounding 18th-century neighbourhood. Some critics also say the theatre's interior design is far more original, providing six stages and seating for some 2000 people. Tickets to shows here will be the hottest ones available once the theatre opens – book ahead to be sure you can get a seat in what's being dubbed 'Russia's most important building project in 70 years'. The theatre is now due to open in 2012, although rumours about delays are rife.

phenomenon of the modern international vodka industry, complete with waxwork models and some very cool bottles. You can guide yourself through the exhibit, or, for twice the price, be accompanied by an English-speaking guide who'll liven things up a bit. If you'd like to sample the exhibits too, take a **tasting tour** (with/without guide R450/300). There's an excellent restaurant in the same building (see p111), and if you eat there, you can visit the museum with a tasting for a very reasonable R150.

GRAND CHORAL SYNAGOGUE — SYNAGOGUE

Map p264 (Большая хоральная синагога; www.jewishpetersburg.ru; Lermontovsky pr 2; admission free; ⌚8am-8pm Sun-Fri, service 10am Sat; Ⓜ Sadovaya) Designed by Vasily Stasov, the striking Grand Choral Synagogue opened in 1893 to provide a central place of worship for St Petersburg's growing Jewish community. Its lavishness (particularly notable in the 47m-high cupola and the decorative wedding chapel) indicates the pivotal role that Jews played in imperial St Petersburg. The synagogue was fully revamped in 2003 with money donated by an American benefactor. Visitors are welcome except on the Sabbath and other holy days. Men and married women should cover their heads upon entering.

Also on-site are the **Small Synagogue** (⌚11am-4pm Mon-Thu, 11am-1pm Fri & Sun), the Jewish restaurant Lechaim (p112) and the store Kosher Shop (p115). In summer, the synagogue also hosts performances with a Jewish cantor and other musicians performing *chaaznut* and *klezmer* music. The synagogue organises English-language tours of the building, as well as longer tours of 'Jewish St Petersburg', all of which need to be organised in advance – see the website.

FREE NABOKOV MUSEUM — MUSEUM

Map p264 (Музей Набокова; www.nabokovmuseum.org; Bolshaya Morskaya ul 47; admission free; ⌚11am-6pm Tue-Fri, noon-5pm Sat & Sun; Ⓜ Admiralteyskaya) This lovely 19th-century town house was the suitably grand childhood home of Vladimir Nabokov, infamous author of *Lolita* and arguably the most versatile and least classifiable of modern Russian writers. Here Nabokov lived with his wealthy family from his birth in 1899 until the revolution in 1917, when they very sensibly left the country. The house features heavily in Nabokov's autobiography *Speak, Memory,* in which he refers to it as a 'paradise lost'. Indeed, he never returned, dying abroad in 1977. There's actually relatively little to see in the museum itself, save for some charming interiors (don't miss the gorgeous stained-glass windows in the stairwell, which are not technically part of the museum, but staff will often allow you to take a peek). Nabokov artefacts on display include family photographs, first editions of his books and parts of his extensive butterfly collection, as well as a couple of rooms given over to temporary art exhibits.

RUMYANTSEV MANSION MUSEUM

Map p264 (Особняк Румянцева; www.spbmuseum.ru, in Russian; Angliyskaya nab 44; adult/student R110/70; ⏲11am-6pm Thu-Tue; ⓂAdmiralteyskaya) History buffs should not miss this oft-overlooked but superb local museum. It is housed in the majestic 1826 mansion of Count Nikolai Petrovich Rumyantsev, a famous diplomat, politician and statesman, as well as an amateur historian whose personal research library became the basis for the Russian State Library in Moscow. The history of the mansion and its owners is fascinating in itself, and the few restored staterooms at the front of the house suggest daily life for the Rumyantsevs was a pretty opulent affair.

Part of the State Museum of the History of St Petersburg, the mansion contains an exhibition of 20th-century history, including displays devoted to the 1921 New Economic Policy (NEP), the industrialisation and development of the 1930s, and the Siege of Leningrad during WWII. Exhibitions are unusual in that they depict everyday life in the city during these historic periods. While each room has an explanatory panel in English, the individual labelling is in Russian only.

POPOV COMMUNICATIONS MUSEUM MUSEUM

Map p264 (Музей связи Попова; www.rustelecom-museum.ru, in Russian; Pochtamtsky per 4; adult/student R100/50; ⏲10.30am-6pm Tue-Sat; ⓂAdmiralteyskaya) Housed in the fabulous 18th-century palace of Chancellor Bezborodko, this museum of communications is the perfect addition to Pochtamtskaya ul (Postal St). It is named for Professor AS Popov, inventor of the radio, and it covers all manner of communication, from the Pony Express up through the modern era (on-site computers offer 30 minutes of free internet access to all museum guests). Exhibits are interactive and interesting, including an antique telephone switchboard that still works, the first civil communications satellite Luch-15, which occupies a prominent place in the atrium, and plenty of multimedia explanations of how things work. Stamp collectors will have a field day admiring the national philatelic collection.

MUSEUM OF THE HISTORY OF RELIGION MUSEUM

Map p264 (Государственный музей истории религии; www.gmir.ru; Pochtamtskaya ul 14; adult R220; ⏲11am-6pm Thu-Tue; ⓂAdmiralteyskaya) Back in the day, this was called the Museum of Atheism; it had a very strong anti-religious bias and it was housed in the Kazan Cathedral. Now the name has changed, as has the location, but the fascinating exhibition remains, describing the history of various world religions, including the Russian Orthodox Church. Recent exhibits, such as one featuring Soviet anti-religious posters, show that the museum has put its historic bias behind it.

MANEGE CENTRAL EXHIBITION HALL EXHIBITION HALL

Map p264 (Центральный выставочный зал Манеж; www.manege.spb.ru, in Russian; Isaakievskaya pl 1; admission R50-100; ⏲11am-7pm Fri-Wed; ⓂAdmiralteyskaya) Formerly the Horse Guards' Riding School, this large white neoclassical building was constructed between 1804 and 1807 from a design by Giacomo Quarenghi. It now houses rotating art exhibitions, often featuring contemporary and local artists. Particularly interesting is the annual December retrospective of painting, sculpture and installation pieces produced by St Petersburg artists.

ALEXANDER BLOK HOUSE-MUSEUM MUSEUM

Map p264 (Музей-квартира Блока; www.spbmuseum.ru; ul Dekabristov 57; admission R90; ⏲11am-6pm Thu-Mon, 11am-5pm Tue; ⓂSadovaya) This museum occupies the flat where poet Alexander Blok spent the last eight years of his life (1912–20). The revolutionary Blok believed that individualism had caused a decline in society's ethics, a situation that would only be rectified by a communist revolution.

The 4th floor has been preserved much as it was when Blok lived here with his wife Lyubov (daughter of Mendeleev). After touring the simple but historic home, descend to the 2nd floor, where Blok's mother lived. When the poet fell ill in 1920, his family moved into this apartment where he finally died a year later. Here, a literary exhibition demonstrates the influence of Blok's work, as well as some original copies of his poems. The room where Blok died contains his death mask and a drawing of Blok on his deathbed, sketched on the last page of the poet's pad. Chamber concerts are occasionally performed here – they're worthwhile for the subdued charm of the flats and the lovely views out onto the Pryazhka River.

NEW HOLLAND HITORIC BUILDINGS

Map p264 (Новая Голландия; www.newhollandsp.com; cnr nab kanala Kryukova & Bolshaya Morskaya ul; MSpasskaya) This island has been closed to the public for the vast majority of the last three centuries, and its structures appear to be little more than ruins at present. Its fortunes are about to change, however, as Russian billionaire Roman Abramovich acquired the island in 2010 and is planning to redevelop it into a cultural and commercial centre, which, it is hotly rumoured, will also house his own enormous contemporary art collection.

In Peter's time, the complex was used for ship-building (its name refers to the place where he learned the trade). In the 19th century, a large basin was built in the middle of the island. Here experiments were conducted by scientist Alexey Krylov in an attempt to build a boat that couldn't be capsized. In 1915 the navy built a radio transmitter here – the most powerful in Russia at the time – but it's been derelict and inaccessible ever since. If you walk by, look out for the impressive red-brick and granite arch, designed by Jean-Baptiste Vallin de la Mothe in the late 18th century, one of the city's best examples of Russian classicism.

HOUSE OF MUSIC PALACE

Map p264 (Дом музыки; 400 1400; www.spdm.ru; nab reki Moyki 211; 11am-5pm Tue & Thu; MSpasskaya) This fabulous and fully restored mansion at the very far end of the Moyka River belonged to Grand Duke Alexey, the son of Alexander II. The wrought-iron and stone fence is one of its most stunning features, with the Grand Duke's monogram adorning the central gates. The palace was built in 1895 by Maximilian Messmacher, and each facade represents a different architectural style, perhaps reflective of the character of Grand Duke Alexey himself. The interior is equally diverse, and since renovation has housed the House of Music (Dom Muzyki), where popular classical concerts are regularly held. Tours of the house (R350) usually leave at noon and 4pm on Tuesdays and Thursdays, but these dates vary and tickets often sell out in advance, so check the website.

EATING

Sennaya

SUMETA CAUCASIAN €

Map p264 (Сумета; ul Yefimova 5; mains R200-400; 11am-11pm; MSadovaya;) Even if you've never had Dagestani food, you'll see plenty of familiar Caucasian dishes in this quiet but friendly place, from Lula kebab (minced-meat kebab) to fried eggplant with garlic and walnuts in sour cream. The house speciality here is *khinkal,* a delicious, juicy meat dumpling. Try the pumpkin *chudu* (large pancake) or the selection of Caucasian wines for something new.

TESTO ITALIAN €€

Map p264 (Тесто; www.testogastronomica.ru; per Grivtsova 5/29; mains R200-300; MSennaya Ploshchad;) This place is good value and yet takes Italian cookery very seriously. Choose from a wide range of homemade pastas and top them with your favourite sauce, whether tomato-based bolognese or a rich, creamy salmon sauce. A few options for soup, salad and pizza round out the menu, but the pasta is the main drawcard. The modern basement space is not too fancy, but has plenty of charm.

KARAVAN CENTRAL ASIAN €€€

Map p264 (Караван; www.caravan2000.ru; Voznesensky pr 46; mains R200-950; noon-2am; MSadovaya;) Despite the kitschy decor (think camel in the corner), Karavan is a superb Central Asian restaurant with a lovely location overlooking the Fontanka River. Open grills line the dining room, giving an optimum view (and scent) of the kebabs that are on the menu. Service is attentive and efficient.

FASOL RUSSIAN-EUROPEAN €€

Map p264 (Фасоль; Gorokhovaya ul 17; mains R250-500; MSennaya Ploshchad;) This chic minimalist cafe is an oasis of good-value food and stylish taste in the middle of rather down-at-heel Gorokhovaya ul. The large menu offers modern takes on Russian dishes with a distinct European edge, making it a good compromise between hearty local fare and more sophisticated European dining.

CONCHITA BONITA MEXICAN €€

Map p264 (Gorokhovaya ul 39; mains R200-400; 24hr Tue-Sat, noon-midnight Mon & Sun; M Sennaya Ploshchad;) Nestled in a tiny basement and blasted with loud music is this Mexican restaurant, a good place for burritos, quesadillas, fajitas and other filling Tex-Mex dishes. There's a good-value daily business lunch for R145, and while it's far from authentic, it's a pretty good attempt by local standards.

Kolomna

TOP CHOICE TEPLO INTERNATIONAL €€

Map p264 (570 1974; www.v-teple.ru; ul Bolshaya Morskaya 45; mains R250-650; 9am-11pm, from 11am Sat, from 1pm Sun; M Admiralteyskaya;) This much-feted, eclectic and original restaurant, housed in the House of Composers and next door to the childhood home of Vladimir Nabokov, has got it all just right. The venue itself is a lot of fun to nose around, with multiple small rooms, nooks and crannies, and full of unexpected props from table football to a child's play room. Service is friendly and fast (when it's not too busy) and the peppy, inventive menu has something for everyone – there's a heavy Italian presence, but dishes come from all over the world and there's plenty of vegetarian choice. Reservations are usually essential, so call ahead.

TOP CHOICE MANSARD INTERNATIONAL €€€

Map p264 (946 4303; www.ginza-mansarda.ru; ul Pochtamskaya 3; mains R500-1400; M Admiralteyskaya;) This extraordinary addition to St Petersburg's eating scene definitely has the best views in town – you can almost touch the dome of St Isaac's Cathedral from the beautifully designed main room. But it's no one-trick pony; the superb menu is assuredly international, and its chefs are equally adept at producing langoustine and asparagus risotto as they are at a gourmet chicken Kiev. Book ahead to be sure of a table with a view.

TOP CHOICE RUSSIAN VODKA ROOM NO 1 RUSSIAN €€

Map p264 (www.vodkaroom.ru; Konnogvardeysky bul 4; mains R450-800; M Admiralteyskaya;) This charming, welcoming place is the restaurant of the Russian Vodka Museum (see p107), but it's good enough to be a destination in its own right. The interior enjoys a grand old-world feel, as does the menu: leg of roast suckling pig, stewed venison tongue and whole fried Gatchina trout take you back to imperial tastes and opulence. As you'd expect there's a huge vodka list (shots R100 to R500) and the knowledgeable staff will help you match your meal to one of the many bottles they sell.

ENTRÉE FRENCH €€

Map p264 (Nikolskaya pl 6; sandwiches R200, mains R400-700; M Sennaya Ploshchad) A very welcome addition to this beautiful though somewhat desolate part of St Petersburg's historic centre, Entrée comes in two parts. The cafe to the right has delicious cakes and sandwiches, an attractive tiled counter and, for some reason, Michael Douglas' signature scrawled on the wall. To the right is a far more formal restaurant with a classic but clever French menu and a huge wine list. Service could be a little friendlier, but otherwise this place is a great find.

TOP CHOICE SADKO RUSSIAN €€

Map p264 (903 2373; www.sadko-rst.ru; ul Glinki 2; mains R330-650; M Sennaya Ploshchad;) Serving all the Russian favourites, this impressive restaurant's decor applies traditional floral designs to a slick contemporary style. It's immensely popular with tourists (reservations are recommended in the evenings), as it's an obvious pre- or post-Mariinsky Theatre dining option. There's a great children's room and a full children's menu to boot, so families are very well catered for. The waiters, many of them music students at the local conservatory, give impromptu vocal performances.

THE IDIOT VEGETARIAN €€

Map p264 (www.idiot-spb.com; nab reki Moyki 82; mains R600-900; 11am-1am; M Sennaya Ploshchad;) Something of a tourist favourite, the Idiot is definitely a charming place and has been providing brunch (R360) for travellers for years now. Insidiously vegetarian (you may not even notice that there's no meat on the menu), this is more about atmosphere, relaxation and fun (helped along by the complementary vodka at the end of each meal). The cosy subterranean space, the antique furnishings and crowded bookshelves make it an extremely pleasant place to come to eat or drink.

BACKSTAGE RUSSIAN €€€

Map p264 (За сценой; 327 0684; Teatralnaya pl 18/10; mains R750-1000; Sadovaya;) The Mariinsky's official restaurant is tucked away, rather out of sight, on one corner of Teatralnaya pl. The decor is stage-worthy, and the food is excellent; sample dishes include fried Dover sole and venison with savoy cabbage and cranberry sauce. Famous opera singers and ballet dancers have written all over the walls, though it's probably best to refrain unless you count yourself among the stars. Reservations for the evenings are recommended.

STROGANOFF STEAK HOUSE STEAKHOUSE €€

Map p264 (314 5514; www.stroganoffsteakhouse.ru; Konnogvardeysky bul 5; mains R400-1000; Sennaya Ploshchad;) Beef lovers can indulge their habit at this 12,000-sq-metre restaurant, the city's biggest. Thanks to clever design, though, it doesn't feel overwhelmingly large or impersonal. The steaks are large enough to share. There's a fun children's playroom here, making it good for young families.

NOBLE NEST RUSSIAN-FRENCH €€€

Map p264 (Дворянское гнездо; 312 0911; www.dvgnezdo.ru; ul Dekabristov 21; mains R1000-3000; Sennaya Ploshchad;) This is the doyenne of the St Petersburg haute cuisine world, housed in the Trianon of the Yusupov Palace (p105). It's exceptionally stuffy (men shouldn't even think of entering without a tie), but – as previous diners such as Bill Clinton will no doubt tell you – the Russian-French cuisine is exceptional. Reservations are recommended.

STOLLE BAKERY €

Map p264 (Столле; www.stolle.ru; ul Dekabristov 33; pies R50-200; 8am-10pm; Sadovaya;) One of several outlets throughout the city, Stolle is a great place to come for coffee or dessert after an evening at the theatre. Black-and-white photos adorn the light-coloured walls, while jazz music wafts in the air. There is another outlet further up **ul Dekabristov** (ul Dekabristov 19; 8am-10pm), although its basement setting is not quite as inviting. See p72 for a full review.

CROCODILE INTERNATIONAL €€

Map p264 (Крокодил; Galernaya ul 18; mains R300-500; Admiralteyskaya;) The original and most interesting of the two restaurants in St Petersburg by this name, this charming eatery is a top choice for lunch or dinner, as long as you are not in a rush. Enjoy a dimly lit but artsy interior (including a piano just waiting to be played) and an interesting, eclectic menu with dishes such as eel soup, veal fillet in grape sauce and lamb cooked in a white wine sauce and star anise. Another, rather less atmospheric location is on **ul Kazanskaya** (ul Kazanskaya 46; 11am-11pm; Sennaya Pl).

LECHAIM JEWISH-RUSSIAN €€

Map p264 (www.eng.jewishpetersburg.ru; Lermontovsky pr 2; mains R200-600; noon-11pm Sun-Fri; Sennaya Ploshchad;) Hidden away beneath the Grand Choral Synagogue (p108), this nonprofit kosher restaurant is the city's best place for traditional Jewish cooking, although you have to search for it somewhat amid all the Russian and Georgian kosher dishes. The dining room is a pleasant space with mosaic floors and chandeliers, but the ambience is rather dulled by the muzak.

SCHÜMLI CAFE €

Map p264 (Kazanskaya ul 40; 9am-10pm; Sennaya Ploshchad) With its large range of coffees, sumptuous selection of cakes and – best of all – freshly made Belgian waffles, this small but friendly cafe is a great place to regain flagging energy when wandering around the city.

DRINKING & NIGHTLIFE

Sennaya

STIRKA BAR

Map p264 (Стирка; www.40gradusov.ru; Kazanskaya ul 26; 10am-1am; Nevsky Prospekt) This friendly joint has three washing machines, so you can drop off a load and have a few beers while you wait for it to finish. A novel idea, though one few people seem to take advantage of. Stirka is mainly a casual dive bar where people drop in for drinks and the odd art show or live performance.

BARDAK BAR

Map p264 (Бардак; www.bardak-bar.com; ul Grivtsova 11; noon-3am Sun-Thu, till 6am Fri & Sat; Sennaya Ploshchad) One of the few recommendable bars around insalubrious

Sennaya pl, Bardak nevertheless has a fairly grizzled student clientele. The exposed brick walls plastered with photos, rickety mezzanine level and dishevelled but hip crowd add up to explain why this groovy little bar was named after the Russian word for 'mess'.

Kolomna

HUNDERTWASSER BAR BAR

Map p264 (www.hundertwasserbar.com; Teatralnaya pl 4; ⌚noon-11.30pm; Ⓜ Sadovaya) This new addition to the Mariinsky's drinking scene is popular with students from the Rimsky-Korsakov Conservatory across the street and often hosts informal jam sessions. Even when these aren't going on, this is a very pleasant, bohemian spot to drink, with two comfortable rooms stuffed full of old furniture that are both perfect for lounging.

SHAMROCK PUB

Map p264 (www.shamrock.spb.ru; ul Dekabristov 27; ⌚9am-2am; Ⓜ Sadovaya) It may seem odd to pop in for a pint after watching ballerinas dance across *Swan Lake,* but that is what many theatre-goers do. This friendly Irish-owned pub opposite the Mariinsky Theatre attracts a steady stream of foreigners and locals.

ENTERTAINMENT

MARIINSKY THEATRE THEATRE

Map p264 (www.mariinsky.ru; Teatralnaya pl 1; tickets R1000-5000; ⌚box office 11am-7pm, performances 7pm; Ⓜ Sennaya Ploshchad) The most celebrated and spectacular venue for ballet and opera in St Petersburg, the Mariinsky Theatre is an attraction in its own right, whether or not you manage to get tickets to see a performance. Known as the Kirov Ballet during the Soviet era, the dance company confusingly still tours the world under this name, as its Soviet-era association with Nureyev, Baryshnikov et al brings more ticket sales.

Despite this odd tie to the past, the current general and artistic director Valery Gergiev has led the venue bravely into the modern world, and construction work on the New Mariinsky Theatre is finally finishing for its opening in 2012. It's the first new opera house to have been built in Russia since imperial times. Tickets can be bought online, in person or through ticket offices all over town, but should be bought in advance during the summer months, and at any time if you'd like to see a premiere or a famous classical work from the Mariinsky's repertoire.

YUSUPOV PALACE THEATRE THEATRE

Map p264 (www.yusupov-palace.ru; nab reki Moyki 94; tickets R500-2500; Ⓜ Sadovaya) Housed inside the outrageously ornate Yusupov Palace (p105), this elaborate yet intimate venue was the home entertainment centre for one of the city's foremost aristocratic families. While you can visit the theatre when you tour the palace, seeing a performance here is a treat, as you can imagine yourself the personal guest of crazy Prince Felix himself. The shows are a mixed bag – usually a 'Gala Evening' that features fragments of various Russian classics.

MARIINSKY CONCERT HALL CONCERT HALL

Map p264 (www.mariinsky.ru; ul Pisareva 20; tickets R400-3000; Ⓜ Sadovaya) Opened in 2007, this concert hall is a magnificent multifaceted creation. It manages to preserve the

CATCH OF THE DAY

Every year, shortly after the ice melts on the Neva River, the *koryushki* (freshwater smelt) swim up the river to spawn. To Petersburgers, this annual event – usually in early May – is a time of celebration, symbolising the end of a long, dark winter and the beginning of gorging on fish, whether fried, dried, smoked or pickled.

The *koryushka* is sometimes called the 'cucumber fish' for its distinctive smell (which disappears after cooking). For a few short weeks, this delicious fish appears on restaurant menus and in private homes. The city even hosts an annual *koryushki* festival at the Peter and Paul Fortress. Across the city, cooks get busy: breading this mild-flavoured fish with flour, salt and sunflower oil, frying it up in a pan, and serving it with a slightly sweet tomato sauce or straight up. It's a popular snack *k pivu* (with beer) or, of course, with vodka.

WORTH A DETOUR

THE GAY SOUTH

While the main gay bars and clubs, **Central Station** (p76), **Golubaya Ustritsa** (p75) and **The Club** (p95) are all in the city centre, two further fun establishments (admittedly rather off the beaten path) are well worth the effort of getting to, especially if you're looking for St Petersburg's small lesbian scene.

3L (www.triel.spb.ru; Moskovsky pr 107-9; cover R300; ⌚10pm-5.30am Wed & Fri-Sun; Ⓜ Moskovskiye Vorota) is St Petersburg's best-known lesbian club and has been running for over a decade now. It has recently moved south from the city centre and is now looking better than ever. Run in general as a female-only space, men are welcome with girls, but the cover for men is exorbitant (R800 when we dropped by!).

A more mixed space is right next door in the same courtyard: **Malevich** (www.malevich-club.ru; Moskovsky pr 107-9; cover free-R300; ⌚11pm-6am Wed & Fri-Sun; Ⓜ Moskovskiye Vorota; Wi-Fi) is a fun, mixed and laid-back cafe-cum-club (it's open as a cafe and social space 6pm to 11pm Wednesday to Sunday too) with a community spirit – art exhibits, social groups and other events are regularly held in the early evenings – but after 11pm it's all about drinking and dancing. Both clubs are right next to the metro station in the courtyard of Moskovsky pr 107–9.

historic brick facade of the set and scenery warehouse that previously stood on this spot, while the modern main entrance, facing ul Dekabristov, is all tinted glass and angular lines, hardly hinting at the beautiful old building behind. Its array of classical orchestral performances is superb, but be aware that it's a modern venue, and won't provide your typical 'night at the Mariinsky' atmosphere.

RIMSKY-KORSAKOV CONSERVATORY — MUSIC SCHOOL

Map p264 (www.conservatory.ru; Teatralnaya pl 3; tickets R200-R2000; Ⓜ Sadovaya) This illustrious music school – opposite the Mariinsky – was the first public music school in Russia. Founded in 1862, it counts Pyotr Tchaikovsky among its alumni and Nikolai Rimsky-Korsakov among its former faculty. Dmitry Shostakovich and Sergei Prokofiev are graduates of this institution, as are countless contemporary artistic figures, such as Mariinsky director Valery Gergiev. The Bolshoy Zal (Big Hall) on the 3rd floor is an excellent place to see the performances by up-and-coming musicians, which take place throughout the academic year, while the Maly Zal (Small Hall) often hosts free concerts from present students and alumni; check when you're in town for what's on.

FEEL YOURSELF RUSSIAN — MUSICAL THEATRE

Map p264 (www.folkshow.ru; Nikolayevsky Palace, ul Truda 4; tickets R1400; ⌚show 6.30pm; Ⓜ Admiralteyskaya) Terrible title, but not a bad show of traditional Russian folk dancing and music. The two-hour show features four different folk groups, complete with accordion, balalaika and Cossack dancers. It is worth attending to get a look inside the spectacular Nikolayevsky Palace, if nothing else.

SHOPPING

MARIINSKY ART SHOP — SOUVENIRS

Map p264 (www.mariinsky.ru; Mariinsky Theatre, Teatralnaya pl 1; ⌚11am-6pm on performance days, also open during interval; Ⓜ Sadovaya) Opera and ballet lovers will delight at the theatre-themed souvenirs for sale in the Mariinsky gift shop. None of it is cheap, but where else can you get a 'Property of Kirov Ballet' T-shirt? Also on sale: a comprehensive collection of CDs, DVDs, books and posters that you won't find elsewhere.

BEE-KEEPING — FOOD & DRINK

Map p264 (Пчеловодство; Sadovaya ul 51; Ⓜ Sennaya Ploshchad) Step into this sweet shop and you won't be able to resist taking home some honey. You can sample many different flavours of honey *(myod)* from all over Russia, and there are also natural remedies, creams and teas made from beeswax and pollen.

MIR ESPRESSO — FOOD & DRINK

Map p264 (Мир Эспрессо; www.mirespresso-spb.ru; ul Dekabristov 12/10; Ⓜ Sadovaya) Come for the aroma and stay for the amazing coffee from all over the world. There are espresso machines and every type of coffee maker and caffeine-related accessory.

SENNOY MARKET FOOD & DRINK

Map p264 (Moskovsky pr 4; ⌚8am-7pm; Ⓜ Sennaya Ploshchad) Cheaper and less atmospheric than Kuznechny Market (p99), Sennoy Market is also centrally located. You'll find fruit and veggies, as well as fresh-caught fish and fresh-cut meat.

SENNAYA SHOPPING CENTRE

Map p264 (www.sennaya.ru, in Russian; ul Yefimova 3; ⌚10am-9pm; Ⓜ Sennaya Ploshchad) This unnervingly American-style mall a short walk from Sennaya pl has pretty much everything in it, though the emphasis is firmly on fashion. There's also a big food court and a bowling alley (p115).

KOSHER SHOP FOOD & DRINK

Map p264 (www.jewishpetersburg.ru; Lermontovsky pr 2; Ⓜ Sennaya Ploshchad) Serving St Petersburg's Jewish community, the Kosher Shop is conveniently located next to the Grand Choral Synagogue (p108). Although its emphasis is on kosher food, the shop also sells books about Judaism in many languages, plus Jewish music and art.

GALLERY OF DOLLS SOUVENIRS

Map p264 (Галерея кукол; Bolshaya Morskaya ul 53/8; ⌚noon-7pm Tue-Sat; Ⓜ Sennaya Ploshchad) Featuring ballerinas and babushkas, clowns and knights, this gallery depicts just about every fairy-tale character and political persona in doll form. The highly creative figures are more like art than toys and make unusual souvenirs (although they're admittedly an acquired taste).

SPORTS & ACTIVITIES

KAZACHIYE BANI BANYA

Map p264 (Казачие бани; www.kazbani.ru; Bolshoy Kazachy per 11; per hr R1000; ⌚24hr; Ⓜ Pushkinskaya) Following a trend that is occurring throughout the city, the communal *banya* is something of an afterthought here. The vast majority of the venue is given over to very swanky, private *bani,* which are an excellent option for a group of up to 10 people.

RENTBIKE BIKE HIRE

Map p264 (☎932 1486; www.rentbike.org; nab kanala Griboyedova 57/65; ⌚noon-10pm; Ⓜ Sennaya Ploshchad) This centrally located company rents out well-maintained bikes at good rates (R600 per day). It will also deliver to your hotel for free if you're staying in the city centre.

BOWLING CITY LEISURE CLUB

Map p264 (www.bowlingcity.ru; ul Yefimova 3; per hr R400-1000; ⌚24hr; Ⓜ Sennaya Ploshchad) This is the most central outlet of a network of leisure clubs providing countless entertainment options including bowling and billiards. Besides the 36 bowling lanes, there is karaoke, a sports bar and pool tables. Rates vary according to time, meaning that it's more expensive to play in the evenings and on weekends.

PLANET FITNESS – SENNAYA GYM

Map p264 (www.fitness.ru; Kazanskaya ul 37; ⌚7am-11pm Mon-Fri, 9am-9pm Sat & Sun; Ⓜ Sadovaya) While rates and facilities differ dramatically between Planet Fitness locations, the outlet near Isaakievskaya pl is among the most central and least costly. Facilities include weights and cardio equipment, as well as a steamy sauna.

Vasilyevsky Island

Neighbourhood Top Five

❶ Take in one of the best views of the city from the historic **Strelka** (p118), the spit of land that crowns Vasilyevsky Island, has a superb Neva panorama and boasts flaming rostral columns during national holidays.

❷ Explore Peter the Great's private collection of anatomical oddities at the ghoulish **Kunstkamera** (p118).

❸ Check out St Petersburg's best new art space, the huge **Erarta Museum of Contemporary Art** (p118), where you'll see Russian works from the late Soviet and post-Soviet era.

❹ Visit the fascinating **Menshikov Palace** (p120), St Petersburg's first stone building.

❺ Hear tales of Soviet exploration in the Arctic aboard the retired **Icebreaker Krasin** (p120).

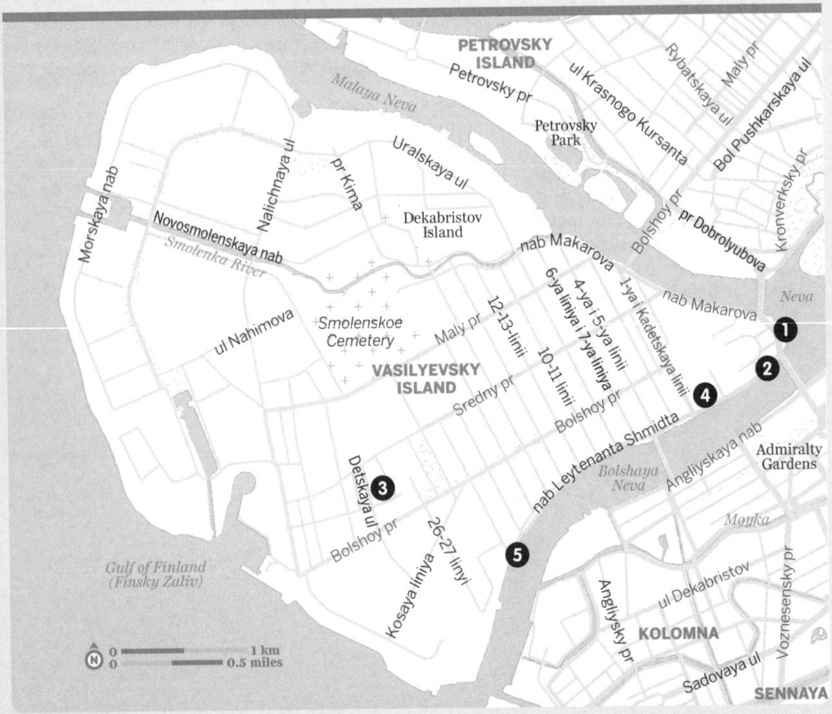

For more detail of this area, see Map p266

Explore: Vasilyevsky Island

Peter the Great originally intended this large triangular island to be the heart of his city. As such, it is among the oldest neighbourhoods in St Petersburg, especially the eastern tip known as the Strelka ('tongue of land'), which is crammed with institutions, museums and the sprawling campus of St Petersburg State University.

Further back from the Strelka, the island is an orderly, residential place, with a grid-system of wide roads full of shops, restaurants and cafes. It makes a great base for travellers, with fast connections to the centre, and plenty to do locally in the evenings.

The northern and western end of the island is rather postindustrial and remote, with the city's ferry port and the LenExpo exhibition centre blighting the landscape. However, in the past few years regeneration has come, with the fantastic new Erarta Museum of Contemporary Art well and truly putting the area on the map for more inquisitive travellers.

Local Life

- **Cool Street** Hang with the locals on 6-ya and 7-ya liniya, the main pedestrian and commercial street of Vasilyevsky Island. Full of cafes, bars, restaurants and shops, this is where to escape the tourist crowds at the Strelka.
- **Bridge Advice** If you're staying on Vasilyevsky Island, remember that in the summer months the bridges go up at night and you can't cross. Dvortsovy most stays up all night (1.25am to 4.50am), but Blagoveshchensky most has a short break and is down from 2.45am until 3.10am.

Getting There & Away

- **Metro** Vasilyevsky Island is served by two metro stations, both on Line 3. By far the most useful is Vasileostrovskaya, at the island's heart, while Primorskaya serves the far-flung northwestern corner of the island.
- **Bus** The number 7 bus goes between Primorskaya to pl Vosstaniya, via Nalichnaya ul, all of Bolshoy pr and Nevsky pr. Trolleybus 10 and 11 run similar routes.
- **Marshrutka** From Vasileostrovskaya metro station, the following *marshrutky* zip to the far end of Sredny pr: K30, K44, K62, K120, K128, K237, K690.

Lonely Planet's Top Tip

This tip might sound slightly nuts, but trust us. If you're heading to Vasileostrovskaya metro station from the city centre at any time during rush hour, be sure to get on the very last carriage (ie the one at the back end of the train), as this is nearest to the escalator when you arrive at the station. The platform at this very busy station is always swamped with people and you'll have to wait for minutes before being able to get on the escalator unless you use this sneaky trick.

Best Places to Eat

- Restoran (p122)
- Gintarus (p122)
- Russky Kitsch (p123)
- Sakartvelo (p122)

For reviews, see p122

Best Places to Drink

- Helsinki Bar (p123)
- Grad Petrov (p122)
- Black & White (p123)
- Stolle (p122)

For reviews, see p123

Best Museums

- Erarta Museum of Contemporary Art (p118)
- Kunstkamera (p118)
- Museum of Zoology (p120)
- Menshikov Palace (p120)

For reviews, see p118

SIGHTS

STRELKA — VIEWPOINT

Map p266 Among the oldest parts of Vasilyevsky Island, this eastern tip is where Peter the Great wanted his new city's administrative and intellectual centre to be. In fact, the Strelka became the focus of St Petersburg's maritime trade, symbolised by the colonnaded Customs House (now the Pushkin House, p122). The two Rostral Columns, archetypal St Petersburg landmarks, are studded with ships' prows and four seated sculptures representing four of Russia's great rivers: the Neva, the Volga, the Dnieper and the Volkhov. These were oil-fired navigation beacons in the 1800s (their gas torches are still lit on some holidays). The Strelka has one of the best views in the city, with the Peter and Paul Fortress to the left and the Hermitage, the Admiralty and St Isaac's Cathedral to the right.

KUNSTKAMERA — MUSEUM

Map p266 (Кунсткамера; ☎328 1412; www.kunstkamera.ru; Universitetskaya nab 3; adult/student R200/50; ⏲11am-6pm Tue-Sun, closed last Tue of the month; Ⓜ Admiralteyskaya) Also known as the Museum of Ethnology and Anthropology, the city's first museum was founded in 1714 by Peter himself. It is famous largely for its ghoulish collection of monstrosities, preserved 'freaks', two-headed mutant foeti, deformed animals and odd body parts, all collected by Peter with the aim of educating the notoriously superstitious Russian people. He wanted to demonstrate that the malformations were not the result of the evil eye or sorcery, but rather caused by 'internal damage as well as fear and the beliefs of the mother during pregnancy' – a marginally more enlightened view. This fascinating place is an essential St Petersburg sight, although not one for the faint-hearted. Think twice about bringing young children here and definitely give Kunstkamera a wide berth if you are pregnant yourself. Indeed, where else can you see specimens with such charming names as 'double-faced monster with brain hernia'?

Most people rush to see the sad specimens, largely ignoring the other interesting exhibitions on native peoples from around the world. Wonderfully kitsch dioramas exhibit rare objects and cultural practices from Asia, Oceania, Africa and the Americas. The

TOP SIGHTS ERARTA MUSEUM & GALLERIES OF CONTEMPORARY ART

This fantastic new contemporary art museum has suddenly made this far-flung and otherwise totally dead area of Vasilyevsky Island a destination in itself. Opened in 2010 and housed in a superbly converted Stalinist building, the museum divides neatly into two parts, spread over five floors. On the left-hand side is the permanent collection of some 2000 works of Russian art produced between the 1950s and the present day, while on the right-hand side the same number of floors house temporary exhibits, where the work is usually for sale. Your ticket includes entrance to the entire permanent collection and the first three floors of the temporary exhibits, but those on the 4th and 5th floors are an extra R150 each.

The permanent collection is an excellent survey of the past half-century of Russian art, and is particularly strong on late Soviet underground art. One nice curatorial touch is the frequent inclusion of objects depicted in paintings in real life – a bowl of apples will sit, for example, in front of a painting entitled *Apple Picking*. It's all terribly sleek, beautifully presented and the best place in St Petersburg to get a feel for contemporary Russian art. To get there from the metro, cross the road and take bus 6.

DON'T MISS

- *A Plank Bed*, Savely Lapitsky
- *USSR*, Yegeny Sarasov
- *Night Shift*, Nikolai Vikulov
- *Funeral of a Commissar*, Pyotr Gorban

PRACTICALITIES

- Map p266
- www.erarta.com, in Russian
- 29-aya liniya 2
- adult/under 21yr R300/150
- ⏲10am-10pm Thu-Tue
- Ⓜ Vasileostrovskaya

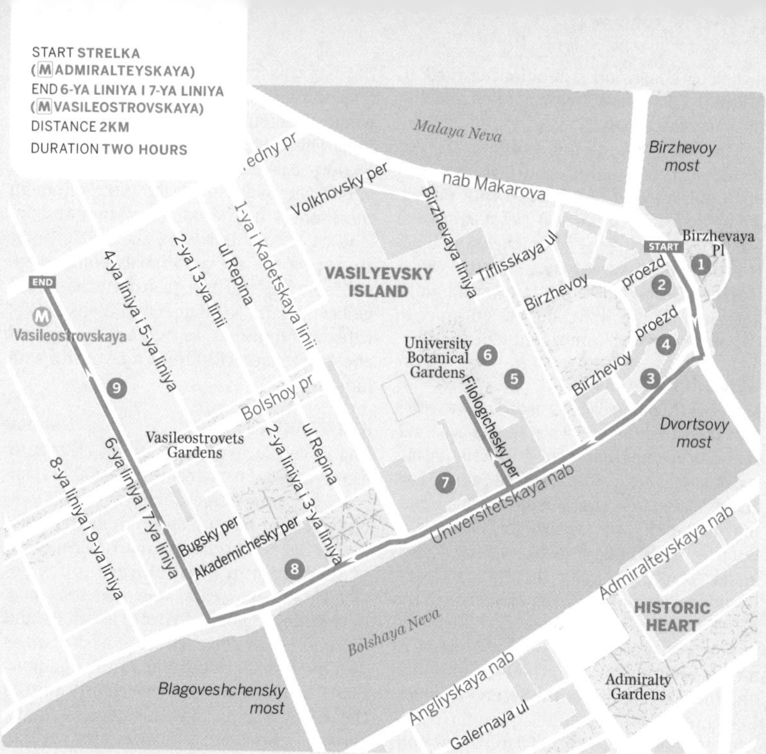

Neighbourhood Walk

Vasilyevsky Island

The eastern nose of Vasilyevsky Island, the 1 **Strelka**, boasts an unparalleled panorama, looking out over the Peter and Paul Fortress, the Hermitage, the Admiralty and St Isaac's Cathedral. A recent addition is the dancing fountain in the middle of the Neva. Overlooking the park, the old stock exchange now houses the 2 **Central Naval Museum**.

The Museum of Anthropology & Ethnography, 3 **Kunstkamera** was Russia's first museum, set up by Peter to dispel common superstitions about illness and disease. The collection of deformed foeti and animals is impressive, if a little disturbing. Next door is the equally impressive 4 **Museum of Zoology**.

At Peter's behest, Domenico Trezzini built the magnificent 5 **Twelve Colleges**, now St Petersburg State University, in 1722. The emperor based his bureaucracy here; separate entrances for each ministry signified their independence, while the unified facade highlighted collective goals. It is now part of the university, housing the 6 **Mendeleev Museum** among others. Behind these buildings, the grounds contain the beautiful university botanical gardens.

Peter originally gifted the entirety of Vasilyevsky Island to his best friend, Prince Menshikov, who proceeded to build the fabulous 7 **Menshikov Palace** on the north bank of the Neva. Menshikov's humble origins gave him a taste for opulence, and the interior is the best-preserved Petrine decor in the city.

Two Egyptian sphinx monuments mark the entrance to the institutional 8 **Academy of Arts Museum**, which houses 250 years' worth of artistic expression. On display are works by academy students and faculty over the years, as well as temporary exhibitions. A beautiful old library – lined with dusty volumes and packed with dark wood furniture – is open for visiting researchers.

Pedestrian-friendly 9 **6-ya liniya i 7-ya liniya** is one of the city's most pleasant places to sit at a sidewalk cafe and watch the world go by. Check out the charming Church of St Andrew, before sampling the goods at one of the sweet sidewalk cafes.

3rd floor houses an exhibition devoted to Mikhail Lomonosov, with a re-creation of his study-laboratory.

The top floors of the museum are not included in your admission price and are open only as part of a **guided tour** (in English for up to 4 people R2300, call in advance to book) of the Academy of Science's first **astronomical observatory** and the great **Gottorp Globe** (1654–64), a rotating globe and planetarium all in one. The entrance to the museum is on Tamozhenny per.

MENSHIKOV PALACE PALACE

Map p266 (Меншиковский дворец; www.hermitagemuseum.org; Universitetskaya nab 15; adult/student R60/free, free admission 1st Thu of the month, audio tour R150; ⌚10.30am-6pm Tue-Sat, until 5pm Sun; Ⓜ Vasileostrovskaya) The first stone building in the city, the Menshikov Palace was built to the grandiose tastes of Prince Alexander Menshikov, Peter the Great's closest friend and the first governor of St Petersburg. Menshikov was of humble origins (he is said to have sold pies on the streets of Moscow as a child), but his talent for both organisation and intrigue made him the second-most important person in the Russian Empire by the time of Peter's death in 1725. His palace, built mainly between 1710 and 1714, was the city's smartest residence at the time (compare it to Peter the Great's tiny Summer Palace). Peter used the palace for official functions and its interiors are some of the oldest and best preserved in the city.

It is now a branch of the Hermitage and while only a relatively small part of the palace is open to visitors, it's well worth coming here to see the impressively restored interiors. The 1st floor displays some stunning Dutch tile work, intended to fortify the rooms against humidity to help ease Menshikov's tuberculosis. Original furniture and the personal effects of Menshikov are on display. Each room has a fact sheet in English explaining its history, which you can borrow. Vavara's Chamber is particularly evocative of how the aristocracy lived during Peter's time. The main room in the palace is the magnificent Grand Hall, where balls and banquets were held.

MUSEUM OF ZOOLOGY MUSEUM

Map p266 (Зоологический музей; www.zin.ru; Universitetskaya nab 1/3; adult/student R200/70, free last Thu each month; ⌚11am-6pm Wed-Mon; Ⓜ Admiralteyskaya; 👪) One of the biggest and best of its kind in the world, the Museum of Zoology was founded in 1832 and has some amazing exhibits, including a vast blue whale skeleton that greets you in the first hall. The highlight is unquestionably the 44,000-year-old woolly mammoth thawed out of the Siberian ice in 1902, although there are a further three mammoths, including a baby one – all incredible finds. On top of the extraordinarily comprehensive collection of beasts from around the globe, upstairs you'll also find thousands of categorised insects, as well as a live **insect zoo** (adult/student R100/50), a favourite with kids.

ICEBREAKER KRASIN MUSEUM

Map p266 (Ледокол Красин; www.krassin.ru; nab Leytenanta Shmita; admission R200; ⌚11am-6pm Wed-Sun; Ⓜ Vasileostrovskaya) The *Krasin*, built in 1917, has a history almost as volatile as the 20th century: she was captured by the British in 1918, returned to the Soviet Union two years later and took part in a large number of Arctic missions and rescues in her long career. The *Krasin* is also the last surviving ship of the infamous PQ-15 convoy that sent aid from Britain to the USSR during WWII. She was finally decommissioned in 1971, and now you can visit the icebreaker's floating museum on a guided tour that leaves every hour on the hour from 11am to 5pm. Special tours of the engine room are available at 1pm and 3pm on Saturday and Sunday.

TWELVE COLLEGES UNIVERSITY

Map p266 (Двенадцать коллегий; Mendeleevskaya liniya 2; Ⓜ Vasileostrovskaya) Completed in 1744 and marked by a statue of scientist-poet Mikhail Lomonosov (1711–65), the 400m-long Twelve Colleges is one of St Petersburg's oldest buildings. It was originally meant for Peter's government ministries, but it is now part of the university, which stretches out behind it. Within these walls populist philosopher Nikolai Chernyshevsky studied, Alexander Popov created some of the world's first radio waves and a young Vladimir Putin earned a degree in law. This is also where Dmitry Mendeleev invented the periodic table of elements, and the building now contains the **Mendeleev Museum** (Mendeleevskaya liniya 2; admission R30; ⌚11am-3.30pm Mon-Fri). His cosy study has been lovingly preserved and you can see his desk (where he always stood rather than sat) and some early drafts of the periodic table.

PEOPLE'S WILL D-2 SUBMARINE MUSEUM
MUSEUM

Map p266 (Подводная лодка Д-2 Народоволец; Shkipersky protok 10; adult/student R300/150; ⏲11am-6pm Wed-Sun; Ⓜ Vasileostrovskaya) Opened as a fun, unique museum, the *People's Will (Narodovolets)* D-2 Submarine was one of the first six (diesel-fuelled) submarines built in the Soviet Union. It was in action between 1931 and 1956, and sank five German ships. Mandatory tours (in Russian) depart on the hour to take you through the sub to see how the crew of 53 lived and worked.

TEMPLE OF THE ASSUMPTION
CHURCH

Map p266 (Успенское подворье монастыря Оптина пустынь; cnr nab Leytenanta Shmidta & 14-ya liniya i 15-ya liniya; admission free; ⏲daily; Ⓜ Vasileostrovskaya) This stunning 1895 neo-Byzantine church was built by architect Vasily Kosyakov on the site of a former monastery. It was closed during the Soviet period, and from 1957 the building became the city's first – and very popular – year-round skating rink. The 7.7m, 861kg metal cross on the roof was only replaced in 1998. At the time of writing the exterior and interior were nearing completion after years of restoration, and the church is looking beautiful both inside and out. Enter through the courtyard.

NOVY MUSEUM
MUSEUM

Map p266 (Новый музей; www.novymuseum.ru, in Russian; 6-ya liniya 29; adult/student R200/100; ⏲11am-7pm Wed-Fri, noon-8pm Sat & Sun; Ⓜ Vasileostrovskaya) This interesting addition to Vasilyevsky Island's museum and arts scene is, as its name suggests, brand new. It was established by local businessman and art collector Aslan Chekhoev as space to show his private collection of Soviet underground and contemporary Russian art. In a fabulous period building conversion, it's been beautifully realised and boasts an interesting program of changing temporary exhibits as well as lecture series (sadly only in Russian).

ACADEMY OF ARTS MUSEUM
MUSEUM

Map p266 (Музей Академии Художеств; www.nimrah.ru; Universitetskaya nab 17; adult/student R300/150; ⏲11am-6pm Wed-Sun; Ⓜ Vasileostrovskaya) Two 3500-year-old sphinx monuments guard the entrance of the Russian Academy of Arts, and art lovers should not bypass the museum of this time-tested institution, which contains works by students and faculty since the academy's founding in 1857. This is the original location of the academy, where boys would live from the age of five until they graduated at age 15. It was an experiment to create a new species of human: the artist. For the most part, it worked; many great Russian artists were trained here, including Ilya Repin, Karl Bryullov and Anton Losenko. But the curriculum was designed with the idea that the artist must serve the state, and this conservatism led to a reaction against it. In 1863, some 14 students left to found a new movement known as the Wanderers (Peredvizhniki), which went on to revolutionise Russian art.

Nonetheless, the Academy of Arts has many achievements to show off, including numerous studies, drawings and paintings by academy members. On the 3rd floor you can examine the models for the original versions of Smolny Cathedral, St Isaac's Cathedral and the Alexander Nevsky Monastery. And if you had any doubt that the Academy of Arts is an august academic institution, take a peek into the fabulous old library. When you enter through the main door take the flight of stairs on your left up to the 2nd floor, where you can buy tickets.

FREE GEOLOGICAL MUSEUM
MUSEUM

Map p266 (Геологический музей; Sredny pr 74; admission free; ⏲10am-4pm Mon-Fri; Ⓜ Vasileostrovskaya) Located in the upper floors of the All-Russian Geological Science and Research Institute, this huge museum contains thousands of fossils, rocks and gems. The precious and semiprecious stones alone are dazzling: sparkling amethyst crystals (including one from the Altai mountains that is 1.5m long); huge chunks of malachite from the Urals; and a gorgeous gypsum 'rose' from Astrakhan. Also on display are prehistoric rocks and fossils, dinosaur fragments, animal skulls and mammoth tusks. The centrepiece of the museum is a huge map of the Soviet Union made entirely of precious gems, which won the Paris World Exposition Grand Prix in 1937.

On entering the building, you'll have to call ☎7446 on the in-house phone, and say you'd like to visit the museum *('ya hachoo pasyeteet moozáy')* and someone will come down to escort you.

CENTRAL NAVAL MUSEUM
MUSEUM

Map p266 (Центральный военно-морской музей; www.navalmuseum.ru; Birzhevaya pl 4; adult/student R400/200; ⏲11am-6pm Wed-Sun;

Ⓜ Admiralteyskaya) Housed in the Old Stock Exchange, the Central Naval Museum is a grand, expansive museum full of maps, model ships, flags and photos. It covers the history of the Russian navy up to the present, though sadly it's hard to recommend to anyone other than die-hard naval enthusiasts, as the foreigner price means it costs as much as the Hermitage, and it's by no way as interesting. The highlight of the display is *Botik,* Peter's first boat and, in his own words, the 'grandfather of the Russian Navy'.

PUSHKIN HOUSE MUSEUM

Map p266 (Пушкинский;www.pushkinskij dom.ru; nab Makarova 4; adult/student R350/200, tour R120; ⌚11am-4pm Mon-Fri; Ⓜ Vasileostrovskaya) The old customs house, topped with statues and a dome, is now home to the Institute of Russian Literature. Fondly called Pushkin House, the handsome building contains a small literary museum with dusty exhibits on Tolstoy, Gogol, Lermontov and Turgenev, as well as a room dedicated to the writers of the Silver Age. Call in advance for an English-language tour.

EATING

Vasilyevsky Island offers plenty of choice for the discerning diner. There's a particular glut of places near the Strelka and around the metro station Vasileostrovskaya.

TOP CHOICE **RESTORAN** RUSSIAN €€

Map p266 (Ресторанъ; www.elbagroup.ru; Tamozhenny per 2; mains R300-1200; Ⓜ Admiralteyskaya; 📋) Natural light filters in through large street-level windows, filling the spacious hall, and cream-coloured linens and hardwood floors make for a chic, contemporary decor. It's an interesting contrast to the name of the restaurant (the old-fashioned Russian spelling harks back to the days of Romanov splendour). The menu manages to combine the best of *haute russe* cuisine with enough modern flare to keep things interesting; try duck baked with apples or traditional Russian chicken pie with pickled cep mushrooms.

OLD CUSTOMS HOUSE RUSSIAN €€€

Map p266 (Старая таможня; Tamozhenny per 1; mains R950-1800; ⌚1pm-1am; Ⓜ Admiralteyskaya; 📶📋) This restaurant is not actually set in the old customs house, although it is around the corner in the historic building that houses St Petersburg's first museum (Kunstkamera). Famous for its wine list and excellent food, this restaurant is where you will see St Petersburg's uppermost classes partaking of filet mignon and caviar crepes.

STOLLE RUSSIAN €

Map p266 (www.stolle.ru; 1-ya liniya 50; mains R100-200; ⌚10am-10pm; Ⓜ Vasileostrovskaya; 📋👪) This cosy pie shop and cafe was the first in this chain. Aptly enough for a cafe that sells Saxon-style pies, it's located in the heart of St Petersburg's old German neighbourhood. For a full review, see p72.

GINTARUS LITHUANIAN €€

Map p266 (Sredny pr 5; mains R300-600; Ⓜ Vasileostrovskaya; 📋) Sumptuously decorated in dark woods and enjoying a very homely feel, this Lithuanian restaurant is a great spot for a smart and interesting meal. If Lithuanian cuisine doesn't exactly get your mouth watering, then there are plenty of other dishes, including a range of delicious soups and lots of grilled meats.

GRAD PETROV GERMAN €€

Map p266 (Градъ Петровъ; www.gradpetrov.com; Univesitetskaya nab 5; meals R400-1000; ⌚noon-1am; Ⓜ Admiralteyskaya; 📋) 'Peter's City' is a classy German restaurant with an impressive menu and cosy decor, and there's a separate bar where you can drink home-brewed Pilsners and Weizens. The menu is all about meat, and particularly sausages. See if you can manage the 1m-long Thüringer, served with onion sauce and red cabbage.

IMPERATOR RESTAURANT RUSSIAN €€

Map p266 (Император ресторан; Universitetskaya nab 5; mains R150-300; ⌚11am-11pm; Ⓜ Admiralteyskaya; 📋) Given its expensive nearby competition and the smartness of the area, this place is a great deal and a convenient lunch stop between the museums of the Strelka. The meaty menu has Russian and Caucasian standards and there's a good value R200 business lunch. Add to that a pleasant summer terrace and this is a winner.

SAKARTVELO GEORGIAN €€

Map p266 (Сакартвело; 12-ya liniya 13; mains R250-500; Ⓜ Vasileostrovskaya) This is Vasilyevsky Island's best Georgian restaurant – a friendly place on a residential backstreet, where sumptuous Caucasian feasts are served up at any time of day, backed up by live music most evenings. Delivery is also available.

RUSSKY KITSCH
RUSSIAN €€

Map p266 (www.concord-catering.ru; Universitetskaya nab 25; mains R350-800; Ⓜ Vasileostrovskaya;) The centrepiece of this crazy cafe is a ceiling fresco of a shameless Fidel Castro and Leonid Brezhnev entwined in a passionate embrace. It's the biggest and best example of a kitsch-laden venue, just as the name promises. The walls and ceilings are plastered with funny photo collages, featuring scenes from Soviet socialist realism alongside other anachronisms. Whether or not this is your style, there's a full Russian menu that runs from bliny to stewed fish and salmon pie. The glass-enclosed porch overlooking the Neva is a delightful place to sip a coffee.

MAMA ROMA
ITALIAN €€

Map p266 (www.mamaroma.ru; Sredny pr 6; mains R180-500; 11am-1am; Ⓜ Vasileostrovskaya;) Reliable Italian fare from decent pizza and fresh gnocchi to polenta, risotto and grills of all kinds, not to mention an excellent breakfast selection. The enormous photo menu makes ordering a doddle.

BLACK & WHITE
CAFE €

Map p266 (www.blackwhite.ru; 6-ya liniya 25; 8.30am-1am; Ⓜ Vasileostrovskaya) This sleek and welcoming coffee shop has a prime location on Vasilyevsky Island's main strip. The sidewalk seating offers the perfect place to sip your organic Colombian and watch the world go by. There's also a tasty breakfast menu and a good-value business lunch.

DRINKING & NIGHTLIFE

HELSINKI BAR
BAR

Map p266 (www.helsinkibar.ru; Kadetskaya liniya 31; noon-2am; Ⓜ Vasileostrovskaya) A slice of neighbouring Finland in the heart of St Petersburg, Helsinki is hands down the coolest place to drink on the island. The vibe is retro, with vinyl-spinning DJs, '70s ads on the walls, vintage furniture and Finnish home cooking. At weekends it stays open as long as people are still buying drinks – a great late-night option if you're staying locally and don't want to worry about the bridges.

GRAD PETROV
PUB

Map p266 (Градъ Петровъ; www.gradpetrov.com; Universitetskaya nab 5; noon-last customer; Ⓜ Admiralteyskaya) Fresh-brewed lager, Weizen, Pilsner, Dunkel and Hefeweizen – it's reason enough to stop by this upmarket microbrewery on Vasilyevsky Island. To top it off, the outdoor tables offer amazing views of St Isaac's Cathedral and the Admiralty across the Neva River.

SPORTS & ACTIVITIES

WATERVILLE AQUAPARK
WATER PARK

Off Map p266 (324 4700; www.waterville.ru; ul Korablestroiteley 14; adult/child Mon-Fri R660/470, Sat & Sun R960/680; 9am-11pm; Ⓜ Primorskaya;) This huge complex inside the Park Inn Pribaltiyskaya Hotel features miles of waterslides and rides, waterfalls, jet streams and wave pools. There is something for everyone here, as special pools for younger children have shallow waters and warmer temperatures, while a two-lane 25m pool is dedicated to water aerobics and lap-swimming. Also on-site: an international 'sweating complex' featuring Russian *banya*, Finnish sauna, Turkish *hammam* and Indian sauna. Prices quoted are for four hours of fun, but all-day admission is also available.

FITNESS HOUSE
GYM

Map p266 (www.fitnesshouse.spb.ru; nab Makarova 2; one-time entry R1000, one-month membership R5000; 7am-11pm Mon-Fri, 9am-10pm Sat & Sun; Ⓜ Admiralteyskaya) In a prominent place opposite the Strelka, this upscale gym offers a slew of fitness classes, from yoga to pilates to body sculpting. The huge complex has a dedicated room for every kind of equipment, including bike machines, cardio equipment and free weights.

VMF POOL
POOL

Map p266 (322 4505; Sredny pr 87; entry R550; 7am-10pm Mon-Sat, 8am-9pm Sun, closed 1 Jun–31 Aug; Ⓜ Vasileostrovskaya) This old-school facility is somewhat out in the wilds of Vasilyevsky Island and is very expensive given that it's more than a little dilapidated. However, it's an Olympic-sized pool and an excellent place to swim laps.

Petrograd & Vyborg Sides

PETROGRAD SIDE | VYBORG SIDE

Neighbourhood Top Five

❶ See the final resting place of the Romanovs, climb the bell tower for stunning views and enjoy the large range of museums and exhibits scattered around the **Peter and Paul Fortress** (p126).

❷ If the Hermitage left you wanting more, visit the state-of-the-art **Hermitage Storage Facility** (p132).

❸ Spend a day relaxing on the charming, wooded **Kirovsky Islands** (p131) – perfect for picnicking, boating and sunbathing.

❹ Make a detour to the historic **Sampsonievsky Cathedral** (p134) for one of the city's most beautiful church interiors.

❺ See how the Soviet elite really lived at the markedly unproletarian apartment that now houses the **Kirov Museum** (p130).

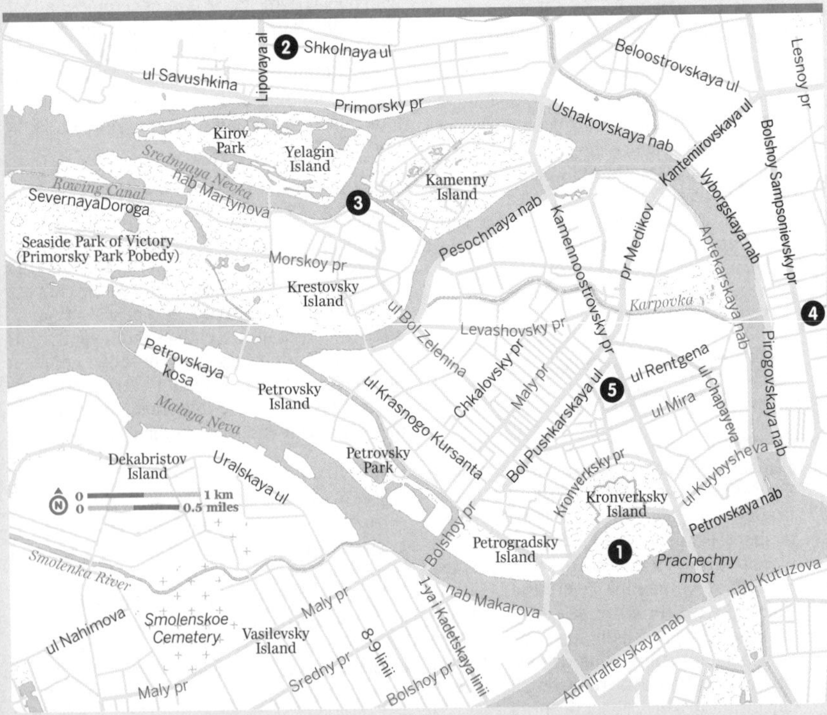

For more detail of this area, see Map p268

Explore: Petrograd & Vyborg Sides

The Petrograd Side, where Peter's city was first founded and from where it grew into the modern city it is today, is a fascinating place packed with historical sites and stunning Style Moderne architecture. It includes little Zayachy Island, home to the Peter and Paul Fortress, St Petersburg's most historic complex, as well as the three Kirovsky Islands – Yelagin, Krestovsky and Kamenny – three charming, wooded Neva delta islands that function today as the city's biggest park.

The enormous Vyborg Side encompasses all the land on the right bank of the Neva River, and is a sprawling, industrial area running from Okhta, across the river from the Alexander Nevsky Monastery all the way out to the Gulf of Finland. Its centre, if the diffuse area can even be said to have one, is around the Finland Station. The Vyborg Side has been consistently in the news recently, due to the controversial plans to build a 400m-high skyscraper here.

Local Life

➡ **Parks** If the weather's good, join the locals as they take to the Kirovsky Islands for fairground rides, boating, sunbathing and cycling through the woods – it's a total escape from the city just three metro stops from the city centre.

➡ **Free Art** Come and see the Hermitage Storage Facility for free on the first Thursday of the month. Even outside of this time it's a great bargain at R60.

➡ **Sunbathe Standing** A must for people watching as much as tanning, join the crowds on the beach at Zayachy Island where the serious sunbathers tan standing up.

Getting There & Away

➡ **Metro** The Petrograd Side is served by Gorkovskaya and Petrogradskaya on Line 2, and by Sportivnaya, Chkalovskaya and Krestovsky Ostrov on Line 5. The Vyborg Side has some 20 metro stations on it, mainly serving far-flung residential areas.

➡ **Bus** Bus 10 runs from the Vyborg Side at Chernaya Rechka, down Bolshoy pr on the Petrograd Side and on into the Historic Heart.

➡ **Marshrutka** *Marshrutka* 346 runs the length of Bolshoy pr and then turns left onto Kamennoostrovsky pr and on to the Vyborg Side.

Lonely Planet's Top Tip

Don't miss the Petrograd Side or Vyborg Side if you'd like to see the real St Petersburg – a far cry from the uniform beauty of the historic heart. The Petrograd Side is a good place to see the everyday life of the middle classes in the city and, while the Vyborg Side around pl Lenina is a vision of a post-industrial nightmare, your average Joes live in the Soviet housing estates further along the metro line – travel to the end of lines 1 or 2 and you'll see real city life.

Best Places to Eat

➡ Mesto (p135)
➡ Chekhov (p135)
➡ Staraya Derevnya (p135)
➡ Salkhino (p136)
➡ Makaronniki (p136)

For reviews, see p135 ➡

Best Parks

➡ Yelagin Island (p132)
➡ Kamenny Island (p132)
➡ Botanical Gardens (p130)
➡ Seaside Park of Victory (p132)

For reviews, see p129 ➡

Best Museums

➡ Hermitage Storage Facility (p132)
➡ The Commandant's House (p127)
➡ Kirov Museum (p130)
➡ Museum of Political History (p129)

For reviews, see p129 ➡

JONATHAN SMITH / LONELY PLANET IMAGES ©

TOP SIGHTS
PETER & PAUL FORTRESS

This large complex of defensive walls houses a former prison, museums and a cathedral, and is the kernel from which St Petersburg grew into the world city it is today. Anyone with any interest in the city's history or the Romanov dynasty, should definitely make sure they don't miss the Peter and Paul Fortress.

On little Zayachy Island, where Peter the Great first broke ground for St Petersburg, construction of the Peter and Paul Fortress began in 1703. Having captured this formerly Swedish settlement on the Neva, Peter set to turn the outpost into a modern Western city. While the fortress was built as a defence against the Swedes, it has never been utilised in the city's defence – unless you count incarceration of political 'criminals' as national defence.

SS Peter & Paul Cathedral

The **SS Peter and Paul Cathedral** (adult/student R200/90; ⏲May-Sep) has an impressive baroque interior, quite different from other Orthodox churches. It's today famous as the last resting place for nearly the entire Romanov dynasty. Peter I's grave is at the front on the right. Nicholas II and his family – minus Alexey and Maria – were the latest and most controversial additions in 1998.

The 122.5m-high **bell tower** (adult/student R130/70; ⏲tours noon, 11.30pm, 1pm, 2.30pm & 4pm May-Sep) remains the city's tallest structure. It offers a small exhibition about the renovation of the tower, as well as an up-close inspection of the bell-ringing mechanism. The main reason to climb all these steps, of course, is for the magnificent 360-degree panorama views of the city. The bell tower is open only by guided tour, which is only available

DON'T MISS...

- SS Peter and Paul Cathedral
- Trubetskoy Bastion
- The Commandant's House
- The Beach
- Rubbing Peter the Great's right forefinger for luck

PRACTICALITIES

- Map p268
- www.spbmuseum.ru
- Zayachy Island
- adult/student R350/170 combined entrance ticket valid for two days
- ⏲grounds 6am-10pm, museums 11am-6pm Thu-Tue
- Ⓜ Gorkovskaya

in Russian and takes an hour. Tickets for the tour are sold at the small boat house in front of the cathedral.

The Trubetskoy Bastion

In the fort's southwest corner are the grim cells of the **Trubetskoy Bastion** (entry to cells alone adult/student R170/70; ⏲11am-6pm Thu-Tue), where Peter the Great supervised the torture to death of his son and later tsars put political prisoners. Inmates included Lenin's brother Alexander Ulyanov, who was hanged for attempting to murder Tsar Alexander III, as well as Maxim Gorky, Leon Trotsky and Mikhail Bakunin. Even Fyodor Dostoevsky spent time here for membership of the illegal Petrashevsky Circle. The cells have been reconstructed and so are equipped much as they would have been in the late 19th century. Short biographies of the various inmates are posted on the doors.

The Commandant's House & Neva Gate

The **Commandant's House** (adult/student R100/60) contains a fascinating museum that charts the history of the St Petersburg region from medieval times to 1918. What starts as a fairly standard-issue plod through the city's history really comes alive once you're upstairs, with modern, interactive exhibits, even though there's still a lack of explanations in English.

In the south wall is the **Neva Gate**, a later addition (1787), where prisoners were loaded on boats for execution or exile. Notice the plaques here showing water levels of famous (and obviously devastating) floods. Outside there are fine views of the whole central waterfront, including the Hermitage. Along the wall to the left, throughout the year on sunny days, you can witness a motley crew of upright sunbathers (standing is supposed to give you a *proper* tan); in winter this is the territory of the Walrus Club, the crazy crew that chops a hole in the ice so they can take a dip (see p129). At noon every day a cannon is fired from Naryshkin Bastion.

Other Sights

Between the cathedral and the Senior Officers' Barracks is Mikhail Shemyakin's **Peter the Great statue**, which depicts him seated with strangely proportioned head and hands. When the statue was unveiled in 1991 it caused outrage among the citizens of St Petersburg, for whom Peter remains a saintly figure. Local lore has it that rubbing his right forefinger will bring good luck.

VISITING THE FORTRESS

Enter the fortress from the eastern side of the island. Just inside the main gate is a useful information office, where you can pick up a free map in English and buy tickets. You can also buy an overall ticket (adult/student R350/170), which allows access to all of the exhibitions on the island (except the bell tower, paid for separately) for two days.

Another good-value ticket, valid just for one day, includes entry to the two main sights of the fortress: the SS Peter and Paul Cathedral and the Trubetskoy Bastion (adult/student R280/150).

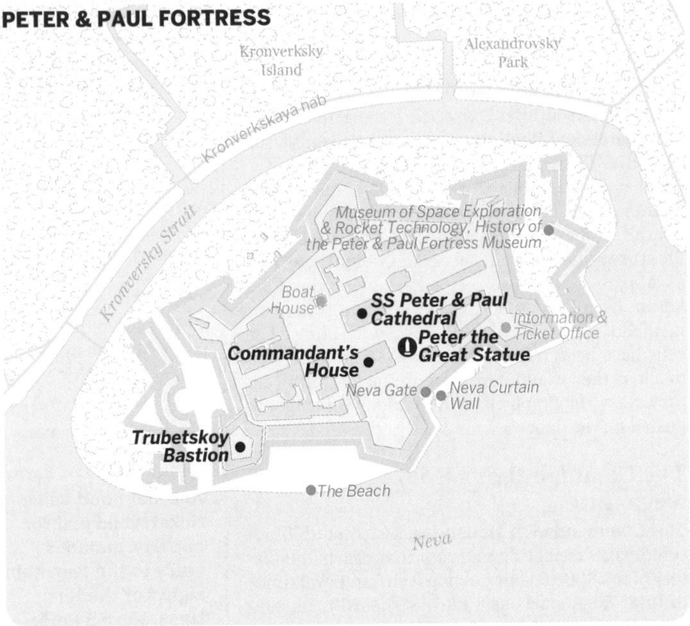

The **Neva Curtain Wall** (included on the complete ticket) houses five rooms containing exhibits about the history of the fortress, including a 10-minute film. You can also walk along the fortress wall, once you part with a pretty cheeky R150 at the main ticket office. The views towards the Hermitage are great, however.

Other Museums

There's a plethora of quirky museums on-site, none unmissable, but all have their own interest, including the Museum of Space Exploration & Rocket Technology (R50), History of the Peter & Paul Fortress Museum (R50) and various other temporary exhibits and galleries.

While there are plenty of snacks and drinks on sale within the fortress grounds, they're expensive and food quality isn't the best – so stock up on drinks before you come.

SIGHTS

Petrogradsky Island

During WWI, the city of St Petersburg changed its name to the less Germanic 'Petrograd'. At this time, the large island north of Zayachy became a fashionable place to live, and the name stuck to the island, if not the city. Today, this fabulous district boasts sparkling architecture, a lively commercial district and plenty of refreshing, uncrowded, green space. Many glorious mansions remain from its early development: stroll up Kamennoostrovsky pr for a Style Moderne treat. Look closely for architectural gems around Avstriyskaya pl, with its castlelike edifices, and around pl Lva Tolstogo, especially the whimsical, turreted Tower House.

PETER'S CABIN — HISTORICAL BUILDING

Map p268 (Домик Пётра Великого; Petrovskaya nab 6; adult/student R200/70; ⏲10am-5pm Wed-Mon; ⓂGorkovskaya) In a patch of trees east of the fortress is a stone building protecting a charming log cottage known as Peter's Cabin, St Petersburg's oldest surviving structure. The log cabin itself was supposedly built in three days in May 1703 for Peter to live in while he supervised the construction of the fortress and city.

The cabin has always been a sentimental site for St Petersburg. During WWII, Soviet soldiers would take an oath of allegiance to the city here, vowing to protect it from the Germans, before disappearing to the front. After the Siege of Leningrad, this was the first museum to reopen to the public.

The little cabin feels more like a shrine than a museum, but confirms Peter's love for the simple life with its unpretentious, homely feel, visibly influenced by the time he spent in Holland. Look out for the bronze bust of Peter by Parmen Zabello in the garden.

MUSEUM OF POLITICAL HISTORY — MUSEUM

Map p268 (Музей политической истории России; ☎313 6163; www.polithistory.ru; ul Kuybysheva 4; adult/student R200/100, English guide R700 (max 5 people); ⏲10am-6pm Fri-Wed; ⓂGorkovskaya) The Kshesinskaya Palace (built 1904) contains the Museum of Political History. Indeed, the building *is* political history – it was briefly the headquarters of the Bolsheviks and Lenin often gave speeches from the balcony. The elegant Style Moderne palace had previously belonged to Mathilda Kshesinskaya, famous ballet dancer and one-time lover of Nicholas II in his pre-tsar days.

Of special note are the rare satirical caricatures of Lenin that were published in magazines between the 1917 revolutions (the same drawings a few months later would have got the artist imprisoned or worse). By contrast, the Lenin memorial room is unchanged since Soviet days, with an almost religious atmosphere. You can visit Lenin's one-time office where he worked between the February and October Revolutions.

The main exhibition tackles Russian politics from the Brezhnev era to the present day. It's excellently curated, with explanations in English. Elsewhere, both the pre- and post-revolutionary period are covered in scrupulous (almost forensic) detail.

WALRUS CLUB

In the cold of winter, the Neva River is frozen solid, except for a pool formed by a 12-sq-metre hole in the ice. Ignoring the bitter wind, an enthusiastic young man strips down to his shorts and plunges into the pool, while a small crowd gathers round. He emerges from the icy waters and stands proudly with his arms above his head in the sign for Victory. Welcome to the Walrus Club, a group of hearty souls who exhort the health benefits of taking a daily dip.

This scene unfolds at the southeastern corner of Zayachy Island, in front of the Peter and Paul Fortress. A friendly blue walrus is painted on the fortress wall. Many of the ice swimmers, known as *morzhi* (walruses), have been paying regular visits to this spot for decades. They claim the practice eliminates muscle pains and boosts energy. More than a few *morzhi* – advancing in age – claim the icy dip improves their libido.

There is good news for all walrus wannabes: this is not an exclusive club – all are invited to take the plunge!

MOSQUE MOSQUE

Map p268 (Соборная мечеть; Kronverksky pr 7; Ⓜ Gorkovskaya) This beautiful working mosque (built 1910–14) was modelled on Samarkand's Gur-e Amir Mausoleum. Its fluted azure dome and minarets are stunning and surprisingly prominent in the city's skyline. The mosque is not generally open to the public, however, as *jamat* (congregation) members are highly protective of their mosque. However, if you are respectfully dressed (women should wear a head covering), you can walk through the gate at the northeast side and ask the guard for entry. If you are asked in, remove your shoes, do not talk and do not take photos.

KIROV MUSEUM MUSEUM

Map p268 (Музей Кирова; www.kirovmuseum.ru; Kamennoostrovsky pr 26/28; admission R90; ⌚11am-6pm Thu-Tue; Ⓜ Petrogradskaya) Sergei Kirov, Leningrad party boss and one of the most powerful men in Russia in the early 1930s, spent 10 years of his life at this decidedly unproletarian apartment, until his murder at Stalin's behest in 1934 sparked a wave of deadly repression in the country. The apartment is now a fascinating museum showing how the Bolshevik elite really lived: take a quick journey back to the days of Soviet glory, including choice examples of 1920s technology, such as the first-ever Soviet-produced typewriter and a conspicuously noncommunist GE fridge, complete with plastic food inside.

Many of Kirov's personal items are on display, including gifts from Leningrad workers, such as a portrait made completely out of feathers. His office from the Smolny Institute has been fully reconstructed in one of the rooms. A gory but reverential display shows the clothes that Kirov wore when he was killed. The tiny hole in the back of his cap was where he was shot (blood stains intact) and the torn seam on his jacket's left breast was where doctors tried to revive his heart.

When you enter the building, take the lift to the 5th floor to buy your ticket and then go down to the 4th floor to enter the museum.

BOTANICAL GARDENS BOTANICAL GARDENS

Map p268 (Ботанический сад; ul Professora Popova 2; grounds adult/child R40/20, greenhouse R180/90; ⌚grounds 10am-6pm daily May-Sep, greenhouse 11am-4pm Sat-Thu May-Sep; Ⓜ Petrogradskaya) On eastern Aptekarsky (Apothecary) Island, this quiet jungle was once a garden of medicinal plants that gave the island its name. The gardens date to 1714, when they were founded by Peter the Great himself. The botanical gardens contain 26 greenhouses on a 22-hectare site. It is a lovely place to stroll and a fascinating place to visit – and not just for botanists. At the turn of the 20th century, these were the second-biggest botanical gardens in the world, behind London's Kew Gardens. However, 90% of the plants died during WWII, which makes the present collection all the more impressive (you will recognise the 'veterans' by their war medals).

A highlight is the tsaritsa nochi *(Selenicereus pteranthus)*, a flowering cactus that blossoms only one night a year, usually in mid-June. On this night, the gardens stay open until morning for visitors to gawk at the marvel and sip champagne.

The entrance is on the corner of Aptekarsky per and nab reki Karpovki.

ALEXANDROVSKY PARK PARK

Map p268 (Ⓜ Gorkovskaya; 👪) As you make your way from the metro to the fortress on Zayachy Island, you will undoubtedly pass through this bustling park. Don't come here looking for peace and quiet – it is too close to traffic and perpetually thronged with people – but if you have kids in tow, there are a few entertainment options worth considering.

The **Planetarium** (Планетарий; www.planetary-spb.ru in Russian; Alexandrovsky Park 4; adult/child R250/140; ⌚noon-6pm; Ⓜ Gorkovskaya) has 50-minute shows on the hour throughout the day, as well as an observatory and several different halls. The **Leningradsky Zoo** (Ленинградский зоопарк; www.spbzoo.ru; Alexandrovsky Park 1; adult/child R350/100; ⌚summer 10am-8pm daily, winter 10am-5pm Tue-Sun; 👪) is full of rather bored-looking animals and happy kids, but is overall very worth visiting for its range of species, including a large number of polar bears.

ARTILLERY MUSEUM MUSEUM

Map p268 (Военно-исторический музей Артиллерии; www.artillery-museum.ru; Alexandrovsky Park 7; adult/student courtyard R50/20, museum R300/150; ⌚11am-6pm Wed-Sun; Ⓜ Gorkovskaya; 👪) The Artillery Museum is housed in the fort's original arsenal, across the moat from the Peter and Paul Fortress. It chronicles Russia's military history, with examples of weapons dating all the way back to the Stone Age. The centrepiece is Lenin's armoured car, which he rode in triumph from the Finland Station. Even if you are not impressed by guns and bombs, who can resist climbing around on the tanks and trucks that adorn the courtyard?

FREE **CRUISER AURORA** MUSEUM

Map p268 (Крейсер Аврора; www.aurora.org.ru; Petrovskaya nab; 10.30am-4pm Tue-Thu, Sat & Sun; M Gorkovskaya;) Moored on the Bolshaya Nevka is the *Aurora,* a mothballed cruiser from the Russo-Japanese War, built in 1900. From a downstream mooring on the night of 25 October 1917, its crew fired a blank round from the forward gun as a signal for the start of the assault on the Winter Palace. During WWII the *Aurora* was sunk by German bombs but was later raised and repaired. Now, restored and painted in pretty colours, it's a living museum that swarms with kids on weekends. It's possible to see the crew's quarters as well as endless communist propaganda and a collection of friendship banners from around the world.

FREE **SIGMUND FREUD MUSEUM OF DREAMS** MUSEUM

Map p268 (Музей сновидений Фрейда; www.freud.ru; Bolshoy pr 18A; noon-5pm Tue & Sun; M Sportivnaya) This odd conceptual exhibition, based on abstractions and ideas, not artefacts, is an outgrowth of the Psychoanalytic Institute that houses it. The two-room exhibition aims to stimulate your subconscious as you struggle to read the display symbolising what Freud himself would have dreamt. Illustrations of Freud's patients' dreams and quotations line the dimly lit, incense-scented hall. English is spoken.

CHALIAPIN HOUSE MUSEUM MUSEUM

Map p268 (Дом-музей Шаляпина; www.theatremuseum.ru; ul Graftio 2B; adult/student R100/50; noon-6pm Wed-Sun; M Petrogradskaya) Opera buffs will want to make the journey out to this house-museum (a branch of the State Museum of Theatre & Music) where the great singer Fyodor Chaliapin lived before fleeing the Soviet Union in 1922. The kindly babushkas (clearly music lovers) will probably play some of the singer's recordings for you as you peruse his personal effects.

FREE **TOY MUSEUM** MUSEUM

Map p268 (Музей игрушки; nab reki Karpovki 32; 11am-6pm Tue-Sun; M Petrogradskaya) Since 1997, this privately run museum has been collecting toys from all over Russia and presenting them in three sections – folk toys, factory toys and artisanal toys. Examples of the latter include toys made in Sergiev Posad, home of the ubiquitous *matryoshka* (nesting doll), a creation often assumed to be far older than it is, being created for the first time only in the 19th century. The Toy Museum is charming and often has very interesting temporary exhibitions too.

YELIZAROV MUSEUM MUSEUM

Map p268 (Музей-квартира Елизаровых; ul Lenina 52, flat 24; adult/student R200/100; 11am-4pm Mon-Tue & Thu-Sat; M Chkalovskaya) This unique building (known locally as the 'boat house' due to its uncanny similarities externally to a large cruise liner) was built in 1913 at the height of St Petersburg's lust for Style Moderne. It would otherwise be unremarkable were it not for the fact that Lenin's wife's family lived here and the great revolutionary himself laid low here before the revolution while organising the workers.

The flat's delightful turn-of-the-20th-century fittings have been preserved intact, and by the look of things, Lenin had a very bourgeois time of it. See the bathroom, where Vladimir Ilyich had a daily splash and the telephone that today still bears Lenin's home phone number. Tap in 24 at the front door and then go up the stairs to the 3rd floor when you're buzzed in.

PETERSBURG AVANT-GARDE MUSEUM MUSEUM

(Музея петербургского авангарда; ul Professora Popova 10; adult/student R70/50; 11am-6pm Mon & Thu-Sun, 11am-5pm Tue; M Petrogradskaya) Also known as the House of Matyushin, this small museum occupies a charming grey-painted wooden cottage dating from the mid-19th century that was once the home of avant-garde artist Mikhail Matyushin (1861–1934). Displays relating to Matyushin's work and that of his coterie can be found inside.

Kirovsky Islands

This is the collective name for the three outer delta islands of the Petrograd Side – Kamenny, Yelagin and Krestovsky. Once marshy forests, the islands were granted to 18th- and 19th-century court favourites and developed into elegant playgrounds. Still mostly parkland, they are leafy venues for picnics, river sports and White Nights' cavorting, as well as home to St Petersburg's super rich.

Yelagin Island is an especially attractive oasis, as it is closed to cars. Krestovsky and Kamenny Islands are also pleasant places to stroll, as there is plenty of parkland, as well as a sort of New Russian suburbia. The metro station Krestovsky Ostrov provides easy access to both Krestovsky and Yelagin Islands; for Kamenny you can walk across the bridge from metro station Chyornaya Rechka on the Vyborg Side.

KAMENNY ISLAND ISLAND

Map p268 (MChyornaya Rechka) Century-old dachas (country cottages; now inhabited by very wealthy locals) line the lanes that twist their way around Kamenny (Stone) Island. The wooded island is punctuated by a series of canals, lakes and ponds, and is pleasant for strolling any time of year. At the east end of the island the **Church of St John the Baptist** (built 1776–81) has been charmingly restored. Behind it, Catherine the Great built the big, classical **Kamennoostrovsky Palace** for her son; it is now a weedy military sanatorium (off limits to casual callers).

The rest of the island is a woodsy, mostly residential neighbourhood. For years a dead oak, supposedly planted by Peter the Great, stood in the middle of the Krestovka embankment. The old oak has been removed and replaced with a young, healthy tree; but it is still known as **Peter's Tree**.

YELAGIN ISLAND ISLAND

Map p268 (www.elaginpark.spb.ru, in Russian; admission Mon-Fri free, Sat & Sun adult/student R50/30; 6am-10pm; MKrestovsky Ostrov) This island is basically a giant park – a delightful car-free (and even bike-free at weekends) zone that is a fantastic place to wander. It was landscaped by the architect Carlo Rossi, so you can expect the loveliest of settings. The centrepiece is the **Yelagin Palace** (Yelagin ostrov 1; admission R200; 10am-6pm Wed-Sun), also by Rossi, which Alexander I built for his mother, Empress Maria. The very beautiful restored interiors of the main house include old furnishings on loan from the Grand Europe and Astoria Hotels; don't miss the stupendous 1890s carved-walnut ensemble in the study and the incredible inlaid-wood floors. Other nearby estate buildings sometimes host temporary exhibitions too.

The rest of the island is a lovely network of paths, greenery, lakes and channels. At the northern end of the island, you can rent rowing boats (per hour R300) to explore the ponds or in-line skates to explore the paths; in winter it's an ideal setting for sledding, skiing and skating (see p139). At the west end, a plaza looks out to the Gulf of Finland: sunsets are resplendent from here.

KRESTOVSKY ISLAND ISLAND

Map p268 (MKrestovsky Ostrov) The biggest of the three northern islands, Krestovsky consists mostly of the vast **Seaside Park of Victory** (Primorsky Park Pobedy), dotted with sports fields. Not far from the metro station, **Divo Ostrov** (www.divo-ostrov.ru; admission free, rides R50-100; 11am-8pm daily Jun-Aug, 11am-8pm Sat & Sun Sep-May; MKrestovsky Ostrov;) is a low-rent Disney-style amusement park with exciting fairground rides that kids will adore. You can also rent bikes and rollerblades here.

Vyborg Side

HERMITAGE STORAGE FACILITY MUSEUM

Map p268 (Реставрационно-хранительский центр Старая деревня; 340 1026; www.hermitagemuseum.com; Zausadebnaya ul 37A; admission R60; tours 11am, 1pm, 1.30pm & 3.30pm Wed-Sun; MStaraya Derevnya) If you left the Hermitage wanting more, the museum's restoration and storage facility provides a superb reason for dragging yourself out to northern St Petersburg. Inside the state-of-the-art complex you'll be led through a handful of rooms housing but a fraction of the museum's collection. This is not a formal exhibition as such, but the guides are knowledgeable and the examples chosen for display (paintings, furniture, and carriages) are wonderful. The highlight is undoubtedly the gorgeous wool and silk embroidered Turkish ceremonial tent, presented to Catherine the Great by the Sultan Slim III in 1793. Beside it stands an equally impressive modern diplomatic gift: a massive wood carving of the mythical garuda bird, given by Indonesia to the city for its 300th anniversary.

The Hermitage has big plans for this site and construction of an enormous golden-yellow glass facility was being completed at the time of research. The storage facility is directly behind the big shopping centre opposite the metro station.

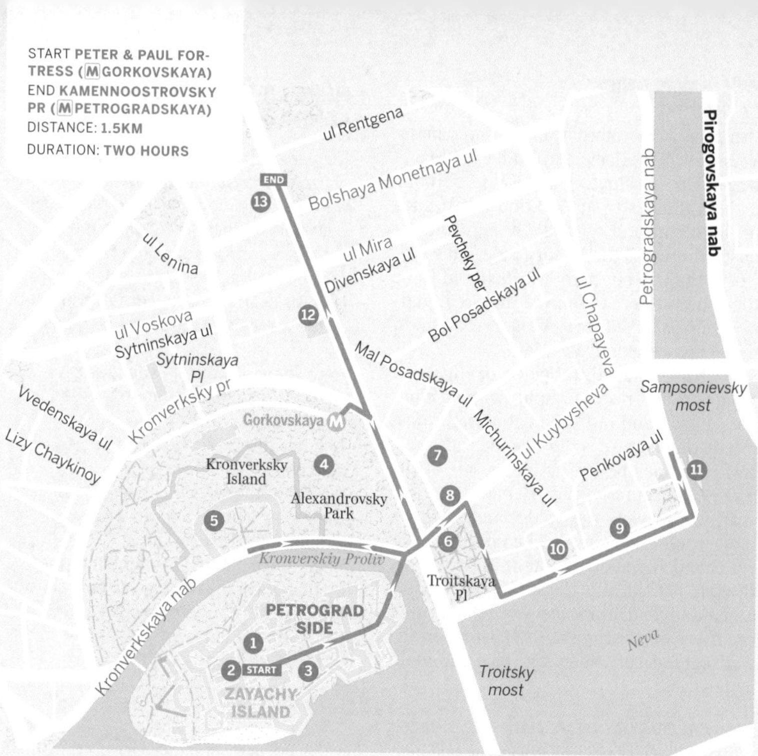

Neighbourhood Walk

Zayachy & Petrogradsky

St Petersburg was founded on 1 **Zayachy Island**, within the walls of the city's first defensive installation, the 2 **Peter and Paul Fortress**. Make sure you check out the 3 **SS Peter & Paul Cathedral**, the last resting place of Peter the Great and almost every tsar since.

The circular 4 **Alexandrovsky Park** surrounds Zayachy Island on three sides, so you'll have to pass through it on your way. It contains a small amusement park, a zoo, a planetarium and plenty of other fun for people of all ages.

Hawks flock to the massive 5 **Artillery Museum**, appropriately placed along the moat opposite the fortress. Its enormous exhibition features weapons through the ages, as well as plenty of tanks and bombers to climb on in the courtyard.

The central square of Peter's early city, 6 **Troitskaya pl** (Trinity Sq) formerly had as its centrepiece the enormous Trinity Cathedral, where Peter attended Mass. The cathedral was destroyed and now the square's most striking building is the 7 **Mosque**. The palace of ballerina Mathilda Kshesinskaya now houses the 8 **Museum of Political History**.

9 **Petrovskaya nab** is home to two historic landmarks. 10 **Peter's Cabin** is considered the oldest structure in the city and the city's soul. Off the island's eastern tip, the 11 **Cruiser Aurora** is a legendary battleship, surviving since the Russo-Japanese War.

Stroll up the stylish 12 **Kamennoostrovsky pr** to get a sense of Petrograd's ever-growing vibrancy. It is packed with shops (see p138), theatres and restaurants (see p135), not to mention the ever-popular 13 **Kirov Museum**.

FREE **SAMPSONIEVSKY CATHEDRAL** CATHEDRAL

Map p268 (www.cathedral.ru; Bolshoy Sampsonievsky pr 41; ⏲11am-6pm Thu-Tue; Ⓜ Vyborgskaya) This fascinating light-blue baroque cathedral dates from 1740 and is a beautiful highlight of a remarkably ugly and industrial area of the Vyborg Side – it's well worth the trip out here. It is believed to be the church where Catherine the Great married her one-eyed lover Grigory Potemkin in a secret ceremony in 1774.

Today it's a delightful place, having been repainted and restored to its original glory both inside and out. The cathedral's most interesting feature is the calendar of saints, two enormous panels on either side of the nave, each representing six months of the year, where every day is decorated with a mini-icon of its saint(s). The enormous silver chandelier above the altar is also something to behold, as is the stunning baroque, green-and-golden iconostasis. Don't miss the frieze of a young Peter the Great on the wall behind you when you face the main iconostasis.

HERE LIE THE PEOPLE OF LENINGRAD

No place better captures the horror of the holocaust that took place in wartime Leningrad than Piskaryovskoe Cemetery. Defiant, yet moving, music emanates from the speakers; a devastated Mother Russia casts her eyes over the destruction and the inscription on the wall behind the sculpture reads:

Here lie the people of Leningrad
Here are the citizens – men, women and children
And besides them the Red Army soldiers
Who gave their lives
Defending you, Leningrad,
Cradle of the Revolution,
Their noble names we cannot number
So many lie beneath the eternal granite
But of those honoured by this stone
Let no one forget
Let nothing be forgotten.

Olga Bergolts, Siege survivor

PISKARYOVSKOE CEMETERY CEMETERY

(Пискарёвское мемориальное кладбище; www.pmemorial.ru; pr Nepokoryonnikh 72; ⏲10am-5pm; Ⓜ Ploshchad Muzhestva) It's hard work getting to this rather remote cemetery, but as the main burial place for the victims of the Nazi blockade in WWII, it is a poignant memorial to the tragedy.

Originally, this area was just an enormous pit where unnamed and unmarked bodies were dumped. Some half a million people were laid to rest here between 1941 and 1943, during the siege (see p190). In 1960 the remodelled cemetery was opened and has been an integral part of the city's soul ever since. Every year on Victory Day (9 May) the cemetery is packed out with mourners, many of whom survived the blockade or lost close relatives to starvation.

From metro station Ploshchad Muzhestva, take *marshrutka* 123 in the direction of Ladozhskaya metro, which passes by the entrance to the cemetery.

BUDDHIST TEMPLE TEMPLE

Map p268 (www.dazan.spb.ru; Primorsky pr 91; ⏲10am-7pm Thu-Tue; Ⓜ Staraya Derevnya) This beautiful *datsan* (temple) was built between 1909 and 1915 at the instigation of Pyotr Badmaev, a Buddhist physician to Tsar Nicholas II. Money was raised from all over Russia, and as far afield as Thailand and England, by various Buddhist organisations; it even gained the support of the Dalai Lama in Lhasa.

In the 1930s the communists shut the temple, arrested many of the monks and used the building as a military radio station. In the 1960s it was taken over by the Zoological Institute and used as laboratories. Thankfully, however, the damage was not particularly profound and the *datsan* was returned to the city's small Buddhist community in 1990, since when it has been renovated. Visitors are welcome.

FINLAND STATION HISTORICAL BUILDING

Map p268 (Финляндский вокзал; pl Lenina 6; Ⓜ Ploshchad Lenina) Finland Station is where Lenin finally arrived in 1917 after 17 years in exile abroad. Here he gave his legendary speech from the top of an armoured car to a crowd who had heard of, but never seen the man. After fleeing a second time he again arrived here from Finland, this time disguised as a railway fireman, and the locomotive he rode in is displayed on the platform. It's not really the same station, as it was rebuilt in the 1970s in the drabbest possible Soviet style. However, its historic significance remains. Walk out onto the square that still bears Lenin's name and you'll see a marvellous statue of the man himself at the far end.

KRESTY PRISON HISTORICAL BUILDING

Map p268 (Тюрьма Кресты; www.kresty.ru; Arsenalnaya nab 7; admission R350; ⌚tours noon, 1.30pm & 3pm Sat & Sun year-round, plus 4.30pm Sat & Sun May-Oct; Ⓜ Ploshchad Lenina) Kresty is St Petersburg's main holding prison; if you're busted here, Kresty's where they take you to await whatever it is that awaits you. You wouldn't want to find out; conditions are much better now than when the prison was at its most crowded, but it is still hardly a pleasant place.

Kresty is the oldest working prison in Russia, built in 1892. Tours visit the holding areas, the grounds and a small museum. This definitely constitutes a unique day out in the city. You will have the chance to see the six-bunk cells and the frightening solitary-confinement closets. Inmates are on-site – working, walking or peeking out at you through slats in their cells. Visitors are told not to interact with them. The little museum has exhibitions on past residents (including Trotsky and the entire Provisional Government from 1917), as well as art made by prisoners with lots of time on their hands.

Each tour can accommodate up to 25 people, so it's worth arriving early and claiming your spot in the queue (your passport must be shown on entry). Tours are in Russian only, although several tour operators organise excursions in English (see p221).

SITE OF PUSHKIN'S DUEL HISTORICAL SITE

(Место дуэли Пушкина; Kolomyazhsky pr; Ⓜ Chyornaya Rechka) This is a point of literary pilgrimage for lovers of Russia's poetic genius, Alexander Pushkin, who was killed in a duel with the Frenchman Georges d'Anthès on 8 February 1837. The story has developed a certain mythology around it in the past two centuries: see p67 for details. A marble monument now stands on the place where Pushkin was shot and there are always fresh flowers here.

From the metro station at Chyornaya Rechka, walk down Torzhkovskaya ul and turn left at the first light on Novosibirskaya ul. Walk straight to the end of the road, cross the train tracks and enter the park. The monument is across the park to the left.

EATING

The Petrograd Side – well heeled and middle class – has a large number of excellent restaurants including plenty of vegetarian choices, two good Georgian restaurants and one of our favourite Russian eateries in the city. Choice on the Vyborg Side is not nearly so rich, but there are a couple of good, if rather remotely located, options.

TOP CHOICE MESTO INTERNATIONAL €€

Map p268 (Kronverksky pr 59; mains R300-600; ⌚11am-midnight; Ⓜ Gorkovskaya; 📶📋🖋) Despite looking brand new, this Petrograd Side place has been quietly winning fans for a decade now. After a recent refit it's looking better than ever though, with art deco fittings, a beautiful glass and marble counter and upholstered benches you could almost fall asleep on. The menu is eccentric but interesting: filling shepherd's pie, châteaubriand and beef Wellington are supplemented by more imaginative dishes such as green gazpacho and pumpkin and prawn soup, and the restaurant's tagline – 'we have a small menu and fresh produce' – certainly rings true. There's breakfast served between 11am and 1pm and in the evening the owner will often play the piano, rounding off a great little Petrograd find.

TOP CHOICE CHEKHOV RUSSIAN €€

Map p268 (Чехов; Petropavlovskaya ul 4; mains R350-700; Ⓜ Petrogradskaya; 📋) Despite a totally nondescript appearance from the street, this Russian restaurant's charming interior perfectly recalls that of a 19th-century dacha and makes for a wonderful setting for any meal. The menu (not to mention the staff's attire) is very traditional and features lovingly prepared Russian classics.

TOP CHOICE STARAYA DEREVNYA RUSSIAN €€

Map p268 (Старая деревня; ☎431 0000; www.sderevnya.ru; ul Savushkina 72; mains R300-500; ⌚1-10pm; Ⓜ Chyornaya Rechka) This tiny, family-run hideaway is well off the beaten track, but its intimate atmosphere and delectable food are one-of-a-kind. Try old Russian recipes such as beef in plum and nut sauce or ham in oranges. The small size of the restaurant guarantees personal service, but reservations are a must. From the metro station, take any tram down ul Savushkina and get off at the third stop.

VOLNA
INTERNATIONAL €€

Map p268 (Волна; www.volna.su; Petrovskaya nab 5; mains R200-500; MGorkovskaya;) Opposite Peter's Cabin, the oldest structure in the city, is this sleek and wonderfully laid-back lounge restaurant with a great terrace perfect for a relaxed lunch over a bottle of wine. Inside it's a bit more upmarket, but remains unfussy. The large menu ranges from risotto, salads and pasta to a selection of Asian dishes from the wok.

LE MENU
VEGETARIAN €€

Map p268 (pr Dobrolyubova 1; mains R100-300; 9am-11pm; MGorkovskaya;) This smart new cafe is brought to you by the passionate vegetarians who run veggie-chain Troitsky Most. In fact there's near identical fare here, the only difference is that the setting is worlds away – all wooden floorboards and chandeliers, for those who appreciate meatless meals in style.

SALKHINO
GEORGIAN €€

Map p268 (Салхино; Kronverksky pr 25; mains R300-600; MGorkovskaya;) An excellent Georgian restaurant, Salkhino serves big portions of delicious food in a convivial, arty setting where you feel more like a guest in someone's house than a customer. Pastel-coloured walls are adorned with paintings by local artists and the menu of home-cooked Georgian meals will keep everyone happy.

MAKARONNIKI
ITALIAN €€

Map p268 (Макаронники; www.makaronniki.ru; pr Dobrolyubova 16; mains R300-1000; MSportivnaya;) With its extremely unlikely location at the top of a business centre, you really do have to know about this surprisingly cool and charming Italian place on the roof. The location actually seems incidental – don't expect any life-changing views from here – but the menu of modern Italian food, from pasta and pizza to rabbit served with cabbage and osso bucco, and a laid-back and whimsical feel make this a place to detour for.

LES AMIS DE JEAN-JACQUES ROUSSEAU
FRENCH €€

Map p268 (Жан-Жак Руссо; www.jan-jak.com; Gatchinskaya ul 2; mains R300-600; MPetrogradskaya;) You can't beat this delightful wine bar for eating and drinking like they do in Paris. The menu boasts excellent, affordable bistro fare, including breakfast (served all day on weekends), as well as a huge selection of French wines. The cosy, comfortable interior and sidewalk seating are equally inviting, so take a seat and pour yourself a glass of Bordeaux.

TBILISO
GEORGIAN €€€

Map p268 (Тбилисо; Sytninskaya ul 10; mains R300-1250; MGorkovskaya;) Decidedly upscale as far as Georgian restaurants go, Tbiliso has a great interior with tiled tables and big booths, made more private by intricate latticework between them. This place is a beloved St Petersburg institution, thanks to its top-notch cooking and Georgian chefs. Classics such as *khachapuri* (cheese bread) and chicken *tabaka* (flattened chicken cooked in spices) are sumptuously prepared, and there's a huge range of wines – look no further for a real blow-out meal.

NA RECHKE
RUSSIAN €€€

Map p268 (На речке; www.ginzaproject.ru; Olgina ul 8; mains R500-1900; MKrestovsky Ostrov;) 'On the River' is the latest outpost of the ever-growing Ginza Project restaurant group and it makes for a great lunch place if you're spending a lazy day on the Kirovsky Islands. Housed in a rather strange, somewhat cobbled-together looking place overlooking the river, inside it's a charming lounge-style restaurant with a big terrace serving up superb Russian home cooking, with (perhaps unsurprisingly) a heavy focus on fish.

NA ZDOROVIE!
RUSSIAN €€

Map p268 (На Здоровье!; http://old.concord-catering.ru/restaurants/na-zdorovie/; Bolshoy pr 13; mains R400-600; MSportivnaya;) This playful restaurant's decor draws on pre- and post-revolutionary folklore, allowing you to eat like 'the tsars and the Soviet dictators'. The menu is made up of old Russian recipes that have been recreated here, including veal stuffed with cherries, and perch served with cheese, lemon and dill. It's definitely a place to try some more unusual Russian dishes in a *very* Russian setting.

YAKATORIYA
JAPANESE €€

Map p268 (www.yakitoriya.spb.ru; Petrovskaya nab 4; meals R300-500; MGorkovskaya) A second branch of Moscow's favourite sushi chain is on Petrogradsky Island. See p74 for a full review.

UNDERGROUND ART

If you've had your fill of museums and palaces in St Petersburg, an ideal way to spend a rainy day is to take a tour of underground art. Metro line 1 (that's the red line on the official metro map) between the Pl Vosstaniya and Avtovo metro stations is striking for its station designs, which include the following:

Avtovo The red and gold mosaic at the end of the platform is only the beginning of the grandeur. Marble and cut-glass clad columns hold up the roof, while a relief of soldiers stands in the temple-like entrance.

Baltiyskaya Look for a naval theme here, with a wavy motif on the mouldings along the platform ceiling and a vivid marble mosaic at the end of the platform depicting the volley from the *Aurora* in 1917.

Kirovsky Zavod This station is named after the nearby engineering plant; the decoration along the platform also takes its inspiration from the oil wells and industry. A scowling bust of Lenin is at the end of the platform.

Narvskaya Perhaps the city's coolest station, Narvskaya features a fantastic sculptured relief of Lenin and rejoicing proletariat over the escalators, as well as lovely carvings of miners, engineers, sailors, artists and teachers on the platform columns.

Pl Vosstaniya Lenin and Stalin are depicted together in the roundels at either end of the platform. Look out for Lenin on a tank and Lenin with the Kronshtadt sailors.

Pushkinskaya A statue of the poet stands at the end of the platform and a moulding of his head is above the escalators. Nip out of the station to view the nearby Style Moderne Vitebsk Station.

Tekhnologichesky Institut On the platform heading south are reliefs of famous Russian scientists, while the northbound platform announces the dates of Russia's major scientific achievements along the columns.

TROITSKY MOST — VEGETARIAN €

Map p268 (Троицкий Мост; Kamennoostrovsky pr 9/2; mains R100-300; ⏲9am-11pm; Ⓜ Gorkovskaya) The original branch of the vegetarian chain is located on Petrogradsky Island, just a few blocks north of the bridge for which it is named. See p93 for a full review.

BALTIC BREAD — BAKERY €

Map p268 (Балтийский хлеб; www.baltic-bread.ru; Bolshoy pr 80; snacks R100-200; ⏲9am-10pm; Ⓜ Petrogradskaya) For a great breakfast option or maybe a late-afternoon pick-me-up, head to the Petrograd outlet of this St Petersburg favourite. See p91 for a full review.

DRINKING & NIGHTLIFE

Petrograd and Vyborg Sides have very slim pickings for drinking and nightlife. However, there are a couple of places worth mentioning.

TUNNEL CLUB — NIGHTCLUB

Map p268 (www.tunnelclub.ru; cnr Zverinskaya ul & Lybansky per; cover R100-230; ⏲midnight-6am Thu-Sat, midnight-3am Sun-Wed; Ⓜ Sportivnaya) Back in the 1990s, Tunnel pioneered techno music in St Petersburg, a bastion of old-school rock-and-roll. Closed for several years, the military-themed club reopened in the bomb shelter where it was first born. The setting is still spooky but somehow appropriate for the techno and dubstep that goes down here.

TORN OFF BALLS — BAR

Map p268 (www.xxxxbar.ru; Pirogovskaya nab 5/2; free before midnight, afterwards admission R200-500; ⏲5pm-10am; Ⓜ Ploshchad Lenina) This horribly named bar attracts (rather than repulses) lots of men who, in the words of the bar, 'have seen it all before'. The idea is that the all-female crew of dominatrices will drum some discipline into the drinkers and diners here – expect floorshows, lots of high heels and potentially a hard spanking.

ENTERTAINMENT

JAM HALL ON PETROGRADSKY — CINEMA

Map p268 (www.jamhall.ru; Kamennoostrovsky pr 42; MPetrogradskaya) Now this is the kind of place that could never have existed in 20th-century Russia. An old palace of culture has been transformed into a luxury cinema experience. With plush sofa-style seating, tables for your drinks and a well-stocked bar on-site, this is the future – and we like it. Pity it mainly shows Hollywood blockbusters dubbed into Russian.

ORLANDINA — LIVE MUSIC

Map p268 (www.orlandina.ru; Instrumentalnaya ul 3; cover R150-300; ⌚4-11pm; MPetrogradskaya) Opened and owned by the small indie record label, Caravan records, this underground club is a pretty slick spot, a great venue for concerts, but also a good place to chill out with the cool crowd at the bar.

BALTIC HOUSE — THEATRE

Map p268 (Балтийский дом; www.baltichouse.spb.ru; Alexandrovsky Park 4; MGorkovskaya) Known under the Soviets as Lenin Komsomol Theatre, this large venue has long hosted an annual festival of plays from the Baltic countries. Renamed in 1991, Baltic House also stages Russian and European plays, as well as a new and growing repertoire of experimental theatre.

SHOPPING

While the Petrograd Side has far fewer shopping options than the historic heart, it is nonetheless an inviting place to shop, its sidewalks lined with food stores, clothing boutiques and the odd speciality shop. The Vyborg Side, by comparison, has very little shopping worth mentioning, with two very big exceptions – the superb Udelnaya Fair, St Petersburg's best flea market, and Imperial Porcelain, the factory outlet for the tsar's own china maker.

TOP CHOICE UDELNAYA FAIR — SOUVENIRS

(Удельная ярмарка; Vyborg Side; ⌚8am-5pm Sat & Sun; MUdelnaya) St Petersburg's only well-established flea market is one shopping experience truly worth travelling for. A treasure trove of Soviet ephemera, prerevolutionary antiques, WWII artefacts and bonkers kitsch from all eras, the sheer size of the place means you'll really have to comb it to find the gems (lots of people simply turn up to sell complete junk from their attics). Exit the metro station to the right and follow the crowds across the train tracks. You'll soon pass a large permanent market, which is of very little interest – continue beyond this and you'll come to a huge area of independent stalls, all totally varying in quality and content. Come in good time, as you may well want to spend several hours here.

DAY & NIGHT — FASHION

Map p268 (www.day-night.ru; Malaya Posadskaya ul 6; MGorkovskaya) The main boutique of a whole chain in the city, Day & Night looks like the set of *Alien* designed by Stella McCartney, and it's certainly one of St Petersburg's premier fashion experiences. Inside you'll find an absolutely top range of international designers: Balenciaga, Givenchy, Bernhard Willhelm, Jil Sander and even Victoria Beckham dresses. Bring your credit card.

SYTNY MARKET — MARKET

Map p268 (Сытный рынок; ☎233 2293; Sytninskaya pl 3/5; ⌚8am-6pm; MGorkovskaya) This colourful market on the Petrograd Side sells everything from vegetables, fruit, meat and fish inside to electronics, clothing and knick-knacks outside. Its name means 'sated' market, quite understandably.

MODEL SHOP — SOUVENIRS

Map p268 (Artillery Museum, Alexandrovsky Park 7; MGorkovskaya) Inside the Artillery Museum (p130; though you don't need to pay for entry to get access to the shop), this is a must for model plane, train and automobile fans. There's a huge range of mainly Russian models in stock and the staff is extremely helpful.

IMPERIAL PORCELAIN — PORCELAIN

(www.ipm.ru, in Russian; pr Obukhovsky Oborony 151; MLomonosovskaya) Dating back to the mid-18th century, this is the company that used to make tea sets for the Russian royal family. Formerly known as Lomonosov China, the company continues to produce innovative designs – the speciality being contemporary takes on traditional themes. The stuff is expensive, but the quality is high and the designs are spectacular (if you like the Russian style, which can seem somewhat on the gaudy side for some). The factory outlet offers discounted prices that are significantly cheaper than those you'll find at Imperial

Porcelain's city centre outlet. To get here, turn left out of the metro station and walk under the bridge. Turn left on the embankment and you'll see the factory ahead.

SPORTS & ACTIVITIES

KRUGLIYE BANI BANYA

Map p268 (Круглые бани; ☎communal 550 0985, private 297 6409; ul Karbysheva 29A; ⏰8am-10pm Fri-Tue; Ⓜ Ploshchad Muzhestva) Among the city's classiest communal bathhouses, the Krugliye Bani (Circle Baths) has a heated circular open-air pool. The 'lux' *banya* is an upgraded communal option, segregated by gender with certain days designated for men or women, so call in advance to find out the schedule. Otherwise, you can reserve a private *parilka* (steam room) for up to four people, open around the clock.

PLANET FITNESS – PETROGRAD SIDE GYM, SWIMMING POOL

Map p268 (www.fitness.ru; Petrogradskaya nab 18; one-time entry R1000-1300; ⏰6am-2am; Ⓜ Petrogradskaya) The city's biggest Planet Fitness outlet is on the Petrograd Side in the prestigious City Centre business centre. Its facilities include a big swimming pool, tennis courts and the requisite machines. Classes include standards such as yoga and spinning, as well as more exotic fare like kickboxing and karate. For relaxation, finish up with a massage or a visit to the sauna. Rates are cheaper before 5pm.

SPORTS COMPLEX GYM, SWIMMING POOL

Map p268 (Дом физической культуры ПГУПС; www.dfkpgups.ru; Kronverksky pr 9A; entry R300; ⏰6.30am-11pm; Ⓜ Gorkovskaya) While the new chains of private fitness centres cater to St Petersburg's wealthy classes, most people with athletic tendencies spend time at places such as this sports complex, which is the Russian version of the YMCA. It's not as shiny and new as the private clubs, but the 25m swimming pool under a glass roof is heavenly. Other facilities include weights, aerobics classes and clubs for every sport imaginable.

YELAGIN ISLAND OUTDOOR ACTIVITIES

Map p268 (www.elaginpark.spb.ru, in Russian; ice skating per hr R150-250; ⏰ice skating 11am-9pm; Ⓜ Krestovsky Ostrov) This car-free island becomes a winter wonderland in colder temperatures, with sledding, cross-country skiing and ice skating. Skis and skates are both available for hire. In summer months, it's a great place to rent in-line skates as there is no traffic to contend with. See p132 for more information on the island.

PETROVSKY STADIUM SPECTATOR SPORTS

Map p268 (Спортивный комплекс Петровский; www.petrovsky.spb.ru; Petrovsky ostrov 2; Ⓜ Sportivnaya) Zenit, St Petersburg's top football team, plays at this huge stadium on Petrovsky Island (a small island on the Petrograd Side). Tickets can usually be purchased at designated ticket outlets or at the stadium – check the website for the schedule or look for posters plastered around town.

JUBILEE SPORTS PALACE SPECTATOR SPORTS

Map p268 (Юбилейный дворец спорта; www.yubi.ru; pr Dobrolyubova 18; Ⓜ Sportivnaya) This 7000-seat stadium is home to the local basketball team, Spartak, who play here from October to April, but it also houses an **ice rink** (entry R300-400) in the summer months.

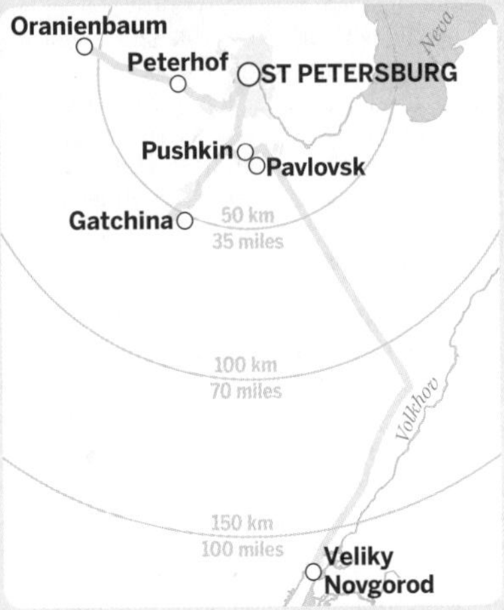

Day Trips from St Petersburg

Peterhof p141

The most popular day trip from St Petersburg is to Peter the Great's spectacular summer palace and grounds on the Gulf of Finland, easily reached by hydrofoil from outside the Hermitage.

Pushkin & Pavlovsk p144

Two beautiful palaces and grounds next door to one another, this is a great day trip to see the summer palaces of Catherine the Great and Tsar Paul I.

Gatchina p148

The leafy park at Gatchina is one of the wildest and most beautiful of all the tsarist palace grounds, while the huge palace itself is a fascinating place to explore, even boasting an underground tunnel.

Oranienbaum p151

Beyond Peterhof is Prince Menshikov's vast estate, which has some truly lovely gardens and is a great place to wander, despite the full renovation it's currently undergoing.

Veliky Novgorod p152

Best as an overnight trip from St Petersburg, Novgorod is one of Russia's most ancient cities, boasting a beautiful Kremlin and a fascinating history.

Peterhof
Петергоф

Explore

The fountains are incredible, the palace is a stunner and the grounds are great for walking and picnicking, so it's no surprise that Peter the Great's summer palace is usually the first-choice day trip for visitors to St Petersburg. Over the years Peter's successors continued to build and expand – pretty much constantly – to create the astounding ensemble seen today. Comparisons to Versailles abound and it's easy to see why: the sheer scale of the main palace, with its incredible cascades and gardens, were heavily influenced by Louis XIV's summer residence. What it isn't though, is undiscovered – and in summer months the place heaves with crowds (not to mention mosquitoes in the swampy gardens) – so come early, or later in the day to avoid the worst of the coach tours.

The Best...

- **Sight** Grand Palace (p142)
- **Place to Eat** Shtandart Restaurant (p144)
- **Place to Drink** Monplaisir Café (p144)

Top Tip

Remember to bring mosquito repellent or to keep your legs and arms covered if you're here during the summer months; the mosquitoes in the palace grounds are fierce.

Getting There & Away

Hydrofoil From May to September, Meteor hydrofoils leave every 20 minutes from outside the Hermitage (adult single/return R500/800, student single/return R450/700). The trip takes 30 minutes. The first hydrofoil leaves at 9.30am, the last hydrofoil back leaves Peterhof at 7pm.

Marshrutka Take *marshrutka* 300 or 424 (R30) from Avtovo metro station, or 103 from Leninsky Prospekt metro station. All pass through the town of Petrodvorets, immediately outside Peterhof. Tell the driver you want to go *'v dvaryéts'* (to the palace) and you'll be let off nearby.

Train Trains (R56, 30 minutes) leave St Petersburg's Baltic Station every 15 to 30 minutes. You need to get off at the Novy Petrodvorets (not Stary Petrodvorets). From here it's a 20-minute walk to Peterhof.

Need to Know

- **Area Code** ☎812
- **Location** 29km west of St Petersburg

SIGHTS

LOWER PARK — PARK

(Нижний парк; www.peterhofmuseum.ru; adult/student R400/200; ⏲park 9am-8pm, fountains 10am-6pm) The vast palace and grounds you see today are a far cry from the original cabin Peter the Great had built to oversee construction of his naval base at Kronshtadt. He liked the place so much that he built a villa, Monplaisir, and then a series of palaces across the estate. Now it's the palace grounds – with an incredible symphony of gravity-powered golden fountains, beautiful waterways and interesting historical buildings – that make Peterhof St Petersburg's most popular day trip.

Sadly, however, it's not cheap. Instead of buying one ticket to the entire park, you're charged a general entry to the grounds and then again for every single thing you'd like to see. You'll also pay at least 100% more than locals, so choose carefully. Inexplicably, many museums also have different closing days, although all buildings are open Friday to Sunday. All tours and posted information are in Russian, so buy an information booklet at the kiosks near the entrances. Almost all of the buildings require an extra ticket to take photographs or videos.

WATER AVENUE — CANAL

Crisscrossed by bridges and bedecked by smaller sprays, Water Ave is a canal leading from the hydrofoil dock to the palace. It culminates in the magnificent **Grand Cascade**, a symphony of over 140 fountains engineered in part by Peter himself. The central statue of Samson tearing open a lion's jaws celebrates – as so many things in St Petersburg do – Peter's victory over the Swedes at Poltava. Shooting up 62m, it was unveiled by Rastrelli for the 25th anniversary of the battle in 1735.

Peterhof

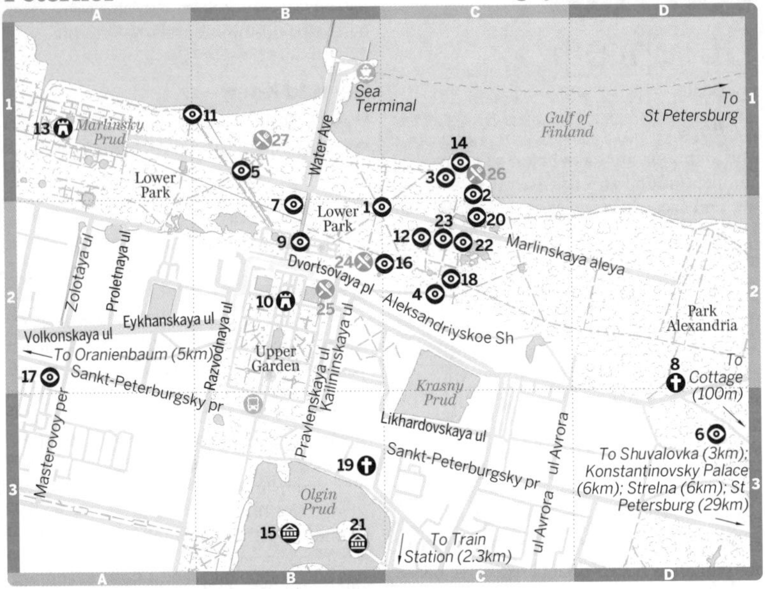

GRAND PALACE HISTORICAL BUILDING

(Большой дворец; adult/student R500/250, audioguide R500; ⏲10.30am-noon & 2.30-4.15pm Tue-Sun, closed last Tue of month) The Grand Palace is an imposing edifice, although with 30-something rooms, it's not as large as many tsarist palaces. It's open to foreign tourists only between 10.30am and noon, and 2.30pm to 4.15pm, so come here first if you're interested in going inside. Tickets are sold near the lobby where you pick up your *tapochki* (slippers to wear over shoes to avoid damaging the wooden floors).

While Peter's palace was relatively modest, Rastrelli grossly enlarged the building for Empress Elizabeth. Later, Catherine the Great toned things down a little with a redecoration, although that's not really apparent from the glittering halls and art-filled galleries that are here today. All of the paintings, furniture and chandeliers are original, as everything was removed from the premises before the Germans arrived. The Chesme Hall is full of huge paintings of Russia's destruction of the Turkish fleet at Çesme in 1770. Other highlights include the East and West Chinese Cabinets, Picture Hall and Peter's study.

After WWII, Peterhof was largely left in ruins. Hitler had intended to throw a party here when his plans to occupy the Astoria Hotel were thwarted. He drew up pompous invitations, which obviously incensed his Soviet foes. Stalin's response was to pre-empt any such celebration by bombing the estate himself, in the winter of 1941–42. So it is ironic but true that most of the damage at Peterhof occurred at the hands of the Soviets. What you see today is largely a reconstruction; in fact, the main palace was completely gutted, as only a few of its walls were left standing.

MONPLAISIR HISTORICAL BUILDING

(Монплезир; adult/student R360/180, combined ticket for 3 buildings adult/student R1000/500; ⏲10.30am-5pm Tue & Thu-Sun May-Sep, Sat & Sun Oct-Apr) This far more humble, sea-facing villa was always Peter the Great's favourite retreat. It's easy to see why: it's wood-panelled, snug and elegant, peaceful even when there's a crowd – which there used to be all the time, what with Peter's mandatory partying ('misbehaving' guests were required to gulp down huge quantities of wine).

Also in this complex is an annexe called the **Catherine Building** (Екатерининский корпус; adult/student R360/180; ⏲10.30am-6pm), which was built by Rastrelli between 1747 and 1755. Its name derives from the fact that Catherine the Great was living here –

Peterhof

Sights **p141**

1	Adam Fountain	B2
2	Bath Building	C1
3	Catherine Building	C1
4	Chess Mountain	C2
5	Eve Fountain	B1
6	Farmer's Palace	D3
7	Favotitka the Dog	B2
8	Gothic Chapel	D2
9	Grand Cascade	B2
10	Grand Palace	B2
11	Hermitage	B1
12	Little Oak Fountain	C2
13	Marly Palace	A1
14	Monplaisir	C1
15	Olgin Pavilion	B3
16	Orangery	C2
17	Raketa Petrodvorets Watch Factory & Museum	A2
18	Rimsky Fountains	C2
19	St Peter and Paul Cathedral	B3
20	Sun Fountain	C2
21	Tsatitsyn Pavilion	B3
22	Umbrella	C2
23	Water Alley Fountain	C2

Eating **p144**

24	Grand Orangerie	B2
25	Kafe Dvortsovoye	B2
26	Monplaisir Café	C1
27	Shtandart Restaurant	B1

rather conveniently – when her husband Peter III was overthrown. The interior contains the bedroom and study of Alexander I, as well as the huge Yellow Hall. On the right side is the magnificent **Bath Building** (Банный корпус; adult/student R360/180; 10.30am-6pm Thu-Tue), built by Quarenghi in 1800, which is nothing special inside. Look out for some more trick fountains in the garden in front of the buildings.

HERMITAGE HISTORICAL BUILDING

(Эрмитаж; adult/student R150/100, combined ticket for 2 buildings adult/student R250/120; 9am-6pm Wed-Mon) Along the shore to the west, the 1725 Hermitage is a two-storey yellow-and-white box featuring the ultimate in private dining: special elevators hoist a fully laid table into the imperial presence on the 2nd floor, thereby eliminating any hindrance by servants. The elevators are circular and directly in front of each diner, whose plate would be lowered, replenished and replaced.

Further west is yet another palace, **Marly** (adult/student R150/100; 10am-6pm Tue-Sun), inspired by the French hunting lodge of the same name so loved by Louis XIV.

PARK ALEXANDRIA PARK

(adult/student R100/50; 9am-8pm) Even on summer weekends, the rambling and overgrown Park Alexandria is peaceful and practically empty. Built for Tsar Nicholas I (and named for his tsarina), these grounds offer a sweet retreat from the crowds. Originally named for Alexander Nevsky, the **gothic chapel** (adult/student R140/70; 10.30am-6pm Tue-Sun) was completed in 1834 as the private chapel of Nicholas I. Nearby is the **cottage** (adult/student R250/120; 10.30am-6pm Tue-Sun) that was built around the same time as his summer residence. Also part of this same ensemble is the beautifully restored **Farmer's Palace** (adult/student R400/200; 10.30am-6pm), built here in 1831 as a pavilion in the park and designed to reify pastoral fantasies of rural life for the royal family. It became the home of the teenage Tsarevich Alexander (later Alexander II), who loved it throughout his life.

PETERHOF TOWN TOWN

In case you have not had enough, there is more to see in the centre of the town of Peterhof (also known as Petrodvorets). You'll need to leave the Lower Park grounds (and won't be able to re-enter to get to the hydrofoil without buying a new ticket) to do this. In front of the Grand Palace is the **Upper Garden** (admission free), which backs onto the Grand Palace. It is far more manicured (and far drier) than the Lower Park, and it makes a wonderful place to stroll, occupying the grounds between the palace and the town.

Wander down Pravlenskaya ul and you'll find yourself in the middle of town. It's well worth wandering past the handsome **St Peter & Paul Cathedral** and continuing around the edge of Olgin Prud (Olga's pond) to **Tsaritsyn and Olgin Pavilions** (adult/student R540/270; 10.30am-6pm, last entry at 4pm), two buildings sitting on islands in the middle of the pond. Nicholas I had these elaborate pavilions built for his wife (Alexandra Fyodorovna) and daughter (Olga Nikolayevna) respectively. Only recently restored and reopened, they boast unique Mediterranean architectural styles reminiscent of Pompeii.

Further down Sankt-Peterburgsky pr is the **Raketa Petrodvorets Watch Factory** (www.raketa.su; Sankt-Peterburgsky pr 60;

⌚boutique 10am-5pm Mon-Fri), one of the town's biggest employers, which has an on-site shop selling *very* cool watches.

EATING

SHTANDART RESTAURANT RUSSIAN €€
(www.restaurantshtandart.spb.ru; mains R300-500; ⌚10am-6pm; 📋) This large and upmarket restaurant overlooks the Gulf of Finland, just west of the boat dock, with plenty of seating both inside and out. It has a large and meaty menu full of interesting and well-realised Russian fare.

GRAND ORANGERIE RUSSIAN €€
(set menus R450-700; ⌚10am-6pm; 📋) An elegant choice, if you want to be served lunch, is this cafe in the charming orangery. It gets busy at lunch, so you may have to queue. The menu is packed with Russian classics and there's also a good cake selection.

MONPLAISIR CAFÉ RUSSIAN €
(mains R200-350; ⌚10am-6pm) For a quick sandwich or snack, head to this pleasant cafe next to Peter's favourite retreat. A few outdoor tables catch the breeze off the Gulf.

KAFE DVORTSOVOYE RUSSIAN €€
(Кафе Дворцовое; mains R350-700; ⌚10am-6pm) If you want to eat in the palace itself, then this fancy cafe is for you. Prices are high, but you're paying for the location – a stone's throw from the entrance to the Grand Palace.

Pushkin & Pavlovsk
Пушкин и Павловск

Explore

The sumptuous palaces and sprawling parks at Pushkin and Pavlovsk are entrenched in Russian history and have been immortalised in literature; few places in Russia are more strongly associated with the country's history and culture than they are. These two neighbouring complexes can be combined in a day's visit. If you are not in the mood to rush, however, there is plenty at either of them to keep you entertained for an entire day. Pushkin is understandably the big hitter with plenty of tour groups and crowds thanks to the beautiful Tsarskoe Selo ('the tsar's village') complex, which contains the staggeringly impressive Catherine Palace and sumptuous grounds. Pavlovsk, just a short bus ride away, is far less visited and much quieter as a result, but its grounds are arguably even lovelier and make for a perfect place to get lost in.

The Best...

- **Sight** Catherine Palace (p145)
- **Place to Eat** Daniel (p148)
- **Place to Wander** Pavlovsk Park (p147)

Top Tip

At the Catherine Palace, if you're not in a group, start lining up in good time for the individual visiting slots which run from noon to 2pm and 4pm to 5pm, otherwise you may miss your chance to go inside.

Getting There & Away

Marshrutka To get to Pushkin and Pavlovsk, take *marshrutka* 286, 299, 342 or K545 from outside Moskovskaya metro station. Take the station exit marked 'Buses for the airport'. The buses stop regularly here and go to both Pushkin (R30) and Pavlovsk (R32).

Train Suburban trains run from Vitebsk Station (Vitebsky vokzal) in St Petersburg, but they're infrequent except for weekends. For Pushkin get off at Detskoe Selo (Детское село; R42, 30 minutes) and for Pavlovsk (R55, 40 minutes) at Pavlovsk Station (Павловск).

Need to Know

- **Area Code** ☎812
- **Location** 25km (Pushkin) and 29km (Pavlovsk) south of St Petersburg

Pushkin

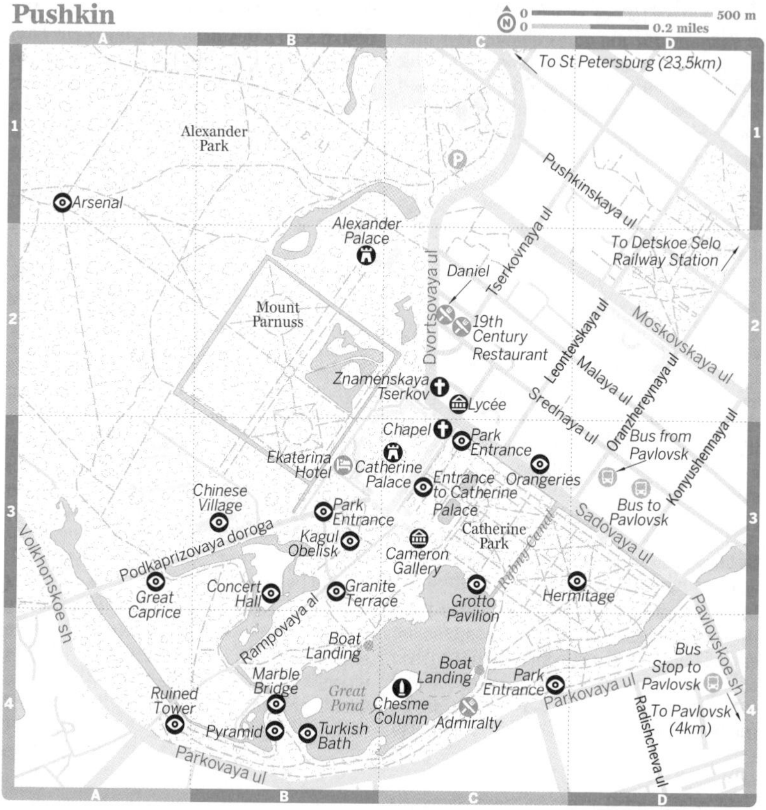

SIGHTS

CATHERINE PALACE PALACE

(Екатерининский дворец; www.tzar.ru; Sadovaya ul 7, Tsarskoe Selo; adult/student R320/160; ⏲10am-5pm Wed-Mon, individuals noon-2pm & 4-5pm, closed last Mon of month) The centrepiece of Tsarskoe Selo, created under Empresses Elizabeth and Catherine the Great between 1744 and 1796, is the vast baroque Catherine Palace, designed by Rastrelli and named after Elizabeth's mother, Peter the Great's second wife. As at the Winter Palace, Catherine the Great had many of Rastrelli's original interiors remodelled in classical style. Most of the gaudy exterior and 20-odd rooms of the palace have been beautifully restored – compare them to the photographs of the devastation left by the Germans.

While the palace opens for individual visitors (as opposed to groups) only at noon, it is usually necessary to queue up well in advance. All visitors are ushered into groups led by a tour guide; arrangements can sometimes be made for tours in English, but don't count on it. Everyone has to go on a guided tour here but it's easy to slip away once you're inside the palace and go around at your own pace.

Tours start with the white **State Staircase** (1860). South of here, only three rooms have been restored: the **Gentlemen-in-Waiting's Dining Room**, the dazzling **Great Hall**, the largest in the palace, and an **antechamber** with some huge blue-and-white Dutch ovens.

North of the State Staircase, you will pass through the **State Dining Room**, the **Crimson** and **Green Pilaster Rooms** and the **Picture Gallery**. The **reception room of Alexander I** contains portraits of his esteemed predecessors.

The highlight is Rastrelli's amazing **Amber Room**, completely covered with gilded woodcarvings, mirrors, agate and jasper mosaics (see p149).

Most of the palace's north end is the early classical work of architect Charles Cameron, including the elegant **Green Dining Room**, the **Blue Drawing Room**, **Chinese Blue Drawing Room** and **Choir Anteroom**, whose gold silk, woven with swans and pheasants, is the original from the 18th century.

Once you finish your tour, you can head to the southern **Zubov Wing** (Zubovsky korpus; adult/student R200/100; ⌚10am-5pm Thu-Tue), which houses special exhibitions.

CATHERINE PARK — PARK

(Екатерининский парк; adult/student R100/50; ⌚9am-6pm) Around the Catherine Palace extends the lovely Catherine Park. The main entrance is on Sadovaya ul, next to the palace chapel. It extends around the ornamental Great Pond and contains an array of interesting buildings, follies and pavilions.

Near Catherine Palace, the **Cameron Gallery** (adult/student R100/50; ⌚10am-5pm Thu-Tue) has rotating exhibitions. Between the gallery and the palace, notice the south-pointing ramp that Cameron added for the ageing empress to walk down into the park.

The park's outer section focuses on the **Great Pond**. In summer you can take a **ferry boat** (adult/child R200/100; ⌚11am-6pm May-Sep) to the little island to visit the **Chesme Column**. Beside the pond, the blue baroque **Grotto Pavilion** (admission free; ⌚10am-5pm Fri-Wed) houses temporary exhibitions in summer. A walk around the Great Pond will reveal other buildings that the royals built over the years, including the very incongruous-looking Turkish Bath with its minaret-style tower, the wonderful Marble Bridge, the Chinese Pavilion and a Concert Hall isolated on an island, where **concerts** (incl ferry transport R350; ⌚May-Sep) take place every Saturday at 5pm from May to September.

ALEXANDER PALACE & PARK — PALACE, PARK

A short distance north of the Catherine Palace, and surrounded by the overgrown and tranquil **Alexander Park** (admission free) is the classical **Alexander Palace** (Dvortsovaya ul 2; adult/student R100/50; ⌚10am-5pm Wed-Mon, closed last Wed of the month). It was built by Quarenghi between 1792 and 1796 for the future Alexander I, but Nicholas II, the last Russian tsar, was its main tenant and made it his favourite residence for much of his reign. Only three rooms are open to visitors, but they're impressive, with a huge tiger skin carpet and an extremely ropey portrait of a young Queen Victoria to boot. It's a poignant and

MAKE A WISH

Cast your kopek into any one of 150 fountains that adorn the grounds at Peterhof. Besides the Grand Cascade and Samson Fountain, here are some of our favourites.

Adam & Eve These two – prominently placed on either side of Water Ave – are the only outdoor sculptures remaining from the Petrine era.

Chess Mountain Flanked by a staircase, this black-and-white tiled chute is adorned with colourful dragons spitting water instead of fire.

Favoritka the Dog Often overlooked, this sweet fountain features four bronze ducks, swimming in circles, as they are chased by a silly-looking bulldog, seemingly shooting them with water.

Little Oak These gangly oak trees are rigged to spray when somebody approaches.

Rimsky Fountains Like two massive marble glasses bubbling over with champagne, these two beauties spray water 10m into the air, then into the pools below.

Sun Perched on a rotating axis, a disk radiates streams of water, creating the effect of sunrays.

Umbrella This circular bench looks like a pleasant shady spot. But anyone who sits down for a rest will discover that the umbrella drops a sheet of water from its edge, so you'll be shaded but soused.

Water Alley Most of the time this looks like a regular shady path through the Lower Gardens. But at designated times, when hidden fountains are turned on, the walkway (and anybody walking there) gets wet!

forgotten place that doesn't get many tourists and is a welcome contrast to the Catherine Palace.

PAVLOVSK PALACE PALACE

(Павловский дворец; www.pavlovskmuseum.ru; ul Revolutsii, Pavlovsk; adult/student R500/300; ⌚10am-5pm) Between 1781 and 1786, on orders from Catherine the Great, architect Charles Cameron designed the Pavlovsk Palace in Pavlovsk. The palace was designated for Catherine's son Paul (hence the name, Pavlovsk), and it was his second wife, Maria Fyodorovna, who orchestrated the design of the interiors. It served as a royal residence until 1917. Tragically, the original palace was burnt down two weeks after liberation following WWII when a careless Soviet soldier's cigarette set off German mines (the Soviets blamed the Germans). As at Tsarskoe Selo, its restoration is remarkable.

The finest rooms are on the middle floor of the central block. Cameron designed the round **Italian Hall** beneath the dome and the **Grecian Hall** to its west, though the lovely green fluted columns were added by his assistant Vincenzo Brenna. Flanking these are two private suites designed mainly by Brenna: Paul's along the north side of the block and Maria Fyodorovna's on the south. The **Hall of War** of the insane, military-obsessed Paul contrasts with Maria's **Hall of Peace**, decorated with musical instruments and flowers.

On the middle floor of the south block are Paul's **Throne Room** and the Hall of the Maltese Knights of St John, of whom he was the Grand Master.

If you decide to skip the palace, you may simply wish to wander around the serene **park grounds** (adult/student R150/80; ⌚9.30am-5pm, until 6pm Sat & Sun) – and as you'll have to pay to enter them just to access the palace, it's worth exploring and seeing what you come across. Filled with rivers and ponds, tree-lined avenues, classical statues and hidden temples, it's a delightful place to get lost. Highlights include the **Rose Pavilion** (adult/student R150/80) and the **Private Garden** (adult/student R100/50), with its beautifully arranged flowerbeds and impressive sculpture of the Three Graces.

EATING

The palaces at Tsarskoe Selo and Pavlovsk both have pretty mediocre eating options on their grounds, but there's plenty more choice nearby, especially in Pushkin.

Pavlovsk

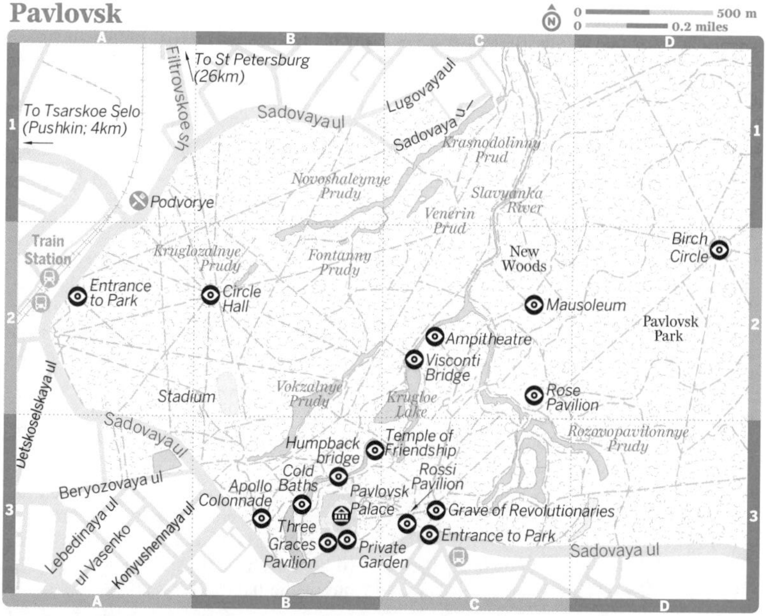

SLEEPING IN PUSHKIN & PAVLOVSK

➡ **Ekaterina Hotel** (☎466 8042; www.hotelekaterina.ru; Sadovaya ul 5, Tsarskoe Selo; r incl breakfast from R3500; ❄📶) Located inside the old servants' block at the Catherine Palace, this small, midrange hotel offers great views on the building's gilded facade. Rooms are modern and reasonably spacious. Best of all though, by staying here you can enjoy the grounds at Tsarskoe Selo after the day-tripping crowds have gone home.

DANIEL INTERNATIONAL €€€

(Даниель; www.apriorico.com; Srednaya ul 2/3; mains R700-1300; ⌚11am-11pm) Look no further for a blow-out gastronomic feast within stumbling distance of the Catherine Palace. Swedish chef Eric Viedgård conjures culinary magic with his seasonally changing menu in an elegant contemporary space with heritage touches.

19TH CENTURY RESTAURANT RUSSIAN €€

(Ресторан 19-й векъ; www.restaurantpushkin.ru; Srednaya ul 2, Pushkin; mains R400-600) Admire the owner's impressive collection of miniature bottles of alcohol at the entrance, before choosing one of four differently decorated dining rooms in which to eat a traditional Russian meal.

PODVORYE RUSSIAN €€

(Подьворе; www.podvoyre.ru; Filtrovskoye sh 16, Pavlovsk; mains R600-1000) This ersatz, traditional Russian log cabin is a short walk in the direction back towards Pushkin from Pavlovsk station. Podvorye dishes up huge portions of delicious Russian food with a side order of live Russian music and dancing. Apparently, President Putin is a regular here.

ADMIRALTY RUSSIAN €€

(Адмиралтейство; ☎465 3549; admiral.gutsait.ru; Catherine Park; mains R400-800) Housed in the old brick Admiralty building overlooking the Great Pond in Catherine Park, this atmospheric restaurant serves traditional and tasty Russian food. The tower-like building does not have a lot of room, and is often used for wedding banquets, so reservations are recommended.

Gatchina
Гатчина

Explore

The furthest flung of the imperial palaces surrounding St Petersburg, Gatchina is rather different from the rest on many counts. First of all, it's in the middle of a busy town, meaning that it doesn't feel grandly isolated like so many tsarist boltholes. Secondly, the extensive landscaped grounds are all public, meaning that you're more likely to encounter picnicking locals than tour groups as you walk around. That said, Gatchina's grounds are perhaps the most beautiful of all the imperial parks and the restored palace, complete with its dark and dramatic history, is a fascinating place to explore. There are a few sights worth seeing in the town of Gatchina itself, so you can easily spend a whole day here.

The Best...

➡ **Sight** Great Gatchina Palace (p149)

➡ **Place to Eat** Kafe Piramida (p150)

➡ **Quirky Sight** Birch House (p149)

Top Tip

Unlike all the other tsarist palaces around St Petersburg, Gatchina's park is public, so it can be far more crowded than, for example, Pavlovsk or Oranienbaum. Avoid the weekends if you'd prefer to enjoy the grounds without crowds of picnicking Russians.

Getting There & Away

Bus From Moskovskaya metro station, bus 100 (R70, one hour) runs regularly. Buses wait on ul Altayskaya and stop just short of Gatchina Park. Tell the driver you want to go to the palace – *'v dvoryéts'*.

Marshrutka *Marshrutky* K18 and 431 (R50) also run this route from outside Moskovskaya metro station and stop right by the park.

Train There are trains to Gatchina Baltiysky (R86, one hour) from the Baltic Station (Baltiysky vokzal) every one to two hours. The train station is directly in front of the palace.

Need to Know

- **Area Code** ☎812
- **Location** 45km south of St Petersburg

SIGHTS

GREAT GATCHINA PALACE HISTORICAL BUILDING

(Большой гатчинский дворец; adult/student R200/80; ⏲10am-5pm Tue-Sun, closed 1st Tue of month) Shaped in a graceful curve around a central turret, the Great Gatchina Palace certainly lives up to its name – its enormous (if surprisingly plain) facade is quite a sight to behold, overlooking a vast parade ground and backing onto the huge landscaped grounds. Built by Rinaldi between 1766 and 1781 in an early classicism style for Catherine the Great's favourite Grigory Orlov, the palace curiously combines motifs of a medieval fortress with elements commonly seen in Russian imperial residences. It's hard to call it beautiful, but there's no doubt that it's extremely impressive. After Orlov's death in 1783, Catherine the Great bought the palace from his heirs and gifted it to her son Paul, who redesigned the exterior between 1792 and 1798.

The 10 State Rooms on the 2nd floor are impressive, including **Paul I's Throne Room**, hung with huge tapestries, and his wife **Maria Fyodorovna's Throne Room**, the walls of which are covered in paintings. Most impressive of all is the **White Hall**, a Rinaldi creation from the 1770s that was redone by Brenna in the 1790s, on the balcony of which is an impressive collection of sundials.

The walk from the state rooms through the **Chesme Gallery** gives you an interesting insight into how the palace looked after WWII. Do not miss the incredible underground tunnel that leads to the lake, and if you'd like a stellar view of the park, climb the **Signal Tower** (Сигнальная башня; adult/student R30/20).

GATCHINA PARK PARK

(Гатчинский парк; admission free; ⏲dawn-dusk) The palace estate at Gatchina is more overgrown, less touristy and more romantic than that of any of the other palaces. The park has many winding paths through birch groves and across bridges to islands in the large **White Lake**. Look out for the frankly bizarre **Birch House** (adult/student R30/20; ⏲11am-7pm Tue-Sun), which was a present from Maria Fyodorovna to Paul I. With a rough facade made of birch logs, the interior is actually very refined, with a beautiful hardwood floor made from timbers from around the world. Perhaps unsurprisingly though, Paul I later built a neoclassical 'mask' to hide the Birch House's facade from the view of casual strollers.

Down on the lake, the **Venus Pavilion** (adult/student R30/20; ⏲11am-7pm Tue-Sun) is a beautiful spot jutting out into the water with an elaborately painted interior. Continue around the lake to find the best picnicking spots – it's even possible to swim in a second lake (see where the locals go) if the weather is good.

THE MYSTERY OF THE AMBER ROOM

The original Amber Room was created from exquisitely engraved amber panels given to Peter the Great by King Friederich Wilhelm I of Prussia in 1716. Rastrelli later combined the panels with gilded woodcarvings, mirrors, agate and jasper mosaics to decorate one of the rooms of the Catherine Palace. Plundered by the Nazis during WWII, the room's decorative panels were last exhibited in Königsberg's castle in 1941. Four years later, with the castle in ruins, the Amber Room was presumed destroyed. Or was it?

In 2004, as Putin and then German Chancellor Gerhardt Schröder presided over the opening of the new US$18 million Amber Room, restored largely with German funds, rumours about the original panels continued to swirl. There are those who believe that parts, if not all, of the original Amber Room remain hidden away (see www.amberroom.org). The mystery gained traction in February 2008 as attention focused on the possible contents of an artificial cavern discovered near the village of Deutschneudorf on Germany's border with the Czech Republic. Nothing conclusive has yet to be unearthed here, though, so the mystery continues.

GATCHINA TOWN TOWN

In the nearby town there are a couple of interesting churches. The baroque **Pavlovsk Cathedral** (Павловский собор; ul Sobornaya), at the end of the pedestrianised shopping street off the central pr 25 Oktyabrya, has a grandly restored interior with a soaring central dome. A short walk west is the **Pokrovsky Cathedral** (Покровский собор; Krasnaya ul), a red-brick building with bright blue domes.

EATING

There are no eating options in the palace or grounds themselves, but as the place was made for picnicking your bet is to bring your own lunch. However, if you haven't done so, there are a couple of options in the town.

KAFE PIRAMIDA RUSSIAN €

(Кафе Пирамида; ul Sobornaya 3A; mains R150-250; ⏲10am-11pm; 🅔) Serving a wide range of traditional Russian dishes as well as delicious cakes and coffees, this cosy place is near the Pavlovsk Cathedral.

SLAVYANSKY DVOR RUSSIAN €

(Славянский двор; ul Dostoevskogo 2; mains R200-350; ⏲11am-midnight Mon-Thu, 11am-3am Fri-Sun) Housed in a restored historic building near the Pokrovsky Cathedral, this traditional Russian place (its name means the Slavic Yard) will do you a filling meal at any time throughout the day.

STRELNA СТРЕЛЬНА

The small village of Strelna, about 6km east of Peterhof, is the site of another palace dreamed up by Peter I. Although construction began in the 18th century, current Prime Minister Vladimir Putin deserves credit for completing this project.

Peter's original plan was to construct a small palace surrounded by water, for use as a summer home. He commissioned Jean Baptiste LeBlond to build the palace and park, but the famed French architect died before he made much progress on the project. Work came to a standstill when Peter turned his attention to Peterhof, as that site was better suited for his fountain fantasy. Years later, at the request of Empress Elizabeth, her favourite architect Rastrelli attempted to expand and elaborate on the existing palace at Strelna. But he too was distracted – this time by construction at Tsarskoe Selo – and it was never really finished. In 1797 Emperor Paul I presented this half-built palace to his son, Grand Duke Constantine Pavlovich. Construction of the Konstantinovsky Palace was finally completed several years later.

The estate fell into disrepair during the Soviet period, occupied by a children's camp and a secondary school. It was devastated by German occupation during WWII, and then left to languish for more than half a century.

In the lead-up to the tercentennial in 2003, President Putin decreed that the property would be rebuilt and converted to a presidential palace – in other words, the 'Palace of Putin'. Using LeBlond's original design, the **park** (admission R150) was landscaped with canals, bridges and fountains, as well as Peter's intended island chateau. Studded with sculpture, it makes a lovely place for a stroll or picnic.

Konstantinovsky Palace (☎438 5360; www.konstantinpalace.ru, in Russian; Berezovaya al 3; adult/student R400/200; ⏲10am-5pm Thu-Tue) has also been fully restored. Excursions visit the fabulous state rooms, including the Blue Room and the over-the-top ornate Marble Room, as well as the ceremonial guest rooms of the president and the first lady. Most impressively, visitors can take a peek into the wine cellar. Apparently, as far back as 1755 these premises were used to house the emperor's collection of Hungarian wine, when the Winter Palace was under construction. These days the cellar contains a collection of more than 13,000 bottles from all over the world.

Also known as the Congress Palace, it is often used for official functions, hosting heads of state and other important delegations. For this reason, it's important to call in advance to confirm that the grounds and palace will be open when you wish to visit. If you'd like to sleep like a tsar, consider staying at the Baltic Star Hotel (see the boxed text, p164).

Oranienbaum Ораниенбаум

Need to Know

- **Area Code** ☎812
- **Location** 41km west of St Petersburg

Explore

Anyone interested in Prince Menshikov, best friend of Peter the Great, and the first governor of St Petersburg, will be fascinated by this testament to his growing vanity. While Peter was building Monplaisir at Peterhof, Menshikov began his own palace at Oranienbaum (Orange Tree), 12km further down the coast. Peter was unfazed by the fact that his subordinate's palace in St Petersburg (Menshikov Palace, p120) was grander than his own, and Menshikov also outdid his master in creating this fabulous retreat. While not particularly opulent compared to the palaces that Elizabeth and Catherine the Great favoured, by Petrine standards Oranienbaum was off the scale. Today, Oranienbaum (which is also known by its Soviet-era name, Lomonosov) is in the midst of a vast restoration project, but it remains a great place to visit for strolling in the beautiful grounds.

The Best...

- **Sight** Great Palace (p151)
- **Place to Eat** Okhota (p152)
- **Quirky Sight** Deer park (in between the palace grounds and the Chinese Palace)

Top Tip

It's very easy to combine Oranienbaum with a visit to Peterhof. From the palace at Peterhof, walk down to the main road and pick up any *marshrutky* with Гатчина written on it. Tell the driver you want to go *'v gátchinsky dvaryéts'*.

Getting There & Away

Marshrutka These depart from Avtovo metro station (R70, 50 minutes).

Train The train from St Petersburg's Baltic Station to Petrodvorets continues to Oranienbaum (R62, one hour). Get off at Lomonosov Station, an hour from St Petersburg, and walk diagonally across the little park in front. Keep going up to the main road, turn right, pass the unmissable Archangel Michael Cathedral and the park entrance is on your left.

SIGHTS

GREAT PALACE — HISTORICAL BUILDING

(Большой дворец) Currently undergoing a vast interior and exterior renovation, this impressive palace will soon be looking incredible. It was not possible to visit the palace at the time of writing, but just wandering around its exterior, peeping through the windows and glimpsing the large, sunken formal gardens that extend in front of it are interesting enough.

Following Peter's death and Menshikov's exile, the palace served briefly as a hospital and then passed to Tsar Peter III. Of course, Peter III didn't much like ruling Russia, so he spent a lot of time here before he was dispatched in a coup led by his wife, the future Catherine the Great.

ORANIENBAUM PARK — PARK

(Музей-заповедник Ораниенбаум; www.oranienbaum.org) Spared Nazi occupation, after WWII Oranienbaum was renamed for the scientist-poet Mikhail Lomonosov. Now known as Oranienbaum again, it doubles as a museum and **public park** (adult/student R140/70; ⌚9am-8pm), with lots of beautiful pathways, ornamental lakes and other follies and pavilions to enjoy.

Beyond the beautiful lake, the **Palace of Peter III** (Дворец Петра III; adult/student R140/70; ⌚10.30am-6pm Wed-Mon May-Oct), also called Peterstadt, is a boxy toy palace, with rich interiors. It was restored in the late 1950s and early 1960s, but is in dire need of attention again and its salmon pink walls are now flaking and chipped. Approach the 'palace' through the monumental **Gate of Honour**, all that remains of a small-scale fortress where Peter amused himself drilling his soldiers.

Worth a peek also is Catherine's over-the-top **Chinese Palace** (Китайский дворец), designed by Antonio Rinaldi. It was closed for renovation at the time of research, so it's bound to be looking fabulous in the near future. Rococo on the inside and baroque on the outside, the private retreat features painted ceilings and fine inlaid-wood floors and walls.

In the meadows between the Palace of Peter III and the Chinese Palace is a small **Deer Park**, where you can see deer being reared for eventual release into the grounds.

EATING

With kilometres of quiet paths through pine woods and sombre gardens, Oranienbaum is a lovely place for a picnic. Otherwise, the one nearby eating option faces the main entrance to the palace on the main road.

OKHOTA RUSSIAN **€€**

(Охота; Dvortsovy pr 65A; mains R400-800) If the name didn't give it away (*okhota* means 'hunt'), you'll get the message from the herd of stuffed animals hanging from the walls and ceilings: game is the order of the day at this smart Russian restaurant.

Veliky Novgorod Великий Новгород

Explore

Straddling the placid Volkhov River, Veliky Novgorod (usually shortened to plain Novgorod) makes for a fascinating side trip from St Petersburg. It's one of Russia's most attractive and tourist-friendly destinations and offers a great opportunity to see life in a more normal city than highly atypical St Petersburg. Novgorod, which misleadingly translates as 'new town', was actually founded in the 9th century. It's a tremendously important centre of medieval Russian cul-

Veliky Novgorod

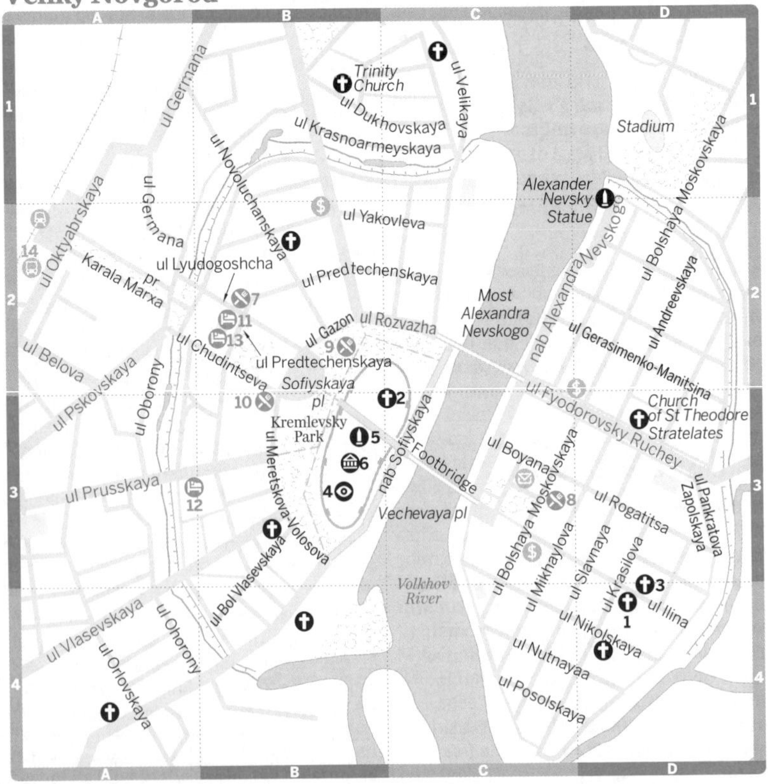

ture and by the 12th century had become Russia's biggest and most powerful city, a legacy that lives on in its impressive kremlin and numerous beautiful old churches and museums. Today it's a laid-back, well-to-do kind of place with one foot in the present and one foot very much in the past.

The Best...

- **Sight** Kremlin (p153)
- **Place to Eat** Nice People (p154)
- **Place to Sleep** Hotel Volkhov (p155)

Top Tip

Novgorod is a popular weekend getaway for Petersburgers, so to avoid the crowds try to plan your visit on a weekday.

Getting There & Away

Bus From St Petersburg's Avtovokzal No 2 you can take buses to Novgorod (R250, 3½ hours, 14 daily), arriving at Novgorod's bus station, which is right next to the train station.

Train *Elektrichki* run from St Petersburg's Moscow Station (R400, three daily, three hours) to Novgorod na Volkhove's station.

Veliky Novgorod

Need to Know

- **Area Code** ☎8162
- **Location** 186km southeast of St Petersburg

SIGHTS

KREMLIN HISTORICAL BUILDING

(admission free; ⏲6am-midnight) On the west bank of the Volkhov River, and surrounded by a pleasant wooded park, this is one of Russia's oldest kremlins. Originally called the Detinets, the fortification dates back to the 9th century, though it was later rebuilt with brick in the 14th-century form that still stands today.

CATHEDRAL OF ST SOPHIA ORTHODOX CHURCH

(Софийский собор; ⏲8am-8pm, services 10am & 6pm Sun) This working cathedral, the kremlin's focal point, was finished in 1050. It has a simple, fortresslike exterior designed to withstand attack or fire (flames had taken out an earlier, wooden church on the site). The onion domes were probably added during the 14th century – even so, they are perhaps the first example of this most Russian architectural detail. The west doors, dating from the 12th century, have tiny cast-bronze biblical scenes and even portraits of the artists. The icons inside date from the 14th century; older ones are in the museum opposite.

NOVGOROD STATE UNITED MUSEUM MUSEUM

(Новгородский государственный объединённый музей-заповедник; www.novgorodmuseum.ru; adult/student R140/80; ⏲10am-6pm Wed-Mon) The highlight of this museum is its galleries of icons, one of the largest collections anywhere. Around 260 pieces have been placed in chronological order, allowing you to see the progression of skills and techniques through the centuries. Downstairs in the history exhibition (with little signage in English) birch bark manuscripts are displayed, some of them 800 years old. Letters, documents and drawings on birch bark by people of all ages and social classes indicate that literacy was widespread in medieval Novgorod.

In the Russian woodcarving exhibits you can see everything from the mundane (kitchen utensils and furniture) to more detailed religious objects. In a separate exhibition are glittering pieces from Novgorod's **gold treasury** (adult/student R100/60), some dating back to the 6th century AD.

MILLENNIUM OF RUSSIA MONUMENT — MONUMENT

This 16m-high, 300-tonne sculpture was unveiled in 1862 on the 1000th anniversary of the Varangian Prince Rurik's arrival. A veritable who's who of Russian history over the last millennium, it depicts some 127 figures – rulers, statesmen, artists, scholars and a few fortunate hangers-on as well.

The women at the top are Mother Russia and the Russian Orthodox Church. Around the middle, clockwise from the south, are Rurik, Prince Vladimir of Kyiv (who introduced Christianity), tsars Mikhail Romanov, Peter the Great and Ivan III, and Dmitry Donskoy trampling a Mongol Tatar. In the bottom band on the east side are nobles and rulers, including Catherine the Great with an armload of laurels for all her lovers. Alexander Nevsky and other military heroes are on the north side, and literary and artistic figures are on the west.

CHURCH OF THE TRANSFIGURATION OF OUR SAVIOUR — MUSEUM

(Церковь Спаса Преображения на Ильине улице; ul Ilina; adult/student R100/60; ⏲10am-5pm Wed-Sun, closed last Thu of month) This church is famous for housing the only surviving frescoes by legendary Byzantine painter Theophanes the Greek (they came close to extinction when the church served as a Nazi machine-gun nest). Restoration has exposed as much of the frescoes as possible, though they are still faint. A small exhibit upstairs includes reproductions with explanations in Russian. Note Theophanes' signature use of white warlike paint around the eyes and noses of his figures, and their piercing expressions.

Opposite is the **Cathedral of Our Lady of the Sign** (Знаменский собор; adult/student R70/40; ⏲10am-5pm Thu-Tue), a 17th-century Moscow-style complex, its interior also festooned with somewhat more vivid frescoes.

EATING

During summertime, several open-air cafes facing the kremlin's west side make pleasant spots for a drink.

TOP CHOICE NICE PEOPLE — INTERNATIONAL €€

(www.gonicepeople.ru; ul Meretskova-Volosova 1/1; mains R300-600; ⏲8am-midnight; 📶🗐) Light floods into this appealing corner cafe-bar where there's a warm welcome from English-speaking staff. Their speciality DIY salads have a choice of six types of lettuce, 27 toppings and seven dressings. There are a lot of other tasty things and daily specials written up on the walls.

THE SAVIOUR OF NOVGOROD

The most important icon in the Cathedral of St Sophia is that of Novgorod's patron saint, **Our Lady of the Sign** (Знамения Божьей Матери), which, according to legend, saved the city from destruction in 1170. Accounts vary, but tend to go something like this...

The Prince of Suzdal and his large army were preparing to attack Novgorod. Things looked pretty bleak for the Novgorodians, and the bishop desperately prayed for the city's salvation. The night before the attack, he had a vision that an icon of the Virgin could save Novgorod, so he had the icon moved from the church to a pillar of the fortress. Not surprisingly, the icon was hit with an arrow shortly after the siege began. It then turned back to face Novgorod; tears were in the Virgin's eyes. Darkness fell upon the land, and the army from Suzdal began attacking one another in confusion. The Novgorodians then rode out from the city and attacked, quickly dispatching their enemies.

There may be a grain of truth in all this: a close look at the icon reveals a notch over the saint's left eye, said to be where the original arrow hit. And, if you visit the Novgorod State United Museum, check out the 15th-century painting depicting three scenes from the battle. It's one of the first icons ever painted of a Russian historical event.

SLEEPING IN VELIKY NOVGOROD

➡ **Hotel Volkhov** (Гостиница Волхов; ☎225 500; www.hotel-volkhov.ru; ul Predtechenskaya 24; s/d from R1950/2900; @) This centrally located modern hotel runs like a well-oiled machine with nicely furnished rooms, pleasant English speaking staff, laundry service and free wi-fi. A sauna (extra fee) is available to guests.

➡ **Hotel Akron** (Гостиница Акрон; ☎736 908; www.hotel-akron.ru; ul Predtechenskaya 24; s/d from R1550/2200) Similar to the Volkhov next door, but with lower prices and no elevator. Rooms have modern bathrooms, cable TV and fridge. Friendly service is also a plus.

➡ **Hotel Cruise** (Гостиница Круиз; ☎772 283; nsm_kruis@mail.ru; ul Prusskaya 11; dm per bed R500, d with bathroom from R2400) A Jekyll and Hyde operation, the Cruise is both a down-at-heel hostel *and* a spiffy boutique style hotel. The older hostel part offers dorm rooms with three single beds that share a bathroom down the hall; if you want to stay alone in one of these rooms, pay R1000. The spacious refurbished 'lux' rooms are very stylish with limed hardwood floors and slick furnishings.

CAFÉ LE CHOCOLAT INTERNATIONAL €€
(www.cafelechocolat.ru; ul Lyudogoshcha 8; mains R250-650; 9am-11pm) White leather couches, blood-red walls and black and white photos set the scene for this chic cafe. The menu features some tantalising options, including dozens of sushi platters, a range of breakfasts, desserts, creative cocktails and fruit teas.

DOM BERGA RUSSIAN €€
(Дом Берга; www.cafe.nov.ru/bergs-house; ul Bolshaya Moskovskaya 24; cafe/restaurant meals from R50/500; cafe 9am-9pm, restaurant noon-midnight) Enjoy expertly prepared Russian dishes in this handsome brick building – there's a choice between simple cafe and fancier restaurant. Portions are a little small and pricey but it's all very palatable and elegantly done.

ILMEN RUSSIAN €€
(Ильмень; ul Gazon 2; mains R200-400) The ground floor has a little deli/bakery for takeaway snacks, and a self-serve bistro, with outdoor area in summer, for cheap sit-down eats. Upstairs, the more formal restaurant Holmgard has a menu packed with Russian dishes including freshly made kebabs.

Sleeping

Accommodation in St Petersburg doesn't come cheap, and it pays to book well in advance, as places fill up during the White Nights and throughout the summer. The hospitality industry has improved enormously in the past decade, with Soviet hotels now a phenomenon of the past, replaced by a range of youth hostels and mini-hotels, and plenty of luxury choice.

Hotels

There has been a revolution in hotel accommodation in St Petersburg in recent times and a large expansion of modern, professionally run establishments. Old Soviet fleapits have been reconstructed as contemporary and appealing hotels, some of the city centre's most desperately derelict buildings have been rebuilt as boutique or luxury properties and the overall standards of service have risen enormously. That said, most hotels are still fairly expensive, with a lack of good midrange places in the city centre. Though they do exist, they tend to get booked up well in advance (particularly during the summer months), so plan ahead if you want to stay in the historic heart. There are plenty of hotels in other neighbourhoods though: Smolny, Vladimirskaya, Vasilyevsky Island and the Petrograd Side are all popular locations with relatively easy access to the rest of the city (as long as you're near a metro station).

Mini Hotels

Mini-hotels are a real St Petersburg phenomenon. While most aspiring hoteliers are not able to pay for the renovation and conversion of entire buildings themselves, lots of small-time entrepreneurs have been able to buy an apartment or two and create a three- to eight-room hotel in otherwise totally unremarkable residential buildings. Due to their individuality and the care that often goes into their running, mini-hotels are some of the best places to stay in the city. They also tend to be well located in the centre of the city where demand for rooms is highest. On the downside, they are by their very nature rather small places, so rooms book up quickly.

Hostels

Once a city with just a handful of very average, far-flung and depressing hostels, St Petersburg now positively spoils budget travellers with a wide range of places to sleep for under R1000 a night. Central, well run, safe, clean and with free wireless, this new generation of hostels will be a very welcome surprise to anyone coming to Russia for the first time. Hostels here tend to be run by enthusiastic staff who themselves have travelled widely and are passionate about backpacking. More than almost anywhere else though, you do really need to book ahead to ensure you get a place at the hostel you want.

Apartments

As hotels for individual travellers tend to be fairly expensive even in midrange categories, renting an apartment is a great option and St Petersburg is full of large apartments that are regularly rented out to tourists. Like mini-hotels, they tend to be right in the city centre, and in general come equipped with wireless internet, washing machines and kitchens. Security is generally very good, with multiple locks on doors, entry phones and well-lit corridors – a far cry from how renting apartments used to be. See p163 for a list of recommended letting agencies.

Lonely Planet's Favourites

Casa Leto (p159) A truly charming Italianate boutique hotel between the Hermitage & St Isaac's.

W Hotel (p159) This luxurious stunner is the coolest new arrival on the city's hotel scene.

Alexander House (p165) A beautiful privately run hotel overlooking the Kryukov Canal.

Andrey & Sasha's Homestay (p165) The best possible cultural immersion with passionate and fun hosts.

Rossi Hotel (p159) A gorgeous boutique hotel overlooking the charming Fontanka River.

Rachmaninov Hotel (p42) Sublime location and great value for money behind the Kazan Cathedral.

Best by Budget

€

Friends Hostel (p160)

Hostel Ligovsky 74 (p163)

Hostel Life (p163)

Green Apple Hotel (p165)

€€

Arkadia (p166)

Tradition Hotel (p168)

Northern Lights (p166)

Hotel Vera (p164)

€€€

Grand Hotel Europe (p159)

Hotel Astoria (p160)

Kempinski Hotel Moyka 22 (p160)

Angleterre Hotel (p159)

Best for Kids

Pio on Mokhovaya (p163)

Sokos Hotel Palace Bridge (p167)

Puppet Hostel (p165)

Pushka Inn (p161)

Best Located for the Hermitage

Nord Hostel (p162)

Location Hostel (p161)

Guest House Nevsky 3 (p159)

Hotel Nauka (p163)

Fortecia Peter (p162)

Best Value for Money

Polikoff Hotel (p161)

3MostA (p160)

Golden Age Retro Hotel (p166)

Petro Palace Hotel (p160)

House in Kolomna (p166)

Best Mini-Hotels

Nevsky Prospekt B&B (p162)

Anichkov Pension (p161)

Austrian Yard Hotel (p164)

Fortecia Peter (p162)

Best for Canal Views

Kempinski Hotel Moyka 22 (p160)

Pushka Inn (p161)

3MostA (p160)

Graffiti Hostel (p166)

NEED TO KNOW

Price Ranges

In our listings we've used the following price codes to represent the price of the cheapest room available during the high season (usually May to July):

€	less than R3000
€€	R3000–8000
€€€	more than R8000

Reservations

➡ It is usually essential to reserve at least a month (and preferably more) in advance for accommodation during the White Nights (late May to early July).

➡ Booking online via the hotel website is usually the cheapest method, as there are few accommodation websites worth bothering with, and most hotels post their best rates online.

Tipping

Tipping hotel staff and porters will only be expected in the very top hotels in St Petersburg, although for good service it will always be appreciated, of course.

Breakfast

Breakfast is nearly always a buffet *(shvetsky stol)* in St Petersburg, and except in four- and five-star hotels, will usually be fairly unexciting, with limited choice.

Where to Stay

Neighbourhood	For	Against
Historic Heart	Quite frankly, this is where you want to be if you have the chance. Everything is here, right on your doorstep, and it takes a maximum of 20 minutes to get anywhere within this neighbourhood on foot.	Accommodation here can be more expensive.
Smolny & Vosstaniya	Equally in the thick of things as the Historic Heart, this happening part of town around the lower half of Nevsky Pr is home to much of St Petersburg's youth culture and artistic life.	Smolny, in particular, can feel surprisingly remote from the rest of the city due to bad transport links and its own backwater ambience.
Sennaya & Kolomna	Far quieter and less busy than the Historic Heart, while still definitely historic and central itself. Great for access to the Mariinsky Theatre.	Distances on foot can be very long, especially if you're staying in Kolomna, where there's no metro.
Vasilyevsky Island	A very pleasant residential area. Very well connected to the rest of the city as long as you're within easy walking distance of one of the two metro stations here.	If you're not near the metro, you will feel very isolated out here. If you are looking to party in St Petersburg during the summer months, this is not a good option as the bridges rise at night.
Petrograd & Vyborg Sides	The Petrograd Side is both central and very pleasant, with lots of local sights and easy transport links to the centre of town.	If you are looking to party in St Petersburg during the summer months, this is not a good option as the bridges rise at night.

Historic Heart

TOP CHOICE **W HOTEL** LUXURY HOTEL €€€

Map p254 (☎610 6161; www.wstpetersburg.com; Voznesensky pr 6; r from R14,700; MAdmiralteyskaya;) When one of the world's coolest hotel brands opened its first Russian hotel in 2011, it unsurprisingly became the talk of the town, and it's not hard to see why when you walk into the dazzling reception area of this 137-room property. The rooms, in several different categories, are all spacious and very luxuriously appointed, if not always terribly subtle in style. The marble bathrooms are gorgeous, and each room comes with luxuries such as iPhone docks, a Netspresso coffee maker and – what else – flat-screen TV in both the room itself and the bathroom. The views from the rooftop MiXup Bar (p75) are superb, the basement Alain Ducasse restaurant MiX in St Petersburg (p72) is one of the top tables in the city and to round it all off, the basement houses a huge, beautiful spa containing a sauna, jacuzzi, treatment rooms and a swimming pool. Definitely the coolest address in St Petersburg.

TOP CHOICE **ROSSI HOTEL** BOUTIQUE HOTEL €€

Map p254 (☎635 6333; www.rossihotels.com; nab reki Fontanki 55; s/d/ste incl breakfast from R5000/9000/10,500; MGostiny Dvor;) This fantastic new addition to the local hotel scene is a beautifully restored building on one of St Petersburg's prettiest squares. The 46 rooms are all designed differently, but their brightness and moulded ceilings are uniform. Antique beds, super sleek bathrooms, exposed brick walls and lots of cool designer touches create a great blend of old and new, while the very best rooms have superb views over the Fontanka River.

TOP CHOICE **CASA LETO** BOUTIQUE HOTEL €€€

Map p254 (☎314 6622; www.casaleto.com; Bolshaya Morskaya ul 34; r incl breakfast R9500-12,000; MAdmiralteyskaya;) A dramatically lit stone stairwell sets the scene for this discreet and stylish boutique hotel. The Anglo-Italian owners have named the five guest rooms after famous St Petersburg architects. With soft pastel shades and plenty of antiques, the spacious, high-ceilinged quarters are deserving of such namesakes. Guests enjoy plenty of five-star perks, such as king-size beds, Molton Brown toiletries, heated floors and free international phone calls.

RACHMANINOV HOTEL BOUTIQUE HOTEL €€

Map p254 (☎571 7618; www.hotelrachmaninov.com; Kazanskaya ul 5; r incl breakfast from R6900; MNevsky Prospekt;) Perfectly located and run by friendly staff, the Rachmaninov Hotel is one for those in the know. Stuffed full of antiques, the rooms have been recently renovated and feel pleasantly old world with their hardwood floors and attractive Russian furnishings. In a move of questionable taste, each bedroom door has been individually painted by a local artist, but this aside, it's a great little spot.

GRAND HOTEL EUROPE LUXURY HOTEL €€€

Map p254 (☎329 6000; www.grandhoteleurope.com; Mikhailovskaya ul 1/7; r from R15,000, ste from €25,000; MGostiny Dvor; @) One of the world's most iconic hotels, the Grand Hotel Europe lives up to its name. Since 1830, when Carlo Rossi united three adjacent buildings with the grandiose facade we see today, little has been allowed to change in this heritage building. No two rooms are the same, but most are spacious and elegant in design. The junior suites are particularly lovely with original patterned parquet floors and smatterings of antiques. Regular guests quite rightly swear by the terrace rooms that afford spectacular views across the city's rooftops.

GUEST HOUSE NEVSKY 3 MINI-HOTEL €€

Map p254 (☎710 6776; www.nevsky3.ru; Nevsky pr 3; s/d incl breakfast R4700/5300; MAdmiralteyskaya;) This tiny place has just four individually decorated rooms and gets rave reviews from guests. Each room has a fridge, TV, safe and a fan, and overlooks a surprisingly quiet courtyard just moments from the Hermitage. Guests are able to use the shared kitchen, making self-catering a doddle, and the washer-dryer is also free to use. As with so many mini-hotels, it's hard to even know this one is here. Go into the courtyard of Nevsky pr 3, and call apartment 10 on the intercom beyond the entrance to the bookshop Staraya Kniga (p79).

ANGLETERRE HOTEL LUXURY HOTEL €€€

Map p254 (☎494 5666; www.angleterrehotel.com; ul Malaya Morskaya 24; r from R9000; MAdmiralteyskaya;) Breathtaking views of St Isaac's Cathedral can be had from the luxurious, beautifully designed rooms at this classic St Petersburg hotel. With supremely comfortable king-sized beds, huge bathrooms and a confidently understated style, it's no wonder that this luxury hotel is a firm favourite with VIPs. There's a great fitness centre and pool that are free for guests, and three restaurants, including a caviar bar and an excellent Italian place, Borsalino, on the ground floor.

HOTEL ASTORIA LUXURY HOTEL €€€

Map p254 (494 5757; www.roccofortehotels.com; ul Bolshaya Morskaya 39; r from R11,000, ste R35,000; M Admiralteyskaya;) What the Hotel Astoria has lost of its original Style Moderne decor, it more than compensates for in contemporary style and top-notch service. Little wonder it's beloved by visiting VIPs, from kings to rock stars. The hotel is part of the Rocco Forte Hotels group and the rooms marry the hotel's heritage character with a more modern design. The best of the suites are sprinkled with antiques and have spectacular views onto St Isaac's Cathedral. The same views – at a slightly lower price – are also available next door at the Angleterre Hotel.

TOP CHOICE **FRIENDS HOSTEL** HOSTEL €

Map p254 (571 0151; www.friendsplace.ru; nab kanala Griboyedova 20; dm/d R500/2500; M Nevsky Prospekt;) Named after the long-running TV show, this new chain of hostels is one of the best things to have happened to St Petersburg's budget travel market for ages. All four locations are great, but our favourite is this one, just next to Kazan Cathedral in a quiet courtyard. The new dorms are spotless, all have lockers and share good bathrooms and a kitchen and there are free international calls for all guests. The friendly staff members speak English, are extremely helpful and organise events every day – from pub crawls to historical walks. As well as dorm rooms there are doubles, triples and quads available, not to mention a Friends apartment just down the canal embankment. The following are the other locations: **Friends on Bankovsky** (310 4950; Bankovsky per 3; M Sennaya Pl;), **Friends on Nevsky** (272 7178; Nevsky pr 106; M Mayakovskaya;) and **Friends on Chekhova** (272 7178; ul Chekhova 11; M Mayakovskaya;).

KEMPINSKI HOTEL MOYKA 22 LUXURY HOTEL €€€

Map p254 (335 9111; www.kempinski.com; nab reki Moyki 22; r/ste from R10,000/19,500; M Nevsky Prospekt; @) This superb hotel has a great location on the Moyka River – it's practically on the doorstep of the Hermitage – and has all the comforts you'd expect of an international luxury chain. Rooms have a stylish marine theme, with cherry-wood furniture and a handsome navy blue and gold colour scheme. The 360-degree panorama from the rooftop Belle View restaurant and bar is unbeatable (although you'll pay extra for your breakfast).

PETRO PALACE HOTEL HOTEL €€

Map p254 (571 2880; www.petropalacehotel.com; ul Malaya Morskaya 14; r from R5500; M Admiralteyskaya;) This large, superbly located midrange hotel between St Isaac's Cathedral and the Hermitage has 194 rooms and excellent facilities, including a great basement fitness centre, with a decent pool, Finnish sauna and full gym. Standard rooms are spacious and tastefully designed, but without any real individuality. Unsurprisingly given its size and location, the hotel is popular with groups, though it rarely feels overrun.

3MOSTA BOUTIQUE HOTEL €€

Map p254 (332 3470; www.3mosta.com; nab reki Moyki 3A; s/d from R3000/5000; M Nevsky Prospekt;) This brand-new property is a welcome addition to the historic centre's sleeping options. The name means 'Three Bridges' in Russian, referring to the three nearby bridges over the Moyka River. Surprisingly uncramped given its wonderful location, there are 24 rooms here, and even the standards are of a good size with tasteful furniture, minibars and TVs.

NEW KID ON THE BLOCK

In 2012, the long-awaited **Four Seasons Hotel Lion Palace** (Map p254; www.fourseasons.com; Voznesensky pr 1) will finally open after years of planning, renovation and building works. Housed in the former palace of Prince Lobanov-Rostovsky – a building designed by Montferrand, the architect of next-door St Isaac's Cathedral – the 183-room luxury property is likely to set a new benchmark for high-end accommodation in St Petersburg. With a swimming pool, two enclosed courtyards, an enormous conference centre, ballroom and huge fitness centre, this really will be St Petersburg's most luxurious hotel. Watch this space.

Some rooms have great views across to the Church on the Spilled Blood, and one even has a balcony looking towards it.

NEVSKY HOTELS
MINI-HOTEL €€

Map p254 (☎703 3860; www.hon.ru; ⓂNevsky Prospekt) This prolific chain of mini-hotels has locations all over the historic heart and beyond. Three properties cluster along Bolshaya Konyushennaya ul, a pleasant avenue that runs from Nevsky pr to the Moyka River. **Nevsky Hotel Grand** (☎312 1206; Bolshaya Konyushennaya ul 10; R5900/6800; ❄📶) is not particularly grand, but a perfectly comfortable hotel right in the middle of the city. **Nevsky Hotel Aster** (☎314 7541; Bolshaya Konyushennaya ul 25; s/d R5900/6800; ❄📶) has five suites and 35 rooms. **SkyHotel** (☎600 2120; Bolshaya Konyushennaya ul 17; s/d R2600/3100; ❄📶) is the best value of the lot, though it lacks some amenities.

ANICHKOV PENSION
MINI-HOTEL €€

Map p254 (☎314 7059; www.anichkov.com; Nevsky pr 64, apt 4; s/d/ste incl breakfast from R5860/7200/7860; ⓂGostiny Dvor; ❄📶) On the 3rd floor of a handsome apartment building with an antique lift, this self-styled pension has just six rooms. The standard rooms are fine, but the suites are well worth paying a little more for. The delightful breakfast room offers balcony views of the bridge from which the pension takes its name. In the best tradition of exclusive European pensions, the Anichkov is a place for those in the know – the entrance is actually on Karavannaya ul.

PUSHKA INN
BOUTIQUE HOTEL €€

Map p254 (☎312 0913; www.pushkainn.ru; nab reki Moyki 14; s/d from R4500/6700, apt R10,000-15,000; ⓂAdmiralteyskaya; ❄📶👪) On a particularly picturesque stretch of the Moyka River, this charming inn is housed in a historic 18th-century building, just next door to the Pushkin Flat-Museum (p66). The rooms are decorated in dusky pinks and caramel tones, with wide floorboards and – if you're willing to pay more – lovely views of the Moyka. Multi-bedroom family-style apartments are also available.

LOCATION HOSTEL
HOSTEL €

Map p254 (☎490 6429; www.location-hostel.ru; Admiralteysky pr; dm/d R600/1500; ⓂAdmiralteyskaya; 📶) With a brilliant location virtually on the doorstep of the Hermitage, this arty but small hostel is definitely a good choice for budget travellers. Dorms are quite crowded, with six to eight bunks in them, but there are also some double rooms if you need more space. There's a communal kitchen, rather tatty-looking shared bathrooms and plenty of cool art in the staircase. The young staff members are passionate about the city, and reception works 24 hours, so you can come back whenever you like.

BELVEDER NEVSKY
MINI-HOTEL €€

Map p254 (☎571 8338; www.belveder-nevsky.spb.ru; Bolshaya Konyushennaya ul 29; s/d R3750/4500; ⓂNevsky Prospekt; 📶) A little bit different from the cookie-cutter mini-hotels, this Finnish-managed business hotel takes things to the next level. Automatic doors open onto corridors covered with golden, diamond-patterned wallpaper, while the decoration of the large rooms also veers towards the opulent with gold-striped wallpaper, flowing window drapes and richly patterned bedspreads.

POLIKOFF HOTEL
MINI-HOTEL €€

Map p254 (☎995 3488; www.polikoff.ru; Nevsky pr 64/11; s/d R3000/3800; ⓂGostiny Dvor) A quiet haven of contemporary cool just steps away from Nevsky pr, the Polikoff Hotel can be hard to find. Enter through the brown door at Karavannaya ul 11 and dial 26. You will find a soothing decor that features subdued lighting, blond-wood veneer and the soft brown and cream tones beloved of modern-design hotels. A few smaller rooms are available at reduced rates – a great find for all those style gurus on a budget.

PIO ON GRIBOYEDOV
MINI-HOTEL €€

Map p254 (☎571 9476; www.hotelpio.ru; nab kanala Griboyedova 35, apt 5; s/d/tr/q R3400/3800/4800/5400; ⓂNevsky Prospekt; 📶) This excellent place overlooks Kanal Griboyedova and has six rooms, all of which share three bathrooms and toilets. It's not as hostel-like as it sounds though; it's much more like staying in a large apartment with friends. The communal areas are very pleasant and the rooms are comfortable and clean. Even better is the central location and view: big windows look out onto the canal and bathe the whole place in light.

MOYKA 5
MINI-HOTEL €€

Map p254 (☎601 0636; www.hon.ru; nab reki Moyki 5; s/d R5900/6800; ⓂNevsky Prospekt; ❄📶) Part of the Nevsky Hotels chain (p161), Moyka 5 has a fantastic location on the Moyka River, behind the Church on the Spilled Blood. It's a pretty slick location for a fairly simple hotel, but 24 sterile yet perfectly decent rooms provide all the necessary comforts.

NEVSKY PROSPEKT B&B MINI-HOTEL €

Map p254 (☎921 955 3754; www.bnbrussia.com; Nevsky pr 11, apt 8; s/d with shared bathroom incl breakfast R2500/3300; Ⓜ Admiralteyskaya; 📶) Superbly located and delightfully decorated, this five-room place is among the city's most charming, with tiled stoves, antique furnishings and the oldest functioning radio and TV you're likely to see anywhere. The English-speaking staff will make you feel right at home, serving breakfast and afternoon tea every day. The only downside is the shared bathroom facilities, but for the centrality it's more than worth the price. Airport transfers are included, but visa support is additional.

FORTECIA PETER MINI-HOTEL €€

Map p254 (Фортеция Питер; ☎315 0828; www.fortecia.ru, in Russian; ul Millionnaya 29; r incl breakfast R4500; Ⓜ Admiralteyskaya; ❄📶) In a fantastic location just seconds from the Hermitage, this pleasant eight-room mini-hotel is found in a quiet and unassuming courtyard. Staff are friendly, some English is spoken and the rooms, while a little on the small side, are comfortable and more than a little charming with their exposed brickwork and beams.

STONY ISLAND HOTEL HOTEL €€

Map p254 (☎337 2434; www.stonyisland.com; ul Lomonosova 1; r R6500; Ⓜ Nevsky Prospekt; ❄📶) Right in the thick of the nightlife hotspot of Dumskaya ul, the Stony Island is for anyone who wants to be in the absolute city centre. The 17 minimalist rooms are in four different categories, and many of them are in interesting shapes thanks to the quirky historic building. Inside, there's a fairly good stab at cool decor as well as flat-screen TVs, mini-bars and good bathrooms. Not one for the noise sensitive, but otherwise it's a great choice.

HOTEL GRIFON MINI-HOTEL €€

Map p254 (☎315 4916; www.grifonhotel.ru; nab kanala Griboyedova 35; s/d incl breakfast from R4500/4990; 📶) The furniture and fittings might be rather cheap and boring, but this hotel, named after the famous nearby Griffin Bridge, is friendly and comfy. The 12 rooms are all quite spacious, have TVs and good bathrooms. Wireless access costs R100 per 24 hours.

CUBA HOSTEL HOSTEL €

Map p254 (☎921 7115; www.cubahostel.ru; Kazanskaya ul 5; dm R500-850, d R2600; Ⓜ Nevsky Prospekt; 📶) This fun, funky hostel has a super location behind the Kazan Cathedral. Rainbow-coloured paint covers the walls in dorm rooms that are equipped with metal bunk beds and private lockers. Rooms sleep four to 10 people and prices vary accordingly. Bathrooms are cramped, but very clean. Staff members are young, speak English and are eager to please. There's a kitchen and washing machine available for guests. The entrance is next to the red British phone box on the street.

COMFORT HOTEL HOTEL €€

Map p254 (☎314 6523; www.comfort-hotel.ru; Bolshaya Morskaya ul 25; s/d incl breakfast from R5200/6200; Ⓜ Admiralteyskaya; ❄📶) This aptly named hotel is indeed comfortable, with 18 cosy rooms, all decorated in a simple style with indifferent and rather cheap furniture. The location is excellent, however, midway between St Isaac's Cathedral and Nevsky pr.

HERZEN HOTEL HOTEL €€

Map p254 (☎315 5550; www.herzen-hotel.ru; Bolshaya Morskaya ul 25; s/d incl breakfast R5100-6000; ❄📶) In the same building as the Comfort Hotel, this is a slightly larger place of similar standards. Its furniture is similarly tasteless, especially in the 'improved' rooms where they've tried to be trendy. You're paying for location here though, and it's got an excellent one.

NORD HOSTEL HOSTEL €

Map p254 (☎571 0342; www.nordhostel.com; Bolshaya Morskaya ul 10; dm/d R950/3000; Ⓜ Nevsky Prospekt; 📶) The ideal location of this discreetly marked hostel – just under the archway from Dvortsovaya pl – is almost too good to be true. An impressive stairwell leads to the friendly if rather cramped 1st-floor hostel, which offers one 10-bed dorm as well as a private double room. All of the rooms have high ceilings, Ikea-style furniture and plenty of natural light, creating a pleasant enough atmosphere. Other facilities include lockers, kitchen, laundry and – should you feel a tune coming on – a piano. Note that check-in is only between 9am and 2pm, and 5pm and 9pm.

MINI HOTEL DOLCE VITA MINI-HOTEL €

Map p254 (702 8288; www.hotel-dolce.ru, in Russian; nab kanala Griboyedova 38; d/tw/tr R2300/2400/3600; MNevsky Prospekt;) The rooms here may be Soviet style and charmless, but the location is fantastic and you won't find any cheaper en suite rooms in such a central location. No English is spoken, though the staff here do their best and can be quite charming once you've broken the ice.

HOTEL NAUKA HOTEL €

Map p254 (315 8696; www.hotel-nauka.ru; Millionnaya ul 27; s R800-900, d R1600-1800, tr/q R2250/2800; MAdmiralteyskaya;) Despite a renovation, the Academy of Science's hotel has effortlessly retained its Soviet air. But with the Hermitage on the doorstep and the bargain basement prices, who are we to complain? Advance booking is advised as the hotel can fill up with impecunious academics who, no doubt, feel very much at home in its university-dorm-style rooms. Bathrooms are shared, though there's a fridge and TV in each room. Nobody really speaks English but that's definitely part of the fun.

Smolny & Vosstaniya

TOP CHOICE **HOSTEL LIGOVSKY 74** HOSTEL €

Map p260 (329 1274; www.hostel74.ru; Ligovsky pr 74, Vosstaniya; dm/r R600/1500, design rooms R2500; MLigovsky Prospekt;) Come and stay in St Petersburg's coolest art gallery and cultural space – the 3rd floor of Loft Project ETAGI (p87) is given over to this superfriendly hostel. Some of the dorms here are enormous (one has 20 beds in it!) but the facilities are spotless, and include washing machines and a small kitchen. As well as the dorms there are three 'design rooms' that are boutique hotel quality at budget price. Reserve ahead – these are nearly always booked up in advance.

TOP CHOICE **HOSTEL LIFE** HOSTEL €

Map p260 (318 1808; www.hostel-life.ru; Nevsky pr 47, Vosstaniya; dm R800-1000, s/d R2200/2600; MMayakovskaya;) A fantastic hostel right in the heart of the city, Life opened in 2010 and is a thoroughly modern, progressive place. From the moment you arrive you're made to feel at home – slippers are provided – and the premises are spacious and bright. The 15 rooms range from doubles to dorms sleeping eight and Room 7 has an amazing corner window on Nevsky pr – surely the best view available for this low price! There's a big kitchen, clean bathrooms, free laundry and professional English-speaking staff – all in all, a great option.

PIO ON MOKHOVAYA MINI-HOTEL €€

Map p258 (273 3585; www.hotelpio.ru; apt 10, Mokhovaya ul 39, Smolny; s/d/tr/q R3800/4400/5600/6400; MMayakovskaya;) This lovely lodging is the sister property to the Pio on Griboyedov (p161). While it lacks the perfect location and canal views, it's actually far more spacious, stylish and comfortable than the other property. It's also very child friendly, with family groups warmly welcomed and provided for. Prices are slightly higher here because each of the 11 rooms has a bathroom. Bonus: there is also a Finnish sauna on-site.

HELVETIA HOTEL & SUITES HOTEL €€

Map p260 (326 2009; www.helvetiahotel.ru; ul Marata 11, Vosstaniya; r incl breakfast from R6000; MMayakovskaya;) Pass through the wrought-iron gates into a wonderfully private and professionally run oasis of calm and class. Next to the Swiss consulate and just a shopping-bag swing away from Nevsky pr, Helvetia occupies a mansion designed by Swiss architect Augusto Lange in 1828. The courtyard is a delightful place to escape the city's bustle. Guest rooms are less atmospheric, but make up for it in comfort. With two on-site restaurants, this is a great place to eat too, and the buffet breakfast is excellent.

KRISTOFF HOTEL HOTEL €€

Map p260 (571 3692; www.kristoff.ru; Zagorodny pr 9, Vosstaniya; r incl breakfast from R3500; MDostoevskaya;) This 31-room hotel at a busy confluence of shopping streets near the heart of Vladimirskaya is a safe

ACCOMMODATION AGENCIES

The following recommended agencies can help you with short-term accommodation in St Petersburg.

Bed & Breakfast (www.bednbreakfast.sp.ru)

City Realty (www.cityrealtyrussia.com)

HOFA (www.hofa.ru)

Travel Russia (www.travelrussia.su)

Intro by Irina (www.introbyirina.com)

and comfortable good-value place to stay. The rooms are smartly decorated (even if they're not particularly memorable) and the service from the English-speaking staff is friendly and efficient. There's also the popular and cosy restaurant downstairs (where breakfast is served), which, handily, is open round the clock.

FIFTH CORNER — MINI-HOTEL €€

Map p260 (☎380 8181; www.5ugol.ru; Zagorodny pr 13, Vosstaniya; r incl breakfast from R4500; ⓂVladimirskaya; ❄📶) Named after the junction of streets that it overlooks, this stylish hotel has been refurbished and its lobby is looking better than ever. Its rooms are quite different: warmer toned and perhaps less design-conscious, but very comfortable all the same. The on-site restaurant has an equally groovy design that makes it a great place for breakfast or a nightcap.

AUSTRIAN YARD HOTEL — MINI-HOTEL €€

Map p258 (☎579 8235; www.austrianyard.com; Furshtatskaya ul 45, Smolny; s/d from R4050/4200; ⓂChernyshevskaya) You must book ahead to stay in the super-secluded place located next to the Austrian consulate. It has four rooms – one on each floor – and they're all good ones. Each is stylishly designed with bright modern furnishings and kitchenettes. There's a little sauna in the courtyard, and a second similar hotel, **Austrian Yard II** (☎273 6065; Furshtatskaya ul 16), just down the road.

HOTEL VERA — HOTEL €€

Map p258 (☎702 6190; www.hotelvera.ru; Suvorovsky pr 25/16, Smolny; s/d incl breakfast from R3600/4990; ⓂPloshchad Vosstaniya; ❄📶) Housed in a fabulous 1903 building, this well-run option has slanted ceilings, stained-glass windows, ceramic-tile stoves and ornate mouldings that remember its art deco origins. It's not all stuck in the past, however. There are satellite TVs and fridges in rooms, and bathrooms are thoroughly modern. Request a room on the courtyard, as those overlooking busy Suvorovsky pr can be noisy.

NEVSKY FORUM — BOUTIQUE HOTEL €€€

Map p260 (☎333 0222; www.forumhotel.ru; Nevsky pr 69, Smolny; s/d incl breakfast from R8100/9900, designer s/d R10,300/11,300; ⓂMayakovskaya; ❄📶) This smart bolthole has the whole range of facilities and comforts you'd expect, but compared to the other luxury properties in town, it caters to a more cost-conscious traveller. All 20 rooms are spacious and comfortable, with king-size beds, big double-glazed windows and environmentally friendly cork flooring. Trendsetters should look to the 'designer' rooms, which are individually decorated in a hip, modern style.

> ### SLEEP LIKE A TSAR
>
> If you've always wanted to sleep in a tsarist palace, here is your chance. Peter the Great built his summer palace at Strelna (p150), a town about 24km from St Petersburg, and now it is Putin's presidential palace, used for international meetings and state visits. Putin houses his guests on the grounds at the **Baltic Star Hotel** (☎438 5700; www.balticstar-hotel.ru; Beriozovaya al 3; r from R4500, ste R10,000, cottage R80,000; ❄📶🏊). If it's not otherwise occupied, you could stay here too. Besides the 100 well-appointed rooms in the main hotel, there are 18 VIP cottages on the shore of the Gulf of Finland, each equipped with a private dining room, study, sauna, swimming pool and, of course, staff quarters for your entourage.

BROTHERS KARAMAZOV — BOUTIQUE HOTEL €€

Map p260 (☎335 1185; www.karamazovhotel.ru; Sotsialisticheskaya ul 11a, Vosstaniya; s/d from R5500/6500; ⓂVladimirskaya; ❄📶) Pack a copy of Dostoevsky's final novel to read while staying at this appealing boutique hotel – the great man penned *The Brothers K* while living in the neighbourhood. In homage, the hotel's 28 charming rooms are all named after different female Dostoevsky characters to help you answer that age-old question: which 19th-century fallen woman are you?

GREENWICH HOTEL — MINI-HOTEL €€

Map p258 (☎273 0817; www.greenwich-hotel.ru; Kovensky per 14-4, Smolny; s/d incl breakfast R4200/4400; ⓂPloshchad Vosstaniya; ❄📶) Tucked away on a quiet side street, this bizarre little hotel claims to be a slice of England in Russia. The reception area is designed to look like you've entered a pub, complete with a red phone box in it (very commonly found in pubs, of course), all a homage to the owner's own sojourn in South London. The overall effect may be rather

Mary Poppins-ish, but the eight rooms, cluttered full of Victoriana, actually have plenty of charm and the location is good.

ARBAT NORD HOTEL BOUTIQUE HOTEL €€

Map p258 (☎703 1899; www.arbat-nord.ru; Artilleriyskaya ul 4, Smolny; s/d incl breakfast R6700/7200; Ⓜ Chernyshevskaya; ❄@📶) Facing the unsightly concrete Hotel Rus, the sleek modern Arbat Nord seems to be showing its neighbour how to run a good establishment. The modern rooms are decorated in gold and green hues, and even though the furniture is fairly cheap, there's plenty of space. Efficient English-speaking staff are on hand, but wireless costs extra.

GREEN APPLE HOTEL MINI-HOTEL €

Map p258 (☎272 1023; www.greenapplehotel.ru; ul Korolenko 14, Smolny; s/d/tr incl breakfast from R2700/3200/3700; Ⓜ Chernyshevskaya; ❄📶) This stylish, thoroughly modern 15-room hotel in the sleepy backstreets of Liteyny is a welcoming place to stay. Some of the best-value rooms are the so-called *ekonomchiks* (little economy rooms), which sleep three people (the third bed is on a mezzanine). They're a great bargain.

ART HOTEL BOUTIQUE HOTEL €€

Map p258 (☎740 7585; www.art-hotel.ru; Mokhovaya ul 27-29, Smolny; s/d from R4000/4800; Ⓜ Chernyshevskaya; 📶) An ornate wrought-iron gate guards the courtyard of this pre-revolutionary apartment building, now displaying a sort of dilapidated grandeur. Follow the signs to this misleadingly named hotel, which retains a straightforward elegance in its 14 rooms, but has nothing particularly arty about it. Indeed, the mood is bourgeois-on-a-budget, with heavy pleated drapes framing the windows, crystal chandeliers and mouldings decorating the ceilings, and a ceramic tile stove in the corridor.

NILS BED & BREAKFAST HOME-STAY €

Map p258 (☎923 0575; www.rentroom.org; 5-ya Sovetskaya ul 21, Smolny; s/d/tr from R1400/2800/3400; Ⓜ Ploshchad Vosstaniya; 📶) Nils' B&B is an excellent option at a great price. Four spacious rooms share two modern bathrooms, as well as a beautiful light-filled common area and kitchen. Nils renovated this place himself, taking great care to preserve the mouldings, wooden floors and other architectural elements. He now exhibits the same consideration in taking care of his guests.

HOTEL SUVOROV MINI-HOTEL €€

Map p258 (☎271 0859; www.suvorovhotel.spb.ru; 5-ya Sovetskaya ul 3/13, Smolny; s/d/ste R3100/3600/3800; Ⓜ Ploshchad Vosstaniya; ❄📶) On a quiet street and behind the enormous Oktyabrsky Concert Hall, this small but welcoming hotel offers excellent value. Housed on the ground floor of an attractive classical building, 20 comfortable rooms offer all the amenities you need, in a modern (albeit bland) setting.

PUPPET HOSTEL HOSTEL €

Map p258 (☎272 5401; www.hostel-puppet.ru; ul Nekrasova 12, Smolny; dm/d R600/800; Ⓜ Mayakovskaya; 📶) This HI-affiliated place once offered accommodation for itinerant puppeteers, so it is not recommended for pupaphobes. Other budget-minded travellers, however, might appreciate the free tickets to the next-door Bolshoy Puppet Theatre (p97) – a fringe benefit for guests. The hostel also offers clean, basic rooms with two to five beds, standard Soviet decor and shared bathroom and kitchen facilities. The staff are friendly, though not always in English. Visa support is available for an extra charge.

Sennaya & Kolomna

TOP CHOICE **ALEXANDER HOUSE** BOUTIQUE HOTEL €€€

Map p264 (☎334 3540; www.a-house.ru; nab kanala Kryukova 27, Kolomna; r/ste from R9500/11,000, apt from R15,000; Ⓜ Sennaya Ploshchad; ❄📶) Owners Alexander and Natalya have converted this historic building opposite Nikolsky Cathedral, styling each of the 14 spacious rooms after their favourite international cities. The themes are not laboured: a ceramic iguana clinging to the ceiling beam in the Barcelona suite; a tropical feel to Bali; Moorish touches in Marrakesh. And yes, a room named St Petersburg, with exposed brick walls and windows overlooking the canal. Lovely common areas include a fireplace-warmed lounge and a vine-laden courtyard containing a guests-only restaurant.

TOP CHOICE **ANDREY & SASHA'S HOMESTAY** HOME-STAY €

Map p264 (☎315 3330, 921 409 6701; asamatuga@mail.ru; nab kanala Griboyedova 49, Sennaya; s/d R2400/2800; Ⓜ Sadovaya) Energetic owners and Italophiles Andrey and Sasha extend the warmest of welcomes to travellers who pass through St Petersburg. This is the biggest of three apartments they rent out (by the room or in their entirety) – all are centrally located and eclectically decorated with lots of designer touches and an eye for beautiful furniture. Andrey and Sasha have chipped back plaster to the brick walls, laid terracotta tile floors (with underfloor heating) and installed iron candelabras. The bedrooms (two to four in each apartment) seem bigger than they actually are, thanks to the use of enormous mirrors. Bathrooms are shared, as are kitchen facilities. Socialising is definitely encouraged, and your hosts will likely invite you to join them sipping wine by the fire or drinking coffee on the rooftop.

ARKADIA BOUTIQUE HOTEL €€

Map p264 (571 6173; www.arkadiahotel.ru; nab reki Moyki 58, Sennaya; s/d from R4100/5100; Admiralteyskaya;) On the banks of the Moyka River, hidden away inside a quiet flower-filled courtyard, this bright yellow hotel provides a welcome respite from the city's crowds. Warm hues, wood floors and natural lighting characterise the guest rooms; though the on-site sauna and plunge pool are not free for guests, they do get a 20% discount. Aside from the owners' obvious fondness for plastic plants, this place is a winner.

NORTHERN LIGHTS MINI-HOTEL €€

Map p264 (571 9199; www.nlightsrussia.com; ul Bolshaya Morskaya 50, Kolomna; r incl breakfast with shared bathroom R3000, s/d incl breakfast with private bathroom R4000/4300; Admiralteyskaya;) Opposite the childhood home of Vladimir Nabokov is this very pleasant, friendly mini-hotel at the end of an impressive old staircase. There are just five rooms here: three have their own bathrooms and air-con, while two share facilities and are fan-cooled. All rooms are tastefully decorated and include cable TV and DVD players.

NEVSKY BREEZE HOTEL HOTEL €€

Map p264 (570 1146; www.hon.ru; ul Galernaya 12, Kolomna; s/d R5900/6800; Admiralteyskaya;) This fantastically located hotel is part of the Nevsky Hotels chain (see p161) and is in one of the city centre's most charming streets, just one block back from the Neva River. The 33 rooms are comfortable and simple, all with private bathrooms but without fridges. It's thoroughly contemporary inside, and little mileage is made out of the historic building, but despite this it's a very popular choice.

DOSTOEVSKY HOUSE HOTEL MINI-HOTEL €€

Map p264 (314 8231; www.ddspb.ru; ul Kaznacheyskaya 61/1, Sennaya; r incl breakfast R3600; Sennaya Ploshchad;) Dostoevsky lived in this house next to Kanal Griboyedova between 1861 and 1863, although it's probably far nicer here than it was when he set *Crime and Punishment* in the surrounding streets. The 10 rooms here are comfortable but plain, and range from spacious to tiny. There's free tea and coffee throughout your stay and a fan in the room to keep you cool.

GRAFFITI HOSTEL HOSTEL €

Map p264 (714 7038; www.graffitihostel.ru; nab reki Moyki 102, Kolomna; dm from R450, d R2000; Sennaya Ploshchad;) You should have no trouble finding this new hostel. Its fabulously painted exterior sets it apart, and it looks more like a contemporary art installation than a place to bed down for the night. The interior is far more simple – basic, even – but the shared bathrooms are clean enough and some even have views of St Isaac's Cathedral from their balconies!

GOLDEN AGE RETRO HOTEL MINI-HOTEL €

Map p264 (Золотая Середина; 315 1212; www.retrohotel.ru; Grazhdanskaya ul 16, Sennaya; s/d with shared bathroom R1700/2150, with private bathroom R2500/2900; Sadovaya;) Tucked into a quiet courtyard in the narrow streets north of Sennaya pl, this friendly little hotel is one of St Pete's best bargains. A few antiques are scattered around to justify its 'retro' claims, but most furniture and all facilities are quite modern, with a kitchen for guest use as well as a washing machine. To access the hotel (which clearly has something against signage), ring 88 at the Grazhdanskaya ul 16 entry phone (even though the official street address is different) and then go up to flat 14 on the 2nd floor.

HOUSE IN KOLOMNA MINI-HOTEL €

Map p264 (Домик в Коломне; 710 8351; www.colomnahotel.ru, in Russian; nab kanala Griboyedova 174A, Kolomna; s/d with shared bathroom R1500/1900, with private bathroom R2300/2600; Sadovaya;) Pushkin's family once rented rooms in this house and the great writer even wrote a short story called *The Little House in Kolomna*. The associations with Pushkin end there, though, as the interior and atmosphere evoke a Russian flat from the 1970s, complete with brown furnishings and lots of plants. You're a bit out of the way here, but at these prices it's a good deal. The hotel is totally unsigned – go into the courtyard behind house 174A and ring the unmarked bell on your left.

HOSTEL ON SADOVAYA HOSTEL €

Map p264 (Гостиница на Садовой; ☎314 4510; www.sadovaya53.ru; Sadovaya ul 53, Sennaya; s/d R2400/3600; MSadovaya) Back in the day, Communist party apparatchiks used to stay here when they came to visit Leningrad. These days, budget travellers can enjoy the same Soviet service and style, and the amount of English spoken remains almost nil. Don't expect anything like a traditional hostel, but rooms are clean and have private facilities. It's handy for the metro, even if the immediate area isn't particularly beautiful.

MATISOV DOMIK HOTEL €€

Map p264 (☎495 0242; www.matisov.com; nab reki Pryazhka 3/1, Kolomna; s/d incl breakfast from R3500/4100; MSadovaya;) Only about a 10-minute walk west of the Mariinsky Theatre, this rather unattractive modern hotel has an idyllic location right on the lovely Pryazhka River. The monochromatic rooms have cheap modern furniture and are a long way from charming, but the staff members are very helpful. It's located rather awkwardly on tiny Madison Island, a 20-minute walk from just about anything else.

Vasilyevsky Island

SOKOS HOTEL VASILYEVSKY HOTEL €€

Map p266 (☎335 2290; www.sokoshotels.com; 8-ya liniya 11-13; r from R6700; MVasileostrovskaya;) Open since 2008, this surprisingly enormous hotel has more than 200 rooms, although you hardly notice it from the street. It's a sleek, well-designed place aimed at business travellers and the upper end of the holiday market. The rooms are spacious, with nice design touches, while the large Repin Lounge downstairs takes care of all food and drink needs. It's a short walk from the main shopping street of Vasilyevsky Island and the metro.

COURTYARD MARRIOT HOTEL €€€

Map p266 (☎380 4011; www.courtyardsaintpetersburg.ru; 2-ya liniya 61; r from R8500; MVasileostrovskaya;) This new addition to Vasilyevsky Island's sleeping options is a stylish business hotel with excellent facilities and professional staff. The rooms are classy, spacious and thoroughly modern, and some on the higher floors have great views. It's a bit of a walk to the metro, but otherwise this is a very comfortable place to stay. The similar **Courtyard St Petersburg Pushkin Hotel** (Map p264; ☎610 5000; nab kanala Griboyedova 166, Kolomna; MSennaya Pl), in Sennaya and Kolomna, is even further from public transport.

NASHOTEL HOTEL €€€

Map p266 (☎323 2231; www.nashotel.ru; 11-ya liniya 50; s/d R8500/9400; MVasileostrovskaya;) Despite being half a decade old, this spotless place still looks like it has just opened. The very tall, beautifully remodelled building on this quiet Vasilyevsky Island side street has a striking exterior and its rooms are blazes of colours, complete with modern furnishings and great views from the higher rooms. Garish touches include some truly dreadful room art and a preponderance of plants throughout, but these gripes aside, this is generally a smart and stylish modern hotel.

ART HOTEL TREZZINI HOTEL €€

Map p266 (☎332 1035; www.trezzini-hotel.com; Bolshoy pr 21; s/d from R4200/6300; MVasileostrovskaya;) Named after Domenico Trezzini, who developed the original architectural plan for Vasilyevsky Island in the 18th century, this place styles itself an 'art' hotel, which means you can expect lots of garish paintings in the lobby. Thankfully the rooms are a little more restrained, although fake rose chandeliers may not be to everyone's taste. Decor issues aside, Trezzini is well located, clean and good value.

SOKOS HOTEL PALACE BRIDGE HOTEL €€€

Map p266 (☎335 2200; www.sokoshotels.com; Birzhevoy per 2-4; r from R9000; MVasileostrovskaya;) Far less a hotel and more a self-contained spa resort, this huge complex is tucked away on a quiet side street just back from the Strelka. It contains a vast pool, no less than eight saunas, several excellent restaurants and wine bars, a bowling alley and a conference centre. Little surprise then that it's popular with families and business people. In fact, it would be very easy not to leave the premises for days on end – though that would rather take the point out of this great location, just a 10-minute walk to the Hermitage.

SHELFORT HOTEL HOTEL €€

Map p266 (☎328 0555; www.shelfort.ru; 3-ya liniya 26; s/d/ste incl breakfast R3550/5050/6500; MVasileostrovskaya;) In a convenient but quiet location close to the metro, this handsome building houses an excellent hotel on the first two floors of this residential building. For those not fortunate enough to score the spacious suites, the regular rooms are still pretty nice, sporting classically simple furnishings, high ceilings and plenty of space. A scattering of antiques gives it a pleasant old-world air.

Petrograd & Vyborg Sides

TOP CHOICE TRADITION HOTEL — HOTEL €€

Map p268 (☎405 8855; www.traditionhotel.ru; pr Dobrolyubova 2; r from R7700; M Sportivnaya; ❄ 📶) Facing the Hermitage across the river, this great little hotel is a consistent traveller favourite and boasts many return guests due to its smiling and extremely helpful staff who really go out of their way for their guests. Its rooms are comfortable and well appointed and the great views across the river make up for its distance from the metro.

APART-HOTEL KRONVERK — HOTEL €€

Map p268 (☎703 3663; www.kronverk.com; ul Blokhina 9; r R4370, apt from R8480; M Sportivnaya; ❄ 📶) If the baroque, rococo and Style Moderne architecture of St Petersburg leaves you hankering after something more contemporary, then here's a place for you. Occupying the upper floors of a slick business centre, the Kronverk offers appealing modern rooms with self-catering facilities. Frosted glass and streamlined black panelling create a crisp reception area where the English-speaking staff are efficient and professional.

HOTEL AURORA — MINI-HOTEL €

Map p268 (☎233 3641; www.hotel-aurora.ru; Malaya Posadskaya ul 15; s/d with shared bathroom R2100/2600, with private bathroom R2600/3100; M Gorkovskaya; 📶) Tucked in behind the Peter and Paul Fortress, this spunky mini-hotel offers affordable, friendly accommodation. The four spacious rooms sport a quaintly charming, Soviet-style decor, with parquet floors, rickety beds and monochrome linens. Nonetheless, shiny new bathrooms and kitchen facilities make this an excellent deal.

Understand St Petersburg

St Petersburg Today

Not since the paint first dried on Rastrelli's buildings in the late 18th century has St Petersburg looked so good. Twenty years of massive investment after 70 years of neglect under the Soviets has certainly paid off, and its facades are bursts of beautifully painted pastels and primes once again. But glimpse inside the buildings and you'll see there's a lot of work yet to be done: overall the city remains poor, despite a burgeoning middle class, and many challenges – economic and political – lie ahead.

Best on Film

Brother (1997) Sergei Bodrov Jr fights the mafia on the mean streets of St Petersburg.

Russian Ark (2002) Alexander Sukorov's one-shot meditation on Russian history filmed inside the Hermitage.

Irony of Fate (1975) Perhaps the best loved Leningrad comedy of all time.

The Stroll (2003) A delightfully playful film in which three friends wander from situation to situation on the streets of St Petersburg.

Onegin (1999) Pushkin's epic tale of lost love and regret is beautifully retold by Martha Fiennes.

Best in Print

Crime and Punishment (Fyodor Dostoevsky, 1866) The quintessential St Petersburg novel explores the mind of the deluded Rodion Raskolnikov.

Speak, Memory (Vladimir Nabokov, 1951) A wonderfully bittersweet literary memoir of Nabokov's own St Petersburg childhood.

The Nose (Nikolai Gogol, 1836) Follow Major Kovalyov around the city in pursuit of his errant nose.

Ten Days That Shook the World (John Reed, 1919) A remarkable first-hand account of the Russian revolution.

Change at City Hall

In 2011 city governor and long-serving Vladimir Putin lieutenant, Valentina Matvienko, was unceremoniously moved sideways out of the city by the Kremlin, having become a liability for the ruling United Russia Party gearing up for presidential elections in 2012. In her place, former KGB officer and dyed-in-the-wool Putin loyalist Georgy Poltavchenko was appointed acting governor, though most local observers agree that his permanence in the post is almost certainly assured, as Russian governors are appointed by the president rather than elected by the populace. Relatively little is known about Poltavchenko, a former federal-level politician and keen tweeter, but few expect many surprises from a man whose background is so closely involved with Putin's St Petersburg network.

Goodbye, Valentina

Matvienko will not be missed by most. Her apparent indifference to the city's architectural heritage and inability to have snow and icicles cleared – no laughing matter in a city with extreme weather patterns, where falling icicles kill and injure many people each year – led to low opinion-poll ratings and unusual amounts of public anger. While she was certainly a formidable force representing the city and could be both wily and charming, her authoritarian style and inability to brook criticism united a disparate opposition. Public demonstrations against her policies became the norm in the last years of her rule.

For the opposition, Matvienko's most obvious failing was her support for the Okhta Centre (p201), an unpopular and, many argue, entirely unnecessary skyscraper development that was to be built in the city centre. The former governor's unwavering support for the scheme caused her to lose a lot of political capital – and all for nothing, when she finally bowed to a large local protest movement and pressure from Unesco, which feared the city's historic heart (a World Heritage site) would be compromised by a 400m skyscraper being built next to it. The tower, now renamed the Lakhta Centre, will still be built, but far from the city centre (to the relief of many architectural preservationists).

Popular Protest

In recent years small protest movements have been causing waves in a city where political protest remains rare. Chief among these is the Strategy 31 movement, which meets on the 31st of each month to protest the government's disregard for article 31 of the Russian constitution, which guarantees freedom of assembly. Ironically, the protesters are routinely arrested and carted away by the police for exercising their rights.

A case of alleged police brutality during one of these protests in 2010 managed to capture the public's imagination more than any other. Police officer Vadim Boiko, dubbed 'Animal Cop' by the media, was filmed beating peaceful protestors and dragging one woman by the hair. He is currently on trial for exceeding his authority, a rare case of the Russian police being held to account by anyone.

Finally the gay rights movement has been forced to prominence by the violence of the far right groups that routinely attack any form of LGBT demonstration. Sadly, the police have rarely done much more than arrest the gay rights protesters, whose marches continue to be unauthorised by the authorities.

A Showcase City

With Putin's continued stranglehold on politics seemingly continuing, his hometown rides high in its prestige within Russia. As a showcase for the new Russia, it hosts international summits and conferences, and enjoys continued federal investment in infrastructure and redevelopment, making it second only to Moscow.

An important prestige project is the New Mariinsky Theatre (p108), due to open in 2012 after a decade of false starts and new dawns. It may not be the dramatic and iconic Dominique Perrault design that would have placed St Petersburg on the world modern architecture map, but it is shaping up to be an excellent theatre worthy of one of the world's leading ballet and opera troupes. Other major projects are the new Four Seasons Hotel (p160), the city's first world-class luxury hotel; the redevelopment of New Holland (p110) into a cultural and entertainment space by billionaire Roman Abramovich; and the recent opening of a fifth metro line including the Hermitage's much-needed Admiralteyskaya stop.

A stark mix of positive and negative, the city has come a long way from post-communist semi-ruin, and is easily one of Europe's most beautiful cities, but everyone from the Kremlin down agrees there's still a huge distance to go.

if Russia were 100 people

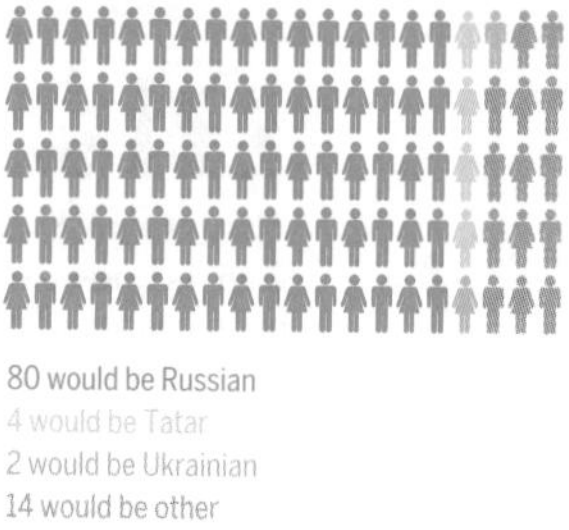

ethnicity

(% of population)

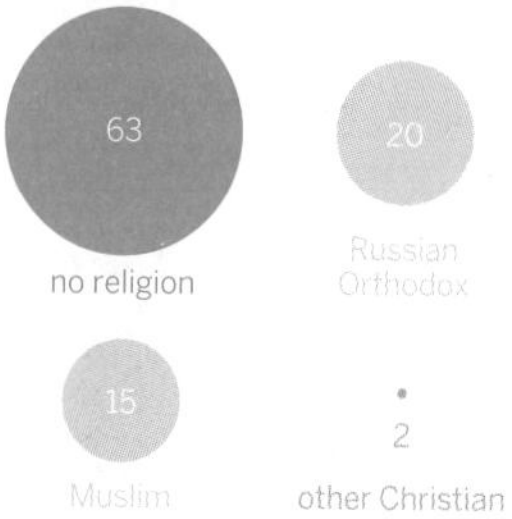

population per sq km

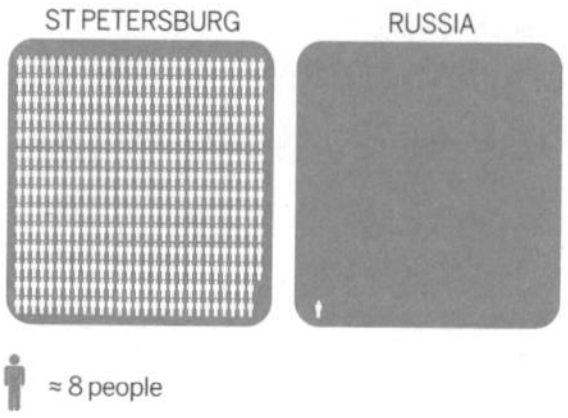

History

The history of St Petersburg (make that Petrograd and Leningrad, as well) is one of struggle. First came a struggle of identity – forcing Russia's inward-looking head to look towards Europe and to recast itself in its image (arguably a task that will never truly be complete). This was followed by a struggle of ideas – whether it be despotism versus reform, communism versus fascism or simply democracy versus autocracy, one that is quietly still being fought today. St Petersburg has been deeply marked by each of these struggles, making its 300-year history one of the world's most eventful.

CITY BY THE SEA

Precocious Prince

For three centuries, Moscow hosted Russia's ruler tsars. The onion-domed capital was shrouded in mystery and intrigue. The precocious Peter never fitted in.

Born in 1672, Peter I was the son of Tsar Alexey I and his second wife, Natalya Naryshkina, and was one of 16 siblings. His spindly frame grew to be an imposing 2m tall and he suffered from a twitchy form of epilepsy. He loved ditching the claustrophobic Kremlin and traipsing through the countryside with his misfit friends, staging mock military manoeuvres and sailing into make-believe naval battles. When his mother arranged a marriage for him to secure the family's aristocratic connections, the teenager reluctantly consented. But a few years later he sent his first wife to a nunnery and took up with a Lithuanian peasant girl, later known as Catherine I, whom he adored and married.

Peter was more than ever convinced that Russians were still living in the dark ages.

Peter was also exceptional for his insatiable curiosity about the outside world. He spent long hours in the city quarter for foreign merchants, who regaled the young prince with tales of the wonders of the modern age. Once on the throne, he became the first tsar to venture beyond the border. Travelling in disguise, Peter and a raucous Russian entourage criss-crossed the continent, meeting with monarchs, dining with dignitaries

TIMELINE

1672

Peter Alexeyevich Romanov is born in Moscow to Alexey Mikhailovich and his second wife Natalya Naryshkina. He grows up to be known as Peter the Great.

1703

On 27 May Peter the Great establishes the Peter and Paul Fortress on Zayachy Island, thus founding the new city of Sankt Pieter Burkh, Russia's 'window to the West'.

1709

A decisive win by Peter's forces at the Battle of Poltava, the main battle of the Great Northern War, marks Russia's ascendancy as the great power in the Baltic, while Sweden begins its decline.

and carousing with commoners. He recruited admirals, academics and artisans to apply their skill in his service. Peter was more than ever convinced that Russians were still living in the dark ages. He vowed to replace superstition with science, backwardness with progress, East with West.

Peter abruptly ended his European expedition when news came of a Kremlin coup. His claim to the throne was illegitimate, some whispered. After his father died, the families of the two tsarinas had clashed over the royal legacy: the Miloslavsky clan claimed lineage back to Ivan and represented the best of old Muscovy, while the upstart Naryshkins were of recent Tatar and distant Scottish bloodlines. When he was only 10 years old, Peter watched in horror as his uncle was murdered by a Moscow mob, stirred by family rivalry. Eventually, a joint settlement was reached by which the boy shared the throne with his dim-witted half-brother, while his ambitious older stepsister acted as regent. In 1689, at the age of 17, Peter was ready: he consigned his stepsister to a nunnery and declared himself tsar. Old Muscovy's resentment of this act prompted the coup, which now brought Peter back from Europe.

Enough was enough. Peter began to impose his strong will on Russia. He vengefully punished the plotters, sending more than 1000 to their death and instilling fear in many thousands. He humiliated and subdued the old elite, forcing aristocrat elders to shave their beards and wear Western clothes. He subordinated the Orthodox Church to earthly political authority, and banished Old Believers who cursed him as the Antichrist. He upended the established social order, forbidding arranged marriages and promoting the humble to high rank. He even changed the date of New Year's Day – from September to January. By now, the undisputed tsar had grown to despise the old capital, and was ready to start afresh.

The Great Northern War

Peter was anxious to turn Russia westward and he saw the Baltic Sea as the channel for change. The problem was that Sweden already dominated the region. It had been more than 400 years since Russia's medieval hero prince, Alexander Nevsky, had defeated the Swedes near the site of Peter's expanding ambition. The territory, however, had long ago passed out of Russian influence. In 1700 Peter put his new army to the test against the powerful Swedish Empire, and the Great Northern War was on. For the next 20 years northern Europe's modernising autocrats, Charles II and Peter, fought for supremacy over the eastern Baltic.

To Peter's dismay, his troops were badly beaten in their first engagement at the Battle of Narva in Estonia, by a smaller, more adept Swedish

For a great biography of the man himself, pick up a copy of Lindsey Hughes' *Peter the Great: A Biography.* Never pulling punches in her detailed retelling of his less-than-laudable personal life and his often barbaric childishness, Hughes manages to present both the genius and failings of Peter I.

PETER THE GREAT

1712–14
At the behest of Peter I, government institutions begin to move from Moscow, and St Petersburg assumes the administrative and ceremonial role as the Russian capital.

1718
Peter the Great's son Alexey dies under torture in the Peter and Paul Fortress, where his father has him interrogated about his purported plan to depose him and reverse his reforms.

1721
Russia and Sweden sign Treaty of Nystad, ending years of competition for control of the Baltic. Russia is on its way to becoming a major world power and entering the modern world.

1725
Thirteen years after St Petersburg was declared the new capital, its population is now 40,000 and as much as 90% of all foreign trade passes through its port.

force. But Russia found allies in Poland, Saxony and Denmark, who diverted Charles' attention. Peter used the opportunity to revamp his army and launch his navy. He established a small Baltic foothold on tiny Hare Island (Zayachy Island) at the mouth of the Neva River, and used it as a base to rout a nearby Swedish garrison. This primitive outpost would become the kernel of Peter's northern capital.

By the time Charles tried to retake the territory, Peter commanded a formidable fighting force. Russia's first naval victory came at the Battle of Hanko, where a galley fleet overwhelmed a Swedish squadron and secured Russian control over the Neva and access to the Gulf. His military chief and boyhood friend, Alexander Menshikov, had a series of impressive battlefield victories, further extending Russian presence on the Baltic coast and causing his Scandinavian foe to flee and the Swedish empire to expire. The Great Northern War shifted the balance of power to the advantage of Peter's Russia. Hostilities officially ended with the signing of the Treaty of Nystad (1721), which formally ceded Sweden's extensive eastern possessions to Russia, including its new capital city, St Petersburg.

When he realised there wasn't enough stone available locally to build his city in polished marble and granite, Peter simply decreed a stone tax, by which all new arrivals to the city were obliged to bring with them a fixed amount of stone before they could enter (not so unusual for a guy who previously issued a tax on beards). Every ship that entered the port also was required to pay a stone tariff. St Petersburg's rocky revenue laws remained in effect for six decades.

Peter's Paradise

Peter did not wait for the war to end before he started building. The wooden palisade encampment on Hare Isle became the red-brick Peter and Paul Fortress (p126). In June 1703 Peter gave the site a name – Sankt Pieter Burkh, in his favourite Dutch tongue and after his patron saint, who stands guard before the gates to paradise.

There was a reason why until now the area had only attracted a few Finnish fishermen for settlement. It was a swamp. The Neva River runs from nearby Lake Ladoga, Europe's largest, and flows into the Gulf of Finland through a low-lying delta of marshy, flood-prone islands, more manageable for moose than man. Although it is close to the Arctic Circle, winds and waters from the Atlantic bring moderate and moist weather. This means that winter, during which the delta freezes up, is relatively short: a matter of no small significance to Peter.

Peter's vision for the new capital was grandiose; so was the task ahead. To find enough dry ground for building, swamps were drained and wetlands filled. To protect the land from flooding, seawalls were built and canals dug. A hands-on autocrat, Peter pitched in with the hammering, sawing and joining. Thousands of fortune-seeking foreigners were imported to lend expertise: architects and engineers to design the city's intricate waterways, and craftsmen and masons to chisel its stone foundations. The hard labour of digging ditches and moving muck was performed by nonvoluntary recruits. Peter pressed 30,000 peasant serfs per year into capital construction gangs, plus Russian convict labourers and

1725

Peter the Great dies of uremia in St Petersburg, having reigned Russia for 42 years of his 52-year life. He had anointed no successor and his wife becomes Catherine I.

JONATHAN SMITH / LONELY PLANET IMAGES ©

Bronze Horseman, *Etienne Falconet*

1727

Catherine I, an illiterate former housemaid, dies after ruling Russia for two years in tandem with Peter's best friend, Prince Menshikov. Peter's grandson becomes Tsar Peter II.

Swedish prisoners of war. The work regimen was strict and living conditions were stark: more than 100,000 died. But those who survived could earn personal freedom and a small piece of marshland to call their own.

Russia's new city by the sea began to take shape, inspired by Peter's recollections of canal-lined Amsterdam. The locus of power was the military stronghold, the Peter and Paul Fortress. Next, he ordered the chief accompaniments of tsarist authority – a church and a prison. The first tavern was the German-owned Triumphant Osteria of the Four Frigates, where Peter would order his favourite drink – vodka with cayenne pepper. The first stone palace belonged to the former Dutch merchant captain and first commander of Russia's Baltic Fleet, Cornelius Cruys. A more impressive dwelling, Menshikov Palace (p120), put up by the territory's first governor-general, Alexander Menshikov, soon adorned the Vasilevsky Island embankment.

Peter abandoned his wooden cabin for a modest Dutch-style townhouse across the river in the new Summer Garden (p69). Nearby, on the future site of the Admiralty, a bustling shipyard was assembling his new navy. Impatient to develop a commercial port, Peter offered a generous reward to the first three ships to drop anchor at the new town docks. The presence of so many foreigners gave the crude swampy settlement a more cosmopolitan feel than the poshest parlours of Moscow.

The wilful spirit of Peter the Great continued to possess the city and bedevil its inhabitants.

In 1712 the tsar officially declared St Petersburg to be the capital. Inspired by the Vatican's crossed keys to paradise, he adopted a city coat of arms that presented crossed anchors topped with an imperial crown. Peter demanded the rest of Russia's ruling elite join him, or else. He said Pieter Burkh was the place they ought to be, so they packed up their carriages and moved to the Baltic Sea. The tsar's royal court, the imperial senate and foreign embassies were relocated. Fearing Peter's wrath, Moscow's old aristocratic families reluctantly began to arrive. Apprehension turned to appal. To them Peter's paradise was a peaty hell. They were ordered to bring their own stones to the party, with which to build elegant mansions and in which to start behaving like Westerners, complete with beardless faces and German dress.

When Peter died of gangrene in 1725, at the age of 52, some thought they might get the chance to abandon his creation, but they were wrong. The wilful spirit of Peter the Great continued to possess the city and bedevil its inhabitants. Within less than a hundred years of its improbable inception, a new magnificent capital would stand on the edge of Europe.

1728

After the death of Peter I and two years of rule by his wife, his grandson Peter II returns the Russian capital back to Moscow.

1730

Peter II dies of smallpox aged 14, three years after ascending the throne. With him the direct male line of the Romanov dynasty ends. Peter the Great's niece, Anna, ascends the throne.

1732

Empress Anna reverses the decision of Peter II and moves the capital to St Petersburg, presiding over the recommencement of the city's construction and development.

1740

Empress Anna dies after a 10-year rule that brought much progress. After a series of intrigues, Peter the Great's daughter Elizabeth ascends the throne after a coup against infant Tsar Ivan VI.

IMPERIAL CAPITAL

Peter the Great's Heirs

By the end of the 18th century St Petersburg would take its place among Europe's grand cities. But in the years immediately following Peter's death, the fate of the Baltic bastion was still uncertain.

While Peter's plans for his imperial capital were clear, those for his personal legacy were murky. His eldest son and heir apparent, Alexey, was estranged from his father early on, suspected of plotting against him later, and eventually tortured to death in the Peter and Paul Fortress. The evidence for treachery was flimsy. On his death bed, Peter tried to dictate a last will, but could not name an heir before his demise. His wife Catherine I assumed the throne for the next two years, with Peter's pal Menshikov acting as de facto tsar. When Catherine died, the reaction started.

The St Petersburg–Moscow power struggle was on. The aristocracy's Old Muscovite faction seized the opportunity to influence the succession. Without his protector, the mighty Menshikov was stripped of all titles and property, and sent packing into Siberian exile. Peter's 11-year-old grandson, Peter II, was chosen as an unlikely heir. Delivering to his enabling patrons, the pliable Peter II returned the capital to Moscow. St Petersburg's population fell by a half and its public works came to rest.

The Romanovs were a delicate dynasty and the teen tsar soon succumbed to smallpox. Moscow's princely power brokers now entrusted the throne to another supposed weakling, Duchess Anna Ivanovna, Peter the Great's niece. But Anna was no pushover and she became the first in a line of tough women rulers. In 1732 Anna declared St Petersburg to be the capital once more, and bade everyone return to the Baltic. Making the offer more enticing, she recommenced glamorous capital construction projects. Wary of scheming Russian elites, she recruited talented German state administrators. Still, the city recovered slowly. A big fire in 1737 left entire neighbourhoods in ruins. Even Anna spent much time ruling from Moscow. St Petersburg remained only half built, its dynamism diminished.

Not until the reign of Peter's second-oldest daughter, the Empress Elizabeth (r 1741–62), did the city's imperial appetite return in full. Elizabeth created one of the most dazzling courts in Europe. She loved the pomp as much as the power. Her 20-year reign was a nonstop aristocratic cabaret. The Empress was a bit eccentric (she was certainly her father's daughter in that respect), enjoying a hedonistic lifestyle that revolved around hunting, drinking and dancing. She most loved hosting elaborate masquerade balls, at which she performed countless costume changes, apparently preferring to end the night in drag. Bawdy though

Peter's fascination with 'freaks' is well documented, but his most outstandingly politically incorrect act remains the dwarf wedding he organised for his faithful servant Iakim Volkov. Peter ordered all the dwarves of Moscow be rounded up and sent to St Petersburg, where, in the Menshikov Palace an entire dwarf wedding ceremony and ball was performed for the amusement of Peter and his assembled court.

1741–61

Empress Elizabeth fulfils her father's goal of a grand European capital, commissioning the construction of countless sumptuous buildings and creating a glittering court.

1754–62

Bartolomeo Rastrelli constructs the Winter Palace as the primary residence of the royal family. Empress Elizabeth dies three months before the building is completed.

1762

Catherine II (later Catherine the Great) is brought to the throne by a coup against her husband Peter III, ushering in the Russian Enlightenment era.

1764

Catherine the Great begins to purchase paintings from European collectors to display in her 'hermitage', the foundation for the State Hermitage Museum collection.

she was, Elizabeth also got the Russian elite hooked on high culture. The court was graced by poets, artists and philosophers. Journalism and theatre gained popularity, and an academy of arts was founded. While her resplendent splurges may have left imperial coffers empty, Elizabeth made her father's majestic dream a reality.

Aristocratic Soul

St Petersburg now displayed all the features of a seriously imperial capital: stately facade, hierarchical heart and aristocratic soul. The city's physical appearance reflected the transition. The centre of power moved across the river to the Neva's south bank. Empress Elizabeth's baroque beauty, the Winter Palace (p44), was meant to impress – and how could it not, with more than a quarter of a million exquisitely embellished square feet. She forbade any new building to rise higher than her 1000-room, 2000-windowed, multicolumned mansion. The immense Palace Square (Dvortsovaya pl; p65) could host as many as 50 parading infantry battalions at once. Across the square was an imposing semicircular structure housing the instruments of statecraft: General Staff, the Treasury and the Foreign Office. Its august archways led out to a beaming boulevard, the city's central artery, Nevsky pr. The commanding Admiralty (p67) stretched along nearly 400m of the south embankment, adorned with ancient heroes such as conqueror Alexander the Great and sea goddess Isis and topped with a gleaming gold spire. The city's monumental mélange reinforced its imperial pretension, with each ruler adding a personal stylistic touch: Peter's restrained baroque, Catherine's refined neoclassicism, Elizabeth's ostentatious rococo.

St Petersburg was a city of ranks, literally. The capital's social hierarchy reflected Peter's image of a well-ordered modern state. To minimise the personal influence of the old nobility, Peter created a Table of Ranks, which formally assigned social status on the basis of service to the emperor. The table included 14 stations in the military forces, civil administration and imperial court. In this system, inheritance was no longer an exclusive means to elite status, as resourceful newcomers were rewarded, too. Living quarters and salary were determined by rank. Each service had its own colour-coded uniforms, with distinguishing pecking-order plumage. Social manners followed suit: a lowly titular counsellor in a shabby overcoat could easily get a collegiate assessor's nose out of joint by addressing him as 'Your Nobleness' instead of the appropriate 'Your High Nobleness'. Not surprisingly, the old aristocratic families still managed to be well represented in the upper echelon.

In 1737 Empress Anna decided to celebrate Russia's victory in the Russo-Turkish War by having a palace carved in ice for herself. The architect Peter Eropkin completed an amazing ice palace with turrets 30m tall. Ever capricious, Anna forced Prince Golitsyn, who had incurred her displeasure, to marry a rather rotund Kalmyk girl inside, before spending the night and consummating the marriage on an ice bed.

ICE PALACE

1773

Emilian Pugachev, a Don Cossack, claims to be the overthrown Peter III and begins a peasant uprising, which is quelled by brute force, curbing the liberal tendencies of Catherine the Great.

1774–75

Yemelyan Pugachov claims to be the Tsar Peter III, begins a Cossack rebellion, and briefly controls a huge swathe of central Russia, unnerving Catherine, who abandons many of her more liberal policies.

1782

The *Bronze Horseman,* a statue of Peter the Great, is unveiled by Catherine before a huge crowd. Absent is the sculptor, Falconet, who has returned to France after a falling-out with Catherine.

1796

Upon the death of Catherine the Great, her embittered son Paul I ascends the throne. One of his first acts as tsar is to decree that women may never again rule Russia.

Despite Peter's meritocratic meddling, St Petersburg was in essence an aristocratic city and life in the capital was infused by blue bloodlines. Although the tsar could upset the balance, for the most part power came by entitlement and property was passed down. Yes, it was possible for the capable and clever to climb the Table of Ranks, but they'd better have a noble patron to give them a boost. The aristocratic elite, who once sneered at Peter's vision of a cosmopolitan capital, eventually came to wallow in it. They imported tastes and manners from their slightly more sophisticated continental cousins. European fashion and philosophy were conspicuously consumed. So far did it go that St Petersburg's aristocrats preferred to speak French to each other. Ancestral connections to kings and queens past became a coveted social commodity. Myths about family origin were eagerly propagated, with the ruling Romanovs taking the cup for uncovering their long-lost genetic link to Julius Caesar.

Enlightened Empress – Despotic Dame

In 1745, at the age of 16, Sophie Augusta of Prussia was betrothed to Duke Peter of Holstein: quite a score for her ambitious mother, as he was a Romanov and heir to the Imperial Russian throne. Sophie moved to St Petersburg, learned to speak Russian, delighted the court with her coy charm, and took the name Catherine when she converted to Orthodoxy. A nice start, but who would guess that a French-tutored fräulein from Stettin would one day reach Peter's lofty status and earn the moniker 'Great'.

More than just a court coquette, Catherine possessed keen political instincts and a strong appetite for power, attributes that had adverse effects on the men in her life. Her husband Tsar Peter III, as it turned out, was a bit of a flake and not terribly interested in ruling. In a plot hatched by her lover, Prince Orlov, Catherine was complicit in a coup that landed her on the throne, lifted Orlov to general-in-chief, and left her helpless husband under guard at a remote estate where he was assassinated shortly afterwards. She followed Peter I's example of paranoid parenting. Indeed, she made her successor son, Grand Duke Paul, so insecure that when he finally took the throne he built a fortified castle, Mikhailovsky Castle (p66), in the middle of the city and locked himself in. Of course, just because you're paranoid doesn't mean they're not after you: Paul's reign was cut short when some disgruntled drunken officers strangled him to death with his bedroom curtains.

Catherine, by contrast, prospered. Despite the details of her unsavoury ascension, she reigned for a satisfying 34 years and presided over a golden age for St Petersburg. Relations between crown and aristocracy were never better. High society strolled through handsome parks, gabbed in

LOVE AFFAIRS

Despite her reputed fondness for anything sexual, including the aforementioned horses, there is little evidence that Catherine the Great's lovers even went into double digits. Her long love affair Grigory Potemkin is fascinatingly described in Simon Sebag Montefiore's *Catherine the Great & Potemkin.*

1799

The birth of poet Alexander Pushkin ushers in the era of Russian romanticism and the Golden Age of Russian literature. Revered as the national bard, Pushkin's legacy endures to this day.

1800

St Petersburg has grown exponentially in its first century, and its population reaches 220,000. By this time, the city has gained all the glory of a cosmopolitan capital.

1801

Tsar Paul is murdered in his bedroom in the fortress-like Mikhailovsky Castle. The coup places his son Alexander on the throne. He vows to continue the reformist policies of his grandmother.

1812–14

Alexander I oversees victory in the Napoleonic Wars and troops occupy Paris. Monuments are strewn about St Petersburg, including the Alexander Column and Narva Gates.

smoky salons and waltzed across glittering ballrooms. The city benefited from her literary leanings, acquiring a splendid public library (p70) and the graceful Smolny Institute (p86), for fine-tuning fair maidens. The Russian Empire, meanwhile, expanded to ever greater distances.

Empress Catherine was a charter member of a club of 18th-century monarchs known as the 'enlightened despots' – dictators who could hum Haydn. On the 'enlightened' side, Catherine corresponded with French philosophers, patronised the arts and sciences, promoted public education and introduced potatoes to the national cuisine. On the 'despotic' side, Catherine connived with fellow enlightened friends to carve up Poland, censored bad news and imprisoned the messengers, tightened serfs' bonds of servitude to their lords, and introduced potatoes to the national cuisine.

> Catherine the Great adopted the Russian language, and, some suggest, not always entirely successfully. One story runs that the German princess spelled the word 'ещё' (more) as истчо (sounding phonetically quite similar) – giving rise to the joke at court: 'How can five spelling mistakes occur in a word of three letters?'

GREAT POWER ST PETERSBURG

1812 Overture

The downside to becoming a great power in European politics is that you become drawn into European wars. Though, in fairness to the Hanovers and Hapsburgs, the Romanovs were pretty good at picking fights on their own. From the 19th century on, Russia was at war and St Petersburg was transformed.

It was Napoleon who coined the military maxim, 'first we engage, then we will see'. That was probably not the best tactic to take with Russia. Tsar Alexander first clashed with Napoleon after joining an ill-fated anti-French alliance with Austria and Prussia. The resulting Treaty of Tilsit was not so bad for Russia – as long as Alexander cooperated with Napoleon's designs against Britain. Alexander reneged; Napoleon avenged. The Little Corporal targeted Moscow, instead of the more heavily-armed St Petersburg. His multinational, 600,000-strong force got there just in time for winter and had little to show for the effort besides vandalising the Kremlin. Hungry, cold and dispirited, they retreated westward, harried by Marshal Kutuzov's troops. The Grande Armée was ground up: only 20,000 survived. Napoleon was booked for an island vacation, while Russia became the continent's most feared nation.

The War of 1812 was a defining event for Russia, stirring nationalist exaltation and orchestral inspiration. Catherine's favourite grandson, Alexander I, presided over a period of prosperity and self-assuredness in the capital. His army's exploits were immortalised in triumphal designs that recalled imperial Rome: the Kazan Cathedral (p65) and the Alexander Column (p65) were shining symbols for a new Russian empire that stretched across half way the globe.

> Contrary to rumour, Catherine the Great categorically did not die underneath a stallion – her death was a far more prosaic affair. She collapsed from a stroke in her bathroom and died tucked up in her bed. No horses are believed to have been present.

1824

The city experiences its worst flood when water levels rise more than 4m. At least 500 people are killed, thousands are injured and more than 300 buildings are destroyed.

1825

Alexander I dies. Reformers assemble on Senate Sq to protest the succession of conservative Nicholas I. The new tsar brutally crushes the Decembrist revolt, killing hundreds.

1836

Construction of Russia's first railway line, from St Petersburg to Tsarskoe Selo, the imperial family's summer residence, begins. Initially trains are horse-drawn.

Catherine Palace (p145)

When Peter I died in 1725, one in six residents was a member of the armed forces; 100 years later the proportion was one in four. St Petersburg was a military capital, a city of immense parade grounds, swaggering elite regiments and epaulette-clad nobility. St Petersburg came to exhibit a patriotic culture that saw the capital as more than just a European city: it was the epicentre of a transcendent Russia whose greatness came from within. The *Bronze Horseman* looked on approvingly.

If you're interested in the bizarre circumstances that led to Pushkin's fatal duel with d'Anthès, read *Pushkin's Buttons*, by Serena Vitale, for the definitive account.

God Preserve Thy People

War did more than confer Great Power status on Russia: it was also a stimulus for new ideas on political reform and social change. In the 19th century, the clash of ideas spilled out of salons and into its streets. On a frosty December morning in 1825, more than 100 soldiers amassed on Senate Sq (now Decembrists' Sq, p106), with the intention of upsetting the royal succession. When Alexander I died unexpectedly without a legitimate heir, the throne was supposed to pass to his liberal-minded brother Constantine, Viceroy of Poland, but he declined, preferring not to complicate his contented life. Instead, the new tsar would be Alexander's youngest brother, Nicholas I, a cranky conservative with a fastidious obsession for barracks-style discipline. The Decembrist revolt was staged by a small cabal of officers, veterans of the Napoleonic Wars, who saw first-hand how people in other countries enjoyed greater freedom

CHECK YOUR CALENDAR

For hundreds of years, Russia was out of sync with the West. Until 1700 Russia dated its years from 'creation', which was determined to be approximately 5508 years before the birth of Christ. So at that time the year 1700 was considered the year 7208 in Russia. Peter, Westward-looking as he was, instituted a reform to date the years from the birth of Christ, as they did in Europe.

Things became complicated again in the 18th century, when most of Europe abandoned the Julian calendar in favour of the Gregorian calendar and Russia did not follow suit. By 1917 Russian dates were 13 days out of sync with European dates, which explains how the October Revolution could have taken place on 7 November.

Finally, the all-powerful Soviet regime made the necessary leap. The last day of January 1918 was followed by 14 February 1918, aligning dates from then on with those in the West.

In this book we use dates corresponding to the current Gregorian calendar that is used worldwide. However, even history is not always straightforward, as other accounts may employ the calendars that were the convention at that time. Tell *that* to your history professor.

1837

Poet Alexander Pushkin is shot in a duel with the Frenchman d'Anthès and later dies at his Moyka River house in St Petersburg, an unfathomable loss to Russian literature, still mourned today.

1849

Author Fyodor Dostoevsky is exiled to Siberia for four years of hard labour after participating in discussions with a liberal intellectual group, the Petrashevsky Circle.

1851

Upon completion of the construction of Nikolaevsky Station (now Moscow Station), the first trains linking Moscow and St Petersburg begin running, introducing rail travel to Russia.

1853–56

Britain and France side against Russia in the Crimean War, a war characterised by inept command and bloody stalemate, until it is finally ended by Alexander II.

and prosperity. They demanded Constantine and a constitution, but instead got exile and execution. The 'people', however, were now part of the discussion.

Russia's pathetic performance in another war prompted another reform attempt, this time initiated by the tsar. In the 1850s, better-equipped British and French armies really stuck it to Russia in a fight over the Crimean peninsula. The new emperor Alexander II concluded from the fiasco that Russia had to catch up with the West, or watch its empire unravel. A slew of reform decrees were issued, promoting public education, military reorganisation and economic modernisation. A sensitive sort, Alexander dropped the death penalty and curtailed corporal punishment. The Tsar Liberator abolished serfdom, kind of – his solution that serfs pay their masters redemptive fees in exchange for freedom pleased no one.

By now the 'people' were becoming less abstract. Political movements that claimed to better understand and represent them were sprouting up. On a Sunday morning in March 1881, several young student members of the Peoples' Will radical sect waited nervously by Kanal Griboyedov as the tsar's procession passed. Their homemade bombs hardly dented the royal armoured coach, but badly wounded scores of spectators and fatally shredded the reforming monarch when he insisted on leaving his carriage to investigate. On the hallowed site, the magnificent and melancholy Church on the Spilled Blood (p64) was constructed, its twisting onion domes trying to steady St Petersburg's uncertain present with Russia's enduring past.

Competition between Russia and Europe's other great powers compelled a state-directed campaign of economic development. St Petersburg became the centre of a robust military-industrial economy, established to fight the wars of the modern age. A ring of ugly sooty smokestacks grew up around the still-handsome city centre. Tough times in the rural villages and job opportunities in the new factories hastened a human flood into the capital. By the 1880s, the population climbed past a million, with hundreds of thousands cramped into slummy suburban squalor. Public health was befouled, public manner was debased. The gap between high society and the lower depths had long been manageable, but now they kept running into each other. The people had arrived.

Focusing on the colourful characters of the imperial period and the dramatic events leading up to the revolution, D Bruce Lincoln's *Sunlight at Midnight* is a definitive history of the period as well as being highly readable and academically rigorous.

REVOLUTION

God Save the Tsar

'We, workers and inhabitants of the city of St Petersburg, our wives, children, and helpless old parents, have come to you, Sovereign, to seek justice and protection.' So read the petition that a large group of workers intended to present to Tsar Nicholas II on a Sunday in January 1905.

1861

The emancipation of serfs frees up labour for the industrial revolution. The flood of workers into the capital leads to overcrowding, poor sanitation, disease epidemics and societal discontent.

1866

Dostoevsky's classic novel of life and death in St Petersburg's poverty-stricken garrets, *Crime and Punishment*, is published, making him Russia's greatest late-19th-century author.

1870

After breaking from the Academy of Arts, a group of upstart artists known as the Peredvizhniki (Wanderers) starts organising travelling exhibitions to widen their audience.

1881

A bomb kills Alexander II as he travels along Kanal Griboyedova. His reactionary son, Alexander III, undoes many of his reforms, but oversees the building of the Trans-Siberian Railway.

Nicholas II ascended the throne in 1894, when his iron-fisted autocratic father, Alexander III, died suddenly. Nicholas was of less steely stuff. Most contemporary accounts agree: he was a good guy and a lousy leader; possessive of his power to decide, except that he could never make up his mind. In 1904 Nicholas followed the foolish advice of a cynical minister, who said that what Russia needed most was a 'small victorious war' to get peoples' minds off their troubles. Unfortunately, the Russo-Japanese War ended in humiliating defeat and the people were more agitated than ever.

By January 1905 the capital was a hotbed of political protest. As many as 100,000 workers were on strike, the city had no electricity and all public facilities were closed. Nicholas and the royals departed for their palace retreat at Tsarskoe Selo (p145). In this charged atmosphere, Father Georgy Gapon, an Orthodox priest who apparently lived a double life as holy man and police agent, organised a peaceful demonstration of workers and their families to protest against the difficult conditions. Their petition called for eight-hour work days and better wages, universal suffrage and an end to the war.

St Petersburg's Top Historic Sites

- *Peter and Paul Fortress (Petrograd & Vyborg Sides)*
- *Winter Palace (Hermitage, Historic Heart)*
- *Alexander Nevsky Monastery (Smolny & Vosstaniya)*
- *Tsarskoe Selo (Pushkin)*

Singing 'God Save the Tsar', the crowd solemnly approached the Winter Palace, hoping to present its requests to the tsar personally. Inside, the mood was jittery: panicky guardsmen fired on the demonstrators, at first as a warning and then directly into the crowd. More than 1000 people were killed by the gunshots or the trampling that followed. Although Nicholas was not even in the palace at the time, the events of Bloody Sunday shattered the myth of the Father Tsar. The Last Emperor was finally able to restore order by issuing the October Manifesto, which promised a constitutional monarchy and civil rights; in fact, not much really changed.

At the start of WWI, nationalist fervour led St Petersburg to change its name to the more Slavic, less German-sounding Petrograd. A hundred years earlier, war with France had made the Russian Empire a great power, but now yet another European war threatened its very survival. The empire was fraying at the seams as the old aristocratic order limped onward into battle. Only the strength of the Bronze Horseman could hold it all together. But Peter's legacy rested on the shoulders of an imperial inheritor who was both half-hearted reformer and irresolute reactionary: the combination proved revolutionary.

CRADLE OF COMMUNISM

Act One: Down with the Autocracy

In 1917, 23 February began like most days in Petrograd since the outbreak of the war. The men went off to the metalworks and arms factories. The women went out to receive the daily bread ration. And the

1883

The dazzling Church on the Spilled Blood is inaugurated as a private place of mourning for the imperial family for the dead Alexander II.

Church on the Spilled Blood (p64)

1890

Queen of Spades, Pyotr Tchaikovsky's opera based on the poem by Alexander Pushkin, premieres at the Mariinsky Theatre, drawing excited crowds and rave reviews.

radical set went out to demonstrate, as it happened to be International Women's Day. Although each left their abode an ordinary individual, by day's end they would meld into the most infamous 'mass' in modern history: the Bronze Horseman's heirs let go of the reigns; the Russian Revolution, a play in three acts, had begun.

After waiting long hours in the winter chill for a little food, the women were told that there would be none. This news coincided with the end of the day shift and a sweaty outpouring from the factory gates. Activist provocateurs joined the fray as the streets swelled with the tired, the hungry and now the angry. The crowd assumed a political purpose. They marched to the river, intent on crossing to the palace side and expressing their discontent to somebody. But they were met at the bridge by gendarmes and guns.

Similar meetings had occurred previously, in July and October, on which occasions the crowd retreated. But now it was February and one did not need a bridge to cross the frozen river. First a brave few, then emboldened small groups, finally a defiant horde of hundreds were traversing the ice-laden Neva toward the Winter Palace.

They congregated in the Palace Sq, demanding bread, peace and an end to autocracy. Inside, contemptuous counts stole glances at the unruly rabble and waited for them to grow tired and disperse. But they did not go home. Instead, they went around the factories and spread the call for a general strike. By the next day a quarter of a million people were rampaging through the city centre. Overwhelmed local police took cover.

When word reached the tsar, he ordered military troops to restore order. But his troops were no longer hardened veterans: they were long dead at the front. Rather, freshly conscripted peasant youths in uniform were sent to put down the uprising. When commanded to fire on the demonstration, they instead broke rank, dropped their guns and joined the mob. At that moment, the 300-year-old Romanov dynasty and 500-year-old tsarist autocracy came to an end.

NICHOLAS & ALEXANDRA

Part love story and part political thriller, Robert Massey's *Nicholas and Alexandra* gives the nitty-gritty on the royal family, Rasputin and the resulting revolution.

Act Two: All Power to the Soviets

Perhaps the least likely political successor to the tsar in February 1917 was the radical socialist Bolshevik Party. The Bolsheviks were on the fringe of the fringe of Russia's political left. Party membership numbered a few thousand, at best. Yet, in less than eight months, the Bolsheviks occupied the Winter Palace, proclaiming Petrograd the capital of a worldwide socialist revolution.

In the days that followed Nicholas' abdication, the Provisional Government was established. It mainly comprised political liberals, representing reform-minded nobles, pragmatic civil servants, and professional

1896

At the coronation of Nicholas II, a stampede by the massive crowd ends with more than a thousand deaths and almost as many injuries.

1896

Anton Chekhov's classic play *The Seagull* opens to poor reviews at the Alexandrinsky Theatre in St Petersburg. The author was apparently so unnerved by the audience's hostility that he left the theatre.

1899

Vladimir Nabokov, the future author of *Lolita*, is born at his family's mansion on Bolshaya Morskaya ul in St Petersburg. He immortalises the house in his autobiography *Speak, Memory*.

1900

By the turn of the 20th century, St Petersburg (population 1,440,000) is Russia's cultural centre. It's also a centre of political unrest.

and business interests. Simultaneously, a rival political force emerged, the Petrograd Soviet. The Soviet (the Russian word for council) was composed of more populist and radical elements, representing the interests of the workers, peasants, soldiers and sailors. Both political bodies were based at the Tauride Palace (p84).

The Provisional Government saw itself as a temporary instrument, whose main task was to create constitutional democracy. It argued over the details of organising an election and convention, rather than deal with the issues that had caused the revolution – bread and peace. At first, the Soviet deferred to the Provisional Government, but this soon changed.

On 3 April, Bolshevik leader Vladimir Lenin arrived at the Finland Station from exile in Switzerland. Lenin's passage across enemy lines

THE MAD MONK

Russia's most legendary letch and holy man was Grigory Rasputin, mystic and healer. He was born in 1869 into poverty in a small village east of the Urals. After a dissolute boyhood and a short-lived marriage, he discovered religion. Rasputin preached (and practised) that the way to divine grace was through sin and redemption: binge drinking and engaging in sexual orgies, and then praying for forgiveness.

St Petersburg's high society was receptive to Rasputin's teachings. Despite his heavy drinking and sexual scandals – or perhaps because of them – he earned the adoration of an army of aristocratic ladies. More notable, Rasputin endeared himself to Emperor Nicholas II and his wife Alexandra, largely as he had the power to ease the pain of their son Alexey, who suffered from haemophilia.

The holy man's scandalous behaviour and his influence over the tsarina evoked the ire of the aristocracy. The powerful Prince Felix Yusupov and the tsar's cousin Grand Duke Dmitry decided that the Siberian peasant must be stopped. On a wintry night in 1916, they invited Rasputin to the sumptuous Yusupov Palace (p105) overlooking the Moyka. They plied the monk with wine and cakes that were laced with potassium cyanide, which seemed to have no effect. In a panic, the perpetrators then shot the priest at close range. Alarmingly, this didn't seem to get the job done either. Rasputin finally drowned when he was tied up in a sheet and dropped into the icy Neva River. He was buried in secret at Pushkin.

Besides mystical powers and lecherous behaviour, Grigory Rasputin is famous for another exceptional attribute: his enormous penis (30cm, if you must know). Legend has it that Rasputin's foes did not stop at murder. Yusupov's maid supposedly found Rasputin's severed organ when cleaning the apartment after the murder.

Which explains the prize artefact at the so-called Museum of Erotica (p86): it is indeed Rasputin's preserved penis. Even in its detached state, the Mad Monk's member is still attracting attention.

1902–04	1905	1906	1914
Clashes in the Far East lead to the Russo-Japanese War, with unexpectedly disastrous results for the Russians. The war diverts resources and stirs up dissent in the capital.	Hundreds of people are killed when troops fire on peaceful protestors presenting a petition to the tsar. Nicholas II is held responsible for the tragedy, dubbed 'Bloody Sunday'.	The first Duma election is held, a decision that is made, but greatly resented, by Nicholas II on the urging of the prime minister. The Duma meets four times a year in the Tauride Palace until 1917.	Russia enters WWI, simultaneously invading Austrian Galicia and German Prussia with minimal success. St Petersburg changes its name to the less Germanic sounding Petrograd.

had been arranged by German generals, who hoped that he would stir things up at home, and thus distract Russia from its participation in the war. As expected, Lenin upset the political status quo as soon as he arrived. His rabid revolutionary rhetoric polarised Petrograd. In the Soviet, the Bolshevik faction went from cooperative to confrontational. But even his radical pals dismissed Lenin as a stinging gadfly, rather than a serious foe. By summer's end, Lenin had proved them wrong.

The Provisional Government not only refused to withdraw from the war but, at the instigation of the allies, launched a new offensive – prompting mass desertions at the front. Meanwhile, the economic situation continued to deteriorate. The same anarchic anger that fuelled the February Revolution was felt on the streets again. Lenin's Bolsheviks were the only political party in sync with the public mood. September elections in the Petrograd Soviet gave the Bolsheviks a majority.

Lenin had spent his entire adult life waiting for this moment. For 20 years he did little else than read, write and rant about revolution. He enjoyed Beethoven, but avoided listening to his music from concern that the sentiment it evoked would make him lose his revolutionary edge. A successful revolution, Lenin observed, had two preconditions: first, the oppressed classes were politically mobilised and ready to act; and, second, the ruling class was internally divided and questioned its will to continue. This politically explosive combination now existed. If the Bolsheviks waited any longer, he feared, the Provisional Government would get its act together and impose a new bourgeois political order, ending his dream of socialist revolution in Russia. On 25 October the Bolsheviks staged their coup. According to Lenin's chief accomplice and coup organiser, Leon Trotsky, 'power was lying in the streets, waiting for someone to pick it up'. Bolshevik Red Guards seized a few buildings and strategic points. The Provisional Government was holed up in the tsar's private dining room in the Winter Palace, protected by a few Cossacks, the Petrograd chapter of the Women's Battalion of Death, and a one-legged commander of a bicycle regiment. Before dessert could be served, their dodgy defences cracked. Mutinous mariners fired a window-shattering salvo from the cruiser *Aurora* (p131) to signal the start of the assault; and the Red Guards – led by Lenin – moved in on the Winter Palace. Three shells struck the building, bullet holes riddled the square side of the palace and a window was shattered on the 3rd floor before the Provisional Government was arrested in the Small Dining Room behind the Malachite Hall. This largely bloodless battle would be celebrated for 70 years as the most glorious moment in history.

At the Tauride Palace the Soviet remained in emergency session late into the night when Lenin announced that the Provisional Government

OCTOBER REVOLUTION

Vsevolod Pudovkin's 1927 silent film *End of St Petersburg* was produced to commemorate the 10th anniversary of the October Revolution and it remains a landmark for Soviet realist cinema.

1915

The first suprematist art show takes place in Petrograd, showcasing Malevich's infamous *Black Square*, creating a critical storm and putting the Russian avant-garde firmly on the map.

1916

After evoking the ire of aristocrats, Grigory Rasputin (the Mad Monk) is invited to Yusupov Palace for cyanide-laced tea by a group of plotters, who then drown him in the icy Moyka River.

1917

The February Revolution results in the abdication of Nicholas II, followed by the Bolshevik coup in October. Vladimir Ilych Lenin seizes power and civil war ensues.

1918

Lenin pulls Russia out of WWI and moves the capital to Moscow. Civil war continues throughout the country, and Petrograd enters a period of political and cultural decline.

had been arrested and the Soviet was now the supreme power in Russia. Half the deputies walked out in disgust. Never one to miss an opportunity, Lenin quickly called a vote to make it official. It passed. Incredibly, the Bolsheviks were now in charge.

Act Three: Consolidating Communism

Nobody really believed the Bolsheviks would be around for long. Even Lenin said that, if they could hold on for just 100 days, their coup would be a success by providing future inspiration. It was one thing to occupy a few palaces in Petrograd, but across the empire's far-flung regions Bolshevik-brand radicalism was not so popular. From 1918 to 1921 civil war raged in Russia: between monarchists and socialists, imperialists and nationalists, aristocrats and commoners, believers and atheists. When it was over, somehow Soviet power was still standing. In the final act of the Russian Revolution, the scene shifted from the Petrograd stage. The imperial capital would never be the same.

In December 1917, an armistice was arranged and peace talks began with the Germans. The Bolsheviks demanded a return to prewar imperial borders, but Germany insisted on the liberation of Poland, where its army was squatting. Trotsky defiantly walked out of negotiations, declaring 'neither war, nor peace'. The German high command was a bit confused and not at all amused – hostilities immediately resumed. Lenin had vowed never to abandon the capital, but that was before a German battle fleet cruised into the Gulf of Finland. Exit stage left. In 1918 the Bolsheviks vacated their new pastel digs in Petrograd and relocated behind the ancient red bricks of Moscow. It was supposed to be temporary (Lenin personally preferred St Petersburg). But Russia was turning inward, and Peter's window to the West was closing.

The aristocratic soul gave up the proletarian body.

Along with the loss of its capital political status, St Petersburg also lost its noble social status. The aristocratic soul gave up the proletarian body. The royal family had always set the standards for high society, but now the royals were on the run. No Romanov stepped forward to claim the once coveted throne. Nicholas II and his family, meanwhile, were placed under house arrest in the Alexander Palace at Tsarskoe Selo (p145), before leaving on a one-way trip to Siberia. The breakdown of the old order made the old elite vulnerable. The tsar's favourite ballerina, Mathilda Kshesinskaya, pleaded in vain as her Style Moderne mansion was commandeered by the Bolsheviks as party headquarters (see p129). The more fortunate families fled with the few valuables they could carry; the less fortunate who stayed were harassed, dispossessed and killed eventually.

1920

The ongoing civil war and the change of capital take their toll in St Petersburg. The population falls to 722,000, one-third of the prerevolutionary figure.

1921

Kronshtadt sailors and soldiers rebel against the increasingly dictatorial regime. They are brutally suppressed and this is the last uprising against Communist rule until the Soviet collapse.

1922

The Soviet Union is officially created, merging Russia, Ukraine, Belarus and the Caucasus into one federal socialist state.

1924

Lenin dies without designating a successor. The city's name is now Leningrad in his honour. Power is assumed by a 'triumvirate' but Stalin increasingly takes control.

The revolution began in Petrograd and ended there in March 1921 when Kronshtadt sailors staged a mutiny. These erstwhile Bolshevik boosters demanded the democracy they had been promised now that the civil war was won. But Lenin, who had since renamed his political party 'the Communists', was reluctant to relinquish political power. The sailors' revolt was brutally suppressed in a full-scale military assault across the frozen bay, confirming the historical adage that revolutions eat their children.

RED PITER

Soviet Second City

Moscow finally reclaimed its coveted ancient title with the caveat that it was now the world's first communist capital. Petrograd consoled itself as the Soviet second city.

The redesignation of the capital prompted the departure of the bureaucracies: the government ministries, the military headquarters, the party apparatus, which took with them a host of loyal servants and servile lackeys. The population dropped by two-thirds from its prewar count. Economic exchange was reduced to begging and bartering. To make matters worse, the food shortages that first sparked the revolution during the war continued well afterwards. Fuel was also in short supply – homes went unheated, factory gates stayed shut and city services were stopped.

The new regime needed a new identity. The old aristocratic labels would not do. The city underwent a name-changing mania – streets, squares and bridges were given more appropriate socialist sobriquets. Once known as Orlov Sq, the plaza fronting Smolny Institute was renamed after the Dictatorship of the Proletariat. Znamenskaya Sq, named after a nearby church, became Uprising Sq (pl Vosstaniya). The city itself was rechristened Leningrad in 1924, to honour the scourge of the old empire. The change ran much deeper: make no mistake, the old aristocratic world was gone. 'For centuries, our grandfathers and fathers have had to clean up their shit,' railed Trotsky. 'Now it is time they clean up ours.' Noble pedigree became a marker for discrimination and exploitation. Family mansions were expropriated; art treasures were seized; churches were closed.

Leningrad was eventually revived with a proletarian transfusion. At the beginning of the 1930s the socialist state launched an intensive campaign of economic development, which reinvigorated the city's industrial sector. New scientific and military research institutes were

Nadezhda Mandelstam, the wife of poet Osip Mandelstam wrote *Hope Against Hope*, an incredibly moving memoir about their lives as dissidents in Stalinist Russia leading up to Osip Mandelstam's death in a transit camp in 1938. The title is a play on words, as *nadezhda* means 'hope' in Russian.

DISSIDENTS

MICHAEL KLINEC / ALAMY ©

Statue of Lenin, Finland Station

1930

Shostokovich's satirical opera *The Nose* premiers at Maly Operny Theatre. He is accused of 'formalism' by Stalinist critics and the opera is not performed again until the 1970s.

1934

Leningrad party boss Sergei Kirov is murdered as he leaves his office at the Smolny Institute. The assassination kicks off the Great Purge, ushering in Stalin's reign of terror.

1937–38

The height of Stalin's great purge, Yezhovshchina, terrorises the whole of Russia, but particularly Leningrad, liquidating much of its local intelligentsia and party organisation.

BONES OF CONTENTION

What happened to the last members of the royal family – even after their execution in 1918 – is a mixture of the macabre, the mysterious and the just plain messy.

The Romanov remains resurfaced in 1976, when a group of local scientists discovered them near Yekaterinburg. So politically sensitive was this issue that the discovery was kept secret until the remains were finally fully excavated in 1991. The bones of nine people were tentatively identified as Tsar Nicholas II, his wife Alexandra, three of their four daughters, the royal doctor and three servants. Absent were any remains of daughter Maria or the royal couple's only son, the tsarevich Alexey.

According to a 1934 report filed by one of the assassin-soldiers, all five children died with their parents when they were shot by a firing squad in Yekaterinburg. The bodies were dumped in an abandoned mine, followed by several grenades intended to collapse the mine shaft. When the mine did not collapse, two of the children's bodies were set on fire, and the others were doused with acid and buried in a swamp. Even then, most of the acid soaked away into the ground – leaving the bones to be uncovered 73 years later.

In mid-1998 the royal remains were finally given a proper burial in the Romanov crypt at SS Peter and Paul Cathedral (p126), alongside their predecessors dating back to Peter the Great. A 19-gun salute bade them a final farewell. President Boris Yeltsin was present, together with many Romanov family members.

The Orthodox Church, however, never acknowledged that these were actually the Romanov remains, and church officials did not attend the burial. Instead, the church canonised the royal family in recognition of their martyrdom.

Despite the controversy, it seemed the story had finally come to an end (however unsatisfying for some). But in 2007 amateur archaeologists in Yekaterinburg found the bodies of two more individuals – a male aged between 10 and 13 and a female aged 18 to 23. The location corresponds with the site described in the 1934 report; and the silver fillings in the teeth are similar to those in the other family members. Genetic tests carried out in 2008 confirmed that these were indeed the remains of the tsarevich Alexey and his sister Maria. After almost a century of mystery, the end of the Russian royal family is finally known.

fitted upon the city's strong higher-education foundations. On the eve of WWII, the population climbed to over three million. Public works projects for the people were undertaken – polished underground metro stations, colossal sports complexes and streamlined constructivist buildings muscled in next to the peeling pastels and cracked baroque of the misty past.

1940

Rapid industrialisation shows results: the population of the city has rebounded, reaching 3.1 million, and Leningrad is now responsible for 11% of Soviet industrial output.

1941

The Nazis invade the Soviet Union and Leningrad is surrounded, blocking residents from all sources of food and fuel, as the city comes under attack.

1942

The Leningrad Radio Orchestra performs the Seventh Symphony by Dmitry Shostakovich. Musicians are given special rations so they can perform, and the music is broadcast throughout the city.

1944

The Germans retreat. Leningrad emerges from its darkest hour, but more than one million are dead from starvation and illness. The city's population has dropped to an estimated 600,000.

Who Murdered Sergei Kirov?

Though no longer the capital, Leningrad still figured prominently in Soviet politics. Its party machine, headquartered in the Smolny Institute, was a plum post in the Communist Party. The First Secretary, head of the Leningrad organisation, was always accorded a seat on the Politburo, the executive board of Soviet power. In the early years Leningrad was a crucial battlefront in the bloody intraparty competition to succeed Lenin.

Lenin died from a stroke at the age of 53, without designating a successor. He was first replaced by a troika of veteran Old Bolsheviks, including Leningrad party head, Alexander Zinoviev. But their stay at the top was brief; they were outmanoeuvred by the most unlikely successor to Lenin's mantle, Josef Stalin, a crude disaffected bureaucrat of Georgian descent.

In 1926 Zinoviev was forced to relinquish his Leningrad seat to Sergei Kirov, a solid Stalin man. The transition reflected deeper changes in the Communist Party: Zinoviev was a haughty Jewish intellectual from the first generation of salon-frequenting socialist talkers, while Kirov was a humble Russian provincial from the second generation of socialist dirty-work doers. Stalin's rise to the top was testimony to his personal appeal to these second-generation Bolsheviks.

Though no longer the capital, Leningrad still figured prominently in Soviet politics.

In high-profile Leningrad, Kirov soon became one of the most popular party bosses. He was a zealous supporter of Stalin's plans for rapid industrialisation, which meant heavy investment in the city. But the manic-paced economic campaign could not be sustained, causing famine and food shortages. Kirov emerged as a proponent of a more moderate course instead of the radical pace that Stalin still insisted on. The growing rift in the leadership was exposed at a 1934 party congress, where a small cabal of regional governors secretly connived to remove Stalin in a bureaucratic coup and replace him with Kirov. It was an offer that Kirov flatly refused.

But it was hard to keep a secret from Stalin. Wary of Kirov's rising appeal, Stalin ordered that he be transferred to party work in Moscow, where he could be watched more closely. Kirov found reasons to delay the appointment. He remained in Leningrad – but not for long. On 1 December 1934 as he left a late-afternoon meeting, Kirov was shot from behind and killed in the corridor outside his Smolny office.

Who murdered Sergei Kirov? The trigger was pulled by Leonid Nikolaev, also a party member – hence his access to the building – and reportedly a disgruntled devotee of the displaced Zinoviev. But circumstantial evidence pointed the finger at Stalin. Kirov's murder was the first act in a much larger drama. According to Stalin, it proved that the party was infiltrated by saboteurs and spies. The ensuing police campaign to

1953

Stalin dies in Moscow, marking the end of decades of terror and the eventual liberalisation of Soviet society.

1955

The first seven stations of the city's metro open 15 years after construction began, hampered initially by war and then by the marshy earth under the city, making the metro a technical marvel.

1956

After the death of Stalin, party leader Nikita Khrushchev makes a 'Secret Speech' denouncing Stalin, thus commencing a period of economic reform and cultural thaw.

1960

A collection of 186 mass graves, the Piskaryovskoe Memorial Cemetery opens in northern Leningrad, with almost 500,000 civilian and military casualties from the blockade.

uncover these hidden enemies became known as the Great Purges, which consumed nearly the entire postrevolutionary Soviet elite. Leningrad intellectuals were especially targeted. More than 50 Hermitage curators were imprisoned, including the Asian art specialist, accused of being an agent of Japanese imperialism, and the medieval armour specialist, accused of harbouring weapons. Successive waves of arrest, exile and execution effectively transformed the Leningrad elite, making it much younger, less assertive and more Soviet. When it was finally over, Stalin stood as personal dictator of unrivalled power – even by tsarist standards.

The Siege

On 22 June 1941 Leningraders were basking in the summer solstice when Foreign Minister Molotov interrupted state radio to announce an 'unprecedented betrayal in the history of civilised nations'. That day, German Nazi forces launched a full-scale military offensive across the Soviet Union's western borders. Stalin's refusal to believe that Hitler would break their nonaggression pact left Leningrad unprepared and vulnerable.

Harrison Salisbury's *The 900 Days: The Siege of Leningrad* is a fascinating forensic reconstruction of the Nazi blockade. It's not for those with a passing interest in the blockade, but for those who want to vicariously suffer through the darkest hours of the city.

The German code-name for its assault on Leningrad was Operation Nordlicht (Operation Northern Lights). The Führer ordered his generals to raze the city rather than incur the cost of feeding and heating its residents in winter. By July German troops had reached the suburbs, inflicting a daily barrage of artillery bombardment and aerial attacks. All Leningraders were mobilised around the clock to dig trenches, erect barricades, board up buildings. The city's factories were dismantled, brick by brick, and shipped to the other side of the Urals. Hermitage staff crated up Catherine's collection for a safer interior location; what they did not get out in time was buried on the grounds of the Summer Garden (see p194). The spires of the Admiralty and Peter and Paul Fortress were camouflaged in coloured netting, which was changed according to the weather and season. The youngest and oldest residents were evacuated; everybody else braced themselves.

At the end of August the Germans captured the east-bound railway: Leningrad was cut off. Instead of a bloody street fight, the Nazi command vowed to starve the city to death. Food stocks were low to begin with but became almost nonexistent after napalm bombs burned down the warehouse district. Moscow dispatched tireless and resourceful Dmitry Pavlov to act as Chief of Food Supply. Pavlov's teams ransacked cellars, broke into box cars and tore up floorboards in search of leftover cans and crumbs. The city's scientists were pressed to develop something edible out of yeast, glue and soap. As supplies dwindled, pets and pests disappeared. A strict ration system was imposed and violators were shot. Workers received 15 ounces (425g) of bread per day; every-

1964

A coup against Khrushchev brings Brezhnev to power; the Years of Stagnation begin. Poet and future Nobel laureate Joseph Brodsky is called a 'social parasite' and exiled.

INTERFOTO / ALAMY ©

Joseph Brodsky

1982

The Leningrad musical underground is lit up by the arrival of Viktor Tsoi's band Kino, who begin to perform live and release their first album, 45.

1985

Reformer Mikhail Gorbachev defeats Leningrad boss Grigory Romanov and is elected general secretary of the party with policies of perestroika (restructuring) and glasnost (openness).

one else got less. It was not enough. The hunger was relentless, causing delirium, disease and death. Hundreds of thousands succumbed to starvation, corpses were strewn atop snow-covered streets, mass graves were dug on the outskirts (see p134).

Relief finally arrived in January, when food supplies began to reach the city from across the frozen Lake Ladoga lifeline. Trucks made the perilous night-time trek on ice roads, fearing the Luftwaffe above and chilled water below. Soviet military advances enabled the supply route to stay open in the spring when the lake thawed. Leningrad survived the worst; still the siege continued. The city endured the enemy's pounding guns for two more years. At last, in January 1944, the Red Army arrived in force. They pulverised the German front with more rockets and shells than were used at Stalingrad. Within days, Leningrad was liberated.

Composer Dmitry Shostakovich premiered his Seventh Symphony for a small circle of friends in his Leningrad flat in 1941. His performance was interrupted by a night raid of German bombers. He stopped and sent his family into the basement, then played on in anguish and defiance as sirens sounded and fires flashed outside. In the spring of 1942 the symphony was performed in Moscow and broadcast by radio to Leningrad, to whom it was dedicated.

The 900 days marked history's longest military siege of a modern city. The city was badly battered but not beaten. The St Petersburg spirit was resilient.

Did people ever laugh under communism? Ben Lewis proves that they did – and how – in his book *Hammer & Tickle: A History of Communism Told Through Communist Jokes*. Brush up on your best NKVD, bread queue and Brezhnev jokes.

HAMMER & TICKLE

THE RETURN OF PETER

From Dissent to Democracy

Throughout the Soviet period, Moscow kept suspicious eyes trained on Leningrad. After WWII, Stalin launched the 'Leningrad Affair', a sinister purge of the Hero City's youthful political and cultural elite, who were falsely accused of trying to create a rival capital. Several thousand were arrested, several hundred were executed. Kremlin apparatchiks were committed to forcing conformity on to the city's free-thinking intellectuals and keeping closed the window to the West. They ultimately failed.

Leningrad's culture club was irrepressible. Like in tsarist times, it teased, goaded and defied its political masters. Stalin terrorised, Khrushchev cajoled and Brezhnev banished, yet the city still became a centre of dissent. As from Radishchev to Pushkin, so from Akhmatova to Brodsky. By the 1970s the city hosted a thriving independent underground of jazz and rock musicians, poets and painters, reformists and radicals. Like the Neva in spring, these cultural currents overflowed

1990
St Petersburg recovers from the mid-century war and benefits from industrial and economic development. In the last decade of the 20th century, its population tops five million.

1991
On Christmas day, Gorbachev announces the dissolution of the Soviet Union. Leningrad's name reverts to St Petersburg after a referendum on the issue.

1997
Mikhail Manevich, vice-governor of the city, is assassinated by a sniper in the middle of the city as he travels to work, marking the height of St Petersburg's lawlessness.

1998
The bodies of the last tsar, Nicholas II, and most of his family are finally buried in the SS Peter and Paul Cathedral after their murder by the Bolsheviks 70 years earlier.

when Mikhail Gorbachev finally came to power and declared a new policy of openness and reform. The Leningrad democratic movement was unleashed.

Gorbachev forced long-time Leningrad party boss Grigory Romanov (no relation to the royals) and his communist cronies into retirement. He held elections for local office that brought to power liberal-minded Anatoly Sobchak, the darling of the progressive intelligentsia and the first popularly elected mayor in the city's history. Leningrad was at the forefront of democratic change, as the old regime staggered towards the exit.

Where Gorbachev sought to breathe new life into Soviet socialism, his rival Boris Yeltsin was intent on killing it. Just two months after Sobchak's historic election, a last gasp of reactionary hardliners staged a coup. While Yeltsin mollified Moscow, a hundred thousand protestors filled Palace Sq in Leningrad. The ambivalent soldiers sent to arrest Sobchak disobeyed orders, and instead escorted him to the local TV station where the mayor denounced the coup and encouraged residents to do the same. Anxiously waiting atop flimsy barricades, anticommunist demonstrators spent the evening in fear of approaching tanks. But the inebriated coup plotters lost their nerve, thanks in large part to the people of Leningrad.

If you can't get enough of Dostoevsky, why not tackle *The Idiot*, which takes place both in St Petersburg and in nearby Pavlovsk. The descriptions are not quite as evocative as those in *Crime and Punishment*, but the characters are equally complex and the debates no less esoteric.

Finding the Future in the Past

In 1991, by popular referendum, the citizens of Leningrad voted resoundingly to change their city's name once more. They chose to restore its original name, the name of its founder, St Petersburg.

As reviled as the communist regime may have been, it still provided a sufficient standard of living, a predictable day at the office and a common target for discontent. The familiar ways of life suddenly changed. The communist collapse caused enormous personal hardship; economic security and social status were put in doubt. Mafia gangs and bureaucratic fangs dug into the emerging market economy, creating contemptible crony capitalism. The democratic movement splintered into petty rivalries and political insignificance. One of its shining stars, Galina Starovoitova, social scientist turned human rights advocate, was brazenly shot dead in her St Petersburg apartment stairwell in 1998. Out on the street, meanwhile, prudish reserve gave way to outlandish exhibitionism. Uncertainty and unfairness found expression in an angry and sometimes xenophobic reaction.

With the old order vanquished, the battle to define the new one was on. The symbols of the contending parties were on display throughout the city. The nouveaux riches quickly claimed Nevsky pr for their

1998

St Petersburg politician and human rights activist Galina Starovoitova is murdered outside her apartment by hitmen, another blow to Russia's reputation as a free and safe society.

1999

President Boris Yeltsin announces his surprise resignation on New Year's Eve, and anoints Prime Minister Vladimir Putin as acting president, thus ushering in a new age in Russian politics.

2000

St Petersburg native Vladimir Putin is elected President of Russia, beginning a new era of far greater central control and 'managed democracy'.

2003

Accused of power abuse and election manipulation, Putin's favoured candidate prevails in elections. Winning 63% of votes, Valentina Matvienko becomes the governor of St Petersburg.

Milano designer get-ups and Bavarian driving machines. The disaffected youth used faded pink courtyard walls to spray-paint Zenith football insignias, swastikas and the two English words they all seem to know. Every major intersection was adorned with gigantic billboard faces of prima ballerinas and pop singers sipping their favourite cups of coffee. And, like all their St Petersburg predecessors, the new ruling elite wants to leave its own distinctive mark on the city: the proposed Gazprom City skyscraper, renamed the Okhta Centre. After all, nothing says 'I own you' quite like a 400m tower of glass and steel (see the boxed text, p201).

Local Spook Makes Good

When St Petersburg native Vladimir Putin was elected president in 2000, speculation was rife that he would transfer the Russian capital back to his home town. When Lenin relocated the capital to Moscow rather hastily in 1918, it was supposed to be a temporary move. Furthermore, the new millennium brought a new regime: what better way to make a significant break with the past? Most importantly, Putin's personal attachment to his home town was significant.

Born in 1952, Putin spent his childhood in the Smolny district. Little Vlad went to school in the neighbourhood and took a law degree at Leningrad State University, before working in Leningrad, Moscow and East Germany for the KGB. In 1990 he returned to his home town, where he was promptly promoted through the ranks of local politics. By 1994 he was deputy to St Petersburg mayor Anatoly Sobchak. In his office in the Smolny Institute, Putin famously replaced the portrait of Lenin with one of Peter the Great. Quite where this apparent reformer went is anyone's guess, but as Putin went from the Smolny to the Kremlin, his newfound reformist instincts clearly became clouded by his atavistic KGB loyalties.

As the city economy slowly recovered from collapse and shock, Sobchak was voted out of office in 1996. Putin was then recruited by fellow Leningrader, Anatoly Chubais, to join him in the capital in the Kremlin administration. After another rapid rise through the ranks, he took over the FSB (the postcommunist KGB). In 1999, after Yeltsin sacked two prime ministers in quick succession, politically unknown Putin was offered the inauspicious post. On New Year's Eve that year Yeltsin finally resigned and Putin was appointed acting president. Putin went on to win two presidential elections, before resigning to become Prime Minister in 2008, due to constitutionally mandated term limits. Since then fellow Petersburger Dmitry Medvedev has been the president of Russia, though it's likely that Putin will have returned to the presidency by the time you read this.

SOVIET JOKE

A Soviet census-taker stops a man along Nevsky pr:

Where were you born?
St Petersburg.

Where did you go to school?
Petrograd.

Where do you live now?
Leningrad.

Where would you like to live?
St Petersburg.

2006

Putin hosts the G8 Summit in St Petersburg, the most significant international political event ever held in the city, marking its reinvention as a ceremonial showpiece for Putin's Russia.

2010

Governor Matvienko announces that after years of protests and international criticism, the controversial 400m-high Okhta Centre will no longer be built in the city centre.

2011

Valentina Matvienko is moved sideways out of the governor's seat in St Petersburg to become the speaker of the Federation Council by President Medvedev.

2011

Former KGB officer and dyed-in-the-wool Putin loyalist Georgy Poltavchenko is appointed acting governor of St Petersburg.

History of the Hermitage

In 1764 Catherine the Great purchased the art collection of Johann Gotzkowski, which contained a large number of now priceless Rubens, Rembrandts and Van Dycks. The capricious empress put the collection on display in the 'small hermitage' where she entertained her guests. Little did anyone know this collection would grow into one of the world's most celebrated art museums, eventually filling the original building, as well as the classical Large Hermitage and the baroque Winter Palace, with millions of artistic masterpieces from around the world.

COLOURS

The Hermitage's distinct appearance, with its two-tone green walls and white painted columns, actually only dates from 1945. Before then it was a number of different colours reflecting the personal taste of the tsars and the changing fashions of the time.

A NEW WINTER PALACE

It was Empress Anna who first engaged a young Bartolomeo Rastrelli to incorporate the existing structures into a proper palace in the 1730s. But even this effort would not satisfy the whims of ever-extravagant Empress Elizabeth. In 1754 she signed a decree ordering the creation of a winter palace, and she closely supervised its design and construction. Her inopportune death in 1761 occurred only a few months before the Winter Palace was finally completed to her design, but her legacy has been confirmed by what is arguably St Petersburg's most strikingly beautiful palace.

Visitors and residents were wowed by the capital's newest addition, 'visible from a distance, rising above the rooftops, the upper storey of the new Winter Palace, adorned with a host of statues', as it was described by one 18th-century visitor to the capital. But the palace, of course, was a private residence. After the death of Empress Elizabeth, Peter III lived here for only three months before he was overthrown in a palace coup and replaced by Catherine the Great. This grand baroque building thenceforth became the official residence of the imperial family.

THE IMPERIAL ART COLLECTION

Collecting art became something of an obsession for Catherine, and she bought some of the most extensive private collections in Europe, including those of Heinrich von Brühl, Lord Robert Walpole and Baron Pierre Crozat. By 1774 Catherine's collection included over 2000 paintings, and at the time of her death in 1796 that number had doubled.

Catherine and her successors didn't much care for Rastrelli's baroque interiors and had most of the rooms completely remodelled in classical style. Catherine also built the Little Hermitage next door – and later the so-called Old Hermitage – to house her growing art collection, and allowed prominent people to privately visit the collection on application. In the 1780s Giacomo Quarenghi added the Hermitage Theatre, which served as the private theatre for the imperial family, and is still used today for intimate classical music concerts.

The early 19th century saw a continued expansion of the collection, particularly in the field of classical antiquity, due both to the continued acquisition of other collections and rich finds being discovered in southern Russia. More acquisitions followed Russia's victory over Napoleon in 1812 and included the private collection of Napoleon's consort, Joséphine de Beauharnais.

In December 1837 a devastating fire broke out in the heating shaft of the Field Marshals' Hall; it burned for over 30 hours and destroyed a large portion of the interior. Most of the imperial belongings were saved, thrown out of windows or dragged outside to sit in the snow. Nicholas I vowed to restore the palace as quickly as possible, employing architect Vasily Stasov and thousands of workers to toil around the clock. Their efforts were not in vain, as the project was completed in a little over a year. Most of the classical interiors in the ceremonial rooms that we see today, including the Grand Hall, the Throne Room and the Armorial Hall, were designed by Stasov.

RUSSIA'S FIRST PUBLIC ART MUSEUM

While Peter the Great opened the Kunstkamera (p118), his private collection of curiosities, to the public in the early 18th century, it was Nicholas I who eventually opened the first public art museum in Russia. During a visit to Germany in 1838 he was impressed by the museums he saw in Munich – specifically, by the idea of buildings that were architectural masterpieces in themselves, designed specifically to house and preserve artistic masterpieces. He employed German architect Leo von Klenze and local boy Vasily Stasov to carry out such a project in the proximity of the Winter Palace. The result was the 'neo-Grecian' New Hermitage, adorned by statues and bas-reliefs depicting great artists, writers and other cultural figures. After 11 years of work, the museum was opened to the public in 1852.

At this time, the first director of the Hermitage was appointed and the collection as a museum, rather than the tsar's private gallery, began to take shape. Various further acquisitions in the late 19th and early 20th centuries meant that the Hermitage had truly arrived as a world-class museum. Particularly important caches of paintings included the two Leonardo da Vinci Madonnas (acquired in 1865 and 1914), Piotr Semionov-Tien-Shansky's enormous collection of Dutch and Flemish art, purchased in 1910, and the Stroganov collection of Italian old masters.

While it may not be the most historically objective film ever made, Sergei Eisenstein's *October* (1928) is a brilliant depiction of the Russian Revolution. The lighting needs of the production left the entire city without electricity during the shoot. The most famous scene, the storming of the Winter Palace, remains an almost unmatched piece of cinematography.

EXPANDING THE COLLECTION

Since Catherine the Great made her first significant artistic purchase in 1764, the imperial art collection had grown consistently as each new ruler procured paintings, sculptures and artefacts to add to the store of treasures. But it was the postrevolutionary period that saw a threefold increase in the collection. In 1917 the Winter Palace and the Hermitage were declared state museums, and throughout the 1920s and 1930s the new Soviet state seized and nationalised countless valuable private collections: those of the Stroganovs, Sheremetyevs, Shuvalovs, Yusupovs and Baron Stieglitz. In 1948 it incorporated the renowned collections of post-Impressionist and Impressionist paintings from of Moscow industrialists Sergei Shchukin and Ivan Morozov. The coffers of the Hermitage swelled.

During WWII, Soviet troops in Germany and Eastern Europe brought home enormous numbers of paintings that had belonged to private collectors. In 1995, after years of keeping the paintings in storage, the Hermitage finally displayed some of this sweet war booty. The exhibition, called 'Hidden Treasures Revealed', is on the 2nd floor of the Winter Palace and consists entirely of art captured from private collections by the Red Army in 1945, including works by Monet, Degas, Renoir, Cézanne, Picasso and Matisse.

THE HERMITAGE TODAY

During WWII a mass exodus of over a million priceless paintings, sculptures and archaeological treasures were evacuated from St Petersburg to Yekaterinburg in the Urals. Meanwhile, the Winter Palace became a temporary shelter for people who had lost their homes in bombings – in 1942 some 12,000 were housed in the museum.

The Hermitage ranks today alongside the Louvre Museum, Museo del Prado and the Metropolitan Museum of Art as one of the great art collections of the world. It maintains outposts in London, Amsterdam and Ferrara, Italy, and frequently shows its paintings in travelling exhibitions around the world. Under the directorship of Mikhail Piotrovsky since 1992, the post-Soviet Hermitage has grown enormously in international stature and expanded its collection on display in St Petersburg.

As well as the Hermitage itself, the State Hermitage Museum includes several other campuses in St Petersburg: the General Staff Building (p66), the Winter Palace of Peter I (p67), the Menshikov Palace (p120), the Imperial Porcelain factory (p138) and, perhaps most significantly, the Hermitage Storage Facility (p132), which, since its opening in 2004, has displayed a huge number of items for which there simply isn't room elsewhere. The complex, already long open, will finally be completed in 2012, and will then be the largest centre of its kind anywhere in the world, with eight different buildings used for displaying, storing and exhibiting parts of the collection that are seen nowhere else.

Plans for the Hermitage include the current conversion of a historic waterfront building on Vasilevsky Island to house yet another branch of the museum in the centre of the city. Muse then, when you pay your 400% mark up on the Russian price for entry to the Hermitage, that your money could be going to far worse places.

Architecture

Peter the Great's intention was to build a city that rivalled Paris and Rome for architectural splendour. He envisioned grand avenues, weaving waterways and magnificent palaces. While he did not live to see this dream become a reality, he made a pretty good start. And his successors, especially Empresses Anna, Elizabeth and Catherine the Great, carried out their own even more elaborate versions of their forebear's plan. Today, central St Petersburg is a veritable museum of 18th- and 19th-century architecture, with enough baroque, classical and empire-style extravagances to keep you ogling indefinitely.

PETRINE BAROQUE

The first major building in the city was the Peter and Paul Fortress (p126), completed in 1704 and still intact today. Peter recruited Domenico Trezzini from Switzerland to oversee early projects. It was Trezzini, more than any other architect, who created the style known as Petrine Baroque, which was heavily influenced by Dutch architecture, of which Peter was enamoured. Trezzini's buildings included the Alexander Nevsky Monastery (p83), the Peter and Paul Cathedral (p126) within the fortress and Twelve Colleges (p120) on Vasilyevsky Island.

Initially, most funding was diverted to the war against Sweden, meaning there wasn't enough money to create the European-style city that Peter dreamed of. Once Russia's victory was secured in 1709, the city began to see feverish development. In 1711, the Grand Perspective (later Nevsky pr) was initially built as a road to transport building supplies from Russia's interior. Nevsky pr was supposed to be a perfectly straight avenue heading to Novgorod. The existing kink (at pl Vosstaniya) is attributed to a miscalculation by builders.

Stone construction was banned outside the new capital, in order to ensure that there would be enough masons free to work on the city. Peter ordered Trezzini to create a unified city plan designed around Vasilyevsky Island. He also recruited Frenchman Jean Baptiste Alexander LeBlond from Paris. The two architects focused their efforts on Vasilyevsky Island, even though most people preferred to live across the river on the higher ground of Admiralty Island. Menshikov Palace (p120) was the finest in the city, and far grander than Peter's Winter Palace (p67).

Top Five Architectural Sights

- *Winter Palace (Hermitage, Historic Heart)*
- *Mariinsky Second Stage (Kolomna)*
- *Chesme Church (southern St Petersburg)*
- *Smolny Cathedral (Smolny)*
- *House of Soviets (southern St Petersburg)*

THE AGE OF RASTRELLI

Empress Anna oversaw the completion of many of Peter's unfinished projects, including the Kunstkamera (p118) and Twelve Colleges (p120). Most significantly, she hired Italian Bartolomeo Rastrelli as chief architect, a decision that more than any other influenced the city's look today. His major projects under Anna's reign were the Manege Central Exhibition Hall (p109) and the Third Summer Palace (since destroyed). Rastrelli's greatest work, however, was yet to come.

Anna left her mark on the face of St Petersburg in many ways. She ordered all nobles to pave the street in front of their properties, thus ensuring the reinforcement of the Neva Embankment and other major thoroughfares. A massive fire in 1737 wiped out the unsightly and run-down wooden housing that surrounded the Winter Palace, thus freeing the historic centre for the centralised city planning that would be implemented under Elizabeth.

Elizabethan St Petersburg was almost entirely the work of Rastrelli, whose Russian baroque style became synonymous with the city. His crowning glory, of course, was the construction and remodelling of the Winter Palace (p67), completed in 1762, shortly after Elizabeth's death.

Rastrelli's second major landmark was Anichkov Palace (p72). After that creation, he became the city's most fashionable architect. Commissions soon followed to build Stroganov Palace (p65), Vorontsov Palace (p70), Kamennoostrovsky Palace (p132), Catherine Palace at Tsarskoe Selo (p145) and the extension of LeBlond's Grand Palace at Peterhof (p142). The sumptuous Smolny Cathedral (p84) is another Rastrelli landmark. His original design included a massive bell tower that would have been the tallest structure in Russia. The death of Empress Elizabeth in 1761 prevented him from completing it.

Rastrelli's baroque style would go out of fashion quickly after Elizabeth's death. But his legacy would endure, as he created some of the most stunning facades in the city, thus contributing to the Italianate appearance of contemporary St Petersburg.

EQUESTRIAN SCULPTURES

While wandering down Nevsky pr, don't miss the beautiful equestrian sculptures on the Anichkov Bridge and check out for yourself a local legend that says the sculptor portrayed a man he didn't like (some say it was Napoleon, others say it was his wife's lover) on the testicles of one of the stallions.

CATHERINE'S RETURN TO CLASSICISM

Despite her fondness for Elizabeth, Catherine the Great was not a fan of her predecessor's increasingly elaborate and sumptuous displays of wealth and power. Catherine's major philosophical interest was the Enlightenment, which had brought the neoclassical style to the fore in Western Europe. As a result, she began her long reign by departing from baroque architecture and introducing neoclassicism to Russia.

The first major neoclassical masterpiece in Catherine's St Petersburg was the Academy of Arts (p121) on Vasilyevsky Island, designed by Jean-Baptiste-Michel Vallin de la Mothe. Catherine employed a wide range of architects, including foreigners such as Vallin de la Mothe, Scot Charles Cameron and Italians Antonio Rinaldi and Giacomo Quarenghi, and home-grown architects such as Ivan Starov and Vasily Bazhenov.

Catherine's plan was to make the palace embankment the centrepiece of the city. To this end, she commissioned the Little Hermitage by Vallin de la Mothe, followed by the Old Hermitage and the Hermitage Theatre (p67) on the other side of the Winter Canal. These buildings on Dvortsovaya pl were followed by Quarenghi's magnificent Marble Palace (p66). Catherine also developed the embankment west of the Winter Palace, now the English Embankment (Angliyskaya nab), creating a marvellous imperial vista for those arriving in the city by boat.

The single most meaningful addition was the *Bronze Horseman* (p106) by Etienne-Maurice Falconet, an equestrian statue dedicated to Peter the Great. It is perched atop an enormous 1500-tonne boulder, known as Thunder Stone, which is from the Gulf of Finland and is supposedly the largest stone ever moved by man.

Other notable additions to the cityscape during Catherine's reign included the new Gostiny Dvor (p70), one of the world's oldest surviving shopping centres. Elizabeth had commissioned Rastrelli to rebuild an arcade that had burned down in 1736; but Catherine removed Rastrelli from the project and had it completed by Vallin de la Mothe, who created a more subtle and understated neoclassical facade. The purest classical construction in St Petersburg was perhaps Vasily Stasov's Tauride Palace (p84), built for Prince Potemkin and surrounded by William Gould's expansive English gardens.

RUSSIAN EMPIRE STYLE

Alexander I (r 1801–25) ushered in the new century with much hope that he would see through Catherine's reforms, becoming the most progressive tsar yet. His most enduring architectural legacy would be the new Alexandrian Empire style, a Russian counterpart of the style that had become popular in prewar Napoleonic France. This style was pioneered by a new generation of architects, most famously Carlo Rossi.

Before the Napoleonic Wars, the two most significant additions to the cityscape were the Strelka, the 'tongue of land' at the tip of Vasilyevsky Island, and Kazan Cathedral, prominently placed on Nevsky pr by Andrei Voronikhin. The Strelka (p118) had long been the subject of designs and proposals as a centrepiece to St Petersburg. Thomas de Thomon finally rebuilt Quarenghi's Stock Exchange and added the much-loved Rostral Columns to the tip of the island. The result was a stunning sight during summer festivities when the columns lit the sky with fire, a tradition that still continues today. The Kazan Cathedral (p65) is a fascinating anomaly in St Petersburg's architectural history. It had been commissioned by Tsar Paul I and reflected his tastes and desire to fuse Catholicism and Orthodoxy. As such it is strikingly un-Russian, borrowing many of its features from the contemporaneous Italian architecture of Rome and Florence.

Catherine's plan was to make the palace embankment the centrepiece of the city

Following the Napoleonic wars, Carlo Rossi initiated several projects of true genius. This Italian architect defined the historic heart of St Petersburg with his imperial buildings – arguably even more than Rastrelli. On Palace Sq, he created the sumptuous General Staff Building (p66), which managed to complement Rastrelli's Winter Palace without outshining it. The building's vast length, punctuated by white columns, and its magnificent triumphal arch make Palace Sq one of the most awe-inspiring urban environments in the world. The final touch to Palace Sq was added by Auguste Montferrand, who designed the Alexander Column (p65), a monument to the 1812 trouncing of Napoleon. Rossi also completed Mikhailovsky Palace (now the Russian Museum; p57) as well as the gardens behind it and Iskusstv pl (now Arts Sq, p69) in front of it.

Rossi's genius continued to shine through the reactionary rule of Nicholas I. In fact, Nicholas was the last of the Romanovs to initiate mass municipal architecture; and so Rossi remained in favour, despite Nicholas' personal preference for the Slavic Revival style that was very popular in Moscow at the time.

Rossi's largest projects under Nicholas were the redesign of Senate Sq (now pl Dekabristov; p106) and Alexandrinskaya Sq (now pl Ostrovskogo; p70), including the Alexandrinsky Theatre (p77) and Theatre St (now ul Zodchego Rossi). The Theatre St ensemble is a masterpiece of proportions: its width (22m) is the same height as its buildings, and the entire street is exactly 10 times the width (220m).

IMPERIAL ST PETERSBURG

Although Rossi continued to transform the city, the building that would redefine the city's skyline was Montferrand's St Isaac's Cathedral (p103).

An Orthodox church built in a classical style, it is the fourth largest cathedral in Europe. Montferrand's unique masterpiece took over three decades to construct and remains the highest building in St Petersburg.

Nicholas' reign saw the construction of St Petersburg's first permanent bridge across the Neva, Blagoveshchensky Most (Annunciation Bridge), and Russia's first railway (linking the capital to Tsarskoe Selo to get the royal family to their summer palace quickly – it's fair to say that the Romanovs didn't quite understand the massive potential of the new technology). A more useful line to Moscow began service in 1851, and Nikolaevsky Station, now known as Moscow Station (Moskovsky vokzal), was built to accommodate it.

The reigns of Alexander II and Alexander III saw few changes to the overall building style in St Petersburg. Industrialisation under Alexander II meant filling in several canals, most significantly the Ligovsky Canal (now Ligovsky pr). A plan to fill in Griboedov Canal proved too expensive to execute and the canal remains one of the city's most charming.

The main contribution of Alexander III was the Church of the Resurrection of Christ, better known as the Church on the Spilled Blood (p64), built on the site of his father's 1881 assassination. Alexander III insisted the church be in the Slavic Revival style, which explains its uncanny similarity to St Basil's Cathedral on Red Square in Moscow. Architects Malyshev and Parland designed its spectacular multicoloured tiling, the first hints of Russian Style Moderne, which by the end of the 19th century would take the city by storm. Painters such as Mikhail Nesterov and Mikhail Vrubel contributed to the interior design.

That the ineffective and conservative Nicholas II presided over one of the city's most exciting architectural periods was pure chance. As the city became richer and richer during the 19th century, the industrialist and merchant classes began building mansions in the feted art nouveau style, known in Russia as Style Moderne. The Petrograd Side was the most fashionable of the era, so that is where the majority of Style Moderne buildings were constructed. The back streets reveal many gems from the late 19th century and early 20th century, including the fabulous mansion of the ballet dancer Mathilda Kshesinskaya, which now houses the Museum of Political History (p129).

ARCHITECTURAL HISTORY

Arthur George's St Petersburg is the first comprehensive popular history of St Petersburg and is a superb read for anyone interested in the city's architectural development. Taking the reader from Petrine Baroque to Stalinism, George is an expert guide to the differing styles that so define the city.

SOVIET LENINGRAD

As in all other spheres of Russian culture, the collapse of the tsarist regime in 1917 led to huge changes in architecture. In the beleaguered city, all major building projects stopped; the palaces of the aristocracy and the mansions of the merchant classes were turned over to the state or split up into communal apartments. As the Germans approached Petrograd in 1918, the title of capital returned to Moscow; the city went into a decline that was to last until the 1990s.

The architectural form that found favour under the Bolsheviks in the 1920s was constructivism. Combining utilitarianism and utopianism, this modern style sought to advance the socialist cause, using technological innovation and slick unembellished design. Pl Stachek is rich with such buildings, such as the Kirov Region Administrative Building on Kirovskaya pl and the incredibly odd Communication Workers' Palace of Culture on the Moyka Canal.

Stalin considered the opulence of the imperial centre of renamed Leningrad to be a potentially corrupting influence on the people. So, from 1927, he began to relocate the centre to the south of the city's historic heart. His traditional neoclassical tastes prevailed. The prime example of Stalinist architecture is the vast House of Soviets (p90), which was meant to be the centrepiece of the new city centre. Noi Trotsky began this magnificent monstrosity in 1936, although it was not finished until after the war (by which time Trotsky had himself been purged). With its columns and bas-reliefs, it is a great example of Stalinist neoclassical design – similar in many ways to the imperial neoclassicism pioneered a century earlier. The House of Soviets was never used as the Leningrad government building, as the plan to relocate the centre was shelved after Stalin's death in 1953.

WWII and Stalin's old age saved many buildings of great importance: the Church on the Spilled Blood, for example, was slated for destruction before the German invasion of the Soviet Union intervened. Many other churches and historical buildings, however, were destroyed.

During the eras of Khrushchev and Brezhnev, St Petersburg's imperial heritage was cautiously respected, as the communist leadership took a step back from Stalin's excesses. Between the 1950s and 1970s, a housing shortage led to the construction of high-rise Soviet apartment buildings, which would cover huge swathes of the city outside the historic centre. For many visitors, this is their first and last view of the city. Examples of archetypal post-Stalinist Soviet architecture include the massive Grand Concert Hall (p97), near pl Vosstaniya, and the nondescript Finland Station (p134), on the Vyborg Side.

CONTEMPORARY ST PETERSBURG

Following the end of communism in the early 1990s, efforts were focused on the reconstruction of imperial-era buildings, many of which were derelict and literally falling down due to 70 years of neglect.

OKHTA CENTRE

No urban development project has caused as many concerns as the notorious Okhta Centre, originally to have been called Gazprom City. At the suggestion of public relations consultants, no doubt, Russia's largest gas company changed the name of its project to Okhta Centre, named after a tributary of the Neva near where the original design was supposed to be.

The name and location may have changed, but the beast has not. The Okhta Centre will be the city's first skyscraper, towering more than 400m over the Neva (that's three times higher than the spire of the SS Peter and Paul Cathedral). The only other structure that even comes close to that height is the 310m TV tower, which is well removed from the historic heart. The Okhta Centre was originally planned to occupy the site of an abandoned factory on the Vyborg Side, just opposite Smolny Cathedral (p84). But such was the (rare) public and international outcry at the plan that in 2010 City Hall backed down and cancelled the project, to the joy of many locals. It was later announced that the building would still be constructed at a new location called Lakhta, a good distance from the historic heart and beyond the Kirovsky Islands on the Vyborg Side. Along with its new location, the project underwent a second name change and is now known as the **Lakhta Centre** (www.proektvlahte.ru).

The project's massive public opposition underscored the lack of democratic choice for residents of Europe's fourth biggest city, whose governor is appointed by the president and only has to be confirmed by the City Legislative Assembly. Many cited the poor handling of the Okhta Centre issue and the massive expenditure of political capital on the project by then governor, Valentina Matvienko, as one of the main reasons the Kremlin decided to remove her in 2011. The completed building will be the tallest structure in Europe, though unsurprisingly many locals are not really that proud of the achievement.

Between 1991 and St Petersburg's tercentennial celebrations in 2003, much of the historic heart was restored at vast expense, although efforts are still continuing today.

Everyone agrees that the total regeneration of New Holland (p110) being undertaken by Roman Abramovich will probably be one of the most exciting of the next decade. The hot rumour is that as well as being a cultural centre, Abramovich will use the island to display his stellar contemporary art collection, which would really put St Petersburg on the map of the international art world.

The governorship of Valentina Matvienko (2003–11) was marked by a shift from preservation to construction, and the city saw a large growth in new building projects during this time, not always to the delight of campaigners for the protection of St Petersburg's architectural heritage, or Unesco, which awarded St Petersburg's historic centre World Heritage status in 1990. The most noteworthy of contemporary architecture projects in St Petersburg are the construction of the Mariinsky Second Stage (p108) next to the Mariinsky Theatre, and, even more controversially, the Okhta Centre (see boxed text, p201). This 403m-tall skyscraper was originally slated to be built next to the Smolny Cathedral but after worldwide condemnation and an unusually strong local protest movement it was relocated far from the city centre.

Arts

Despite the evident European influences, St Petersburg's Russian roots are a more essential source of inspiration for its artistic genius. Musicians and writers have long looked to Russian history, folk culture and other national themes. That St Petersburg produced so many artistic and musical masterpieces is in itself a source of wonder for the city's visitors and inhabitants today. Strolling from one art-filled room to another through the never-ending Winter Palace, listening to a symphony at the Mariinsky or watching a ballerina bend her body into impossible shapes...such is the artistic feast awaiting the visitor to St Petersburg.

BALLET

First introduced in the 17th century, ballet in Russia evolved as an offshoot of French dance combined with Russian folk and peasant dance techniques. In 1738, French dance master Jean Baptiste Lande established the Imperial Ballet School in St Petersburg – a precursor to the famed Vaganova School of Choreography (see p70).

The French dancer and choreographer Marius Petipa (1819–1910) is considered the father of Russian ballet, acting as principal dancer and premier ballet master of the Imperial Theatres and Imperial Ballet. All told, he produced more than 60 full ballets, including the classics *Sleeping Beauty* and *Swan Lake*.

In 1907, Petipa wrote in his diary, 'I can state that I created a ballet company of which everyone said: St Petersburg has the greatest ballet in all Europe.' At the turn of the 20th century, the heyday of Russian ballet, St Petersburg's Imperial Ballet School rose to world prominence, producing superstar after superstar. Names such as Vaslav Nijinsky, Anna Pavlova, Mathilda Kshesinskaya, George Balanchine, Michel Fokine and Olga Spessivtzeva turned the Mariinsky Theatre (p107) into the world's most dynamic display of the art of dance.

Sergei Diaghilev graduated from the St Petersburg Conservatory in 1892, but he abandoned his dream of becoming a composer when his professor, Nikolai Rimsky-Korsakov, told him he had no talent for music. Instead he turned his attention to dance, and his Ballets Russes took Europe by storm. The Petipa-inspired choreography was daring and dynamic, and the stage decor was painted by artists such as Alexander Benois, Mikhail Larionov, Natalya Goncharova and Leon Bakst. The overall effect was an artistic, awe-inducing display unlike anything taking place elsewhere in Europe.

Under the Soviets, ballet was treated as a natural resource. It enjoyed highly privileged status, which allowed schools such as Vaganova and companies such as the Kirov to maintain a level of lavish production and no-expense-spared star-searches. Still, the story of 20th-century Russian ballet is connected with the West, to where so many of its brightest stars emigrated or defected. Anna Pavlova, Vaslav Nijinsky, Rudolf Nureyev, Mikhail Baryshnikov, George Balanchine, Natalya Makarova, Mathilda Kshesinskaya, to name a few, all found fame in Western Europe or America, and most of them ended up living there.

The hot ticket in town is the Mariinsky Second Stage, which should be opening in 2012. Book early at www.mariinsky.ru to guarantee your seats in what will inevitably become one of the leading ballet and opera houses in the world.

MARIINSKY

Of the huge range of productions it's possible to see at the Mariinsky Theatre, Prokofiev's thoroughly modernist ballet *Romeo and Juliet* is perhaps one of the most enjoyable. It premiered on this very stage in 1940 and has changed little since – a true classic.

The Kirov, now known by its pre-revolutionary name, the Mariinsky, has its home at the Mariinsky Theatre (p107) and has been rejuvenated under the fervent directorship of artistic director Valery Gergiev. The Mariinsky's calling card has always been its flawless classical ballet, but in recent years names such as William Forsythe and John Neumeier have brought modern choreography to this establishment. The Mariinsky's credibility on the world stage is set to soar further in 2012 on completion of the Mariinksy Second Stage, being built adjacent to the old one on the Kryukov Canal (see the boxed text, p108).

MUSIC

St Petersburg has a rich musical legacy, dating back to the days when the Group of Five and Pyotr Tchaikovsky composed here. Opera and classical music continue to draw crowds, and the Mariinsky and Philharmonia regularly sell out their performances of home-grown classics. Surprisingly, earlier music, such as baroque and medieval, is not as well known or as well loved. But the directors of the Early Music Festival (p21) have long been campaigning to change that with their excellent annual event.

Music lovers come in all shapes and sizes, however. Even when rock-and-roll was illegal it was played in basements and garages. Now, 20 years after the weight of censorship has been lifted, St Petersburg is the centre of *russky rok,* a magnet for musicians and music lovers, who are drawn to its atmosphere of innovation and creation.

OPERA

For a truly surreal night at the opera, treat yourself to tickets to see the Mariinsky's production of Shostakovich's opera *The Nose*, based on the hilarious socially satirical short story by Nikolai Gogol of a socially-aspirant bureaucrat who wakes up one morning to find his nose has left him and is gadding around town.

Classical Music & Opera

As the cultural heart of Russia, St Petersburg was a natural draw for generations of composers, its rich cultural life acting as inspiration for talent from throughout Russia. Mikhail Glinka is often considered the father of Russian classical music. In 1836 his opera *A Life for the Tsar* premiered in St Petersburg. While European musical influences were evident, the story was based on Russian history, recounting the dramatic tale of a peasant, Ivan Susanin, who sacrificed himself to save Mikhail Romanov.

In the second half of the 19th century, several influential schools – based in the capital – formed, from which emerged some of Russia's most famous composers and finest music. The so-called Group of Five – Modest Mussorgsky, Nikolai Rimsky-Korsakov, Alexander Borodin, César Cui and Mily Balakirev – looked to folk music for uniquely Russian themes. They tried to develop a distinct sound using unusual tonal and harmonic devices. Their main opponent was Anton Rubinstein's conservatively rooted Russian Musical Society, which became the St Petersburg Conservatory in 1861. The competition between the two schools was fierce. Rimsky-Korsakov wrote in his memoirs: 'Rubinstein had a reputation as a pianist, but was thought to have neither talent nor taste as a composer.'

Pyotr Tchaikovsky (1840–93) seemed to find the middle ground, embracing Russian folklore and music as well as the disciplines of the Western European composers. In 1890 Tchaikovsky's *Queen of Spades* premiered at the Mariinsky. His adaptation of the famous Pushkin tale surprised and invigorated the artistic community, especially as his deviations from the original text – infusing it with more cynicism and a brooding sense of doom – tied the piece to contemporary St Petersburg.

Tchaikovsky is widely regarded as the doyen of Russian national composers and his output, including the magnificent *1812 Overture,* his concertos and symphonies, ballets (*Swan Lake, Sleeping Beauty* and *The Nutcracker*), and opera *(Yevgeny Onegin)* are among the world's most popular classical works.

Following in Tchaikovsky's romantic footsteps was the innovative Igor Stravinsky (1882–1971). He fled Russia after the revolution, but his memoirs credit his childhood in St Petersburg as having a major effect on his music. *The Rite of Spring* (which created a furore at its first performance in Paris), *Petrouchka* and *The Firebird* were all influenced by Russian folk music. The official Soviet line was that Stravinsky was a 'political and ideological renegade'; but he was rehabilitated after he visited the USSR and was formally received by Khrushchev himself.

Similarly, the ideological beliefs and experimental style of Dmitry Shostakovich (1906–75) led to him being alternately praised and condemned by the Soviet government. As a student at the Petrograd conservatory, Shostakovich failed his exams in Marxist methodology, but still managed to write his First Symphony before he graduated in 1926. He wrote brooding, bizarrely dissonant works, as well as accessible traditional classical music. After official condemnation by Stalin, his Seventh Symphony (Leningrad Symphony) brought him honour and international standing when it was performed during WWII. The authorities changed their mind and banned his anti-Soviet music in 1948, then 'rehabilitated' him after Stalin's death. These days he is held in high esteem as the namesake of the acclaimed Shostakovich Philharmonia (p77).

Since becoming its artistic director in 1988, Valery Gergiev has revitalised the Mariinsky (p107). The Russian classics still top the list of performances, but Gergiev is also willing to be a little adventurous, taking on operas that had not been performed in half a century or more. Gergiev is also responsible for initiating the Stars of White Nights Festival (p21), an annual event that showcases the best and brightest dancers and musicians.

Five Classic Petersburg Albums:

- *Kino – Gruppa Krovi*
- *Leningrad – Piraty XXI Veka*
- *Akvarium – Peski Peterburga*
- *DDT – Chorny Pyos Peterburg*
- *Dva Samolyota – Ubitsy Sredi Nas*

Rock

Russian music is not all about classical composers. Ever since the 'bourgeois' Beatles filtered through in the 1960s, Russians both young and old have supported the rock revolution. Starved of decent equipment and the chance to record or perform to big audiences, Russian rock groups initially developed underground. By the 1970s – the Soviet hippy era – rock music had developed a huge following among the disaffected, distrustful youth in Leningrad.

Although bands initially imitated their Western counterparts, a real underground sound emerged in Leningrad in the 1980s. Boris Grebenshchikov and his band Akvarium (Aquarium) caused sensations wherever they performed; his folk rock and introspective lyrics became the emotional cry of a generation. Yury Shevchuk and his band DDT emerged as the country's main rock band. The god of Russian rock was Viktor Tsoy and his group Kino. His early death in a 1990 car crash ensured his legend would have a long life. On the anniversary of Tsoy's death (15 August), fans still gather to play his tunes and remember the musician, especially at his grave at the Bogoslovskoe Cemetery, which is located a short distance from the Piskaryovskoe Memorial Cemetery (p134).

For an engaging account of how culture and politics became intertwined during the early Soviet period, read Solomon Volkov's *Shostakovich and Stalin*, which examines the fascinating relationship between two of the main representatives of each field.

Many contemporary favourites in St Petersburg have been playing together since the early days. The most prominent (and perhaps most popular) local fixture is Dva Samolyota (Two Airplanes), a ska band exhibiting influences of Latin-jazz, reggae and afro-beat. These days the group plays together only occasionally, but its members are still fixtures on the local scene.

Switch on Russian MTV and you'll see local versions of boy bands and disco divas all doing their sometimes desultory, sometimes foot-tapping stuff. Meanwhile, St Petersburg clubs are filled with garage bands, new wave, punk, hard rock and electronic groups.

VISUAL ARTS

It should come as no surprise that St Petersburg is an artistic place, having been designed by the leading artists of the day. In the early years, aristocrats and emperors filled their palaces with endless collections of paintings and applied arts, guaranteeing a steady stream of artistic production. These days, hundreds of thousands of visitors come here to see the masterpieces that hang in the Hermitage and the Russian Museum.

But St Petersburg's artistic tradition is not only historical. The city's winding waterways, crumbling castles and colourful characters continue to inspire creative types and in recent years the city has become a nurturing space for artists to work, with plentiful studios, gallery spaces and new museums interested in modern work. Anyone interested in the state of contemporary art in the city should head to Loft Project ETAGI (p87), Erarta Museum (p118) and the Rizzordi Art Foundation (p88). St Petersburg has always been a city of artists and poets, and that legacy endures.

Academy of Arts

Known both as the Imperial Academy of Arts and the St Petersburg Academy of Arts, this official state-run artistic institution was founded in 1757 by Count Ivan Shuvalov, a political adviser, education minister and longtime lover of Empress Elizabeth. It was Catherine the Great who moved the Academy out of Shuvalov's home, commissioning the present neoclassical building on Vasilyevsky Island (see p121).

The Academy was responsible for the education and training of young artists. It focused heavily on French-influenced academic art, which incorporated neoclassicism and romanticism. Painters such as Fyodor Alexeyev and Grigory Chernetsev came out of the Academy of Arts.

Peredvizhniki

In the 19th century, artist Ivan Kramskoy led the so-called 'revolt of 14' whereby a group of upstart artists broke away from the powerful but conservative Academy of Arts. The mutineers considered that art should be a force for national awareness and social change, and they depicted common people and real problems in their paintings. The Peredvizhniki (Wanderers), as they called themselves, travelled around the country in an attempt to widen their audience (thus inspiring their moniker).

The Peredvizhniki included Vasily Surikov, who painted vivid Russian historical scenes, and Nicholas Ghe, who favoured both historical and biblical landscapes. Perhaps the best loved of all Russian artists, Ilya Re-

MY NAME IS SHNUR

Leningrad, the punk band from St Petersburg, was banned from the radio and forbidden from performing in Moscow by its former mayor, Yuri Luzhkov. But such controversy only fuelled its popularity. Lead singer Sergei Shnurov claims 'Our songs are just about the good sides of life – vodka and girls, that is.'

But besides being rowdy and bawdy, the lyricist is known for his ironic insights on contemporary culture. 'Money' satirises society's pervasive consumerism, while 'WWW' is a commentary on the alienation caused by modern technology. Most famously, 'Menya Zovut Shnur' (My Name is Shnur) and its accompanying animated video are a harsh critique of authority.

Nowadays, Leningrad is widely played on Russian radio, thanks in part to filler noise that covers up the most vulgar lyrics. But that doesn't mean the spunky, punky band is going mainstream. Leningrad continues to act in ways that are unexpected, uncouth and outrageous; and the fans wouldn't have it any other way.

pin has works that range from social criticism *(Barge Haulers on the Volga)* to history *(Cossacks Writing a Letter to the Turkish Sultan)* to portraits.

By the end of the 19th century, Russian culture was retreating from Western influences and looking instead to nationalistic themes and folk culture for inspiration. Artists at this time invented the *matryoshka*, the quintessential Russian nesting doll. One of the world's largest collections of *matryoshkas* is on display at the Toy Museum (p131).

Mikhail Vrubel was inspired by Byzantine mosaics and Russian fairy tales. Painters such as Nikolai Roerich and Mikhail Nesterov incorporated mystical themes, influenced by folklore and religious traditions. All of these masters are prominently featured at the Russian Museum (p57).

Avant-Garde

From about 1905 Russian art became a maelstrom of groups, styles and 'isms', as it absorbed decades of European change in a few years. It finally gave birth to its own avant-garde futurist movements.

Mikhail Larionov and Natalya Goncharova were the centre of a Cézanne-influenced group known as the Knave of Diamonds. This husband-wife team went on to develop neo-primitivism, based on popular arts and primitive icons. They worked closely with Sergei Diaghilev, the founder of Ballets Russes, designing costumes and sets for the ballet company that brought together some of the era's greatest dancers, composers and artists.

The most radical members of the Knave of Diamonds formed a group known as Donkey's Tail, which exhibited the influences of cubism and futurism. Larionov and Goncharova were key members of this group, as well as Marc Chagall and Kazimir Malevich.

In 1915 Malevich announced the arrival of suprematism. His abstract geometrical shapes (with the black square representing the ultimate 'zero form') freed artists from having to depict the material world and made art a doorway to higher realities. See one of his four *Black Square* paintings, and other examples of Russian avant-garde, at the Hermitage (p44).

Soviet Art

Futurists turned to the needs of the revolution – education, posters, banners – with enthusiasm. They had a chance to act on their theories of how art shapes society. But at the end of the 1920s abstract art fell out of favour. The Communist Party wanted socialist realism. Images abounded of striving workers, heroic soldiers and healthy toiling peasants, some of which are on display at the Russian Museum. Two million sculptures of Lenin and Stalin dotted the country; Malevich ended up painting portraits and doing designs for Red Square parades.

After Stalin, an avant-garde 'Conceptualist' underground group was allowed to form. Ilya Kabakov painted, or sometimes just arranged, the debris of everyday life to show the gap between the promises and realities of Soviet existence. Erik Bulatov's 'Sotsart' pointed to the devaluation of language by ironically reproducing Soviet slogans or depicting words disappearing over the horizon. In 1962 artists set up a show of 'unofficial' art in Moscow: Khrushchev called it 'dog shit' and sent it back underground. Soviet underground art is particularly well represented in the collection of the brand new Erarta Museum of Contemporary Art (p118).

Neo-Academism & Non-Conformist Art

As the centre of the avant-garde movement in Russia at the turn of the last century, St Petersburg never gave up its ties to barrier-breaking, gut-wrenching, head-scratching art. After the end of communism the city rediscovered its seething artistic underbelly.

Best Artist House-Museums in St Petersburg

Rimsky-Korsakov (Smolny & Vosstaniya)

Chaliapin House Museum (Petrograd & Vyborg Sides)

Anna Akhmatova Museum in the Fountain House (Smolny & Vosstaniya)

Brodsky House Museum (Historic Heart)

Much of St Petersburg's post-Soviet contemporary art revolved around the artistic collective at Pushkinskaya 10 (p88), where artists and musicians continue to congregate and create. This place was 'founded' in the late 1980s, when a bunch of artists and musicians moved into an abandoned building near Pl Vosstaniya. The centre has since developed into an artistic and cultural institution that is unique in Russia, if not the world.

In the early 1990s Timur Novikov founded the Neo-Academic movement as an antidote to 'the barbarism of modernism'. This return to classicism (albeit with a street-level, junk-shop feel) culminated in his foundation of the Museum of the New Academy of Fine Arts, which is housed at Pushkinskaya 10. Although he died in 2002, he continues to cast a long shadow on the city's artistic scene.

Over the years, the hodgepodge of artists, exhibits and studio space at Pushkinskaya 10 has grown. The centre is now officially known as the Free Culture Society, although it's still often referred to by its original address. In 1998 the Free Culture Society opened the Museum of Non-Conformist Art, with its own collection of 'unofficial' art from the 20th and 21st centuries. Most importantly, the various museums and galleries at Pushkinskaya 10 showcase the ever-growing oeuvre of its member artists, including not only paintings but also photographs, sculptures, collages, videos, set and graphic designs and music.

CINEMA

The Lenfilm studio on the Petrograd Side was a centre of the Soviet film industry, producing many much-loved Russian comedies and dramas – most famously, Sergei Eisenstein's *October* (1928). Lenfilm has continued in the post-communist era to work with some success as a commercial film studio. However, the removal of Soviet-era state funding for film-making has inevitably led to torpor in the local industry.

There are, of course, exceptions. Ever since *Russian Ark* (2002), St Petersburg native Alexander Sokurov has been recognised as one of Russia's most talented contemporary directors. The world's first unedited feature film, *Russian Ark* was shot in one unbroken 90-minute frame. Sokurov's films have tackled a wide range of subjects, most significantly the corrupting influence of power, which was explored in a tetralogy of films observing individual cases, including Hitler *(Molokh),* Lenin *(Taurus),* Japanese Emperor Hirohito *(The Sun)* and Faust *(Faust).* Another recent Sokurov production that was critically acclaimed is *Alexandra* (2007), the moving tale of an elderly woman who visits her grandson at an army base in Chechnya. The title role is played by Galina Vishnevskaya, opera doyenne and wife of composer-conductor Mstislav Rostropovich.

Another star of the St Petersburg's film industry is Alexey German, who gained attention with his 1998 film *Khrustalyov! My Car!* Based on a story by Joseph Brodsky, the film tells the tale of a well-loved military doctor who was arrested during Stalin's 'Doctor's Plot'. The 2012 release of *A History of the Arkanar Massacre,* which has been in production for over a decade now, is eagerly awaited.

Other Lenfilm successes include Alexey Balabanov's *Of Freaks and Men,* the joint project of Boris Frumin and Yury Lebedev, *Undercover,* and Andrei Kravchuk's *The Italian,* all of which enjoyed some critical acclaim in the West.

St Petersburg hosts the Festival of Festivals (p21), an annual noncompetitive film event in June. Partly sponsored by Lenfilm, the festival is an attempt to draw film-makers to the city, as well as to draw attention to its films. A smaller but more innovative event is **Message to Man** (www.m2m.iffc.ru), a festival featuring documentaries, shorts and animated films.

LOCAL COLOUR

A charming and whimsical film, Alexei Uchitel's *The Stroll* (Progulka, 2003), follows three young Petersburgers as they wander around the city getting into all sorts of situations from a soccer riot to an argument between friends and a rainstorm. Great for St Petersburg local colour!

THEATRE

While it may not be completely accessible to most travellers due to language barriers, theatre plays a major role in St Petersburg performing arts. At least a dozen drama and comedy theatres dot the city streets, not to mention puppet theatres and musical theatres. As in all areas of the performing arts, contemporary playwrights do not receive as much attention as well-known greats and adaptations of famous literature. Nonetheless, drama has a long history in Russia and St Petersburg, as the cultural capital, has always been at the forefront.

In the early days, theatre was an almost exclusive vehicle of the Orthodox Church, used to spread its message and convert believers. In the 19th century, however, vaudeville found its way to Russia. More often than not, these biting, satirical one-act comedies poked fun at the rich and powerful. Playwrights such as Alexander Pushkin and Mikhail Lermontov decried the use of their art as a tool of propaganda or evangelism. Other writers – Nikolai Gogol, Alexander Griboyedov and Alexander Ostrovsky – took it a step further, writing plays that attacked not just the aristocracy but the bourgeoisie as well. Anton Chekhov wrote for St Petersburg newspapers before writing one-act, vaudevillian works. Yet it is his full-length plays that are his legacy.

Towards the end of the 19th century Maxim Gorky represented an expansion of this trend in anti-establishment theatre. His play *The Song of the Stormy Petrel* raised workers to a level superior to that of the intellectual. This production was the first of what would be many socialist realist performances, thus earning its author the esteem of the Soviet authorities.

The futurists had their day on the stage, mainly in the productions of the energetic and tirelessly inventive director Vsevolod Meyerhold, who was one of the most influential figures of modern theatre. His productions of Alexander Blok's *The Fair Show Booth* (1906) and Vladimir Mayakovsky's *Mystery-Bouffe* (1918) both caused a sensation at the time. Both Anna Akhmatova and Dmitry Shostakovich cited Meyerhold's 1935 production of *Queen of Spades* by Tchaikovsky as one of the era's most influential works.

During the Soviet period, drama was used primarily as a propaganda tool. When foreign plays were performed, it was for a reason – hence the popularity in Russia of *Death of a Salesman,* which showed the inevitable result of Western greed and decadence. However, just after the revolution, theatre artists were given great, if short-lived, freedom to experiment – anything to make theatre accessible to the masses. Avant-garde productions flourished for a while, notably under the mastery of poet and director Igor Terentyev. Artists such as Pavel Filonov and Malevich participated in production and stage design.

Even socialist theatre was strikingly experimental: the Theatre of Worker Youth, under the guidance of Mikhail Sokolovsky, used only amateur actors and encouraged improvisation, sudden plot alterations and interaction with audience members, striving to redefine the theatre-going experience. Free theatre tickets were given out at factories; halls that once echoed with the jangle of their upper-class audience's jewellery were now filled with sailors and workers. The tradition of sending army regiments and schoolchildren to the theatre continues to this day.

Today theatre remains important to the city's intellectuals, but it isn't at the forefront of the arts, receiving little state support and, unlike the ballet or opera, unable to earn revenues from touring abroad. If you're interested in the state of contemporary Russian theatre, the Maly Drama Theatre (p97), Baltic House (p138) and the Priyut Komedianta (p78) are particularly worth checking out.

For a comprehensive rundown of the history of drama from classical staging to the revolutionary works of Meyerhold and Mayakovsky, see Konstantin Rudnitsky's excellent *Russian & Soviet Theatre: Tradition & the Avant-Garde*.

HISTORY OF DRAMA

Literature

St Petersburg's very existence, a brand new city for a brand new Russia, seems sometimes to be the stuff of fiction. Indeed, its early history is woven into the fabric of one of Russia's most famous epic poems, Pushkin's *The Bronze Horseman,* which muses on the fate of the city through the eyes of Falconet's famous equestrian statue of Peter the Great. In just three centuries the city's three incarnations – St Petersburg, Petrograd and Leningrad – have produced more great writers than many cities do over a millennium: Pushkin, Gogol, Dostoevsky, Blok, Akhmatova and Brodsky are all intimately associated with Peter's city.

ROMANTICISM IN THE GOLDEN AGE

Among the many ways that Peter and Catherine the Great brought Westernisation and modernisation to Russia was the introduction of a modern alphabet. Prior to this time, written Russian was used almost exclusively in the Orthodox church, which employed an archaic and incomprehensible Church Slavonic. During the Petrine era, it became increasingly acceptable to use popular language in literature. This development paved the way for two centuries of Russian literary prolificacy, with St Petersburg at its centre.

Romanticism was a reaction against the strict social rules and scientific rationalisation of previous periods, exalting emotion and aesthetics. Nobody embraced Russian romanticism more than the national bard, Alexander Pushkin, who lived and died in St Petersburg. Most famously, his last address on the Moyka River is now a suitably hagiographic museum, its interior preserved exactly as it was at the moment of his death in 1837 (see p66). The duel that killed him is also remembered with a monument on the site (see p135).

Four Statues of Pushkin in St Petersburg

- *Ploshchad Isskustv (Historic Heart)*
- *Pushkin House (Vasilyevsky Island)*
- *ulitsa Pushkinskaya (Smolny & Vosstaniya)*
- *Site of Pushkin's Duel (Petrograd & Vyborg Sides)*

Pushkin's epic poem *Yevgeny Onegin* (*Eugene Onegin* in English) is partly set in the imperial capital. Pushkin savagely ridicules its foppish aristocratic society, despite being a fairly consistent fixture of it himself for most of his adult life. The wonderful short story 'The Queen of Spades' is set in the house of a countess on Nevsky pr and is the weird supernatural tale of a man who uncovers her Mephistophelean gambling trick. Published posthumously, *The Bronze Horseman* is named for the statue of Peter the Great that stands on pl Dekabristov (p106). The story takes place during the great flood of 1824. The main character is the lowly clerk Yevgeny, who has lost his beloved in the flood. Representing the hopes of the common people, he takes on the empire-building spirit of Peter the Great, represented by the animation of the *Bronze Horseman.*

No other figure in world literature is more closely connected with St Petersburg than Fyodor Dostoevsky (1821–81). He was among the first writers to navigate the murky waters of the human subconscious, blending powerful prose with psychology, philosophy and spirituality. Born in Moscow, Dostoevsky moved to the imperial capital in 1838, aged 16, to study, and he began his literary and journalistic career here, living at dozens of addresses in the seedy and poverty-stricken area around Sennaya pl, where many of his novels are set.

His career was halted – but ultimately shaped – by his casual involvement with a group of young free thinkers called the Petrashevsky Circle. Nicholas I decided to make an example of some of these liberals by having them arrested and sentencing them to death. After a few months in the Peter and Paul Fortress prison, Dostoevsky and his cohorts were assembled for execution. As the guns were aimed and ready to fire, the death sentence was suddenly called off – a joke! – and the group was committed instead to a sentence of hard labour in Siberia. After Dostoevsky was pardoned by Alexander II and returned to St Petersburg, he wrote *Notes from the House of the Dead* (1861), a vivid recounting of his prison sojourn.

The ultimate St Petersburg novel and literary classic is Dostoevsky's *Crime and Punishment* (1866). It is a tale of redemption, but also acknowledges the 'other side' of the regal capital: the gritty, dirty city that spawned unsavoury characters and unabashed poverty. It's a great novel to read before visiting St Petersburg, as the Sennaya district in which it's largely set retains its dark and sordid atmosphere a century-and-a-half later.

In his later works, *The Idiot, The Possessed* and *The Brothers Karamazov,* Dostoevsky was explicit in his criticism of the revolutionary movement as being morally bankrupt. A true believer, he asserted that only by following Christ's ideal could humanity be saved. An incorrigible Russophile, Dostoevsky eventually turned against St Petersburg and its European tendencies. His final home near Vladimirskaya pl now houses the Dostoevsky Museum (p87) and he is buried at Tikhvin Cemetery (p83) within the walls of the Alexander Nevsky Monastery, a suitably Orthodox setting for such a devout believer.

Amidst the epic works of Pushkin, Tolstoy and Dostoevsky, the absurdist short-story writer Nikolai Gogol (1809–52) sometimes gets lost. But his troubled genius created some of Russian literature's most memorable characters, including Akaki Akakievich, tragicomic hero of 'The Overcoat', and the brilliant social-climber Major Kovalyev, who chases his errant nose around St Petersburg in the absurdist masterpiece 'The Nose'. Gogol came to St Petersburg from his native Ukraine in 1829, and wrote and lived here for a decade before spending his final years abroad. He was not impressed by the legendary capital: in a letter to his mother he described it as a place where 'people seem more dead than alive' and complained endlessly about the air pressure, which he believed caused illness. He was nevertheless inspired to write a number of absurdist stories, collectively known as *The Petersburg Tales,* which are generally recognised as the zenith of his creativity.

LABYRINTH

If you want to get inside the mind of Petersburg's most surreal writer, try Simon Karlinsky's explosive *The Sexual Labyrinth of Nikolai Gogol*, which argues that the key to understanding the writer was that he was a self-hating homosexual. Supported very strongly by textual analysis, the book is convincing, if rather polemical.

SYMBOLISM IN THE SILVER AGE

The late 19th century saw the rise of the symbolist movement, which emphasised individualism and creativity, purporting that artistic endeavours were exempt from the rules that bound other parts of society. The outstanding figures of this time were the philosopher-poet Vladimir Solovyov (1853–1900), novelist Andrei Bely (1880–1934) and poet Alexander Blok (1880–1921) as well as the poets Sergei Yesenin (1895–1925), Nikolai Gumilev (1886–1921) and Anna Akhmatova (1889–1966). The Stray Dog Café (p76), an underground bar on pl Iskusstv (Arts Sq), was a popular meeting place where Symbolist writers, musicians and artists exchanged ideas and shared their work.

Blok and Bely, who both lived in St Petersburg, were the most renowned writers of the Symbolist movement. While Bely was well known and respected for his essays and philosophical discourses, it is his mysterious novel *Petersburg* for which he is remembered. Its language is both literary and musical: it seems the author was paying as much attention to the sound of his words as to their meaning. The plot, however difficult to follow, revolves around a revolutionary who is hounded by the *Bronze Horseman* (the same statue that harasses Pushkin's character) and is ordered to carry out the assassination of his own father, a high-ranking tsarist official, by his revolutionary cell. Many critics see Bely's masterpiece as a forerunner of Joyce's far later modernist experiments in *Ulysses*, even though *Petersburg* wasn't even translated into English until the 1950s.

Blok took over where Dostoevsky left off, writing of prostitutes, drunks and other characters marginalised by society. Blok sympathised with the revolutions and he was praised by the Bolsheviks once they came to power in 1917. His novel *The Twelve,* published in 1918, is pretty much a love letter to Lenin. However, he later became disenchanted with the revolution and consequently fell out of favour; he died a sad, lonely poet in 1921, before his fall out with the communists could have more serious consequences. In one of his last letters, he wrote, 'She did devour me, lousy, snuffling dear Mother Russia, like a sow devouring her piglet'. The flat where he spent the last eight years of his life is now a museum (see p109).

DOSTOEVSKY

Crime and Punishment may be on everyone's reading list before they head to the northern capital, but another (far shorter) St Petersburg work from Dostoevsky is 'White Nights', a wonderful short story that has been adapted for cinema by no less than nine different directors!

REVOLUTIONARY LITERATURE

The immediate aftermath of 1917 saw a creative upswing in Russia. Inspired by social change, writers carried over these principles into their work, pushing revolutionary ideas and ground-breaking styles.

The trend was temporary, of course. The Bolsheviks were no connoisseurs of culture; and the new leadership did not appreciate literature unless it directly supported the goals of communism. Some writers managed to write within the system, penning some excellent poetry and plays in the 1920s; however, most found little inspiration in the prevailing climate of art 'serving the people'. Stalin announced that writers were 'engineers of the human soul' and as such had a responsibility to write in a partisan direction.

The clampdown on diverse literary styles culminated in the early 1930s with the creation of socialist realism, a literary form created to promote the needs of the state, praise industrialisation and demonise social misfits. While Stalin's propaganda machine was churning out novels with titles such as *How the Steel Was Tempered* and *Cement,* St Petersburg's literary community was secretly writing about life under tyranny. The tradition of underground writing, which had been long established under the Romanovs, once again flourished.

LITERATURE OF DISSENT & EMIGRATION

Throughout the 20th century, many talented writers were faced with silence, exile or death, as a result of the imposing standards of the Soviet system. Many accounts of Soviet life were *samizdat* (literally 'self-publishing') publications, secretly circulated among the literary community. The Soviet Union's most celebrated writers – the likes of Boris Pasternak, Alexander Solzhenitsyn, Mikhail Bulgakov and Andrei Bitov – were silenced in their own country, while their works received international acclaim. Others left Russia in the turmoil of the revolution and its bloody aftermath, including perhaps St Petersburg's greatest 20th-century writer, Vladimir Nabokov.

Born to a supremely wealthy and well-connected St Petersburg family in 1899, the 18-year-old Nabokov was forced to leave St Petersburg in 1917 due to his father's previous role in the Provisional Government. Leaving Russia altogether in 1919, Nabokov was never to return to his homeland and died in Switzerland in 1977. His fascinating autobiography, *Speak, Memory,* is a wonderful recollection of his idyllic Russian childhood amid the gathering clouds of revolution, and the house he grew up in now houses the small, but very worthwhile, Nabokov Museum (p108).

No literary figure is as inextricably linked to the fate of St Petersburg-Petrograd-Leningrad as Anna Akhmatova (1889–1966), the long-suffering poet whose work contains bittersweet depictions of the city she loved. Akhmatova's family was imprisoned and killed, her friends were exiled, tortured and arrested, and her colleagues were constantly hounded – but she refused to leave her beloved city and died there in 1966. Her former residence in the Fountain House now contains the Anna Akhmatova Museum (p84), a fascinating and humbling place.

Akhmatova was the dazzling Petrograd poet of the Silver Age of Russian poetry during the first two decades of the 20th century. She was well-travelled, internationally feted and an incorrigible free spirit who, despite having the chance after the revolution, decided not to leave Russia and go abroad. This decision sealed her fate, and within a few years her ex-husband would be shot by the Bolsheviks, and decades of harassment and proscription would follow as Akhmatova's work was denounced by Communist Party officials as 'the poetry of a crazed lady, chasing back and forth between boudoir and chapel'.

However, as a reward for her cooperation with the authorities in the war effort, Akhmatova was allowed to publish again after WWII. Nonetheless, she was cautious, and she worked in secret on masterpieces such as *Requiem,* her epic poem about the terror. Through all this, her love for her city was unconditional and unblinking. As she wrote in *Poem Without a Hero:* 'The capital on the Neva/Having forgotten its greatness/Like a drunken whore/Did not know who was taking her'. Despite unending official harassment, Akhmatova refused to leave her beloved Leningrad and died there in 1966, having outlived Stalin by over a decade. Her sad life, marked by the arrest and murder of so many friends and even her own son, is given a very poignant memorial at the Anna Akhmatova Monument (p85) opposite the Kresty Holding Prison, where the poet queued up for days on end to get news of her son following one of his many arrests.

Poetry is notoriously hard to translate, but polyglot Vladimir Nabokov very insistently translated *Yegeny Onegin*, Pushkin's most famous work into English, the result of which is largely panned by critics, but a fascinating read all the same. Nabokov's system of translation is unique and great way to understand a work most people consider inaccessible to non-Russians.

When Nikita Khrushchev came to power following Stalin's death in 1953, he relaxed the most oppressive restrictions on artists and writers. As this so-called 'thaw' slowly set in, a group of young poets known as 'Akhmatova's Orphans' started to meet at her apartment to read and discuss their work. The star of the group was the fiercely talented Joseph Brodsky, who seemed to have no fear of the consequences of writing about what was on his mind. In 1964 he was tried for 'social parasitism' (ie being unemployed) and was exiled to the north of Russia. His sentence was shortened after concerted international protests led by French philosopher Jean-Paul Sartre. He returned to Leningrad in 1965, only to immediately resume his thorn-in-the-side activities.

During Brodsky's absence, Khrushchev had been overthrown and replaced by a more conservative Brezhnev. It was Brezhnev who came up with the plan to silence troublemaking writers by sending them into foreign exile. Brodsky was put on a plane to Germany in 1972, and the second wave of Russian émigré writers, which would include fellow St Petersburg writer Sergei Dovlatov, began.

POSTCOMMUNIST ST PETERSBURG WRITING

The postglasnost era of the 1980s and 1990s uncovered a huge library of work that had been suppressed during the Soviet period. Authors such as Yevgeny Zamyatin, Danil Kharms, Anatoly Rybakov, Venedict Erofeev and Andrei Bitov – banned in the Soviet Union – are now recognised for their cutting-edge commentary and significant contributions to world literature.

Surprisingly, however, St Petersburg is not a magnet for Russian writers in the 21st century (unlike artists and musicians). The contemporary literary scene is largely based in Moscow, and, to some degree, abroad, as émigré writers continue to be inspired and disheartened by their motherland.

Action-packed thrillers and detective stories have become wildly popular in the 21st century, with Darya Dontsova, Alexandra Marinina and Boris Akunin ranking among the best-selling and most widely translated authors. Realist writers such as Tatyana Tolstaya and Ludmilla Petrushevskaya engage readers with their moving portraits of everyday people living their everyday lives. Meanwhile, social critics such as Viktor Pelevin continue the Soviet literary tradition of using dark humour and fantastical storylines to provide scathing social commentary.

Hearteningly, love of literature is an integral part of St Petersburg culture: ask any Petersburger what books they like to read and they'll no doubt begin to wax rhapsodically on the Russian classics without any hesitation. Anyone with any degree of education in the city will be able to quote freely from Pushkin or Akhmatova, and reference a clutch of Dostoevsky novels or Nabokov short stories they've read.

NABOKOV'S GOGOL

Another very original interpretation of Gogol can be found in Vladimir Nabokov's wonderful biography, *Nikolai Gogol*. Written in English by the polyglot Nabokov, it discusses in English the impact of much of Gogol's Russian language – something quite inaccessible to most readers!

Survival Guide

Transport

GETTING TO ST PETERSBURG

St Petersburg is well connected to the rest of Europe by plane, train, ferry and bus links. The vast majority of travellers arrive in St Petersburg by air at Pulkovo Airport. Flight time from London and Paris to St Petersburg is three hours, from Berlin it's a two-hour flight, and from Moscow it's an hour.

Train is also a popular way to get here – from Moscow there are overnight sleeper trains as well as fast four-hour day trains. See www.rzd.ru for details. From Helsinki there are four daily Allegro express trains that take you from the Finnish capital to St Petersburg in an impressive 3½ hours. See www.vr.fi for prices and timetables.

An increasing number of travellers arrive at one of St Petersburg's five cruise and ferry terminals. There are regular connections between St Petersburg and Stockholm (22 to 24 hours), Tallinn (14 hours) and Helsinki (10 hours). See www.stpeterline.com for prices and timetables.

Flights, tours and rail tickets can be booked online at lonelyplanet.com/bookings.

Air

Most travellers arrive in St Petersburg at **Pulkovo International Airport** (www.pulkovoairport.ru), 17km south of the city. Pulkovo-1 handles domestic flights, as well as flights to the former Soviet Union. The international terminal is Pulkovo-2, which has daily connections to most major cities in Europe. Both terminals are woefully ill-equipped for the needs of the modern traveller, although Pulkovo-2 did get a spruce-up for the 2003 tercentenary celebrations.

Airlines

All airlines fly from Pulkovo-1 Airport in St Petersburg to three different Moscow airports. Book in advance and you can get tickets as cheap as R2200 one-way, although normally prices are between R3000 and R3600.

Aeroflot (www.aeroflot.ru) Flies into Sheremetyevo Airport in Moscow up to 10 times a day.

Rossiya Airlines (www.rossiya-airlines.com) Based in St Petersburg, this airline flies to Domodedovo Airport in Moscow and operates about eight flights per day between the two cities.

Sky Express (www.skyexpress.ru) Russia's first no-frills budget airline flies into Moscow's Vnukovo Airport, operating two or three daily flights to St Petersburg. Sky Express is the cheapest way to go if you book far enough in advance. In-flight food, beverages, entertainment and other services incur additional costs.

Pulkovo-1

Passengers flying from Moscow or elsewhere in Russia or the former Soviet Union will arrive at this unmodernised Soviet airport. The easiest way into the city centre is to take a taxi (there is no dispatch point – you'll just have to negotiate with the drivers who'll offer you rides). Reckon on paying R700 to R900 depending on where you want to go.

An alternative is to take bus 39 (R21, every 15 minutes, from 5.30am to 12.30am) from outside the terminal building. It connects you to the Moskovskaya metro station from where you can get to anywhere in the city. Buy your ticket on the bus. Alternatively jump into any *marshrutka* (minibus), and check with the driver that it goes to the Moskovskaya metro station (nearly all do).

Pulkovo-2

From the international terminal, taking a taxi to the city centre has never been easier. There is a taxi booking stand in the arrivals area of the airport where staff speak English. Tell them where you're going and you'll be given a slip of paper with the price on it and be taken to a taxi outside. Expect to pay R600 to R800 for a trip to the centre, depending on where exactly you're headed. Drivers usually won't speak

CLIMATE CHANGE & TRAVEL

Every form of transport that relies on carbon-based fuel generates CO_2, the main cause of human-induced climate change. Modern travel is dependent on aeroplanes, which might use less fuel per kilometre per person than most cars but travel much greater distances. The altitude at which aircraft emit gases (including CO_2) and particles also contributes to their climate change impact. Many websites offer 'carbon calculators' that allow people to estimate the carbon emissions generated by their journey and, for those who wish to do so, to offset the impact of the greenhouse gases emitted with contributions to portfolios of climate-friendly initiatives throughout the world. Lonely Planet offsets the carbon footprint of all staff and author travel.

much English, but just hand over the money on arrival – you don't need to tip.

For those on a budget, bus K-13 shuttles you to the nearest metro station, Moskovskaya (R27, every 10 minutes, from 5.30am to 12.30am). Turn left when you leave the arrivals area and the bus stop is between departures and arrivals. The bus terminates at the Moskovskaya metro station, so you don't need to worry about where to get off.

Train

Moscow Station

If you're arriving from Moscow, you'll come to the **Moscow Station** (Московский вокзал; www.moskovsky-vokzal.ru; Nevsky pr 85), in the centre of the city. There are two metro stations close by: Pl Vosstaniya (Line 1) and Mayakovskaya (Line 3). To get here (you can enter both stations through one building) turn left outside the main entrance to the Moscow Station, and the exit is in one side of the building on Ligovsky pr.

Finland Station

Trains from Helsinki arrive at the **Finland Station** (Финляндский вокзал; pl Lenina 6). From here you can connect to anywhere in the city by metro from the Pl Lenina station (Line 1) on the square outside the station.

Ladozhsky Station

Some trains from Helsinki to Moscow stop en route in St Petersburg at the remote **Ladozhsky Station** (Ладожский вокзал; www.lvspb.ru, in Russian; Zanevsky pr 73). It's served by the Ladozhskaya metro station on Line 4.

Boat

There are numerous cruise boats plying the routes between St Petersburg and Moscow, many stopping at some of the Golden Ring cities on the way. Boat operators and agencies include the following:

Infoflot (www.infoflot.com, in Russian) Cruises range from seven to 12 days, some stopping in Yaroslavl, Uglich, Valaam and other towns.

Mosturflot (www.mosturflot.ru, in Russian) Ships cruise between the two capitals in seven days.

Orthodox Cruise Company (www.cruise.ru) Catering to foreigners, the good ship *Anton Chekhov* spends 10 days cruising between the capitals, stopping in Mandroga, Kizhi, Goritsy, Yaroslavl and Uglich.

Rechturflot (www.rtflot.ru, in Russian) Offers a 12-day round-trip option.

Vodohod (www.bestrussiancruises.com) Cruises ranging from 10 to 13 days make stops in Svirstroy, Mandroga, Kizhi, Goritsy, Yarolslavl, Kostroma and Uglich along the way.

Marine Facade Terminal

The Marine Facade Terminal (Морской фасад; www.portspb.ru) at the far end of Vasilyevsky Island is a brand-new facility where most big cruise ships now dock in St Petersburg. It's not in the city centre, but it's not too far to walk to the Primorskaya metro station, from where it's just two stops to Gostiny Dvor (Line 3) in the Historic Heart. Head down Novosmolenskaya nab and you'll reach the station once you've crossed Nalichnaya ul.

Alternatively you can take a taxi. An official dispatch stand is in the arrivals area with fixed rates to various places around town. You'll be given a slip of paper with the price you need to pay the driver: prices average R150 to R300 depending on where in the centre you want to go.

Sea Port

If you're arriving by ferry from Stockholm or Helsinki then you'll arrive at the **Sea Port** (Map p266; Морской вокзал; www.mvokzal.ru; pl Morskoy Slavy 1) in the southern corner of Vasilyevsky Island. It's not served by the metro, so your easiest way into the city centre is to take a taxi. Drivers wait outside the terminal; negotiate with them. Prices average R150 to R300 depending on where in the centre you want to go.

BUYING TICKETS IN ST PETERSBURG

You'll most likely have your onward travel tickets when you arrive in St Petersburg, but if not it's easy to purchase tickets for boat, bus, train and plane travel. First of all, try online – you can buy many train tickets (www.rzd.ru), bus tickets (www.luxexpress.eu) and, of course, nearly all airline tickets via websites.

Buying train tickets in person can be done at any train station (even at a different terminus from where your train departs), although waiting time can be long. More useful is the centrally located **Train Tickets Centre** (Кассы ЖД; Map p254; nab kanala Griboyedova 24; ⌚8am-8pm Mon-Sat, until 4pm Sun; Ⓜ Gostiny Dvor), although lines can be just as long and torturously slow moving. Don't expect anyone to speak English, and make a note of your train time, number and departure date to give to the person behind the glass window.

You can buy ferry tickets for nearly all boats at the **Ferry Centre** (Паромный центр; Map p258; ul Vosstaniya 19; Ⓜ Ploshchad Vosstaniya), a short walk from the Moscow Station. Alternatively, it's possible to buy ferry tickets in the **Sea Port** (Морской вокзал; Map p266; www.mvokzal.ru; pl Morskoy Slavy 1) at the far-flung end of Vasilyevsky Island, as well as online through the ferry companies themselves.

If time is tight, then nearly all travel agencies can organise onward travel tickets for you, although of course there's usually a mark-up on the cost and a delivery fee.

An alternative option is to take bus 7 (R21) from the main road outside. The bus should have Pl Vosstaniya (Пл Восстания) written on it, and it goes all the way down Sredny pr, crosses the Neva at the Hermitage and then goes down Nevsky pr to Pl Vosstaniya.

River Port

Boats from Moscow and elsewhere within Russia arrive at the **River Port** (Речной вокзал; www.mvokzal.ru; pr Obukhovskoy Oborony 195), which is a short walk away from the Proletarskaya metro station. Turn left on to pr Obukhovskoy Oborony and it's five minutes down the road.

Other Ports

There are three other docks where cruise ships sometimes arrive in St Petersburg. Smaller cruise ships usually dock on either the English Embankment Passenger Terminal or the Lieutenant Schmidt Embankment Passenger Terminal. Neither terminal has particularly great facilities, but both are centrally located and you're within easy walking distance from the sights of the Historic Heart.

One far less attractive possibility is docking at the **St Petersburg Sea Port** (Морской порт Санкт-Петербург; www.seaport.spb.ru; Mezhevoy kanal 5), which is the main commercial and industrial port in the city. It's on Gutuyevsky Island and a long way from anything. There are a few taxi drivers working out of here, but they can go quickly if a cruise ship arrives, so you may have to call and order one (see p220). It's technically possible to walk out of the port to the Narvskaya metro station, but reckon on a 30-minute walk through a fairly miserable industrial area. If you decide to walk, head up Obvodny Canal and then turn right onto Staropetrogovsky pr and you'll see Narvskaya metro station on pl Stachek.

Bus

Avtovokzal No 2

St Petersburg's main bus station is confusingly named **Avtovokzal No 2** (Map p260; ☎766 5777; www.avokzal.ru, in Russian; nab Obvodnogo kanala 36), even though there's no Avtovokzal No 1. It has bus connections to cities all over western Russia, including Veliky Novgorod (p152), but most travellers won't use it. If you do happen to arrive here, it's a short walk along the canal to the new metro station Obvodny Kanal (Line 5).

Bus Services

Lux Express (www.luxexpress.eu; Admiral Business Centre, Mitrofanievskoe sh 2; ⌚9am-9pm; Ⓜ Baltiyskaya) runs buses from both Avtovokzal No 2 and from outside the Baltiysky Vokzal. Its buses run very regularly to Tallinn (from R850, 12 daily) and Rīga (from R1000, three daily).

Ecolines (www.ecolines.ru; Podyezdny per 3; Ⓜ Pushkinskaya) runs daily buses from the Vitebsky vokzal to Tallinn (R980), Rīga (R1250) and Kyiv (R1880), and Odesa (R2320).

Other Bus Arrivals

There are several other places where various bus services from Helsinki arrive. These include *marshrutky* from Helsinki, which stop on pl Vosstaniya, right opposite the pl Vosstaniya metro station and Ardis Finnord buses, which arrive at the **Ardis Finnord office** (Italiyanskaya ul 37), an easy walk to the Gostiny Dvor metro station.

GETTING AROUND ST PETERSBURG

St Petersburg can be a frustrating place to get around for visitors: the metro, while an excellent system, actually has relatively few stations in the centre of the city, and distances from stations to nearby sights can be long. Many visitors find buses and *marshrutky* a little daunting, as all the signage is in Russian only and you need to know where you're going, so many people just walk.

Metro

The St Petersburg **Metro** (www.metro.spb.ru; 6am-midnight) is a very efficient five-lined system. The network of some 65 stations is most usefully employed for travelling long distances, especially connecting the suburbs to the city centre.

Look for signs with a big blue 'M' signifying the entrance to the metro. The flat fare for a trip is R25; you will have to buy an additional ticket if you are carrying a significant amount of baggage. If you wish to buy a single journey, ask for *'odin proyezd'* and you will be given a *zheton* (token) to put in the machine.

If you are staying more than a day or two, however, it's worth buying a smart card (R30), which is good for multiple journeys to be used over the course of a fixed time period. Their main advantage is that you won't have to line up to buy tickets – the ticket counters can have very long lines during peak hours.

The metro is fully signed in English throughout the system, so it's quite easy to use even for first-timers in Russia.

A confusing aspect of the St Petersburg metro is that where two lines cross and there is a *perekhod* (transfer), the two stations will have different names. For example, Nevsky Prospekt and Gostiny Dvor are joint stations: to all intents and purposes they are one and the same (ie you don't need to go outside to change), but each has a different name because it's on a different line.

CATCHING THE TRAIN TO MOSCOW

All trains to St Petersburg depart from the Moscow Station. Take your pick from the standard overnight trains or the new super-fast Sapsan trains.

Overnight

There are about 10 overnight trains travelling between St Petersburg and Moscow. Most depart between 10pm and midnight, arriving in the capital the following morning between 6am and 8am. On the more comfortable *firmenny* trains, a 1st-class *lyuks* ticket (two-person cabin) runs from R5200 to R6000, while a 2nd-class *kupe* (four-person cabin) is R2000 to R3000.

Sapsan

These high-speed trains travel at speeds of 200km/h to reach their destination in four hours or less. Trains depart throughout the day. Comfortable 2nd-class seats are R2300 to R2800, while super-spacious 1st-class seats run from R5000 to R5600.

SAMPLE TRAINS FROM ST PETERSBURG TO MOSCOW

NAME & NO	DEPARTURE	DURATION	FARE
1 Krasnaya Strela	11.55pm	8hr	R2600-3000
3 Ekspress	11.59pm	8hr	R2380
5 Nikolaevsky Express	11.30pm	8hr	R2750
53 Grand Express	11.40pm	9hr	R5000-6200
151A Sapsan	6.45am	4hr	1st-/2nd-class R5056/2612
157A Sapsan	1.30pm	4½hr	1st-/2nd-class R2354/4645
161A Sapsan	3.15pm	4hr	1st-/2nd-class R5460/2870
165A Sapsan	7.45pm	4hr	1st-/2nd-class R5530/2870

Bus, Trolleybus & Marshrutka

Buses and particularly *marshrutky* (minibuses) are a very handy way to get around the city and they tend to cover routes that the metro doesn't, making them essential for certain areas of town. Most travellers find taking them a bit daunting, however, as there's no signage in English. On both buses and trolleybuses, you get on and then pay the conductor who comes through the bus. Fares are usually R20 to R25. *Marshrutky* work rather differently: you flag them down (there are no bus stops for *marshrutky*), open the door yourself and jump in, then once you've taken your seat you pay the driver (pass the money via your fellow passengers if you're not sitting within reaching distance). You'll also need to request the stop you want – usually announcing to the driver the name of the street or the place you're going to shortly before you get there. Alternatively, when you want to get off, simply say (or shout!): *'AstanavEEtye pazhalsta!'* (Stop please!) and the driver will pull over as soon as possible.

Taxi

One of the most enduring Soviet traditions is that of 'catching a car'. The shadow economy is thriving and numerous people drive the city streets specifically looking to give people paid lifts in their 1970s Zhigulis and Ladas. See the boxed text (p220) for more information about the cultural norms associated with this form of transport.

Nearly all official taxis are unmetered (though there are plans to introduce these) so if you do flag one down you'll have to go through a similar process of negotiation to that involved in catching a car, only the driver will want more money for being 'official'.

The best way to get a taxi is to order one through a company as prices will be a lot lower than those charged if you flag a driver down on the street. Operators will usually not speak English, so unless you speak Russian you might want your hotel reception to call one of the following numbers for you:

Peterburgskoye Taxi (☎068, 324 7777; www.taxi068.spb.ru, in Russian)

Taxi-4 (☎633 3333; www.taxi-4.ru, in Russian)

Taxi Blues (☎321 8888; www.taxiblues.ru, in Russian)

Taxi Million (☎600 0000; www.6-000-000.ru, in Russian)

Bicycle

Bicycles are becoming more common on the streets of St Petersburg, but cycling is still difficult: pothole-riddled roads and lunatic drivers unaccustomed to cyclists make

CATCHING A CAR

Stand on practically any street and stick out your arm: you can be assured that sooner rather than later a car will stop for you. Usually it's a well-worn little Lada or Zhiguli, but it can be anything – a snazzier car, an off-duty city bus, an army Jeep with driver in camouflage. The drivers may be on their way somewhere, or they may just be trying to supplement their income. These unofficial taxis are the cheapest way to cover distances in the city centre.

So, you've stuck your arm out and a car has stopped. This is where the fun starts. You state your destination, say, *'ulitsa Marata!'* The driver looks away for a second and shouts back *'skolko?'* (how much?) You bark back a price. If he's happy with that amount, he'll say, *'sadites'* (sit down), at which point you get in and drive off. If he's not happy with that price, a period of negotiation might ensue.

If you feel that the driver is trying to rip you off because of your accent, shut the door. If there's more than one person in the car, don't get in. And if the driver seems creepy, let him drive on. There'll be another car coming in a flash. At any time, you are welcome to give a gruff *'nyet'* and slam the door.

Alternatively, the driver might not ask you for a price and just tell you to get in or not, depending on whether he wants to go your way. If that's the case, at the end of the ride you pay him what you think the fare was worth. If your ride is less than five minutes long, R150 to R200 is acceptable. For a greater distance reckon on paying R300.

As a bonus, often these drivers are very interesting characters you wouldn't ordinarily meet on your trip, and chatting with them about the potholes, how much better things were under the Soviets, their days in the army and how much you earn can be great fun.

it a dangerous proposition. You'll notice many cyclists stay entirely on the pavement when they ride, such is the level of danger on the road. Indeed, many drivers seem to consider cyclists to be in the wrong if they're in the road at all, regarding them as a form of pedestrian. Helmets are highly recommended.

That said, the city's relatively compact size means that it is easy to get around by bike – and often much quicker than public transport. Many adventurers swear by their bikes as the ideal form of transport in St Petersburg (at least from May to October).

Especially when you are unfamiliar with traffic patterns, it is advised to stay off the busiest, traffic-clogged roads. Stick to the back streets and pavements. Both sides of the Neva River have wide footpaths (with few pedestrians) that are perfect for pedalling. Car-free Yelagin Island (p132) is another excellent place for cycling, although bikes are not allowed on weekends and holidays. A map of safe cycle routes in the city can be found here: www.i-bike-spb.ru/lanes.

You can hire bikes from Skat Prokat (p100), Friends Hostel (p160) and from Rentbike (p115).

BRIDGE TIMETABLE

From May until November all bridges across the Neva rise at the following times nightly to allow ships to pass through, meaning you cannot cross the river during these times. Therefore, if you're staying on Vasilyevsky Island, the Petrograd Side or the Vyborg Side and go out clubbing in the city centre, you'll need to time your trip home well, or wait until dawn. All times are am.

BRIDGE	UP	DOWN	UP	DOWN
Alexandra Nevskogo	2.20	5.10		
Birzhevoy	2.00	4.55		
Blagoveshchensky	1.25	2.45	3.10	5.00
Bolsheokhtinsky	2.00	5.00		
Dvortsovy (Palace)	1.25	4.50		
Finlyandsky	2.20	5.30		
Grenadersky	2.45	3.45	4.20	4.50
Kantemirovsky	2.45	3.45	4.20	4.50
Liteyny	1.40	4.45		
Sampsonievsky	2.10	2.45	3.20	4.25
Troitsky	1.35	4.50		
Tuchkov	2.00	2.55	3.35	4.55
Volodarsky	2.00	3.45	4.15	5.45

TOURS

In a city as large and foreign as St Petersburg, a lot of travellers prefer (at least initially) to be shown around on a walking tour to kick things off. There are several excellent ones on offer, as well as bike tours, boat tours and a hop-on-hop-off bus that can take you around the main sights of the centre.

Walking Tours

Peter's Walking Tours (☎943 1229; www.peterswalk.com) Established in 1996, Peter Kozyrev's innovative and passionately led tours are highly recommended as a way to see the city with knowledgeable locals. The choice of tours available is enormous. The daily Original Peterswalk is one of the favourites and functions as a do-it-yourself introduction to the city: you tell your guide what aspects of the city you're interested in and they improvise a tour for you then and there. Other tours include a Friday night pub crawl, a Rasputin Walk and a WWII and the Siege of Leningrad tour. Tours depart from Hostel Life (p163), though it's a good idea to book your place beforehand as these walks are justifiably popular.

VB Excursions (☎380 4596; www.vb-excursions.com) Offers excellent walking tours with clued-up students on themes including Dostoevsky and revolutionary St Petersburg. Their 'Back in the USSR' tour (R1150 per person) includes a visit to a typical Soviet apartment for tea and bliny.

Anglo Tourismo (☎325 9906; www.anglotourismo.com) This enthusiastically run company was offering free daily three-hour walking tours of the city centre in the summer of 2011, no doubt to steer travellers to their excellent boat tours. It's a great promotional idea though. Check on the website to see if this is continuing.

Bike Tours

Petersburg Bike Tours (☎943 1229; www.biketour.spb.ru) Run jointly by Peter's Walking Tours (p221) and Skat Prokat (p100), these excellent bike tours are a very popular way to cover large swathes of the city in just a few hours. Most popular is the White Night Bike Tour (R1200 including bike hire), which leaves from Skat Prokat at 10.30pm every Tuesday and Thursday from mid-May until the end of August.

Bus Tours

City Tour (☎718 4769; www.citytourspb.ru) The familiar red 'hop on, hop off' double-decker buses you'll see in most big cities in Europe have finally arrived in St Petersburg and offer a useful service for anyone unable to walk easily. The buses run along Nevsky pr from pl Vosstaniya, drop by the Russian Museum, pass the Hermitage, go over the Strelka, the Petrograd Side and then back to the historic centre, taking in the Church on the Spilled Blood, the Admiralty and St Isaac's Cathedral before going back down Nevsky pr. An adult day ticket costs R450, valid for as many trips as you like.

Liberty (www.libertytour.ru) Specialising in wheelchair-accessible tours in and around St Petersburg, this unique-in-Russia company has specially fitted vans. They can also advise on and book hotels with rooms for the disabled.

Directory A–Z

Business Hours

Throughout this guide, we only supply opening hours for establishments when they differ from the following norms:

Banks 9am-6pm Mon-Fri

Businesses & Shops 10am-9pm Mon-Fri, 10am-7pm Sat & Sun

Bars & Clubs 6pm-6am

Information 9am-6pm

Restaurants 11am or noon-11pm

Museum hours vary widely, as do their weekly days off. Most museums shut their ticket offices an hour before closing time. Many close for a *sanitarny den* (cleaning day), during the last week of every month.

Customs Regulations

Customs controls in Russia are relatively relaxed these days. Searches beyond the perfunctory are quite rare. Apart from the usual restrictions, you are limited by the amount of cash you can bring in. If you are carrying more than US$3000 – or valuables worth that much – you must declare it and proceed through the red channel.

Otherwise, on entering Russia, you can pick up your luggage and go through the green channel, meaning 'nothing to declare'.

If you intend to take home anything vaguely 'arty' (manuscripts, instruments, coins, jewellery) it must be assessed by the **Cultural Security Department** (Map p254; ☎311 5196; Malaya Morskaya ul 17; ⏰11am-5pm Mon-Fri; Ⓜ Admiralteyskaya). Take along your passport, a sales receipt and the item in question. The 'experts' will issue a receipt for tax paid and a certificate stating that the item is not an antique. It is illegal to export anything over 100 years old.

Discount Cards

There are no discount cards currently operating on a citywide basis. If you're a student then bring an ISIC card to get discounts – cards issued by non-Russian universities will normally be refused. The Hermitage is the blissful exception where anyone with a student card from any country gets in for free. Senior citizens (usually anyone over the age of 60) are often also eligible for discounts, so bring your passport with you.

PRACTICALITIES

- **Newspapers & Magazines** Check out **The St Petersburg Times** (www.sptimes.ru) and **In Your Pocket** (www.inyourpocket.com).
- **TV & Radio** As well as the main state TV channels, St Petersburg has several local channels. Satellite TV is available at most top-end hotels.
- **Weights & Measures** Russia uses the metric system.
- **Smoking** Is allowed almost everywhere. Nearly all hotels offer nonsmoking rooms, as do most restaurants.

Electricity

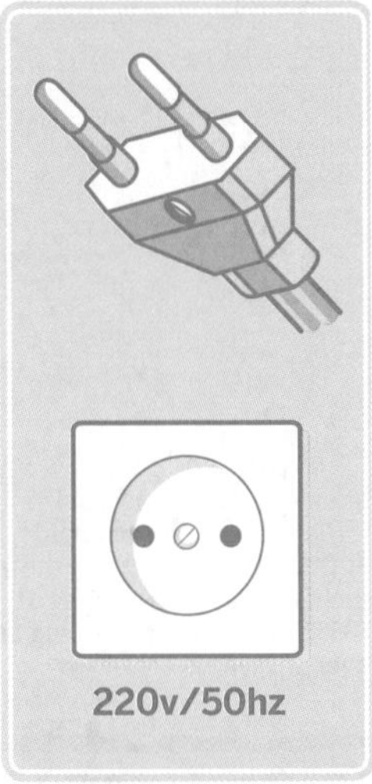

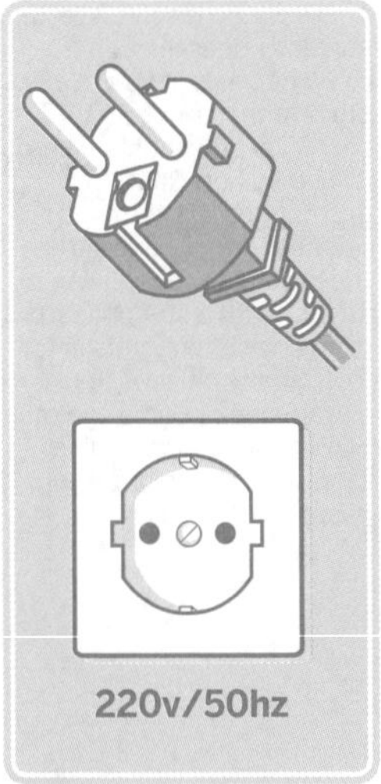

Embassies & Consulates

Despite not being a capital city, St Petersburg has a good level of consular representation from most countries. If your country is not represented here, contact your embassy in Moscow in an emergency.

Australia (Map p254; ☎315 1100; www.russia.embassy.gov.au; nab reki Moyki 11; MAdmiralteyskaya)

Finland (Map p258; ☎331 7600; www.finland.org.ru; Preobrazhenskaya pl 4; MChernyshevskaya)

France (Map p254; ☎332 2270; www.francespb.org; nab reki Moyki 15; MAdmiralteyskaya)

Germany (Map p258; ☎320 2400; www.sankt-petersburg.diplo.de; Furshtatskaya ul 39; MChernyshevskaya)

The Netherlands (Map p254; ☎334 0200; www.nlcg.spb.ru; nab reki Moyki 11; MAdmiralteyskaya)

UK (Map p258; ☎320 3200; www.ukinrussia.fco.gov.uk; pl Proletarskoy Diktatury 5; MChernyshevskaya)

USA (Map p258; ☎331 2600; http://stpetersburg.usconsulate.gov; Furshtatskaya ul 15; MChernyshevskaya)

Emergency

Ambulance (☎03)

Fire department (☎01)

Police (☎02)

Gay & Lesbian Travellers

When it comes to tolerance towards gay travellers, St Petersburg is liberal by Russian standards, but still far behind the rest of Europe. It should be no problem at all to book a double room for same-sex couples, although outside top-end hotels you can expect some curiosity from staff. Same-sex public displays of affection are never a good idea in St Petersburg, however: always err on the side of caution.

There is a busy and growing gay scene, but it remains fairly discreet. Gay pride marches are routinely attacked by far right groups and the police often harass protesters.

Here are a few useful links:

www.gay.ru/english The English version of this site includes club listings and tour guides, plus information on gay history and culture in Russia.

www.lesbi.ru An active site for lesbian issues; Russian only.

www.qguys.ru The most popular gay dating website.

www.xs.gay.ru The local gay and lesbian portal. Russian only.

Health

Health insurance for any trip to St Petersburg is necessary (and often a precondition of getting your visa). Note that, officially at least, most embassies require you purchase travel insurance from a list of companies given on the embassy website. This doesn't appear to be strictly implemented, however: by all means try sending them a copy of a non-approved policy if you already have one.

Health care in the city is very good if you're going private. Using public hospitals is not something you should consider, so even if your local embassy doesn't require valid health insurance, you should definitely purchase it.

St Petersburg does not pose any particular threats to your health, although you should be aware of the risks associated with drinking the tap water (see the boxed text, p226). Also be aware that the city was built on a swamp, which means the mosquitoes are nasty in the summer months. Be sure to bring plenty of insect repellent. You may also want to bring some painkillers with you – those post-vodka mornings can be hard work without them.

Internet Access

Internet access is now very good in St Petersburg. With the exception of some of the top-end and very bottom-end places, nearly all hotels have free wireless internet. Many restaurants, cafes, bars and clubs also have wi-fi – often there won't even be a password, but when there is, simply ask the staff.

If you are travelling without a laptop or smartphone, there are some good old-fashioned internet cafes:

Café Max (Map p260; www.cafemax.ru; Nevsky pr 90; per hr R120; ⌚24hr; Ⓜ Mayakovskaya) A big fancy place with 150 computers, a game zone and a comfy cafe and beer bar. It's located on the 2nd floor.

Internet Cafe (Map p254; Nevsky pr 11; per hr R80; ⌚24hr; Ⓜ Admiralteyskaya) Above Subway.

Russian Museum Internet Centre (Map p254; Nevsky pr 17; per hr R150; ⌚9am-10pm; Ⓜ Gostiny Dvor) Inside the courtyard of the Stroganov Palace.

Legal Matters

It's not unusual to see *militsioners* (police officers) randomly stopping people on the street to check their documents. In recent years, this checking tends to focus on anyone remotely Caucasian-looking and other people with darkish skin, but the police have the right to stop anyone. Unfortunately, readers have complained about police pocketing their passports and demanding bribes. The best way to avoid such unpleasantness is to carry a photocopy of your passport, visa and registration, and present that when a police officer demands to see your *dokumenty*. A photocopy is sufficient for such inquiries, despite what the officer may argue. Threatening to phone your consulate usually clears up any such misunderstandings. For legal purposes, Russians come of age at 18, when they are legally allowed to drink, drive and vote (but not simultaneously). Both heterosexual and homosexual sex is legal at 16.

Medical Services

These private clinics have facilities of an international standard and are pricey, but generally accept major international insurance policies, including direct billing.

Clinics

In case of more serious health issues:

American Medical Clinic (Map p264; ☎740 2090; www.amclinic.ru; nab reki Moyki 78; Ⓜ Sadovaya)

Euromed (Map p258; ☎327 0301; www.euromed.ru; Suvorovsky pr 60; Ⓜ Chernyshevskaya)

Medem International Clinic & Hospital (Map p260; ☎336 3333; www.medem.ru; ul Marata 6; Ⓜ Mayakovskaya)

Pharmacies

Look for the sign АПТЕКА *(apteka)* or the usual green cross to find a pharmacy.

36.6 Pharmacy (http://spb.366.ru) is a chain of 24-hour pharmacies with many branches around the city:

Historic Heart (Map p254; Gorokhovaya ul 16; Ⓜ Sadovaya)

Petrogad Side (Map p268; Bolshoy pr 62; Ⓜ Petrogradskaya)

Smolny (Map p258; Nevsky pr 98; Ⓜ Mayakovskaya)

Money

Russian currency is the rouble, written as рубль or abbreviated as руб. There are 100 kopecks (копеек or коп) in the rouble, and these come in small coins that are worth one, 10 and 50 kopecks. Roubles are issued in coins in amounts of one, two and five roubles. Banknotes come in values of 10, 50, 100, 500, 1000 and 5000 roubles. Small stores, kiosks and many other vendors have difficulty changing large notes, so save those scrappy little ones. The rouble has been relatively stable since it was revalued in 1998. For exchange rates, see the inside front cover.

ATMs

ATMs linked to international networks such as AmEx, Cirrus, Eurocard, MasterCard and Visa can be found everywhere in St Petersburg. Look for the sign БАНКОМАТ *(bankomat)*. Using a credit or debit card, you can always obtain roubles, although US dollars are sometimes available, too.

Changing Money

US dollars and euros are easy to change around St Petersburg, but other currencies will undoubtedly cause more hassle than they are worth. Whatever currency you bring should be in pristine condition. Banks and exchanges do not accept old, tatty bills with rips or tears. For US dollars make certain they are of the new design, which has the large offset portrait. When you visit the exchange office, be prepared to show your passport.

Credit Cards

Credit cards, especially Visa and MasterCard, are widely accepted in hotels, restaurants and shops. You can also use your credit card to get a cash advance at most major banks in St Petersburg. Be aware that many places will want to see photo ID when you use a credit card.

Post

Although service has improved dramatically in recent years, the usual warnings about delays and disappearances of incoming and outgoing mail apply to St Petersburg. Airmail letters take two to three weeks to the UK, and three to four weeks to the USA or Australasia.

To send parcels home, head to the elegant **main post office** (Map p264; Pochtamtskaya ul 9; Ⓜ Admiralteyskaya). Smaller post offices may refuse to send parcels internationally; most importantly, your package is more likely to reach its destination if you send it from the main post office. Bring your item unwrapped: it will be wrapped and sealed with wax for you. You must provide an address in St Petersburg – your hotel name will be fine.

Public Holidays

During the major holiday periods – the first week in January (between New Year's Day and Orthodox Christmas) and the first week or two of May (around May Day and Victory Day) – St Petersburg empties out as many residents retreat from the city for much-needed vacations. Transport is often difficult to book around these periods, but accommodation is usually not a problem. Although many residents leave, the city is a festive place over New Year's and during the May holidays, usually hosting parades, concerts and other events in honour of the holidays. The downside is that many museums and other institutions have shortened hours or are closed altogether during these holiday periods.

By contrast, the Stars of White Nights Festival was designed with tourists in mind: theatres, museums and other institutions often host special events between late May and early July to appeal to the massive influx of visitors during this period. If you are visiting St Petersburg at this time, book your travel and accommodation in advance and expect to pay top rates. In August there are still plenty of tourists around, but residents tend to retreat from the city to recover. Many theatres close for the month of August, as do some of the smaller museums and galleries.

See p20 for an extensive list of special events in the city. The following list is St Petersburg's public holidays.

New Year's Day 1 January

Russian Orthodox Christmas Day 7 January

Defenders of the Motherland Day 23 February

International Women's Day 8 March

Easter Monday April/May (varies)

International Labour Day/ Spring Festival 1 & 2 May

Victory Day 9 May

Russian Independence Day 12 June

Day of Reconciliation and Accord (the rebranded Revolution Day) 7 November

Constitution Day 12 December

Safe Travel

You can disregard the horror stories you hear about the mafia in New Russia. While there has been a problem with crime and corruption since the early 1990s, the criminal elements have no interest in tourists.

TO DRINK OR NOT TO DRINK

Reports about the harmful effects of drinking tap water in St Petersburg have been widely publicised and greatly exaggerated. The city's water supplier, Vodokanal, insists that the water is safe to drink, as do many local residents. Nonetheless, the pipes are antiquated, so the water may contain some metal pollutants. Furthermore, traces of *Giardia lamblia* have been found on a very small scale. GI is a nasty parasite that causes unpleasant stomach cramps, nausea, bloated stomach, diarrhoea and frequent gas. There is no preventative drug, and it is worth taking precautions against contracting it.

To be absolutely safe, only drink water that has been boiled for 10 minutes or filtered through an antimicrobial water filter (PUR brand makes a good portable one). It's probably safe to accept tea or coffee at someone's house, and most restaurants and hotels likely have filtration systems. Bathing, showering and brushing your teeth often cause no problems at all.

If you develop diarrhoea, be sure to drink plenty of fluids, preferably including an oral rehydration solution. Imodium is to be taken only in an emergency; otherwise it's best to let the diarrhoea run its course and eliminate the parasite from the body. Metronidazole (brand name Flagyl) or Tinidazole (known as Fasigyn) are the recommended treatments for *Giardia lamblia*.

A far bigger threat is petty theft, especially the notorious pickpocketing in the city centre. Take care among the crowds on Nevsky pr and in the metro: crowded quarters make for rich pickings for the criminally inclined. Be cautious about taking taxis late at night, especially near bars and clubs that are in isolated areas. Never get into a car that already has two or more people in it.

One far grimmer problem is the rise of the skinhead and neo-Nazi movement in St Petersburg. You are unlikely to encounter these thugs, but you will undoubtedly read about some disgusting acts of violence that have been committed against Asian, Caucasian and other darker-skinned or foreign-looking residents of the city. Non-white travellers should therefore exercise caution when wandering around the city after dark and at any time of day in the suburbs. While this violence peaked around 2005 and has since declined, it's still a very real, if unlikely, threat.

Telephone

Russia's international code is ☎7. The international access code from landline phones in Russia is ☎8 followed by ☎10 after the second tone, then the country code and number. From mobile phones, however, just dial +[country code] to place an international call.

Mobile Phones

Mobile phone numbers start with the country code (☎7), plus three digits that change according to the service provider, followed by a seven-digit number. To call a mobile phone from a landline, the line must be enabled to make paid calls (all local numbers are free from a landline anywhere in Russia). To find out if this is the case, dial ☎8, and then if you hear a second tone you can dial the mobile number in full. If you hear nothing, hang up – you can't call anywhere but local landlines from here.

Main mobile providers include Beeline, Megafon, MTS and Skylink. You can buy a local SIM card at any mobile phone shop, which you can slot into your home handset during your stay. SIM cards cost as little as R200, after which you only pay to make calls, although prices are very low.

Time

St Petersburg is GMT +3 hours, the same as Moscow time. Therefore, when it is midday in St Petersburg, it is 10am in Berlin, 9am in London and 4am in New York. Russia employs daylight savings along with much of the rest of the world.

Toilets

Around nearly all metro stations and tourist attractions there's at least one disgusting blue Portakabin-type toilet manned by an attendant who will charge around R25 for the honour of using it. There are also pay toilets in all main-line train stations and free ones in museums. As a general rule, it's far better to stop for a drink in a cafe or duck into a fancy hotel and use their cleaner facilities.

Tourist Information

Tourist information has finally got halfway decent in St Petersburg, and the **St Petersburg Tourist Information Centre** (Map p254; ☎310 2822; www.ispb.info; ul Sadovaya 14/52; ⏰10am-7pm Mon-Fri, noon-6pm Sat) has its main office just of Nevsky pr as well as several kiosks around the city and desks at both terminals of Pulkovo Airport and the brand-new Marine Façade Terminal on Vasilyevsky Island. All branches have helpful English-speaking staff and a variety of maps, leaflets and tours on offer. The other branches include **Dvortsovaya pl** (Map p254; Dvortsovaya pl 12; ⏰10am-7pm; Ⓜ Admiralteyskaya) and **Pl Vosstaniya** (Map p260; pl Vosstaniya; ⏰10am-7pm; Ⓜ Ploshchad Vosstaniya).

Travellers with Disabilities

Inaccessible transport, lack of ramps and lifts, and no centralised policy for people with physical limitations make Russia a challenging destination for wheelchair-bound visitors. More mobile travellers will have a relatively easier time, but keep in mind that there are obstacles along the way.

Toilets are frequently accessed from stairs in restaurants and museums; distances are great; public transport is extremely crowded; and many footpaths are in a poor condition and hazardous even for the mobile.

This situation is changing (albeit very slowly), as buildings undergo renovations and become more accessible. Most upmarket hotels (especially Western chains) offer accessible rooms and have lifts, and the Hermitage is also now fully accessible.

Visas

Nearly all visitors need a Russian visa in their passports before they travel. The only exceptions are if you're from the handful of nationalities that don't require a visa or if you plan to take advantage of the 72-hour visa on arrival scheme (see the boxed text, p228).

The primary types of visas are tourist visas (for one entry, 30-day stay) or business visas (one-entry, two-entry or multi-entry, for 30- to 90-day stays). You can also get a 'private' visa if you have a personal friend who is inviting you to Russia, but be aware that he or she will undergo some serious hassle to get you an invitation.

The specific requirements of Russian embassies in each country differ slightly, so check with the website of the embassy you're planning to apply through. Be aware that unless you live permanently somewhere outside your own country, you won't usually be able to obtain a Russian visa anywhere but at home.

Generally for all visas you'll need to submit your passport, a photo, an invitation of letter of support from either a hotel or a travel agency, a completed application form (downloadable from the embassy website), and in most cases a certificate of insurance coverage.

The most annoying part of the visa process is the need to provide an invitation or a letter of support. If your hotel doesn't offer this service (most do, though you'll usually need to pay for it), then try one of the following travel agencies.

City Realty (www.cityrealtyrussia.com)

Ost-West Kontaktservice (www.ostwest.com)

Travel Russia (www.travelrussia.su)

Way To Russia (www.waytorussia.net)

Application

Apply as soon as you have all the documents you need (but not more than two months ahead). Processing time ranges from 24 hours to two weeks, depending on how much you are willing to pay.

It's possible to apply at your local Russian consulate by dropping off all the necessary documents with the appropriate payment or by mailing it all (along with a self-addressed, postage-paid envelope for the return). When you receive the visa, check it carefully – especially the expiry, entry and exit dates and any restrictions on entry or exit points.

A third option is to use a visa agency. While more expensive than doing it all yourself it's a great way to delegate the hassles to someone else. Some agencies charge very reasonable fees to submit, track and collect your visa. The following are some recommended ones:

Action-visas.com (www.action-visas.com)

CIBT (www.uk.cibt.com)

Comet Consular Services (www.cometconsular.com)

Real Russia (www.realrussia.co.uk)

Visalink.com.au (www.visalink.com.au)

VisaHQ.com (www.russia.visahq.com)

Zierer Visa Services (www.zvs.com)

Registration

On arrival you receive an immigration card, which you must fill out and get stamped along with your visa. Half the card will be kept by the immigration officer, the other half you should keep with your passport for the rest of your stay. When you are checking in at a hotel, you'll have to surrender your passport and visa so the hotel can register you with OVIR (office of visas and registrations). Usually they are given back the next morning, if not the same day.

If you're not staying at a hotel, register the visa yourself. The easiest way is to take it to a travel agency where staff will usually offer registration for between R500 and R1000. If you are staying in Russia for fewer than seven working days, there is no need to register your visa.

72-HOUR VISA-FREE TRAVEL

St Petersburg is part of a scheme that allows visitors to enter Russia without a pre-arranged visa. Visa-free entry is available only to people arriving by ferry or on a cruise ship and who have pre-booked a tour of the city with companies licensed by the Russian government. The initiative does not allow for you to leave the tour at any point so it's rather restrictive – but it can be a good way to see the city if you're on a cruise and haven't had the time to organise a Russian visa. Operators who run these trips include **St Peter Line** (www.stpeterline.com) and **Saimaa Travel** (www.saimaatravel.fi).

Women Travellers

Sexual harassment on the streets is rare, but it is common in the workplace, the home and personal relations. Foreign women are likely to receive some attention, mostly in the form of genuine, friendly interest. An interested stranger may approach you and ask: *'Mozhno poznakomitsa?'* (May we become acquainted?) Answer with a gentle, but firm, *'Nyet'* (No) and it usually goes no further, although drunken men may persist. The best way to lose an unwelcome suitor is to enter an upmarket hotel or restaurant, where ample security will come to your aid. Women should avoid taking private taxis alone at night.

Russian women dress up and wear lots of make-up on nights out. If you are wearing casual gear, you might feel uncomfortable in a restaurant, club or theatre.

Language

Russian belongs to the Slavonic language family and is closely related to Belarusian and Ukrainian. It has more than 150 million speakers within the Russian Federation and is used as a second language in the former republics of the USSR, with a total number of speakers of more than 270 million people.

Russian is written in the Cyrillic alphabet (see the next page), and it's well worth the effort familiarising yourself with it so that you can read maps, timetables, menus and street signs. Otherwise, just read the coloured pronunciation guides given next to each Russian phrase in this chapter as if they were English, and you'll be understood. Most sounds are the same as in English, and the few differences in pronunciation are explained in the alphabet table. The stressed syllables are indicated with italics.

BASICS

Hello.	Здравствуйте.	*zdrast*·vuy·tye
Goodbye.	До свидания.	da svi·*da*·nya
Excuse me.	Простите.	pras·*ti*·tye
Sorry.	Извините.	iz·vi·*ni*·tye
Please.	Пожалуйста.	pa·*zhal*·sta
Thank you.	Спасибо.	spa·*si*·ba
You're welcome.	Пожалуйста.	pa·*zhal*·sta
Yes.	Да.	da
No.	Нет.	nyet

WANT MORE?

For in-depth language information and handy phrases, check out Lonely Planet's *Russian phrasebook*. You'll find it at **shop.lonelyplanet.com**, or you can buy Lonely Planet's iPhone phrasebooks at the Apple App Store.

How are you?
Как дела? — kak di·*la*

Fine, thank you. And you?
Хорошо, спасибо. А у вас? — kha·ra·*sho* spa·*si*·ba a u vas

What's your name?
Как вас зовут? — kak vas za·*vut*

My name is ...
Меня зовут ... — mi·*nya* *za*·vut ...

Do you speak English?
Вы говорите по-английски? — vi ga·va·*ri*·tye pa·an·*gli*·ski

I don't understand.
Я не понимаю. — ya nye pa·ni·*ma*·yu

ACCOMMODATION

Where's a ...?	Где ...?	gdye ...
boarding house	пансионат	pan·si·a·*nat*
campsite	кемпинг	*kyem*·ping
hotel	гостиница	ga·*sti*·ni·tsa
youth hostel	общежитие	ap·shi·*zhih*·ti·ye

Do you have a ... room?	У вас есть ...?	u vas yest' ...
single	одноместный номер	ad·na·*myest*·nih *no*·mir
double	номер с двуспальней кроватью	*no*·mir z dvu·*spal'*·nyey kra·*va*·tyu

How much is it for ...?	Сколько стоит за ...?	*skol'*·ka *sto*·it za ...
a night	ночь	noch'
two people	двоих	dva·*ikh*

The ... isn't working.	... не работает.	... ne ra·*bo*·ta·yit
heating	Отопление	a·ta·*plye*·ni·ye
hot water	Горячая вода	ga·*rya*·cha·ya va·*da*
light	Свет	svyet

CYRILLIC ALPHABET

Cyrillic	Sound	
А, а	a	as in 'father' (in a stressed syllable); as in 'ago' (in an unstressed syllable)
Б, б	b	as in 'but'
В, в	v	as in 'van'
Г, г	g	as in 'god'
Д, д	d	as in 'dog'
Е, е	ye	as in 'yet' (in a stressed syllable and at the end of a word);
	i	as in 'tin' (in an unstressed syllable)
Ё, ё	yo	as in 'yore' (often printed without dots)
Ж, ж	zh	as the 's' in 'measure'
З, з	z	as in 'zoo'
И, и	i	as the 'ee' in 'meet'
Й, й	y	as in 'boy' (not transliterated after **ы** or **и**)
К, к	k	as in 'kind'
Л, л	l	as in 'lamp'
М, м	m	as in 'mad'
Н, н	n	as in 'not'
О, о	o	as in 'more' (in a stressed syllable);
	a	as in 'hard' (in an unstressed syllable)
П, п	p	as in 'pig'
Р, р	r	as in 'rub' (rolled)
С, с	s	as in 'sing'
Т, т	t	as in 'ten'
У, у	u	as the 'oo' in 'fool'
Ф, ф	f	as in 'fan'
Х, х	kh	as the 'ch' in 'Bach'
Ц, ц	ts	as in 'bits'
Ч, ч	ch	as in 'chin'
Ш, ш	sh	as in 'shop'
Щ, щ	shch	as 'sh-ch' in 'fresh chips'
Ъ, ъ	–	'hard sign' meaning the preceding consonant is pronounced as it's written
Ы, ы	ih	as the 'y' in 'any'
Ь, ь	'	'soft sign' meaning the preceding consonant is pronounced like a faint y
Э, э	e	as in 'end'
Ю, ю	yu	as the 'u' in 'use'
Я, я	ya	as in 'yard' (in a stressed syllable);
	ye	as in 'yearn' (in an unstressed syllable)

DIRECTIONS

Where is ...?	
Где ...?	gdye ...
What's the address?	
Какой адрес?	ka·*koy* a·dris
Could you write it down, please?	
Запишите, пожалуйста.	za·pi·*shih*·tye pa·*zhal*·sta
Can you show me (on the map)?	
Покажите мне, пожалуйста (на карте).	pa·ka·*zhih*·tye mnye pa·*zhal*·sta (na *kar*·tye)

Turn ...	Поверните ...	pa·vir·*ni*·tye ...
at the corner	за угол	za *u*·gal
at the traffic lights	на светофоре	na svi·ta·*fo*·rye
left	налево	na·*lye*·va
right	направо	na·*pra*·va

behind ...	за ...	za ...
far	далеко	da·li·*ko*
in front of ...	перед ...	*pye*·rit ...
near	близко	*blis*·ka
next to ...	рядом с ...	*rya*·dam s ...
opposite ...	напротив ...	na·*pro*·tif ...
straight ahead	прямо	*prya*·ma

EATING & DRINKING

I'd like to reserve a table for ...	Я бы хотел/ хотела заказать столик на … (m/f)	ya bih khat·*yel*/ khat·*ye*·la za·ka·*zat'* *sto*·lik na ...
two people	двоих	dva·*ikh*
eight o'clock	восемь часов	*vo*·sim' chi·*sof*

What would you recommend?	
Что вы рекомендуете?	shto vih ri·ka·min·*du*·it·ye
What's in that dish?	
Что входит в это блюдо?	shto *fkho*·dit v e·ta *blyu*·da
That was delicious!	
Было очень вкусно!	*bih*·la o·chin' *fkus*·na
Please bring the bill.	
Принесите, пожалуйста счёт.	pri·ni·*sit*·ye pa·*zhal*·sta shot

I don't eat ...	Я не ем …	ya nye yem ...
eggs	яиц	*ya*·its
fish	рыбы	*rih*·bih
poultry	птицы	*ptit*·sih
red meat	мяса	*mya*·sa

Key Words

bottle	бутылка	bu·*tihl*·ka
bowl	миска	*mis*·ka
breakfast	завтрак	*zaf*·trak
cold	холодный	kha·*lod*·nih
dinner	ужин	*u*·zhihn
dish	блюдо	*blyu*·da
fork	вилка	*vil*·ka
glass	стакан	sta·*kan*
hot (warm)	жаркий	*zhar*·ki
knife	нож	nosh
lunch	обед	ab·*yet*
menu	меню	min·*yu*
plate	тарелка	tar·*yel*·ka
restaurant	ресторан	ris·ta·*ran*
spoon	ложка	*losh*·ka
with/without	с/без	s/byez

Meat & Fish

beef	говядина	gav·*ya*·di·na
caviar	икра	i·*kra*
chicken	курица	*ku*·rit·sa
duck	утка	*ut*·ka
fish	рыба	*rih*·ba
herring	сельдь	syelt'
lamb	баранина	ba·*ra*·ni·na
meat	мясо	*mya*·sa
oyster	устрица	*ust*·rit·sa
pork	свинина	svi·*ni*·na
prawn	креветка	kriv·*yet*·ka
salmon	лососина	la·sa·*si*·na
turkey	индейка	ind·*yey*·ka
veal	телятина	til·*ya*·ti·na

Fruit & Vegetables

apple	яблоко	*yab*·la·ka
bean	фасоль	fa·*sol'*
cabbage	капуста	ka·*pu*·sta
capsicum	перец	*pye*·rits
carrot	морковь	mar·*kof'*
cauliflower	цветная капуста	tsvit·*na*·ya ka·*pu*·sta
cucumber	огурец	a·gur·*yets*
fruit	фрукты	*fruk*·tih
mushroom	гриб	grip
nut	орех	ar·*yekh*
onion	лук	luk
orange	апельсин	a·pil'·*sin*
peach	персик	*pyer*·sik
pear	груша	*gru*·sha
plum	слива	*sli*·va
potato	картошка	kar·*tosh*·ka
spinach	шпинат	shpi·*nat*
tomato	помидор	pa·mi·*dor*
vegetable	овощ	*o*·vash

Signs

Вход	Entrance
Выход	Exit
Открыт	Open
Закрыт	Closed
Справки	Information
Запрещено	Prohibited
Туалет	Toilets
Мужской (М)	Men
Женский (Ж)	Women

Other

bread	хлеб	khlyep
cheese	сыр	sihr
egg	яйцо	yeyt·*so*
honey	мёд	myot
oil	масло	*mas*·la
pasta	паста	*pa*·sta
pepper	перец	*pye*·rits
rice	рис	ris
salt	соль	sol'
sugar	сахар	*sa*·khar
vinegar	уксус	*uk*·sus

Drinks

beer	пиво	*pi*·va
coffee	кофе	*kof*·ye
(orange) juice	(апельсин-овый) сок	(a·pil'·*si*·na·vih) sok
milk	молоко	ma·la·*ko*
tea	чай	chey
(mineral) water	(минеральная) вода	(mi·ni·*ral'*·na·ya) va·*da*
wine	вино	vi·*no*

EMERGENCIES

Help!	Помогите!	pa·ma·*gi*·tye
Call ...!	Вызовите ...!	*vih*·za·vi·tye ...
a doctor	врача	vra·*cha*
the police	милицию	mi·*li*·tsih·yu

Leave me alone!
Приваливай! pri·*va*·li·vai

There's been an accident.
Произошёл несчастный случай. pra·i·za·*shol* ne·*shas*·nih *slu*·chai

I'm lost.
Я заблудился/заблудилась. (m/f) ya za·blu·*dil*·sa/za·blu·*di*·las'

Where are the toilets?
Где здесь туалет? gdye zdyes' tu·al·*yet*

I'm ill.
Я болен/больна. (m/f) ya *bo*·lin/bal'·*na*

It hurts here.
Здесь болит. zdyes' ba·*lit*

I'm allergic to (antibiotics).
У меня алергия на (антибиотики). u min·*ya* a·lir·*gi*·ya na (an·ti·bi·*o*·ti·ki)

SHOPPING & SERVICES

I need ...
Мне нужно ... mnye *nuzh*·na ...

I'm just looking.
Я просто смотрю. ya *pros*·ta smat·*ryu*

Can I look at it?
Покажите, пожалуйста. pa·ka·*zhih*·tye pa·*zhal*·sta

How much is it?
Сколько стоит? *skol'*·ka *sto*·it

That's too expensive.
Это очень дорого. *e*·ta *o*·chen' *do*·ra·ga

There's a mistake in the bill.
Меня обсчитали. min·*ya* ap·shi·*ta*·li

bank	банк	bank
market	рынок	*rih*·nak
post office	почта	*poch*·ta
telephone office	телефонный пункт	ti·li·*fo*·nih punkt

Question Words

What?	Что?	shto
When?	Когда?	kag·*da*
Where?	Где?	gdye
Which?	Какой?	ka·*koy*
Who?	Кто?	kto
Why?	Почему?	pa·chi·*mu*

TIME, DATES & NUMBERS

What time is it?
Который час? ka·*to*·rih chas

It's (10) o'clock.
(Десять) часов. (*dye*·sit') chi·*sof*

morning	утро	*ut*·ra
afternoon	после обеда	*pos*·lye ab·*ye*·da
evening	вечер	*vye*·chir
yesterday	вчера	vchi·*ra*
today	сегодня	si·*vod*·nya
tomorrow	завтра	*zaft*·ra

Monday	понедельник	pa·ni·*dyel'*·nik
Tuesday	вторник	*ftor*·nik
Wednesday	среда	sri·*da*
Thursday	четверг	chit·*vyerk*
Friday	пятница	*pyat*·ni·tsa
Saturday	суббота	su·*bo*·ta
Sunday	воскресенье	vas·kri·*syen*·ye

January	январь	yan·*var'*
February	февраль	fiv·*ral'*
March	март	mart
April	апрель	ap·*ryel'*
May	май	mai
June	июнь	i·*yun'*
July	июль	i·*yul'*
August	август	*av*·gust
September	сентябрь	sin·*tyabr'*
October	октябрь	ak·*tyabr'*
November	ноябрь	na·*yabr'*
December	декабрь	di·*kabr'*

1	один	a·*din*
2	два	dva
3	три	tri
4	четыре	chi·*tih*·ri
5	пять	pyat'
6	шесть	shest'
7	семь	syem'
8	восемь	*vo*·sim'
9	девять	*dye*·vyat'
10	десять	*dye*·syat'
20	двадцать	*dva*·tsat'
30	тридцать	*tri*·tsat'
40	сорок	*so*·rak
50	пятьдесят	pi·dis·*yat*
60	шестдесят	shihs·dis·*yat*
70	семьдесят	*syem'*·dis·yat

80	восемьдесят	*vo*·sim'·di·sit
90	девяносто	di·vi·*no*·sta
100	сто	sto
1000	тысяча	*tih*·si·cha

TRANSPORT

Public Transport

A ... ticket (to Novgorod).	Билет ... (на Новгород).	bil·*yet* ... (na *nov*·ga·rat)
one-way	в один конец	v a·*din* kan·*yets*
return	в оба конца	v o·ba kan·*tsa*

bus	автобус	af·*to*·bus
train	поезд	*po*·ist
tram	трамвай	tram·*vai*
trolleybus	троллейбус	tra·*lyey*·bus

first	первый	*pyer*·vih
last	последний	pas·*lyed*·ni
metro token	жетон	zhi·*ton*
platform	платформа	plat·*for*·ma
(bus) stop	остановка	a·sta·*nof*·ka
ticket	билет	bil·*yet*
ticket office	билетная касса	bil·*yet*·na·ya *ka*·sa
timetable	расписание	ras·pi·*sa*·ni·ye

When does it leave?
Когда отправляется? — kag·*da* at·prav·*lya*·it·sa

How long does it take to get to ...?
Сколько времени нужно ехать до …? — *skol'*·ka vrye·mi·ni *nuzh*·na *ye*·khat' da ...

Does it stop at ...?
Поезд останавливается в …? — *po*·yist a·sta·*nav*·li·va·yit·sa v ...

Please stop here.
Остановитесь здесь, пожалуйста! — a·sta·na·*vit*·yes' zdyes' pa·*zhal*·sta

Driving & Cycling

I'd like to hire a ...	Я бы хотел/хотела взять ... на прокат. (m/f)	ya bih kha·*tyel*/kha·*tye*·la vzyat' ... na pra·*kat*
4WD	машину с полным приводом	ma·*shih*·nu s *pol*·nihm pri·*vo*·dam
bicycle	велосипед	vi·la·si·*pyet*
car	машину	ma·*shih*·nu
motorbike	мотоцикл	ma·ta·*tsikl*

KEY PATTERNS

To get by in Russian, mix and match these simple patterns with words of your choice:

When's (the next bus)?
Когда (будет следующий автобус)? — kag·*da* (*bu*·dit *slye*·du·yu·shi af·*to*·bus)

Where's (the station)?
Где (станция)? — gdye (*stant*·sih·ya)

Where can I (buy a padlock)?
Где можно (купить нависной замок)? — gdye *mozh*·na (ku·*pit'* na·vis·*noy* za·*mok*)

Do you have (a map)?
Здесь есть (карте)? — zdyes' yest' (*kart*·ye)

I'd like (the menu).
Я бы хотел/хотела (меню). (m/f) — ya bih khat·*yel*/khat·*ye*·la (min·*yu*)

I'd like to (hire a car).
Я бы хотел/хотела (взять машину). (m/f) — ya bih khat·*yel*/khat·*ye*·la (vzyat' ma·*shih*·nu)

Can I (come in)?
Можно (войти)? — mozh·na (vey·ti)

Could you please (write it down)?
(Запишите), пожалуйста. — (za·pi·*shiht*·ye) pa·*zhal*·sta

Do I need (a visa)?
Нужна ли (виза)? — nuzh·*na* li (*vi*·za)

I need (assistance).
Мне нужна (помощь). — mnye nuzh·*na* (*po*·mash)

diesel	дизельное топливо	*di*·zil'·na·ye *to*·pli·va
regular	бензин номер 93	ben·*zin* *no*·mir di·vi·*no*·sta tri
unleaded	очищенный бензин	a·*chi*·shi·nih bin·*zin*

Is this the road to ...?
Эта дорога ведёт в …? — *e*·ta da·*ro*·ga vid·*yot* f ...

Where's a petrol station?
Где заправка? — gdye za·*praf*·ka

Can I park here?
Здесь можно стоять? — zdyes' *mozh*·na sta·*yat'*

I need a mechanic.
Мне нужен автомеханик. — mnye *nu*·zhihn af·ta·mi·*kha*·nik

The car has broken down.
Машина сломалась. — ma·*shih*·na sla·*ma*·las'

I have a flat tyre.
У меня лопнула шина. — u min·*ya* lop·*nu*·la *shih*·na

I've run out of petrol.
У меня кончился бензин. — u min·*ya* *kon*·chil·sa bin·*zin*

GLOSSARY

(m) indicates masculine gender, (f) feminine gender and (n) neuter gender

aeroport – airport
alleya – alley
apteka – pharmacy
avtobus – bus
avtomaticheskie kamery khranenia – left-luggage lockers
avtovokzal – bus station
babushka – grandmother
bankomat – ATM
banya – bathhouse
bolshoy/bolshaya/bolshoye (m/f/n) – big, great, grand
bulvar – boulevard
bylina – epic song
dacha – country cottage
datsan – temple
deklaratsiya – customs declaration
dom – house
duma – parliament
dvorets – palace
elektrichka – suburban train; also *prigorodnye poezd*
galereya – gallery
glasnost – openness; policy of public accountability developed under the leadership of Mikhail Gorbachev
gorod – city, town
kafe – cafe
kamera khranenia – left-luggage office or counter
kanal – canal
kladbische – cemetery
kolonnada – colonnade
kon – horse
korpus – building within a building
koryushki – freshwater smelt
kruglosutochno – open 24 hours
lavra – most senior grade of Russian Orthodox monastery
letny sad – summer garden
liteyny – foundry
maly/malaya/maloye (m/f/n) – small, little
marshrutka – minibus that runs along a fixed route; diminutive form of *marshrutnoye taxi*
Maslenitsa – akin to Mardi Gras; fete that celebrates the end of winter and kicks off Lent
matryoshka – nesting doll; set of painted wooden dolls within dolls
mekh – fur
mesto – seat
militsioner – police officer
militsiya – police
morskoy vokzal – sea station
morzh – literally walrus, but the name commonly given to ice swimmers in the Neva
most – bridge
muzey – museum
naberezhnaya – embankment
novy/novaya (m/f) – new
Novy God – New Year
ostrov – island
parilka – steam room (at a *banya*)
Paskha – Easter
passazhirskiy poezd – passenger train
perekhod – transfer
pereryv – break, recess
perestroika – reconstruction; policy of reconstructing the economy developed under the leadership of Mikhail Gorbachev
pereulok – lane, side street
pivnaya – beer bar
ploshchad – square
prigorodnye poezd – suburban train; also *elektrichka*
proezd – passage
prospekt – avenue
rechnoy vokzal – river station
reka – river
restoran – restaurant
Rozhdestvo – Christmas
rynok – market
ryumochnaya – equivalent of the local pub
samizdat – underground literary manuscript
sanitarny den – literally 'sanitary day'; a day during the last week of every month on which establishments such as museums shut down for cleaning
shosse – highway
skory poezd – fast train; regular long-distance service
sobor – cathedral
stary/staraya/staroye (m/f/n) – old
stolovaya – cafeteria
tapochki – slippers
teatralnaya kassa – theatre kiosk; general theatre box office scattered about the city
troika – sleigh drawn by three horses
tserkov – church
ulitsa – street
uslovie yedenitsiy – standard units, which is equivalent to euros; often abbreviated as y.e.
vagon – carriage (on a train)
veniki – bundle of birch branches used at a *banya* to beat bathers to eliminate toxins and improve circulation
vokzal – station
vyshaya liga – Russia's premier football league
zal – hall
zamok – castle

MENU DECODER

bliny – pancakes блины

borsch – beetroot soup борщ

buterbrod – open-faced sandwich бутерброд

garnir – garnish, or side dish гарнир

ikra (chyornaya, krasnaya) – caviar (black, red) икра (чёрная, красная)

kartoshki – potatoes картошки

kasha – porridge каша

kefir – sour yogurtlike drink кефир

khleb – bread хлеб

kvas – mildly alcoholic fermented-rye-bread drink квас

lapsha – noodle soup лапша

losos – salmon лосось

mineralnaya voda (gazirovannaya, negazirovannaya) – water (sparkling, still) минеральная вода (газированная, негазированная)

moloko – milk молоко

morozhenoye – ice cream мороженое

myaso – meat мясо

obed – lunch обедь

okroshka – cold cucumber soup with a *kvas* base окрошка

ovoshchi – vegetables овощи

ovoshnoy salat – tomato and cucumber salad, literally 'vegetable salad' овошной салат

pelmeni – dumplings filled with meat or vegetables пельмени

pirog or **pirogi** (pl) – pie пирог, пироги

pivo (svetloe, tyomnoe) – beer (light, dark) пиво (светлое, тёмное)

ptitsa – poultry птица

ris – rice рис

ryba – fish рыба

salat olivier – see *stolichny salat* салат Оливье

seld pod shuboy – salad with herring, potatoes, beets and carrots, literally 'herring in a fur coat' сельдь под шубой

shashlyk (myasnoy, kuriny, rybnoy) – kebab (meat, chicken, fish) шашлык (мясной, куриный, рыбной)

shchi – cabbage soup щи

solyanka – a tasty meat soup with salty vegetables and hint of lemon солянка

svekolnik – cold beet soup свекольник

sok – juice сок

stolichny salat – 'capital salad', which contains beef, potatoes and eggs in mayonnaise; also called *salat olivier* столичный салат

tvorog – soft sweet cheese similar to ricotta творог

uzhin – dinner ужин

zavtrak – breakfast завтрак

zakuski – appetisers закуски

Behind the Scenes

SEND US YOUR FEEDBACK

We love to hear from travellers – your comments keep us on our toes and help make our books better. Our well-travelled team reads every word on what you loved or loathed about this book. Although we cannot reply individually to postal submissions, we always guarantee that your feedback goes straight to the appropriate authors, in time for the next edition. Each person who sends us information is thanked in the next edition – and the most useful submissions are rewarded with a free book.

Visit **lonelyplanet.com/contact** to submit your updates and suggestions or to ask for help. Our award-winning website also features inspirational travel stories, news and discussions.

Note: We may edit, reproduce and incorporate your comments in Lonely Planet products such as guidebooks, websites and digital products, so let us know if you don't want your comments reproduced or your name acknowledged. For a copy of our privacy policy visit lonelyplanet.com/privacy.

OUR READERS

Many thanks to the travellers who used the last edition and wrote to us with helpful hints, useful advice and interesting anecdotes:

Nicolas Adams, Tjeerd Ates, Joop Bakker, Jane Binstead, David Bird, Clifford Bland, Jennifer Carter, Romelle Castle, Karen Collyer, Andrew Cox, Chris Derksen, Karen Haas, John Hamilton, Marcia Hammond, Sam Hoben, Steve K, Arthur Kane, Anna Kirk, Josef Lampa, Suzie Mclellan, Leo Paton, Charlotte Seiglow, Elizabeth Smirnova, Annina Von Muralt, Hans Wiedemar and Jan Willem Van Hofwegen.

AUTHOR THANKS

Tom Masters

Big thanks to my best friend in St Petersburg, Simon Patterson, for his good-humoured, vodka-soaked company on every trip I make to the city. Thanks also to Grégory Strub, Anna Knutson, Sergey Chernov, Tobin Auber, Gena Bolgolepov, Dima Dzhafarov, Veronika Altukhova, Dima Makarov, Alexei Dmitriev, Jessica Moroz, Chinawoman & Gang and Slava Gusinsky for all their help and company during this research trip. At Lonely Planet many thanks to Simon Richmond, Mara Vorhees, Anna Tyler, Imogen Hall and all the in-house team in Melbourne for their continued hard work and support.

ACKNOWLEDGMENTS

Climate map data adapted from Peel MC, Finlayson BL & McMahon TA (2007) 'Updated World Map of the Köppen-Geiger Climate Classification', *Hydrology and Earth System Sciences*, 11, 163344.

Illustrations pp46-7 by Javier Zarracina.

Cover photograph: Interior of Church on the Spilled Blood, Izzet Keribar/Lonely Planet Images.
Many of the images in this guide are available for licensing from Lonely Planet Images: www.lonelyplanetimages.com.

THIS BOOK

This 6th edition of Lonely Planet's *St Petersburg* guidebook was researched and written by Tom Masters. Simon Richmond researched and wrote text for Veliky Novgorod. The 5th edition was written by Mara Vorhees, the 4th edition by Tom Masters, the 3rd edition by Steve Kokker, and the 1st and 2nd editions by Nick Selby. This guidebook was commissioned in Lonely Planet's London office, and produced by the following:

Commissioning Editors Imogen Hall, Anna Tyler, Emily K Wolman
Coordinating Editors Susie Ashworth, Victoria Harrison
Coordinating Cartographer Marc Milinkovic
Coordinating Layout Designer Virginia Moreno
Senior Editors Susan Paterson, Angela Tinson
Managing Editor Brigitte Ellemor
Managing Cartographers Shahara Ahmed, Adrian Persoglia
Managing Layout Designer Jane Hart
Assisting Editors Pat Kinsella, Anne Mulvaney
Assisting Cartographer Hunor Csutoros
Cover Research Naomi Parker
Internal Image Research Aude Vauconsant
Language Content Branislava Vladisavljevic

Thanks to Jo Cooke, Janine Eberle, Catherine Eldridge, Ryan Evans, Will Gourlay, Liz Heynes, Laura Jane, David Kemp, Valentina Kremenchutskaya, Annelies Mertens, Wayne Murphy, Trent Paton, Piers Pickard, Lachlan Ross, Michael Ruff, Julie Sheridan, Laura Stansfeld, John Taufa, Gerard Walker, Clifton Wilkinson

NOTES

NOTES

See also separate subindexes for:

- EATING p249
- DRINKING & NIGHTLIFE p249
- ENTERTAINMENT p250
- SHOPPING p250
- SPORTS & ACTIVITIES p250
- SLEEPING p251

Index

Sights p000
Map Pages **p000**
Photo Pages **p000**

L

M

Sights p000
Map Pages **p000**
Photo Pages **p000**

N

Sights p000
Map Pages **p000**
Photo Pages **p000**

EATING

DRINKING & NIGHTLIFE

ENTERTAINMENT

Sights p000
Map Pages **p000**
Photo Pages **p000**

SHOPPING

SPORTS & ACTIVITIES

SLEEPING

St Petersburg Maps

Map Legend

Sights
- Beach
- Buddhist
- Castle
- Christian
- Hindu
- Islamic
- Jewish
- Monument
- Museum/Gallery
- Ruin
- Winery/Vineyard
- Zoo
- Other Sight

Eating
- Eating

Drinking & Nightlife
- Drinking & Nightlife
- Cafe

Entertainment
- Entertainment

Shopping
- Shopping

Sports & Activities
- Diving/Snorkelling
- Canoeing/Kayaking
- Skiing
- Surfing
- Swimming/Pool
- Walking
- Windsurfing
- Other Sports & Activities

Sleeping
- Sleeping
- Camping

Information
- Bank
- Embassy/Consulate
- Hospital/Medical
- Internet
- Police
- Post Office
- Telephone
- Toilet
- Tourist Information
- Other Information

Transport
- Airport
- Border Crossing
- Bus
- Cable Car/Funicular
- Cycling
- Ferry
- Metro
- Monorail
- Parking
- S-Bahn
- Taxi
- Train/Railway
- Tram
- Tube Station
- U-Bahn
- Other Transport

Routes
- Tollway
- Freeway
- Primary
- Secondary
- Tertiary
- Lane
- Unsealed Road
- Plaza/Mall
- Steps
- Tunnel
- Pedestrian Overpass
- Walking Tour
- Walking Tour Detour
- Path

Boundaries
- International
- State/Province
- Disputed
- Regional/Suburb
- Marine Park
- Cliff
- Wall

Geographic
- Hut/Shelter
- Lighthouse
- Lookout
- Mountain/Volcano
- Oasis
- Park
- Pass
- Picnic Area
- Waterfall

Hydrography
- River/Creek
- Intermittent River
- Swamp/Mangrove
- Reef
- Canal
- Water
- Dry/Salt/Intermittent Lake
- Glacier

Areas
- Beach/Desert
- Cemetery (Christian)
- Cemetery (Other)
- Park/Forest
- Sportsground
- Sight (Building)
- Top Sight (Building)

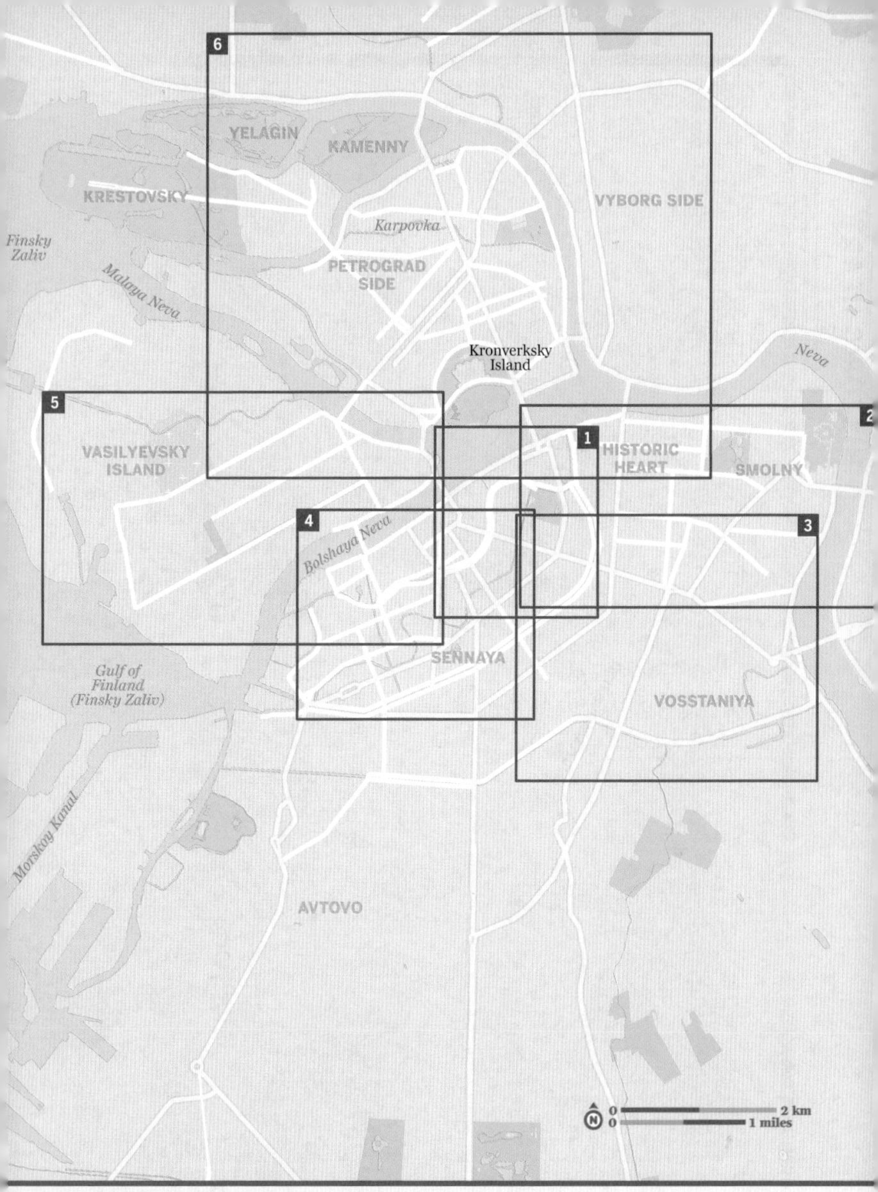
6
YELAGIN
KAMENNY
KRESTOVSKY
VYBORG SIDE
Karpovka
Finsky Zaliv
Malaya Neva
PETROGRAD SIDE
Kronverksky Island
Neva
5
VASILYEVSKY ISLAND
1
HISTORIC HEART
SMOLNY
2
4
3
Bolshaya Neva
SENNAYA
VOSSTANIYA
Gulf of Finland (Finsky Zaliv)
Morskoy Kanal
AVTOVO
0 2 km
0 1 miles

MAP INDEX

HISTORIC HEART

Key on p256

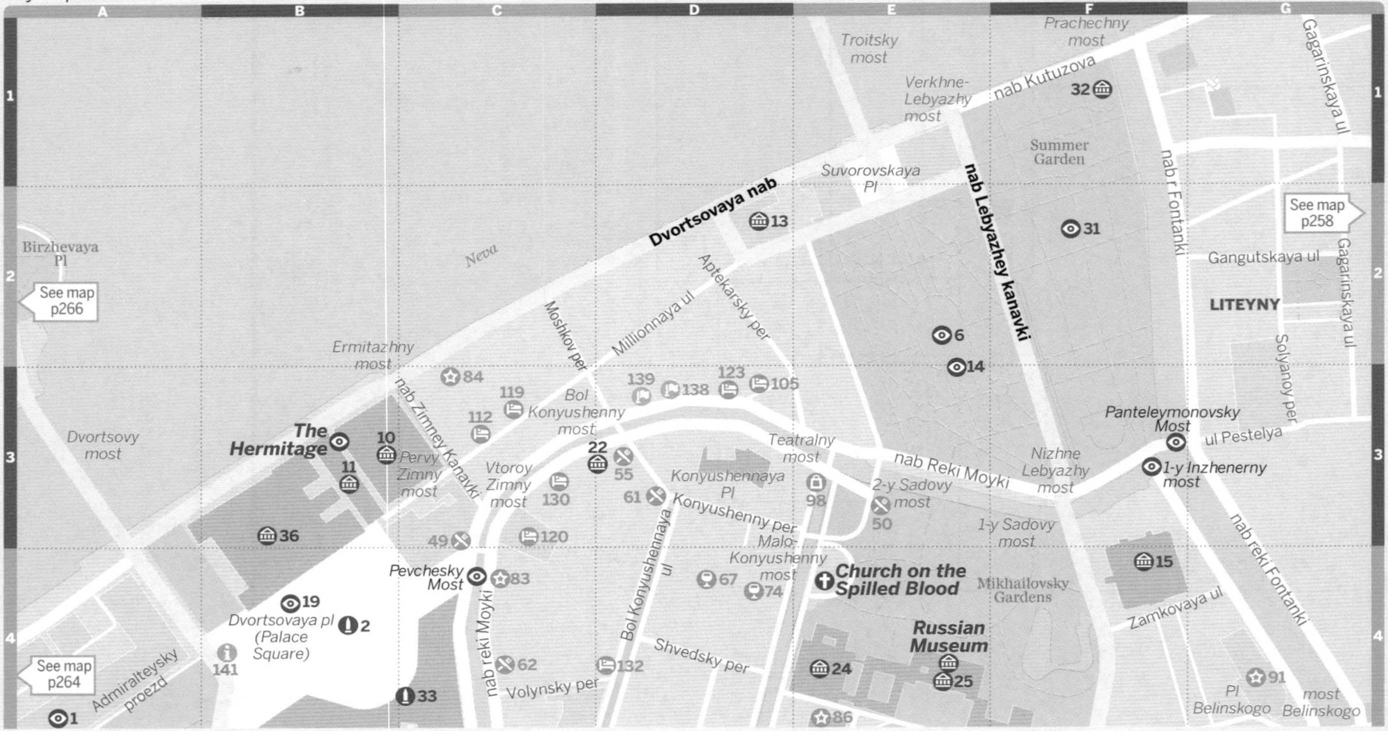

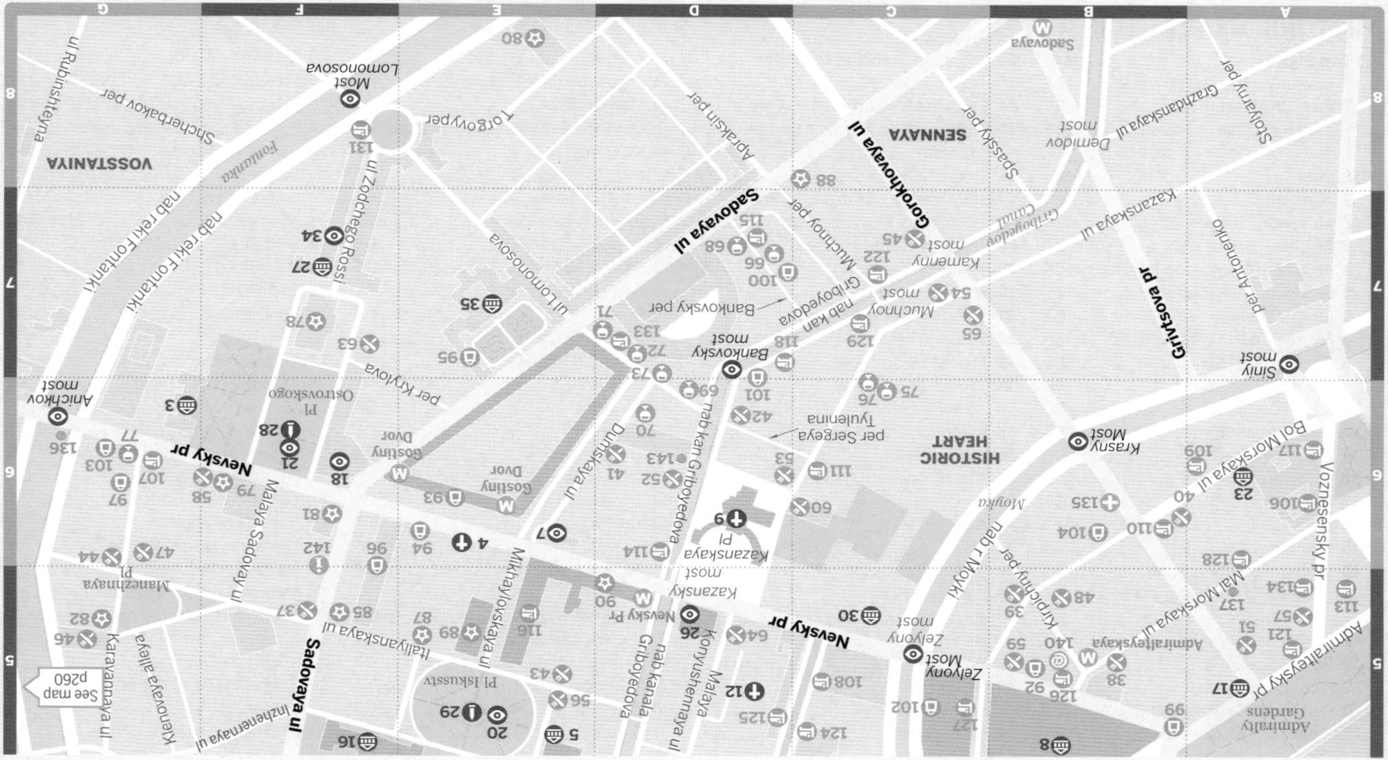
See map p260
Nevsky pr
Sadovaya ul
Gorokhovaya ul
Grivtsova pr
Admiralteysky pr
Voznesensky pr
Bol Morskaya ul
Mal Morskaya ul
Kirpichny per
Admiralteyskaya
Admiralty Gardens
nab r Moyki
Moyka
Zelyony Most
Zelyony most
Krasny Most
Siniy most
HISTORIC HEART
Kazanskaya Pl
Kazansky most
nab kan Griboyedova
nab kanala Griboyedova
Malaya Konyushennaya ul
Nevsky Pr
Bankovsky most
Bankovsky per
per Sergeya Tyulenina
Dumskaya ul
Gostiny Dvor
Mikhaylovskaya ul
Italyanskaya ul
Pl Iskusstv
Inzhenernaya ul
Klenovaya alleya
Karavannaya ul
Manezhnaya Pl
Malaya Sadovaya ul
Pl Ostrovskogo
per Krylova
ul Lomonosova
ul Zodchego Rossi
Torgovy per
Most Lomonosova
Anichkov most
nab reki Fontanki
Fontanka
Shcherbakov per
ul Rubinshteyna
VOSSTANIYA
SENNAYA
Apraksin per
Muchnoy per
Muchnoy most
Kamenny most
Griboyedov Canal
Kazanskaya ul
Spassky per
Demidov most
Grazhdanskaya ul
Stolyarny per
per Antonenko
Sadovaya

HISTORIC HEART *Map on p254*

Top Sights (p44)
Church on the Spilled Blood E4
Russian Museum E4
The Hermitage B3

Sights (p65)
1 Admiralty A4
2 Alexander Column B4
3 Anichkov Palace G6
4 Armenian Church of St Catherine. E6
5 Brodsky House-Museum E5
6 Eternal Flame E2
7 Former Town Duma E6
8 General Staff Building B5
Gostiny Dvor .... (see 93)
9 Kazan Cathedral D6
10 Large Hermitage B3
11 Little Hermitage B3
12 Lutheran Church D5
13 Marble Palace D2
14 Mars Field E3
15 Mikhailovsky Castle F4
16 Museum of Ethnography F5
17 Museum of the History of the Political Police A5
18 National Library of Russia F6
19 Palace Square B4
20 Ploshchad Iskusstv E5
21 Ploshchad Ostrovskogo F6
22 Pushkin Flat-Museum D3
23 Rosphoto State Photography Centre A6
24 Russian Museum (Benois Wing) ... E4
25 Russian Museum (Mikhailovsky Palace) E4
26 Singer Building D5
27 St Petersburg State Museum of Theatre & Music F7
28 Statue of Catherine the Great F6
29 Statue of Pushkin E5
30 Stroganov Palace C5
31 Summer Garden F2
32 Summer Palace of Peter I F1
33 Triumphal Arch C4
34 Vaganova School of Choreography F7
35 Vorontsov Palace E7
36 Winter Palace B3
Winter Palace of Peter I .... (see 84)

Eating (p72)
37 Baku F5
38 Bushe B5
39 Café King Pong B5
40 Entrecôte B6
41 Fat Friar D6
Fiolet .... (see 131)
42 Garçon D6
43 Kalinka Malinka E5
44 Kavkaz Bar G6
45 Kilikia C7
46 Korovabar G5
47 Mama Roma G6
MiX in St Petersburg .... (see 134)
48 Ne Goruy B5
49 NEP C3
50 Park Giuseppe E3
51 Pelmeny Bar A5
52 Pirogovy Dvorik D6
53 Sharlot Café D6
54 Soup Wine C7
55 Stolle D3
56 Stray Dog Café E5
57 Tandoori Nights A5
58 Teremok F6
59 Teremok B5
60 Terrassa C6
61 The Other Side D3
The Other Side .... (see 61)
62 Troitsky Most C4
63 Yakitoriya F7
64 Yolki Palki D5
65 Zoom Café C7

Drinking & Nightlife (p45)
66 Bar Without A Name D7
67 Barakobamabar D4
Belgrad .... (see 70)
68 Bermudy Bar Disco D7
Café Singer .... (see 26)
69 Central Station D6
70 Datscha D6
Fidel .... (see 70)
71 Folks D7
72 Golubaya Ustritsa D7
Lobby Bar .... (see 116)
73 Lomonosov D7
MiXup Bar .... (see 134)
74 Mod Club D4
75 RadioBaby C6
76 Tinkoff C6
77 Tribunal Bar G6

Entertainment (p77)
78 Alexandrinsky Theatre F7
79 Avrora F6
80 Bolshoy Drama Theatre E8
81 Demmeni Marionette Theatre F6
82 Dom Kino G5
83 Glinka Capella House C4
84 Hermitage Theatre C3
85 Komissarzhevskaya Theatre F5
86 Mikhailovsky Theatre E4
87 Musical Comedy Theatre E5
88 Priyut Komedianta Theatre C8
89 Shostakovich Philharmonia Bolshoy Zal E5
90 Shostakovich Philharmonia Maly Zal D5
91 St Petersburg State Circus G4

Shopping (p78)

92 Bukvoed B5
Dom Knigi .... (see 26)
93 Gostiny Dvor E6
94 Grand Palace E6
95 Military Shop E7
96 Passage F6
Prostranstvo Kultury .... (see 96)
97 Retro Shop G6
98 Souvenir Market E3
99 Staraya Kniga B5
100 The People Showroom D7
101 Vinissimo D7
102 Wild Orchid C5
103 Writers' Bookshop G6
104 Yakhont B6

Sleeping (p159)

105 3MostA D3
106 Angleterre Hotel A6
107 Anichkov Pension G6
108 Belveder Nevsky C5
109 Casa Leto A6
110 Comfort Hotel B6
111 Cuba Hostel C6
112 Fortecia Peter C3
113 Four Seasons Hotel Lion Palace A5
114 Friends Hostel D6
115 Friends on Bankovsky D7
116 Grand Hotel Europe E5
Guest House Nevsky 3 .... (see 99)
Herzen Hotel .... (see 110)
117 Hotel Astoria A6
118 Hotel Grifon D7
119 Hotel Nauka C3
120 Kempinski Hotel Moyka 22 .... C3
121 Location Hostel A5
122 Mini Hotel Dolce Vita C7
123 Moyka 5 .... D3
124 Nevsky Hotel Aster C5
125 Nevsky Hotel Grand D5
126 Nevsky Prospekt B&B B5
127 Nord Hostel C5
128 Petro Palace Hotel A6
129 Pio on Griboedov C7
Polikoff Hotel .... (see 107)
130 Pushka Inn C3
Rachmaninov Hotel .... (see 111)
131 Rossi Hotel F8
132 SkyHotel D4
133 Stony Island Hotel D7
134 W Hotel A5

Information (p224)

135 36.6 Pharmacy B6
136 Anglotourism G6
Australian Consulate .... (see 138)
137 Cultural Security Department A5
138 Dutch Consulate D3
139 French Consulate D3
140 Internet Cafe B5
Russian Museum Internet Centre(see
141 Tourist Information Centre B4
142 Tourist Information Centre F6

Transport (p218)

143 Central Train Ticket Office D6

LITEYNY & SMOLNY

Key on p259

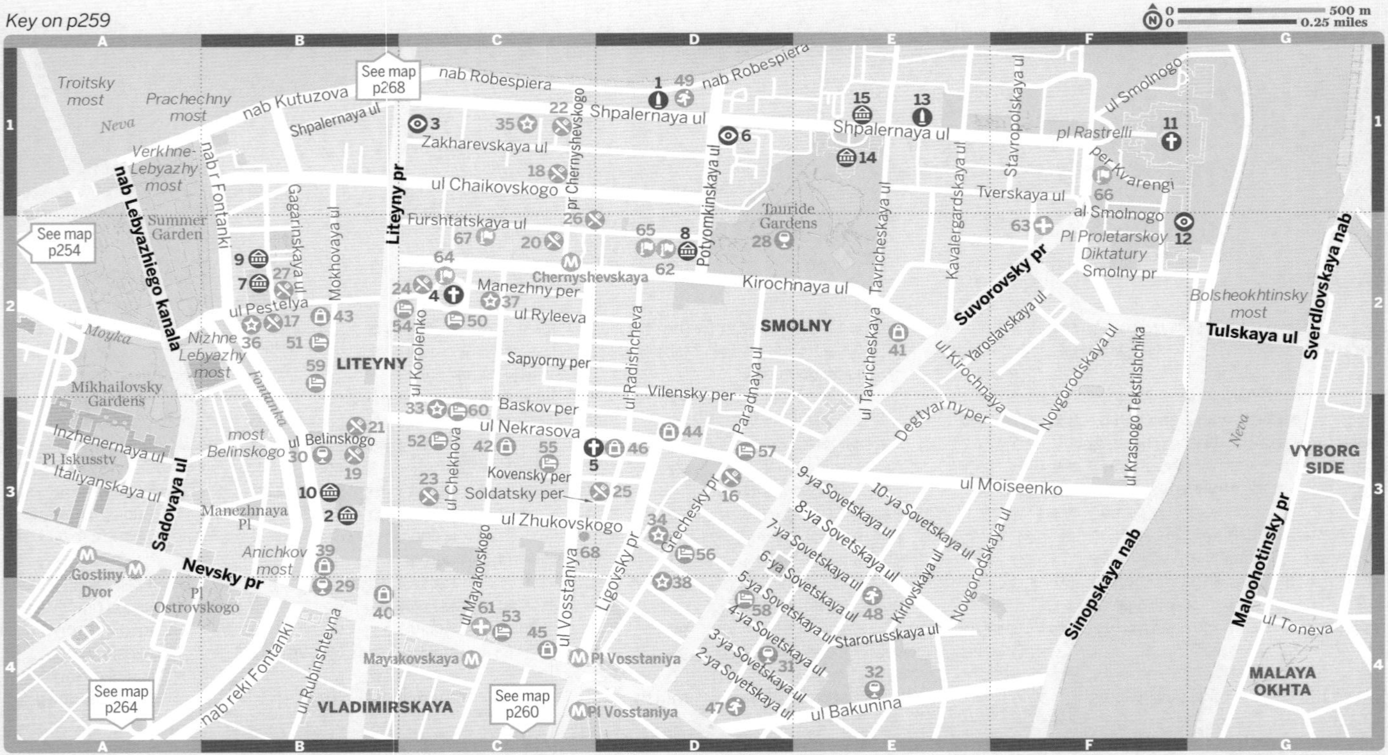
0 500 m
0 0.25 miles
See map p268
See map p254
See map p264
See map p260
Troitsky most
Prachechny most
Neva
Verkhne-Lebyazhy most
nab Kutuzova
nab Robespiera
Shpalernaya ul
Zakharevskaya ul
ul Chaikovskogo
pr Chernyshevskogo
Furshtatskaya ul
Liteyny pr
nab r Fontanki
nab Lebyazhiego kanala
Summer Garden
Gagarinskaya ul
Mokhovaya ul
ul Pestelya
Moyka
Nizhne Lebyazhy most
Fontanka
Mikhailovsky Gardens
LITEYNY
ul Korolenko
Manezhny per
ul Ryleeva
Sapyorny per
Chernyshevskaya
Kirochnaya ul
Potyomkinskaya ul
Tauride Gardens
Tavricheskaya ul
ul Tavricheskaya
Kavalergardskaya ul
Stavropolskaya ul
Tverskaya ul
ul Smolnogo
pl Rastrelli
per Kvarengi
al Smolnogo
Pl Proletarskoy Diktatury
Smolny pr
Suvorovsky pr
Bolsheokhtinsky most
Tulskaya ul
Sverdlovskaya nab
SMOLNY
Yaroslavskaya ul
ul Kirochnaya
Novgorodskaya ul
ul Krasnogo Tekstilshchika
ul Radishcheva
Vilensky per
Paradnaya ul
Degtyarny per
Baskov per
ul Nekrasova
ul Chekhova
Kovensky per
Soldatsky per
ul Zhukovskogo
ul Mayakovskogo
ul Vosstaniya
Ligovsky pr
Grechesky pr
ul Belinskogo
most Belinskogo
Inzhenernaya ul
Pl Iskusstv
Italiyanskaya ul
Sadovaya ul
Manezhnaya Pl
Anichkov most
Nevsky pr
Gostiny Dvor
Pl Ostrovskogo
nab reki Fontanki
ul Rubinshteyna
VLADIMIRSKAYA
Mayakovskaya
Pl Vosstaniya
9-ya Sovetskaya ul
10-ya Sovetskaya ul
8-ya Sovetskaya ul
7-ya Sovetskaya ul
6-ya Sovetskaya ul
5-ya Sovetskaya ul
4-ya Sovetskaya ul
3-ya Sovetskaya ul
2-ya Sovetskaya ul
Kirovskaya ul
Starorusskaya ul
ul Bakunina
ul Moiseenko
Sinopskaya nab
Maloohotinsky pr
VYBORG SIDE
ul Toneva
MALAYA OKHTA

LITEYNY & SMOLNY *Map on p258*

Sights (p84)
1 Anna Akhmatova Monument D1
2 Anna Akhmatova Museum in the Fountain House B3
3 Bolshoy Dom C1
4 Cathedral of the Transfiguration of our Saviour C2
5 Church of St John the Baptist C3
6 Floral Exhibition Hall D1
7 Museum of Decorative & Applied Arts B2
8 Museum of Erotica D2
9 Museum of the Defence & Blockade of Leningrad B2
10 Sheremetyev Palace B3
11 Smolny Cathedral F1
12 Smolny Institute F2
13 Statue of Felix Dzerzhinsky E1
14 Tauride Palace & Gardens E1
15 World of Water Museum E1

Eating (p89)
16 Baltic Bread D3
17 Botanika B2
18 Chaynaya Lozhka C1
19 Fat Frier B3
20 Gin No Taki C2
Il Grappolo .... (see 30)
21 Istoriya B3
22 Jakov C1
23 Kompot Café C3
24 Makarov C2
25 Molokhovet's Dream D3
26 Sunduk C2
27 Vox B2

Drinking & Nightlife (p93)
28 Igrateka D2
29 P.I.E.R.O.G.I. B4
30 Probka B3
31 XXXX D4
32 Zhopa E4

Entertainment (p95)
33 Bolshoy Puppet Theatre C3
34 Grand Concert Hall D3
35 JFC Jazz Club C1
36 Kitaysky Lyotchik Dzhao Da B2
37 Red Fox Jazz Café C2
Smolny Cathedral .... (see 11)
Sunduk .... (see 26)
38 Zoccolo D4

Shopping (p98)
39 Anglia Books B3
40 Borey Art Centre B4
41 Kisselenko Fashion Salon E2
42 Komissionary Magazin C3
43 Liberty Art Gallery B2
44 Maltsevsky Market D3
45 Nevsky Centre C4
Sol-Art .... (see 7)
46 Soldier of Fortune D3

Sports & Activities (p100)
47 Degtyarniye Bani D4
48 Mytninskiye Bani E4
49 Planet Fitness D1

Sleeping (p163)
50 Arbat Nord Hotel C2
51 Art Hotel B2
Austrian Yard Hotel .... (see 62)
52 Friends on Chekhova C3
53 Friends on Nevsky C4
54 Green Apple Hotel C2
55 Greenwich Hotel C3
56 Hotel Suvorov D3
57 Hotel Vera D3
58 Nils Bed & Breakfast D4
59 Pio on Mokhovaya B2
60 Puppet Hostel C3

Information (p224)
61 36.6 Pharmacy C4
62 Austrian Consulate D2
63 Euromed F2
64 Finnish Consulate C2
65 German Consulate D2
66 UK Consulate F1
67 US Consulate C2

Transport (p218)
68 Ferry Centre C3

Key on p262

VLADIMIRSKAYA & VOSSTANIYA

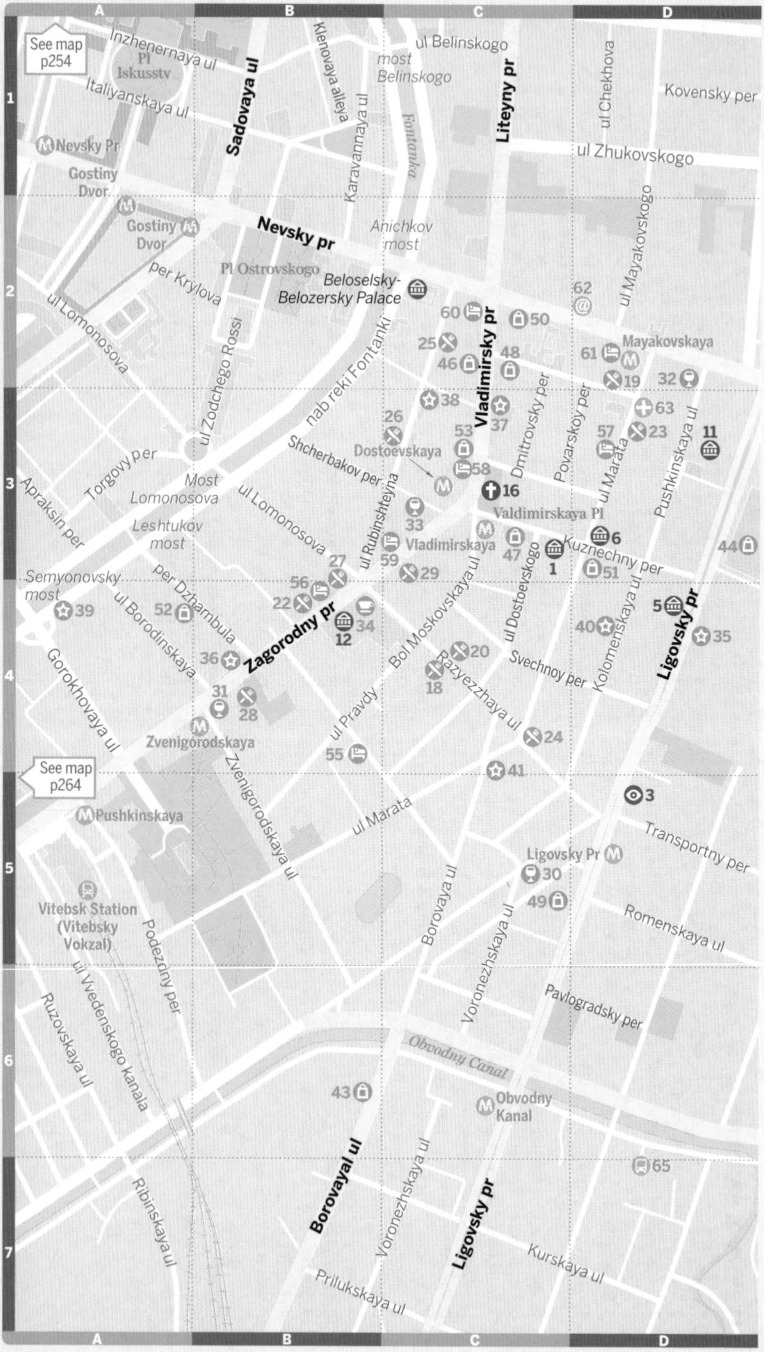

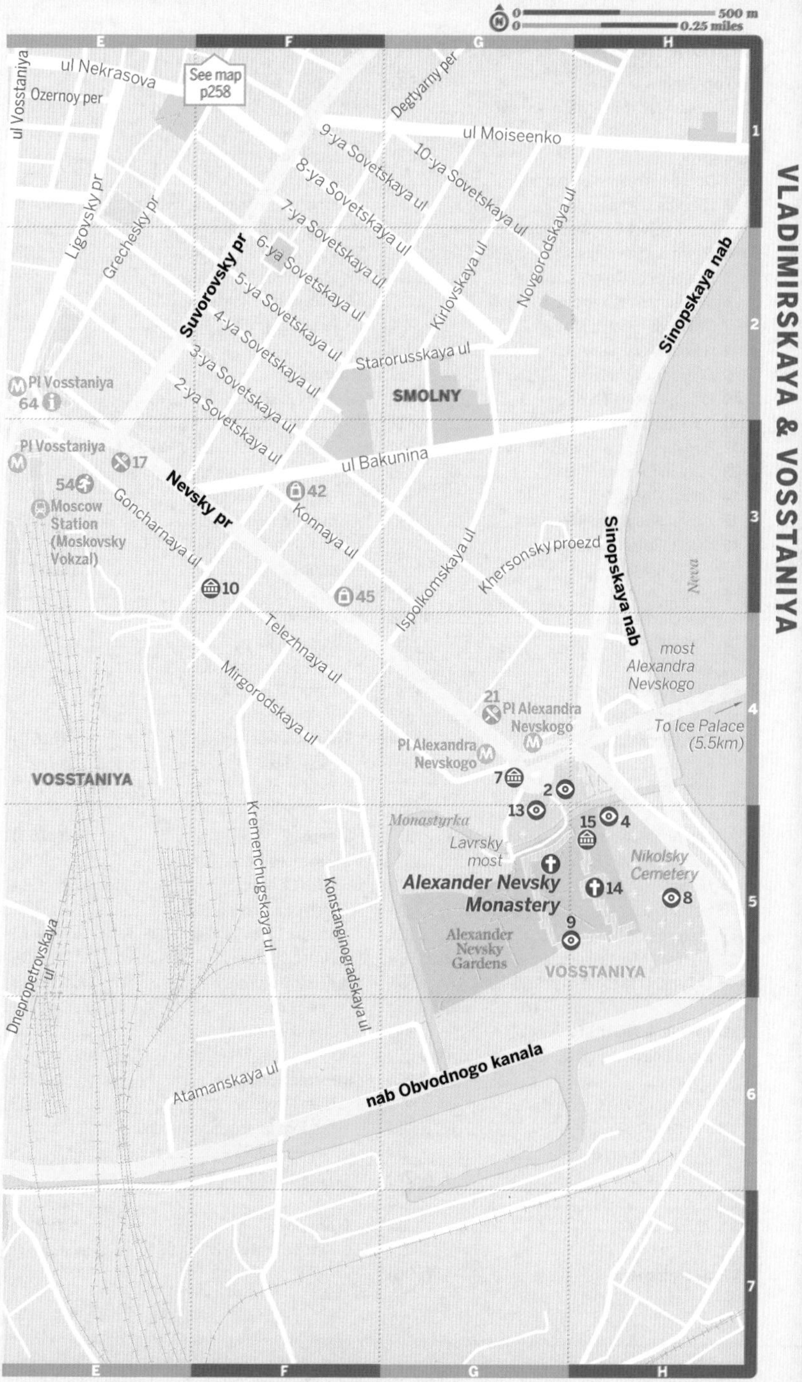

0 500 m
0 0.25 miles
E
F
G
H
1
2
3
4
5
6
7
VLADIMIRSKAYA & VOSSTANIYA
See map p258
ul Vosstaniya
ul Nekrasova
Ozernoy per
Degtyarny per
ul Moiseenko
9-ya Sovetskaya ul
10-ya Sovetskaya ul
8-ya Sovetskaya ul
7-ya Sovetskaya ul
6-ya Sovetskaya ul
5-ya Sovetskaya ul
4-ya Sovetskaya ul
3-ya Sovetskaya ul
2-ya Sovetskaya ul
Ligovsky pr
Grechesky pr
Suvorovsky pr
Kirlovskaya ul
Novgorodskaya ul
Sinopskaya nab
Starorusskaya ul
SMOLNY
Pl Vosstaniya
64
Pl Vosstaniya
17
54
Moscow Station (Moskovsky Vokzal)
Nevsky pr
ul Bakunina
42
Konnaya ul
Goncharnaya ul
10
45
Ispolkomskaya ul
Khersonsky proezd
Sinopskaya nab
Neva
Telezhnaya ul
Mirgorodskaya ul
most Alexandra Nevskogo
21
Pl Alexandra Nevskogo
To Ice Palace (5.5km)
Pl Alexandra Nevskogo
7
2
VOSSTANIYA
13
15
4
Monastyrka
Lavrsky most
Nikolsky Cemetery
Alexander Nevsky Monastery
14
8
9
Alexander Nevsky Gardens
VOSSTANIYA
Kremenchugskaya ul
Konstanginogradskaya ul
Dnepropetrovskaya ul
nab Obvodnogo kanala
Atamanskaya ul

VLADIMIRSKAYA & VOSSTANIYA *Map on p260*

SENNAYA & KOLOMNA *Map on p264*

Key on p263

SENNAYA & KOLOMNA

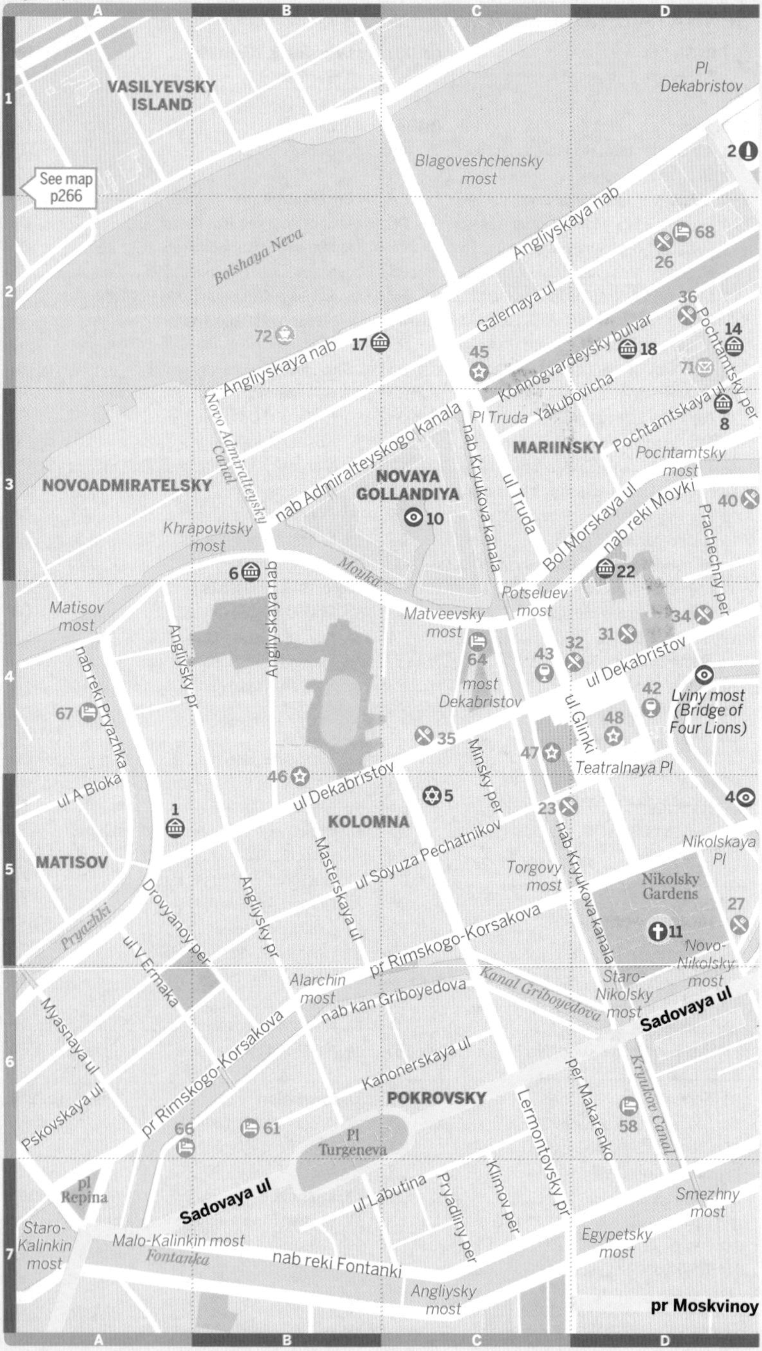

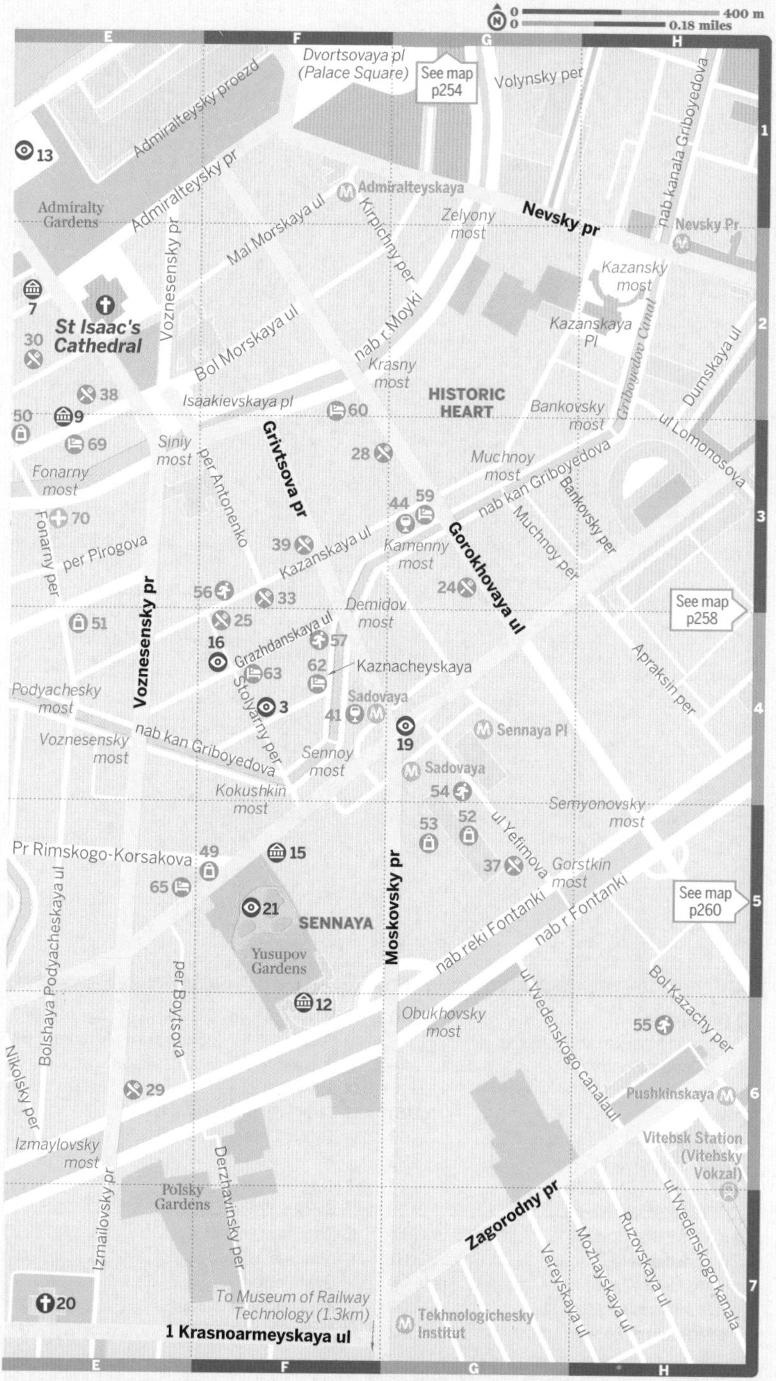
0 400 m
0 0.18 miles
Dvortsovaya pl (Palace Square)
See map p254
Volynsky per
Admiralteysky proezd
Admiralteysky pr
Admiralty Gardens
Admiralteyskaya
Kirpichny per
Mal Morskaya ul
Zelyony most
Nevsky pr
nab kanala Griboyedova
Nevsky Pr
Kazansky most
Kazanskaya Pl
Griboyedov Canal
Voznesensky pr
St Isaac's Cathedral
Bol Morskaya ul
nab r Moyki
Krasny most
HISTORIC HEART
Dumskaya ul
Isaakievskaya pl
Bankovsky most
ul Lomonosova
Siniy most
Grivtsova pr
Muchnoy most
Fonarny most
per Antonenko
nab kan Griboyedova
Bankovsky per
Muchnoy per
Fonarny per
per Pirogova
Kazanskaya ul
Kamenny most
Gorokhovaya ul
Demidov most
See map p258
Grazhdanskaya ul
Kaznacheyskaya
Podyachesky most
Stolyarny per
Sadovaya
Apraksin per
Sennaya Pl
Voznesensky most
Sennoy most
Kokushkin most
Semyonovsky most
ul Yefimova
Pr Rimskogo-Korsakova
Gorstkin most
Moskovsky pr
SENNAYA
Yusupov Gardens
nab reki Fontanki
nab r Fontanki
See map p260
Bolshaya Podyacheskaya ul
per Boytsova
Obukhovsky most
ul Vvedenskogo canalaul
Bol Kazachy per
Nikolsky per
Pushkinskaya
Vitebsk Station (Vitebsky Vokzal)
Izmaylovsky most
Polsky Gardens
Derzhavinsky per
Zagorodny pr
Izmailovsky pr
Vereyskaya ul
Mozhayskaya ul
Ruzovskaya ul
ul Vvedenskogo kanala
To Museum of Railway Technology (1.3km)
Tekhnologichesky Institut
1 Krasnoarmeyskaya ul

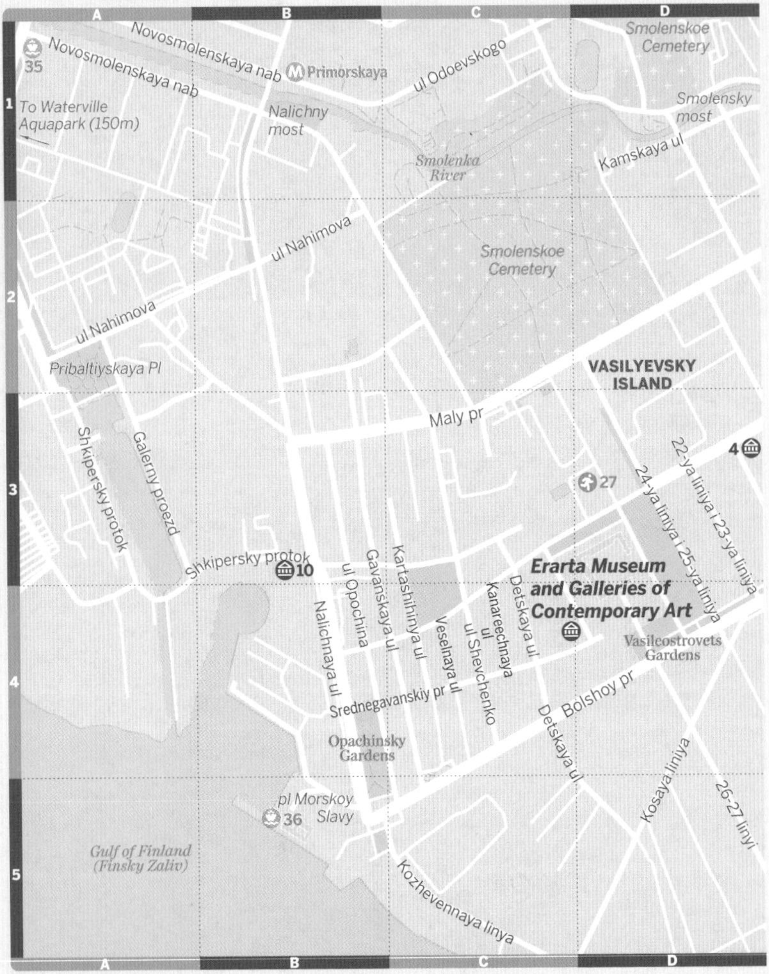

Top Sights (p118)

Erarta Museum and Galleries of Contemporary Art C4

Sights (p118)

1 Academy of Arts Museum G3
2 Central Naval Museum H2
3 Church of St Andrew F3
4 Geological Museum D3
5 Icebreaker Krasin E4
6 Kunstkamera H2
Mendeleev Museum .... (see 14)
7 Menshikov Palace G3
8 Museum of Zoology H2
9 Novy Museum F2
10 People's Will D-2 Submarine Museum B3
11 Pushkin House H2
12 Strelka H2
13 Temple of the Assumption F4
14 Twelve Colleges H2

Eating (p122)

15 Black & White F2
16 Chaynaya Lozhka F2
17 Gintarus G1
18 Grad Petrov H2
Imperator Restaurant .... (see 18)
19 Mama Roma G2

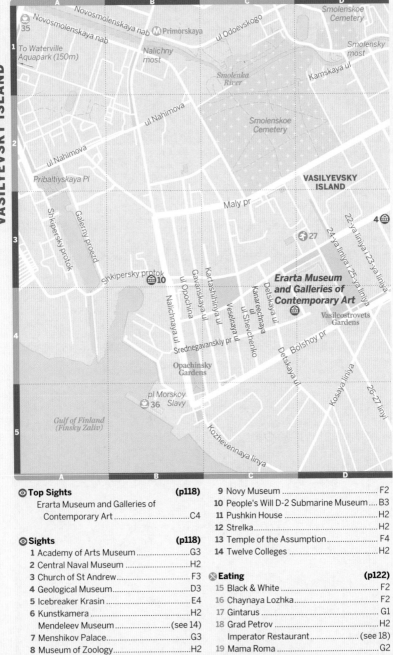

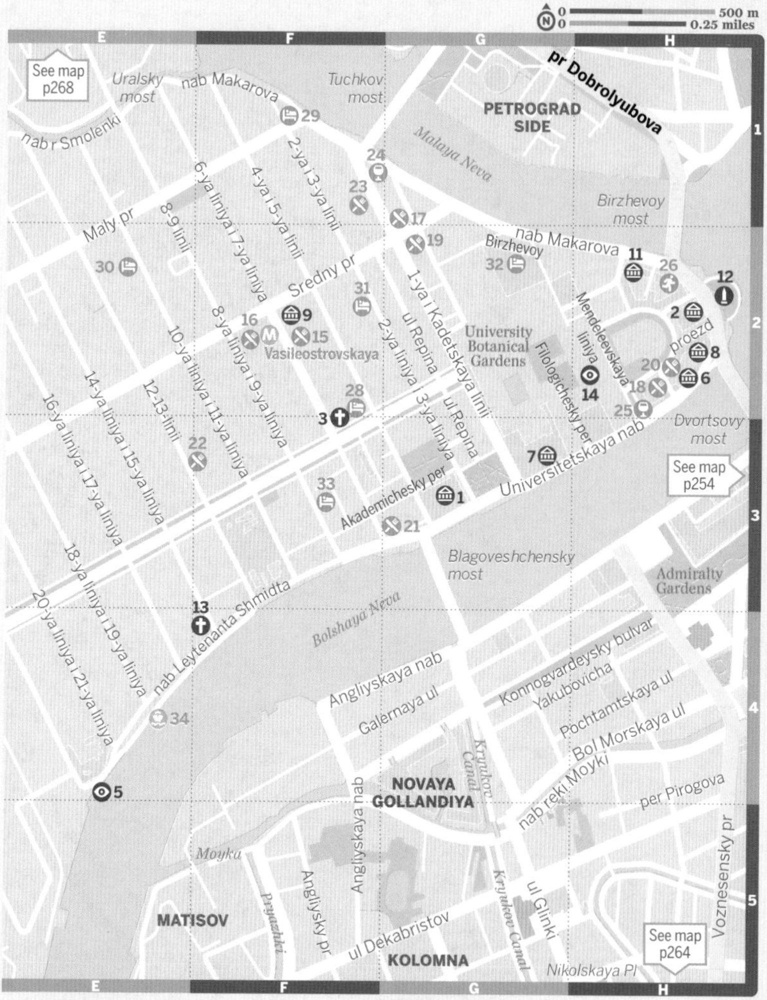

20 Old Customs House H2
21 Russky Kitsch G3
22 Sakartvelo F3
23 Stolle F1

Drinking & Nightlife **(p123)**

24 Helsinki Bar F1
25 Restoran H2

Sports & Activities **(p123)**

26 Fitness House H2
27 VMF Pool D3

Sleeping **(p167)**

28 Art Hotel Trezzini F2
29 Courtyard Marriot F1
30 NasHotel E2
31 Shelfort Hotel F2
32 Sokos Hotel Palace Bridge G2
33 Sokos Hotel Vasilevsky F3

Transport **(p217)**

34 Lieutenant Schmidt Passenger Terminal E4
35 Marine Facade Terminal A1
36 Sea Port (Morskoy Vokzal) B5

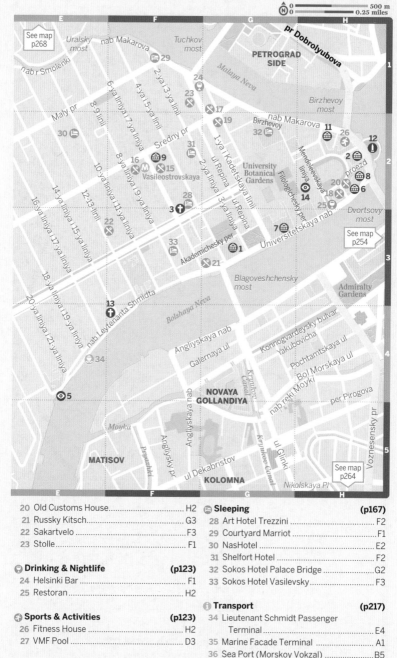

Key on p270

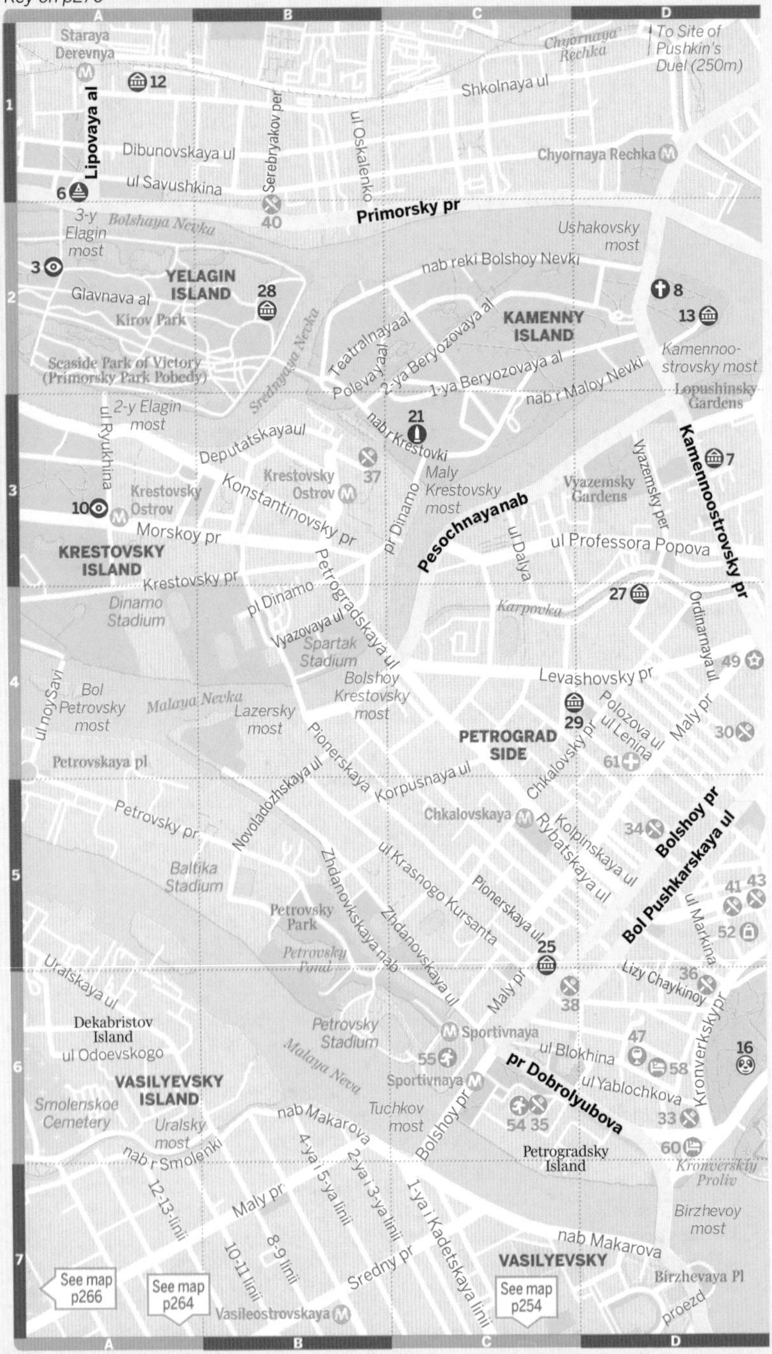
A
B
C
D
1
2
3
4
5
6
7
Staraya Derevnya
12
Lipovaya al
Dibunovskaya ul
ul Savushkina
6
Serebryakov per
ul Oskalenko
40
Primorsky pr
Shkolnaya ul
Chyornaya Rechka
To Site of Pushkin's Duel (250m)
Chyornaya Rechka
3-y Elagin most
Bolshaya Nevka
3
YELAGIN ISLAND
28
Glavnava al
Kirov Park
Seaside Park of Victory (Primorsky Park Pobedy)
Srednyaya Nevka
Ushakovsky most
nab reki Bolshoy Nevki
8
13
KAMENNY ISLAND
Teatralnayaal
Polevayaal
2-ya Beryozovaya al
1-ya Beryozovaya al
nab r Maloy Nevki
Kamennoostrovsky most
Lopushinsky Gardens
2-y Elagin most
ul Ryukhina
Deputatskayaul
21
nab r Krestovki
37
Krestovsky Ostrov
Maly Krestovsky most
Vyazemsky per
Kamennoostrovsky pr
7
Vyazemsky Gardens
10
Krestovsky Ostrov
Konstantinovsky pr
pr Dinamo
Pesochnayanab
ul Dalya
ul Professora Popova
Morskoy pr
KRESTOVSKY ISLAND
Krestovsky pr
Petrogradskaya ul
pl Dinamo
27
Karpovka
Ordinarnaya ul
Dinamo Stadium
Vyazovaya ul
Spartak Stadium
49
Levashovsky pr
Bolshoy Krestovsky most
ul noySavi
Bol Petrovsky most
Malaya Nevka
Lazersky most
29
Polozova ul
ul Lenina
Maly pr
30
PETROGRAD SIDE
Chkalovsky pr
61
Petrovskaya pl
Pionerskaya
Novoladozhskaya ul
Korpusnaya ul
Petrovsky pr
Chkalovskaya
Rybatskaya ul
Kolpinskaya ul
34
Bolshoy pr
Baltika Stadium
Zhdanovskaya nab
ul Krasnogo Kursanta
Pionerskaya ul
Bol Pushkarskaya ul
41
43
ul Markina
52
Petrovsky Park
Petrovsky Pond
Zhdanovskaya ul
25
Uralskaya ul
Maly pr
38
Lizy Chaykinoy
36
Kronverksky pr
Dekabristov Island
ul Odoevskogo
Petrovsky Stadium
Sportivnaya
ul Blokhina
47
16
58
VASILYEVSKY ISLAND
Malaya Neva
55
Sportivnaya
pr Dobrolyubova
ul Yablochkova
Smolenskoe Cemetery
Uralsky most
nab Makarova
Tuchkov most
54
35
Bolshoy pr
33
nab r Smolenki
Petrogradsky Island
60
Kronverksky Proliv
12-13-linii
4-ya i 5-ya linii
2-ya i 3-ya linii
1-ya i Kadetskaya linii
Maly pr
Birzhevoy most
10-11 linii
8-9 linii
nab Makarova
Sredny pr
VASILYEVSKY
Birzhevaya Pl
See map p266
See map p264
Vasileostrovskaya
See map p254
proezd

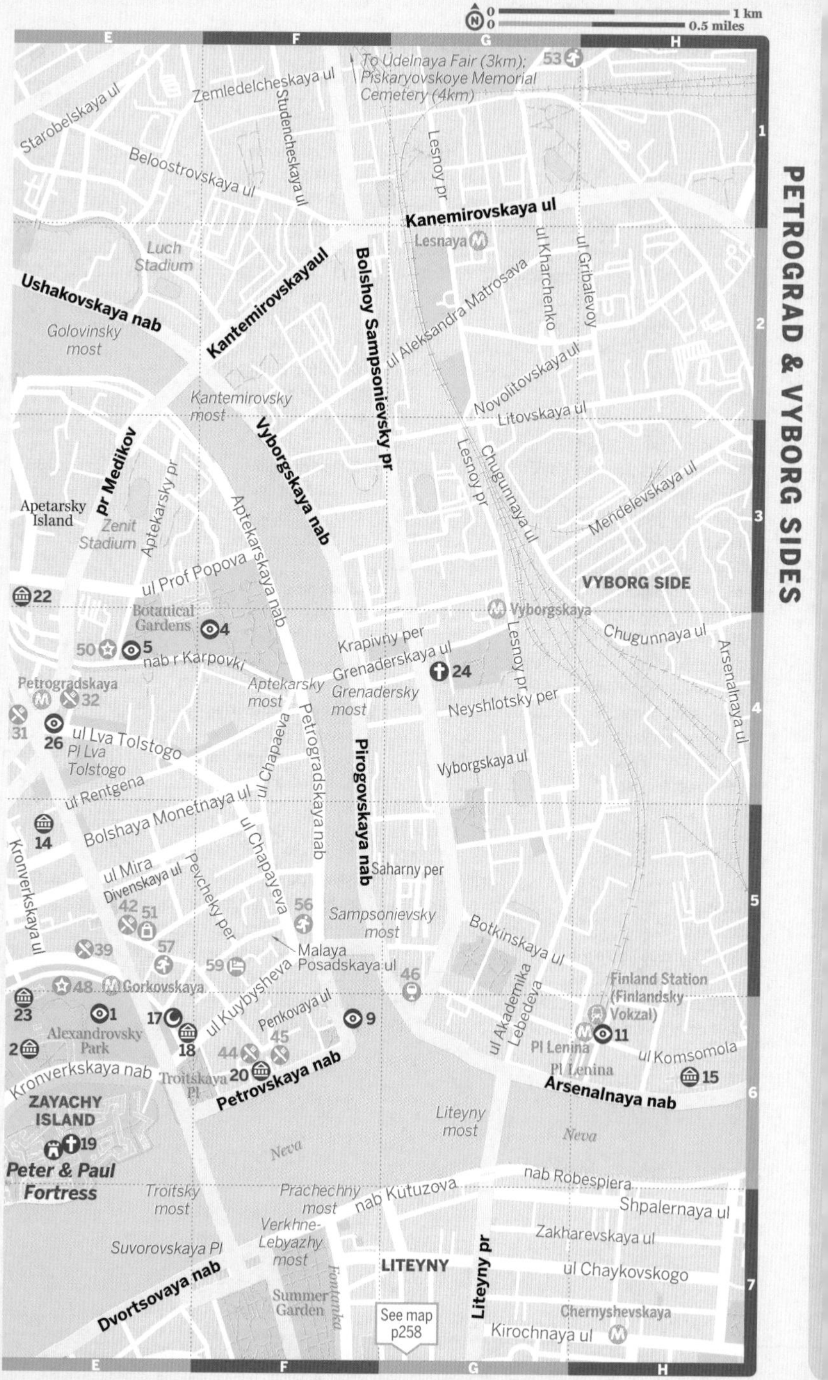
PETROGRAD & VYBORG SIDES
0 1 km
0 0.5 miles
To Udelnaya Fair (3km); Piskaryovskoye Memorial Cemetery (4km)
Zemledelcheskaya ul
Starobelskaya ul
Beloostrovskaya ul
Studencheskaya ul
Lesnoy pr
Kanemirovskaya ul
Lesnaya
Luch Stadium
Ushakovskaya nab
Golovinsky most
Kantemirovskayaul
Bolshoy Sampsonievsky pr
ul Aleksandra Matrosova
ul Kharchenko
ul Gribalevoy
Novolitovskaya ul
Litovskaya ul
Kantemirovsky most
Vyborgskaya nab
pr Medikov
Apetarsky Island
Zenit Stadium
Aptekarsky pr
Aptekarskaya nab
Chugunnaya ul
Mendelevskaya ul
ul Prof Popova
VYBORG SIDE
Botanical Gardens
Vyborgskaya
Chugunnaya ul
Arsenalnaya ul
nab r Karpovki
Krapivny per
Grenaderskaya ul
Aptekarsky most
Grenadersky most
Petrogradskaya
Neyshlotsky per
ul Lva Tolstogo
Pl Lva Tolstogo
ul Chapaeva
Petrogradskaya nab
Pirogovskaya nab
Vyborgskaya ul
ul Rentgena
Bolshaya Monetnaya ul
Kronverkskaya ul
ul Chapayeva
ul Mira
Divenskaya ul
Pevcheky per
Saharny per
Sampsonievsky most
Botkinskaya ul
Malaya Posadskaya ul
Gorkovskaya
ul Kuybysheva
Penkovaya ul
ul Akademika Lebedeva
Finland Station (Finlandsky Vokzal)
Alexandrovsky Park
Pl Lenina
ul Komsomola
Kronverkskaya nab
Troitskaya Pl
Petrovskaya nab
Arsenalnaya nab
ZAYACHY ISLAND
Liteyny most
Neva
Peter & Paul Fortress
Troitsky most
Prachechny most
nab Kutuzova
nab Robespiera
Shpalernaya ul
Verkhne-Lebyazhy most
Zakharevskaya ul
Suvorovskaya Pl
LITEYNY
Liteyny pr
ul Chaykovskogo
Dvortsovaya nab
Summer Garden
Fontanka
See map p258
Chernyshevskaya
Kirochnaya ul
1 2 4 5 9 11 14 15 17 18 19 20 22 23 24 26 31 32 39 42 44 45 46 48 50 51 53 56 57 59
E F G H
1 2 3 4 5 6 7

PETROGRAD & VYBORG SIDES *Map on p268*

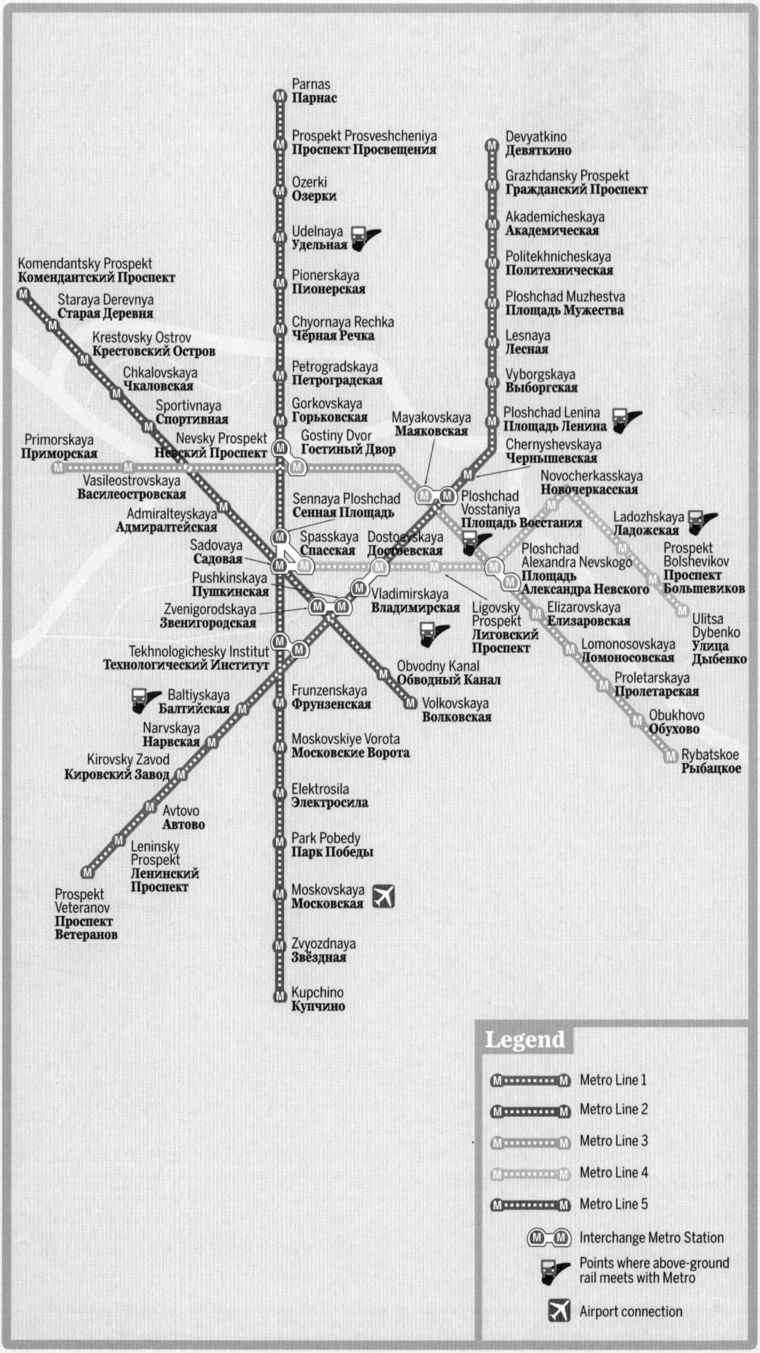
Parnas
Парнас
Prospekt Prosveshcheniya
Проспект Просвещения
Ozerki
Озерки
Udelnaya
Удельная
Pionerskaya
Пионерская
Chyornaya Rechka
Чёрная Речка
Petrogradskaya
Петроградская
Gorkovskaya
Горьковская
Nevsky Prospekt
Невский Проспект
Gostiny Dvor
Гостиный Двор
Sennaya Ploshchad
Сенная Площадь
Spasskaya
Спасская
Sadovaya
Садовая
Tekhnologichesky Institut
Технологический Институт
Frunzenskaya
Фрунзенская
Moskovskiye Vorota
Московские Ворота
Elektrosila
Электросила
Park Pobedy
Парк Победы
Moskovskaya
Московская
Zvyozdnaya
Звёздная
Kupchino
Купчино
Devyatkino
Девяткино
Grazhdansky Prospekt
Гражданский Проспект
Akademicheskaya
Академическая
Politekhnicheskaya
Политехническая
Ploshchad Muzhestva
Площадь Мужества
Lesnaya
Лесная
Vyborgskaya
Выборгская
Ploshchad Lenina
Площадь Ленина
Chernyshevskaya
Чернышевская
Mayakovskaya
Маяковская
Ploshchad Vosstaniya
Площадь Восстания
Dostoevskaya
Достоевская
Vladimirskaya
Владимирская
Pushkinskaya
Пушкинская
Zvenigorodskaya
Звенигородская
Baltiyskaya
Балтийская
Narvskaya
Нарвская
Kirovsky Zavod
Кировский Завод
Avtovo
Автово
Leninsky Prospekt
Ленинский Проспект
Prospekt Veteranov
Проспект Ветеранов
Komendantsky Prospekt
Комендантский Проспект
Staraya Derevnya
Старая Деревня
Krestovsky Ostrov
Крестовский Остров
Chkalovskaya
Чкаловская
Sportivnaya
Спортивная
Admiralteyskaya
Адмиралтейская
Obvodny Kanal
Обводный Канал
Volkovskaya
Волковская
Primorskaya
Приморская
Vasileostrovskaya
Василеостровская
Ploshchad Alexandra Nevskogo
Площадь Александра Невского
Elizarovskaya
Елизаровская
Lomonosovskaya
Ломоносовская
Proletarskaya
Пролетарская
Obukhovo
Обухово
Rybatskoe
Рыбацкое
Novocherkasskaya
Новочеркасская
Ladozhskaya
Ладожская
Prospekt Bolshevikov
Проспект Большевиков
Ulitsa Dybenko
Улица Дыбенко
Ligovsky Prospekt
Лиговский Проспект
Legend
Metro Line 1
Metro Line 2
Metro Line 3
Metro Line 4
Metro Line 5
Interchange Metro Station
Points where above-ground rail meets with Metro
Airport connection

Our Story

A beat-up old car, a few dollars in the pocket and a sense of adventure. In 1972 that's all Tony and Maureen Wheeler needed for the trip of a lifetime – across Europe and Asia overland to Australia. It took several months, and at the end – broke but inspired – they sat at their kitchen table writing and stapling together their first travel guide, *Across Asia on the Cheap*. Within a week they'd sold 1500 copies. Lonely Planet was born.

Today, Lonely Planet has offices in Melbourne, London and Oakland, with more than 600 staff and writers. We share Tony's belief that 'a great guidebook should do three things: inform, educate and amuse'.

Our Writers

Tom Masters

Coordinating Author Tom first came to St Petersburg in 1996 while studying Russian at the School of Slavonic & East European Studies, part of the University of London. He loved the city so much that he came back after graduating and worked as a writer and editor at the *St Petersburg Times*. Since then he's been based in London and Berlin, but returns regularly to Piter to take on documentary work and write freelance articles and Lonely Planet guides.

Read more about Tom at:
lonelyplanet.com/members/tommasters

Simon Richmond

Veliky Novgorod After studying Russian history and politics as part of his university degree, Simon's first visit to the country was in 1994 when he wandered goggle-eyed around gorgeous St Petersburg, and peeked at Lenin's mummified corpse in Red Square. He's since travelled the breadth of the nation from Kamchatka in the far east to Kaliningrad in the far west, stopping off at many points between. An award-winning writer and photographer, Simon is the coauthor of Lonely Planet's *Trans-Siberian Railway* editions 1, 2 and 3; *Russia* editions 3, 5 and 6; and many other titles for the company, ranging from Cape Town to Korea.

Read more about Simon at:
lonelyplanet.com/members/simonrichmond

Published by Lonely Planet Publications Pty Ltd
ABN 36 005 607 983
6th edition – March 2012
ISBN 978 1 74179 327 7

10 9 8 7 6 5 4 3 2
Printed in China